D1519272

COMMENTARY ON *DE GRAMMATICO*

SYNTHESE HISTORICAL LIBRARY

TEXTS AND STUDIES IN THE HISTORY OF

LOGIC AND PHILOSOPHY

VOLUME 8

COMMENTARY ON

DE GRAMMATICO

The Historical-Logical Dimensions of a Dialogue of St. Anselm's

by

DESMOND PAUL HENRY

Dept. of Philosophy, The University, Manchester, England

D. REIDEL PUBLISHING COMPANY

DORDRECHT-HOLLAND / BOSTON-U.S.A.

Library of Congress Catalog Card Number 73–86092

ISBN 90 277 0382 5

Published by D. Reidel Publishing Company,
P.O. Box 17, Dordrecht, Holland

Sold and distributed in the U.S.A., Canada, and Mexico
by D. Reidel Publishing Company, Inc.
306 Dartmouth Street, Boston,
Mass. 02116, U.S.A.

Printed in The Netherlands by D. Reidel, Dordrecht

To: *Louise*
Anne-Marie
Rita
and
Elaine

CONTENTS

ACKNOWLEDGEMENTS

As on many previous occasions I am particularly indebted to Czesław Lejewski for his teaching and advice concerning the Leśniewski systems used in the present work. Such an acknowledgement of indebtedness is particularly appropriate here, since it was as a result of my asking his counsel many years ago concerning a section of the text of *De Grammatico* that he first pointed out to me the utility of many-link functors in elucidating such texts. At the same time I must stress that any shortcomings which may ensue as a consequence of the rather summary exposition of Leśniewski's Ontology contained in §3 are entirely my responsibility.

The editors of the Synthese Historical Library are to be thanked for their kindness in suggesting the publication of this work.

In common with all students of St. Anselm I am deeply grateful to the most learned and genial editor of the saint's works, the late F. S. Schmitt, O.S.B. It is by this kind permission that I have exploited the text of *De Grammatico* provided by him in his edition of Anselm's writings. The same text, along with a summary and translation, has already figured in an earlier work of mine ('The *De Grammatico* of St. Anselm: the Theory of Paronymy', Notre Dame U.P., 1964), and I would like to thank the editors of the Notre Dame series for their permission to re-use this textual material. The prent work is complementary to, and by no means supersedes or abrogates, the earlier one.

Among reviewers of earlier works of mine who by their remarks have contributed to the correction or enhancement of this commentary I should particularly like to mention E. C. Luschei, P. T. Geach, and J. D. Cloud.

Passages from John of Salisbury's *Metalogicon*, as edited by C. C. J. Webb, are reproduced by permission of the Clarendon Press, Oxford.

§0. TRANSLATION AND REFERENCE CONVENTIONS

THE SYMBOL '⊖'

In order that the flavour of the original Latin expressions used by Anselm and other writers may be readily available to the reader, I have not hesitated to intersperse the commentary, as is often customary, with such expressions. So that those unacquainted with the Latin language may not be left with blank understandings at such points, I have added English translations even in places where to do so involves repetition of a rather trite sort. Such additions would ordinarily tend to encumber the printed page with a multiplicity of parentheses, thereby inducing an unnecessarily troubling impression of interruption in the flow of the text. At such junctures I have hence preferred to interpose the sign '⊖' between the Latin and the English, as in, for example, *usus loquendi* ⊖ the current course of utterance. Of course such translation can at times only provide a makeshift rendering of what is in the Latin deliberately or unintentionally ambiguous. In certain circumstances it has been possible to indicate the ambiguity by resorting to the oblique stroke '/' as a separation between the two senses provided in the English version. The usual Latin titles of works referred to have, however, been left untranslated. The same symbol '⊖' has also been used between the English and Latin versions of the expressions reproduced at the head of each commentative note in §7.

INTERNAL REFERENCES

The present work as a whole, and the text of *De Grammatico* presented herein, have both been broken down into numbered sections. Numerals referring to sections of the work apart from the *De Grammatico* text are simple and prefaced by '§' (e.g. §5). References to the text (and hence also to the synopsis of the text) are each made by means of a complex numeral without any further sign prefixed (e.g. '4.5022'). Such text-reference numerals hence each consist of two parts. That part before the full point refers to a main division; that part following the full point refers to a sub-division of the main division. Such numerals have been allocated in such a way that cross-references involving, say, only two digits, can be used as a global indication of all sections the left-hand digits of whose numerals are identical with the reference given; e.g. '2.2' would cross-refer to *all* divisions of the text which have numerals beginning as thus indicated. In §3 sentences in the language of Leśniewski's Ontology are introduced, and are numered serially by means of a full point followed by digits, e.g. '§3.11' refers to that sentence numbered '.11' in §3. References to several such numbered sentences will be made without repetition of the main section number, e.g. '§3.6.7.8' refers to the sentences numbered '.6', '.7' and '.8' within §3. Cross references to such numbered sentences within a given section need not carry the section-number within which they occur, e.g. within §3, the sentence numbered '.11' may simply be cross-referred to as '.11'.

§7 of this work consists of commentary arising directly from details of the text of *De Grammatico* as presented in §6. That such a note or comment is available has been indicated in the text and its translation by the presence of superscript letters allocated in alphabetical order within each of the minimal sub-divisions of the text. Thus that stretch of text numbered '3.21' has the letters '*a*', '*b*', '*c*', '*d*', and '*e*' superscribed at appropriate points within it. Reference to the relevant comment can accordingly be made by prefixing '*n*' to the textual division-number and adding the letter in question; e.g. '*n*3.12*e*' refers to that note centred around the occurrence of '*utrimque*' ⊖ 'on both flanks' in 3.21.

EXTERNAL REFERENCES

Works to which reference is made will be indicated by the italicised *sigla* co-ordinated with the bibliographical details given below. Generally, the *sigla* will be immediately followed by page, column, or paragraph numbers, as in '*W* 55' and '*HL* §3.45'. References to lines or groups of lines in works which have their lines numbered will be made by adding a full point and the individual line-numeral (e.g. '*SN* 34.3') or the initial and terminal line numbers of the groups of lines (as in '*A* 109.2.12'). Where works referred to are in several volumes, or are divided into numbered books or parts, the Roman numeral of the volume, book, or part will be interposed between the *siglum* and the page/line numbers, as in '*S* I 253.15.20'. Apart from *SN* Anselm's own works are not listed below, as their titles are quoted in full. The numbers annexed to the *sigla* '*APH*' and '*APA*' are those serially allotted to the paragraph divisions of the manual edition (Marietti).

BIBLIOGRAPHY

A	Abaelardus, Petrus	*Dialectica* (Ed. De Rijk, 1956)
AC	Aristotle	*Categoriae*
ADCD	Augustine of Hippo	*De Civitate Dei*
ADEE	Aquinas, Thomas	*De Ente et Essentia*
ADI	Aristotle	*De Interpretatione*
ADSE	Aristotle	*De Sophisticis Elenchis*
AGT	Anscombe, G. E. M. and Geach, P. T.	*Three Philosophers* (Oxford, 1961)
AO	Abaelardus, Petrus	*Opera* (Ed. Cousin, 1859)
AP	Aristotle	*Analytica Priora*
APA	Aquinas, Thomas	Commentary on *Analytica Posteriora* (Ed. Spiazzi, 1955)
APH	Aquinas, Thomas	Commentary on *Peri Hermeneias* (=*De Interpretatione*) (Ed. Spiazzi, 1955)
ASCG	Aquinas, Thomas	*Summa Contra Gentiles*
AST	Aquinas, Thomas	*Summa Theologica*
B	Boethius	*Opera Omnia* (*Tomus Posterior*) *PL* 64
BB	Boethius	*In Isagogem Porphyrii Commenta* (Ed. Schepps and Brandt, 1906)
BC	Boethius	*In Categorias Aristotelis libri quatuor* (*B*159–294)
BCP	Boethius	*Commentaria in Porphyrium* (*B* 71–158)
BD	Boethius	*Liber de Divisione* (*B* 875–892)
BDF	Boethius (*sic*)	*Liber de Definitione* (*B* 891–910)
BDIG	Boethius	*In librum Aristotelis de interpretatione, commentaria maiora* (*B* 393–640)
BDIL	Boethius	*In librum Aristotelis de interpretatione, commentaria minora* (*B* 293–392)
BDP	Boethius	*Dialogi in Porphyrium* (*B* 9–70)
BDPN	Boethius	*Liber de persona et de duabus naturis* (*B* 1337–1357)
BDT	Boethius	*De differentiis topicis* (*B* 1173–1216)
BISC	Boethius	*Introductio ad syllogismos categoricos* (*B* 761–794)
BM	Boethius	*Commentarii in librum Aristotelis* ΠΕΡΙ ΕΡΜΗΝΕΙΑΣ (Ed. Meiser, 1877, 1880)
BML	Boehner, P.	*Medieval Logic* (Manchester U.P., 1952)
BQS	Boethius	*Quomodo substantiae bonae sint* (*B* 1311–1314)
BSA	Balmus, C. I.	*Étude sur le style de saint Augustin dans les Confessions et la Cité de Dieu* (Paris, 1930)
BSC	Boethius	*De syllogismo categorico libri duo* (*B* 793–832)

BSE	Boethius (*sic*)	*Interpretatio Elenchorum Sophisticorum Aristotelis* (*B* 1007–1040)
BSH	Boethius	*De Syllogismo Hypothetico libri duo* (*B* 831–876)
BHL	Bocheński, I.	*History of Formal Logic*, tr. Ivo Thomas (Notre Dame U.P., 1961)
BT	Boethius (*sic*)	*Interpretatio Topicorum Aristotelis* (*B* 909–1008)
BTC	Boethius	*Commentaria in Topica Ciceronis* (*B* 1039–1174)
CH	Cicero (*sic*)	*Rhetorica ad Herennium*
CI	Cicero	*De Inventione Rhetorica*
CIA	Cousin, V.	*Ouvrages Inédits d'Abélard* (Paris, 1836)
CM	Carnap, R.	*Meaning and Necessity* (Chicago, 1956)
CR	Church, A.	Review in *Journal of Symbolic Logic*, Vol. 8, No. 2, p. 46, 1943.
CRH	Cloud, J. D.	Review of *HL* in *Philosophical Books* Jan. 1968
CSI	Cassiodorus Senator	*Institutiones* (Ed. Mynors, 1937)
DD	Descartes, R.	*Discours de la Méthode*
DLM	De Rijk, L. M.	*Logica Modernorum* (Assen, 1962, 1967)
G	Garlandus, Compotista	*Dialectica* (Ed. De Rijk, 1959)
GRG	Geach, P. T.	*Reference and Generality* (Cornell, 1962)
HAA	Henry, D. P.	'St. Anselm and Scriptural Analysis' (*Sophia*, Vol. I, No. 3, 1962)
HAD	Henry, D. P.	'St. Anselm on the varieties of "Doing"' (*Theoria*, Vol. XIX, No. 3, 1953)
HAN	Henry, D. P.	'St Anselm's Nonsense' (*Mind*, Vol. LXXII, No. 285, 1963)
HAP	Henry, D. P.	'St. Anselm and Paulus' (*Law Quarterly Review*, 1963)
HAR	Henry, D. P.	'An Anselmian Regress' (*Notre Dame Journal of Formal Logic*, Vol. III, No. 3, 1962)
HDG	Henry, D. P.	*The* De Grammatico *of St. Anslem: the Theory of Paronymy* (Notre Dame U. P., 1964)
HEE	Henry, D. P.	'Being, Essence, and Existence' (*Logique et Analyse*, No. 27, 1964)
HG	Henry, D. P.	'St. Anselm's *De Grammatico*' (*Philosophical Quarterly*, Vol. 10, No. 39, 1960)
HHS	Henry, D. P.	'The Early History of *Suppositio*' (*Franciscan Studies*, 1964)
HL	Henry, D. P.	*The Logic of St. Anselm* (Oxford, 1967)
HLM	Henry, D. P.	*Medieval Logic and Metaphysics* (London, 1972)
HM	Henry, D. P.	'Remarks on St. Anslem's treatment of possibility' (*Spicilegium Beccense* I, 1959)
HMN	Heinnemann, F.	'The Meaning of Negation' (*Proc. of Aristotelian Society*, 1943–4)
HMP	Henry, D. P.	Art. 'Medieval Philosophy' in *Encyclopedia of Philosophy* (Ed. Paul Edwards, New York, 1968)
HN	Henry, D. P.	'Numerically Definite Reasoning in the *Cur Deus Homo*' (*Dominican Studies*, Vol. VI, 1953)
HNA	Henry, D. P.	'St. Anselm and Nothingness' (*Philosophical Quarterly*, 1965)

HOF	Henry, D. P.	'Ockham and the Formal Distinction' (*Franciscan Studies*, 1965)
HOS	Henry, D. P.	'Ockham, *Suppositio*, and Modern Logic' (*Notre Dame Journal of Formal Logic*, Vol. 5, No. 4)
HP	Henry, D. P.	'The *Proslogion* Proofs' (*Philosophical Quarterly*, Vol. 5, 1955)
HR	Henry, D. P.	'St. Anselm's *rustici*' (*Medium Aevum*, Vol. XXXIII, 1964)
HRE	Henry, D. P.	'Was St. Anselm really a Realist?' (*Ratio*, Vol. V, 1963)
HRG	Henry, D. P.	'War St. Anselm wirklich ein Realist?' (*Ratio* (German Edition) Vol. V, 1963)
HRK	Henry, D. P.	Review of *KSL* (*Philosophical Studies* Vol. XVII, 1968)
HSL	Hispanus, Petrus	*Summulae Logicales* (Ed. Bocheński, 1947)
HSP	Hunt, R. W.	'Studies on Priscian in the eleventh and twelfth centuries' (*Medieval and Renaissance Studies*, Vol. I)
HT	Hume, David	*Treatise of Human Nature* (Ed. Selby-Bigge, Oxford, 1896)
HW	Henry, D. P.	'Why *Grammaticus?*' (*Archivum Latinitatis Medii Aevi*. Vol. XXVIII)
JA	Jolivet, J.	*Arts du langage et théologie chez Abélard* (Paris, 1969)
JL	Joseph, H. W. B.	*An Introduction to Logic* (2nd Edn., 1916)
JN	Jalbert, Guy	*Nécessité et Contingence chez saint Thomas d'Aquin et chez ses prédécesseurs* (Ottawa, 1961)
K	Keil, H. (Ed.)	*Grammatici Latini* (Leipzig, 1885–80)
KF	Kapp, E.	*Greek Foundations of Traditional Logic* (Columbia, U.P., 1942)
KSE	Keynes, J. N.	*Studies and Exercises in Formal Logic* (3rd Edn., 1894)
KSL	Kretzmann, N.	*William of Sherwood's Introduction to Logic* (Minnesota, U.P., 1966)
KSS	Kretzmann, N.	*William of Sherwood's Treatise on Syncategorematic Words* (Minnesota U.P., 1968)
LA	Lejewski, C.	'Proper Names' (*Aristotelian Society Supplementary Volume* No. XXXI)
LAS	Łukasiewicz, J.	*Aristotle's Syllogistic* (Oxford, 1951 and 1957)
LE	Locke, John	*Essay Concerning Human Understanding*
LLE	Lejewski, C.	'Logic and Existence' (*British Journal for the Philosophy of Science*, Vol. 5, 1954)
LLL	Luschei, E. C.	*The Logical Systems of Leśniewski* (Amsterdam, 1962)
LR	Lejewski, C.	'On Leśniewski's Ontology' (*Ratio*, Vol. I, 1958)
MB	Moody, E. A.	'Buridan and a Dilemma of Nominalism' (*Harry Austryn Wolfson Jubilee Volume*, English Section, Vol. 2, Jerusalem, 1965)

MGH		*Monumenta Germaniae Historica, Legum*, Folio Tom. 3 (Ed. Perz, 1868)
MID	Minto, W.	*Logic Deductive and Inductive* (London, 1894)
ML	Macdonald, J.	*Lanfranc, a study of his life and writings* (Oxford, 1926)
MLE	Marsh, G. P.	*Lectures on the English Language* (New York, 1861)
MMC	Moody, E. A.	'The Medieval Contribution to Logic' (*Studium Generale*, Vol. 19, 1966)
MMP	Maurice, F. D.	*Medieval Philosophy* (London, 1857)
MSL	Mill, J. S.	*System of Logic* (5th Ed., London, 1862)
PFL	Prior, A. N.	*Formal Logic* (Oxford, 1955 and 1962)
PL	Migne, J. P. (Ed.)	*Patrologia Latina*
QIO	Quintilian	*Institutiones Oratoriae*
RI	Russell, B.	*An Introduction to Mathematical Philosophy* (London, 1919)
S	Schmitt, F. S. (Ed.)	*S. Anselmi Opera Omnia* (Edinburgh, 1946)
SA	Sullivan, M. W.	*Apuleian Logic* (Amsterdam, 1967)
SLB	Southern, R. W.	'Lanfranc of Bec and Berengar of Tours' (*Studies presented to F. M. Powicke*)
SM	Salisbury, John of	*Metalogicon* (Ed. C. C. J. Webb, Oxford, 1929)
SN	Schmitt, F. S.	'Ein neues unvollendetes Werk des hl. Anselm von Canterbury' (*Beiträge zur Geschichte der Philosophie des Mittelalters* Bd. XXXIII, Heft 3)
TA	Tweedale, M. M.	'Abailard and Non-Things' (*Journal of the History of Philosophy* Vol. V, No. 4, 1967)
W	Wittgenstein, L.	*Philosophical Investigations* (tr. G. E. M. Anscombe, 1953)
WJC	Wilson, J. Cook	*Statement and Inference* (Vol. I, Oxford, 1926)

§1. INTRODUCTION

The intent of the present work is chiefly the presentation of a running commentary, preponderantly historical in complexion, on the detail of the text of St. Anselm's dialogue *De Grammatico*. At the same time the making intelligible of that text has demanded the concurrent proffering of logical elucidations. The framework adopted for the latter is the Ontology of S. Leśniewski. The unsuitability of other current systems of logic for the analysis of medieval doctrines has been suggested in *HLM* I. Hereunder the line of analyses proposed in *HDG* (an introductory study of *De Grammatico*) will for the most part be maintained, with only a few modifications. Changes which further study might demand would in any case involve not so much an abrogation of the *HDG* versions, but rather certain complications of detail on the lines indicated in *HLM*, *HEE*, and *HOF̀*. Readers who happen to be out of sympathy either with modern logic as a whole, or with the Leśniewskian systems in particular, may be assured that the historical thread of the commentary remains for the most part unaffected by issues connected with such logics.

Much of the historical material contained in the commentary consists of quotations from the logical works of Boethius. Some of that material may at first sight appear prosaic and tedious. However, there are indications in recent works on medieval logic that there still exists a lack of familiarity with what are, after all, the roots of the terminological and conceptual nerve-fibres which animate medieval logic throughout its existence, and which issue to a large extent from the logical output of Boethius.

Consider, for example, the recent discussion on the origins of the notion of 'distribution' as it occurs in post-medieval logic. A familiar tenet of 'traditional' (i.e. post-medieval) logic is that all universal propositions distribute their subject terms (whereas particular ones do not) and that all negative propositions distribute their predicate terms (whereas affirmative ones do not). For example, in 'All men are mortal' and 'No men are liquid' the subject-terms 'men' in both cases 'refer' to the whole extent of the class of men, and are hence 'distributed', whereas in 'No men are liquid' and 'Some men are not liquid' the predicate terms 'liquid' in both cases 'refer' to the whole extent of the class of liquid things, and are hence likewise 'distributed'. Further, 'All men are mortal' is a *universal affirmative* proposition, 'No men are liquid' is a *universal negative* proposition, 'Some men are mortal' is a *particular affirmative* proposition, and 'Some men are not liquid' is a *particular negative* proposition. The universality or particularity of such categorical propositions is then referred to as their *quantity*, and their affirmativity or negativity as their *quality*. The idea of logical *quantity* is hence an integral part of the doctrine of distribution (*GRG* 3). Now the question at issue is whether or not allusions to 'distributed terms' are post-medieval confusions (*GRG* 63). *KSL* 119–20 suggests at least a thirteenth-century doctrine of distribution, and a twelfth-century origin for the associated notions of quantity and quality. In so suggesting *KSL* supersedes the view that the thirteenth-century Peter of Spain's *Summulae Logicales* (*HSL*) is "the first text in which the notions of quantity and quality occur" (*BHL* 211).

However, as has been pointed out in *HRK* 360, centuries before the medieval era Boethius had used all the notions and terminology now in question (e.g. quantity and quality, *B* 462A–B, *B* 465D–466A, *B* 769B, *B* 799B; distribution, *B* 463C). From this and numerous other examples it would appear that contemporary acquaintance with the Boethian origins of medieval logical terminology is sometimes lacking. It turns out that *De Grammatico* deploys many of the key terms used by the medievals; the commentary presented in §7 below hence embodies a sort of lexikon embracing those terms.

Nevertheless, the interest of *De Grammatico* extends well beyond its function as a collection of terminological examples, as will become evident hereunder, and as I have already tried to make plain elsewhere (*HDG*, *HL* §3, *HG*, *HW*). It is now several years since I ventured to conjecture that this dialogue reflects a rift between logicians, as represented by Boethius, and grammarians, as represented chiefly by Priscian (*HW*, *HDG* §4, *HL* §3.124). This conjecture has been amply confirmed by the more recently published monumental work of L. M. De Rijk (*DLM*; cf. the references thereto provided in *n*1.201*b*, *n*3.800*b*, *n*4.22*c*, and *n*4.234*a*). Since *DLM* traces in great detail the development of what has come to be considered as one of the centrally characteristic accomplishments of medieval logic, namely the doctrine of *suppositio*, it is now possible to see more clearly the place *De Grammatico* occupies in the history of that development. Thus it is in this dialogue that both the interest in fallacies and the contextual approach to the study of meaning which *DLM* I and *DLM* II–I 116 recognise as crucial are already well exemplified.

The commentary presented below may appear to be unduly overloaded with internal cross-references. However, I am unaware of any other method, apart from repetition by means of further distracting footnotes, giving rise to an almost infinite regress, of bringing to bear in a fashion undistorted by summarising all the multiple strands of background information relevant at any given point. Although the references to Boethius are all to the sometimes defective text of Migne (*B*) I have, where possible, emended the text of such references with the help of *BM* and *BB*. For present purposes I have alluded to the Migne version of Aristotle's *Categoriae* as being Boethius' translation. I have also retained the Migne nomenclature for Boethius' works on the syllogism. Questions have been raised on both these features of *PL* 64 (*A* xiii–xvi, *DLM* I 39 n.5) which scarcely affect the present work but which should, of course, be borne in mind.

§2. ST. ANSELM AS A LOGICIAN

There exist various well-known stock stories concerning both the history of medieval logic and the history of medieval philosophy. Hitherto there has been lacking a single guiding thread in terms of which the history of both of these may be systematically unified and clarified. In addition, the history of medieval philosophy has tended to be the monopoly of historians working in terms of the post-medieval literary mode of philosophising, almost totally alien to the logically-spined and lapidary brevity of the medievals themselves. As a result, the historians of medieval philosophy appear to be engaged in the sort of endless and futile mock-battle which Kant ascribes to certain metaphysicians: dangerous adventures, as he says, from which they can never desist, and which yet they can never bring to a termination. A solution to this situation, I would now tentatively propose, lies in the direction of certain reorientations suggested by the study of the logical work of St. Anselm. Indeed, it will be found that the discussion of these problems can illuminate, in a quite salient fashion, the significance of Anselm's logic as a whole, and of *De Grammatico* in particular.

In the first place the impression conveyed by Boehner (*BML* 1) and Bocheński (*BHL* 149) to the effect that medieval logic contains little of any interest before the time of Abelard is surely now beginning to undergo a change. The works of De Rijk, and in particular his most weighty *Logica Modernorum* (DLM), together with recent studies by other authors (*MMC* 444, *HDG*, *HL*) would at any rate tend to dissipate such an impression. While it may be true that such pre-Abelardian material by no means rivalled either in standard or extent the work of Abelard himself, I still feel that it has a peculiar interest of its own. Indeed, in the case of Anselm's contribution, not only are there points at which *De Grammatico*, for all its comparative brevity, outstrips in subtlety corresponding doctrines in Abelard (as certain of the commentative notes will indicate) but there are also some respects in which Anselm sets the scene for the already-mentioned fresh appreciation, in the light of contemporary interests, of the history not only of medieval logic, but of medieval philosophy as well.

For present purposes it will suffice to accept the usual account of the *Logica Vetus* ⊖ Old Logic, the logic available initially to Anselm. According to this account the only Aristotelian works with which he would be aquainted would be the *Categoriae* and *De Interpretatione*. In addition there would be Boethius' commentaries on these and on Porphyry's *Isagoge*, as well as other logical writings of Boethius' own composition. The *Analytica* (prior and posterior), *Topica*, and *De Sophisticis Elenchis*, all from Aristotle, would be unknown to Anselm. Boethius had in fact translated these Aristotelian works into Latin, but the versions published in *B* are now attributed to the post-Anselmian James of Venice.

It is Anselm's cardinal distinction between forms of sentence required by logical considerations and the often misleading impression conveyed by *usus loquenci* ⊖ the current course of utterance (*HG*, *HAN*, *HNA*, *HL* §2.12, *n*4.2341*a*) which sets the scene, not only for many of Anselm's applications of logic, but also for a reminder of certain important characteristics of medieval logic and philosophy as a whole. In *De Grammatico* it turns out that logical considerations may even require the logician to adopt forms of sentence which are at odds with *usus loquendi* ⊖ ordinary usage (cf. *HL* §2.12, *HAN*, *n*1.000*b*, *n*4.2341*b*). Now the whole body of medieval philosophy and logic is notorious for its employment of just such forms of sentence. This reflects the medievals' realisation that for logical or philosophical purposes certain semantical categories which are not available in non-technical speech, or which at least go unrecognised by the grammarian of ordinary language, may be required. What we have here, in fact, is a semi-artificial language: a sort of half-way house between natural language (using this term in its perhaps misleading modern sense) and the fully artificial languages of contemporary logic (*HLM* I §3).

This facet of Anselm's work not only brings him into collision with his grammarian contemporaries (*HW*, *HL* §3.124, *n*1.201*b*, *n*3.800*b*, *n*4.22*c*, *n*4.2341*a*) but also suggests the new guiding thread for the reorientation of the history of medieval logic and philosophy, as promised above. I have already exemplified elsewhere, and especially in *HLM*, the way in which this thread may be used (cf. *HMP* 255–6): the varying degrees of awareness of the contrast between technical language, with its novel parts of speech, and the varieties of *usus loquendi* ⊖ ordinary utterance, may be investigated. Various also are the attitudes which we find being adopted towards this contrast (*HL* §2.2). More important yet, the ways in which this artificialised language could give rise to misunderstanding between thinkers, thereby affecting the whole course of medieval philosophy, may be analysed (*HLM* III §5, §6, *HOF*, *HOS*). The entire field of medieval philosophical and logical writings constitutes an almost totally unexplored territory still awaiting elucidation in terms of this sort of survey. Carried out with the help of the fine and sympathetic co-ordinates made available by Leśniewski logical systems, with their unique sensitivity to diversity of semantical category (cf. §3) such an investigation promises to yield definite conclusions which the more literary type of elucidation (alien in its mode to the logically-structured medieval doctrines) could never hope to achieve. *HLM*, *HDG*, *HL*, *HMP*, *HEE*, and *HOF* represent the beginnings of this process.

To revert, however, to the effect of this cardinal distinction on Anselm's own output: a further result is his systematic statement of a method of proposition-analysis (*SN*, cf. *HL* §4) whereby the true, logical, or real form of a sentence is made explicit and contrasted with the apparent or merely grammatical forms misleadingly countenanced by *usus loquendi* ⊖ the current course of utterance. (One aspect of the theological significance of this contrast lies in the fact that for Anselm Holy Writ itself may sometimes suffer from the defects of *usus loquendi* ⊖ ordinary usage; another aspect will be mentioned below). Outside *SN*, in many of his works, this method of analysis is exploited to good effect by Anselm for the solution of logical and theological problems. Such solutions tend to cluster around certain salient problem-verbs on which turn the sentences to be analysed, e.g. '*facere*' ⊖ 'to bring about' (*HL* §6.2, *HAD*), '*dare*' ⊖ 'to give' (*HL* §6.3), '*debere*' ⊖ 'to be obliged' (*HL* §6.4), and '*velle*' ⊖ 'to will' (*HL* §6.5). Not immediately connected with the system of *SN*, but still within the ambit of the cardinal distinction mentioned above, are masterly analyses of the problems arising from the assumption that '*nihil*' ⊖ 'nothing' is a name like any other name (*n*4.813*b*, *HL* §6.6).

One may well ask: whence had Anselm the inspiration for the creation of this immensely significant distinction? It is interesting to note that both St. Augustine and St. Anselm attribute incapacity for the understanding of the high matters associated with the Trinity to the contamination of thought by the things of sense: *ea quae de corporalibus rebus ... perceperunt ad res incorporeas et spirituales transferre conantur* ⊖ they are impelled to transfer to incorporeal and spiritual matters those things which they have perceived in connection with corporeal objects (*De Trinitate* I, 1) says St. Augustine. Likewise St. Anselm has the well-known passage against those heretics of logic whose reason is so plunged into the imaginations of sense that they cannot rise above the latter, and hence should be expelled from the discussion of the spiritual (*Epistola de Incarnatione Verbi* I). It is, however, symptomatic of Anselm's special interest in logic that he goes on to give prectise details of the sort of incapacity which the sense-bound suffer, where Augustine had contended himself with merely saying that the speech of such persons followed crooked and distorted patterns. For Anselm we are here faced with a logical incapacity of a quite definite sort:

For how shall he who does not yet understand how many men can be specifically one man, understand how in that most hidden and high nature many persons, each of whom is wholly god, are one god? And how can he whose mind is too darkened to distinguish between his horse and its colour distinguish between one god and his many relationships?

Qui enim nondum intelligit quomodo plures homines in specie sint unus homo: qualiter in secretissima et altissima natura comprehendet quomodo plures personae, quarum singula quaeque perfectus est deus, sint unus deus? Et cuius mens obscura est ad diiudicandum inter equum suum et colorem eius: qualiter discernet inter unum deum et plures relationes eius? (*S* II 10.4.9, cf. *HL* 97–8, 106)

Now this mention of the distinction between the horse and its colour takes us immediately back to *De Grammatico* 14. There, in consequence of the logical truth '*albus est habens albedinem*' ⊖ '*white* is ... having whiteness' which has to be given the special logical interpretation described in chapter 21 of the same work, the meaning of the colour-word "white" is shown to be distinguishable from its reference (e.g. a horse). In other words, lack of skill in operating according to Anselm's cardinal distinction between the logical and the usual way of expressing things is the incapacity here in question.

This suggests, but of course in no way proves, that Anselm's distinction was perhaps in part inspired by the gap between discourse concerning the Trinity and the more usual ways of talking – a gap analogous to that already evident in the conflict between logicians and grammarians, noted above. In the face of such powerful evidence of the divergence between ordinary usage (the concern of the grammarian) and the truth in two of its most prominent manifestations, namely in theological and logical discourse, Anselm may have felt that the key to many problems lay in the distinction between the modes of expression required by logic, and the modes tolerable in non-technical contexts; hence the corresponding prominence of the use of this distinction in his own works.

§3. LOGICAL FRAME OF REFERENCE

At various points in the commentary (§7 below) an artifical language drawn from the logical systems of the Polish logician S. Leśniewski will be used for elucidatory purposes. It should be emphasised at the outset that use of such a language is not made in order to astonish non-logicians with an impressive array of squiggles; those who have no taste for this kind of thing may pass on and gain some understanding from the ordinary-language approximations which are usually also available, Much of the commentary is in any case of a historical nature, and hence does not primarily rely on the artificial language. Neither should the use of allusions to Leśniewski be taken to impy that St. Anselm was anticipating Leśniewski's logic. However, as both the thinkers mentioned were concerned with general truths as to how things are, it would not be surprising if at some points they had certain theses in common.

More positively, it would appear that translations of Anselmian statements into a suitable artificial language offers the only hope of coming to anything like a conclusive verdict on the cogency of his doctrines, and this for two main reasons.

First, it so happens that all philosophers and logicians are human beings who are born and grow up into the natural-language community of their tribe or nation. For certain purposes the language of everyday life has to be supplemented by technical language. If the user of the technical language is prepared to display common human politeness, then he will explain his technical language, using non-technical language as his starting point. Many present-day authors are 'impolite' relative to this criterion. They are prepared to put old terms to new uses, and to parade the result as a philosophical discovery of great profundity; the reader is duly impressed, and like the members of the crowd in the story of the king's new clothes feels that it is incumbent upon him to act as though he understood. At least Boethius and the medievals did what they could to explain their new uses of old words, as when Boethius expatiates on the various possible senses of 'in', so as to make his point clear. Even with such good will and ample precautions, however, the point of new or specialised senses for old terms can easily be missed. Whenever a natural language is modified in this way the reader cannot always see his way, and communication is still a shaky business (*HLM* III §5). The extremest form of consideration for the reader, therefore, lies in using as few terms as possible as starting points, and defining the rest in terms of these originals. This is what is at least in principle possible in respect of the excursions into artificial language essayed in the present work. Thus the propositional calculus presupposed may be founded on a single primitive term, and adding to this a further single primitive term for Ontology one advances by means of overtly stated rules of definition to new terms and new categories. It is in the light of the resultant clarity that conjectural analyses of Anselmian statements can be attempted.

The second reason why translation into modern artificial language is desirable arises from the fact that in *De Grammatico* we witness an argument between a *Magister* ⊖ Tutor and *Discipulus* ⊖ Student. The arguments are not merely a succession of assertions and counter-assertions. On the contrary, there are two major general patterns of exchange between the two interlocutors, namely: (i) certain premisses are propounded with which it is assumed the other will agree, and consequences are drawn therefrom; (ii) premisses definitely agreed by the other are shown to have consequences unpalatable to that other. In these and kindred cases, therefore, the drawing of consequences, or inferring, is involved. Hence are required some standards or criteria whereby the validity of such consequence-drawing inferences may be assessed. It is not the case (contrary to the impression which may be conveyed by some philosphers) that just anything follows from anything; rather, conclusion B follows from premiss(es) A when the proposition 'If A then B' is true and A is true. Whether or not this type of 'If ... then ...' proposition is true can be depicted as turning on whether or not the proposition in question is of such a general nature as to be limited to no definite subject-matter apart from what may in a very broad sense be called 'things in general', or is an instance of such general propositions. If this is the case, then logical theories are sufficient to check the validity of the inferences. If this is not the case, then their truth must be checked by reference to the theory appropriate to the subject-matter in question. Anselm's inferences can be represented as being sometimes of the first of these two sorts, sometimes of the second.

Provision will be made below for the consideration of both sorts of case. Here once again, therefore, we are in need of logical theories to which appeal may be made, and once again those of Leśniewski will be of service.

Space does not allow a full exposition of what Leśniewski called *Protothetic* (roughly speaking, propositional calculus with quantifiers and functorial variables). Ideally this, with its single primitive term, should first be introduced. Brevity demands that theses of Protothetic be presupposed herein without explicit statement, but any standard introduction to propositional calculus will be ample foundation for what follows. More detailed attention will be given to Leśniewski's *Ontology*, however, which involves the addition of a further primitive term '$\in$' (or such other as may be chosen, cf. *LR*). In this system the characteristic variables are initially nominal (as contrasted with the propositional variables of Protothetic). Fuller accounts of Ontology are given in *LR*, *HLM* II, *HDG* §6, and *LLL*. For present purposes it is only possible to give the minimum informal notational elucidation.

Lower-case letters of the Latin alphabet will be used as variables for names and name-like expressions (including adjectives and 'descriptions' in the Russellian sense; cf. *RI* XVI and *HLM* II §1). Lower-case letters of the Greek alphabet ('φ', 'ψ', 'χ') will be used as predicate variables; these should not be confused with the other Greek letters used as abbreviations for abstract nouns, to be proposed below. Logical theses will for the most part be prefaced by quantifiers, the latter being either universal (e.g. '$[ab]$ ...' which is read as 'for all *a*, *b*, ...') or particular (e.g. '$[\exists ab]$ ...', read as 'for some *a*, *b*, ...'). Quantification will be 'unrestricted' in the sense outlined in *LLE* and *HLM* II §2. The upshot of this non-restriction is that empty names (i.e. those which refer to nothing) as well as non-empty names (shared or unshared) may be envisaged as substituends in expressions which involve such quantification, and which also involve nominal variables. It is for this reason that the quantifier '$[\exists\ ...]$' is read off as 'for some...' rather than as 'there exists a... such that'. In this way questions of existential commitment may be disengaged from that immediate entanglement with quantification which has bedevilled logic ever since Russell's inception of discussion on 'descriptions'.

The advantages of the use of Ontology as a means for analysing propositions and checking inferences may be initially outlined in the following terms. The inner structure of any proposition (i.e. assertive sentence) may in the first place be roughly represented as '$\varphi(a)$' where 'φ' is a predicate and 'a' a name. (Here 'predicate' means an incomplete expression which, when completed by a name, forms a proposition). Thus '$\varphi(a)$' would be an adequate representation, for most purposes, of the logical form of propositions such as 'Jack runs' 'Pegaus flies' and 'Europeans intermarry', hence the reason why talk about predicates can often obviously amount to talk about verbs, in an ordinary grammatical sense of the latter. However, given the specification of 'predicate' provided above. it is evident that although '$\varphi(a)$' will for some purposes also be adequate for the representation of the form of propositions which are of great length and complexity, there may nevertheless be times when it is necessary to pay further attention to the inner structure of the predicate 'φ', at least to the extent of making explicit the 'is' of such predicates as 'is a runner', 'is a philosopher', and so forth. In such cases the remainder of the predicate apart from the 'is' is evidently a name or name-like expression (e.g. 'runner', 'philosopher') and hence adequately catered for by nominal variables. The indefinite article 'a' may be either for the moment neglected (so that we are in the situation of languages which, like Latin, have no articles) or it may be assimilated to the 'is' as 'is (a)'. After all, we have the same 'is' without the following article in cases wherein the second name-like expression in the sentence is an adjective, as in 'Jack is tall'. There will arise no instance in this present work where the difference between sentences such as the last-quoted one and one such as 'Jack is a philosopher' is of any logical significance.

Now predicates involving 'is' of the sort under consideration form *true* sentences when the name which completes the predicate is an unshared name or name-like expression (i.e. a proper noun or definite description). Other conditions are also required, and we accordingly will find it convenient to enrich our logical symbolism by means of the single primitive term '$\in$', readable in English as 'is' or 'is a', and in Latin by '*est*', and informally characterise it as being a two-argument functor which forms a proposition from two names; it is also such that a proposition of the form '$a \in b$' is true if and only if either 'a' and 'b' each name only the same individual object (as in 'Tully is Cicero') or 'a' names only one individual object and 'b' names several, of which a is one, as in 'Tully is an orator' (cf. *LR* 157). (The move from consideration of sentences whose form is adequately characterisable relative to the purposes in hand as '$\varphi(a)$' to those whose form is characterised in more detail as '$a \in b$' corresponds in part to the medieval rules on the interchange of predications *de secundo adiacete* ⊖ of a second component with predications *de tertio adiacente* ⊖ of a third component, as described in *n*4.8121*a*). No claim is made as to the correspondence between this primitive term and any 'is' of ordinary language. However, it will be found convenient for the analysis of sentences in ordinary language with suitable modifications either to it or to its arguments. At the same time, as *LR* shows, it is not by any means the sole primitive term usuable for the axiomatisation of Ontology.

However, the fact that this '$\in$' may be used as the sole primitive term of a logical theory is one reason why the resulting theory is called 'Ontology'; it is, so to speak, an '*is*-ology' if one characterises it with reference to this primitive term. As already stated, we assume as given in Protothetic those functors from propositional calculus which form propositions from propositions, i.e. '$\equiv$' for 'if and only if', '$\supset$' for 'if ... then ...', '$\vee$' for 'or' and '$\cdot$' for 'and' are all functors which form propositions from two propositional arguments; finally '$\sim$' for 'it's not that...' forms propositions from single propositional arguments. The dot or groups of dots have in fact a dual role; they function both as 'and' and as punctuation. In the latter use they may be thought of as single-ended parentheses the strengths of which vary according to number. For fuller codification of the dotting conventions see *HLM* 32–5, *LR* 160–1, *HDG* 125.

Leśniewski's original axiom of Ontology (hereunder referred to as 'Ax') incorporates the primitive '$\in$' and runs as follows:

Ax. $[ab] :: a \in b \,.\equiv :. [\exists c] \,.\, c \in a :. [c] : c \in a \,.\supset .\, c \in b :. [cd] : c \in a \,.\, d \in a \,.\supset .\, c \in d$

i.e. for all *a* and *b*: *a* is *b* if and only if for some *c*, *c* is *a*, and for all *c*, if *c* is *a* then *c* is *b*, and for all *c* and *d*, if *c* is *a* and *d* is *a* then *c* is *d*.

Rules for definition (*LR* 172–3) will not here be stated. Intuitively, however, it is obvious that the sentences of Ontology which now follow introduce new expressions by reference to the primitive term. First are presented definitions of the functors 'ex( )', 'sol( )', and 'ob( )', each of which forms a proposition from a single nominal argument:

.1 $[a] : \mathrm{ex}(a) \,.\equiv .\, [\exists b] \,.\, b \in a$ (*LR* T1) i.e., for all *a* there exists at least one *a* if and only if for some *b*, *b* is *a*. (First functor of existence).

.2 $[a]:\mathrm{sol}(a).\equiv:[bc]:b\in a.c\in a.\supset.b\in c$ (*LR* T5)

i.e., for all *a* there exists at most one *a* if and only if for all *b* and *c*, if *b* is *a* and *c* is *a* then *b* is *c*. (Second functor of existence).

.3 $[a]:\mathrm{ob}(a).\equiv.[\exists b].a\in b$ (*LR* T16)

i.e. for all *a*, there exists exactly one *a* if and only if for some *b*, *a* is *b*. (Third functor of existence).

(Note that the 'ob( )' defined in .3 may also be read as '... is an object'). In extension of what has already been stated above concerning quantification, it is now evident that statements concerning existence need no longer be immediately embedded in quantificational notation.

The following definitions are of functors ('$\subset$', '$\not\subset$', etc.) which form propositions from two nominal arguments:

.4 $[ab]:.a\subset b.\equiv:[c]:c\in a.\supset.c\in b$ (*LR* T19)

i.e., for all *a* and *b*, all *a* is *b* if and only if for all *c*, if *c* is *a* then *c* is *b*. (Weak Inclusion).

.5 $[ab]:.a\not\subset b.\equiv:[c]:c\in a.\supset.\sim(c\in b)$ (*LR* T23)

i.e., for all *a* and *b*, no *a* is *b* if and only if for all *c*, if *c* is a then it is not that *c* is *b*. (Weak exclusion).

.6 $[ab]:a\triangle b.\equiv.[\exists c].c\in a.c\in b$ (*LR* T20)

i.e., for all *a* and *b*, some *a* is *b* if and only if for some *c*, *c* is *a* and *c* is *b*. (Partial inclusion).

.7 $[ab]:a\not\triangle b.\equiv.[\exists c].c\in a.\sim(c\in b)$ (*LR* T24)

i.e., for all *a* and *b*, some *a* is not *b* if and only if for some *c*, *c* is *a* and it is not that *c* is *b*. (Partial exclusion).

.8 $[ab]:a=b.\equiv.a\in b.b\in a$ (*LR* T25)

i.e., for all *a* and *b*, *a* is the same object as *b* if and only if *a* is *b* and *b* is *a*. (Singular identity).

.9 $[ab]:.a\bigcirc b.\equiv:[c]:c\in a.\equiv.c\in b$ (*LR* T27) i.e., for all *a* and *b*, only all *a* is *b* if and only if for all *c*, *c* is *a* if and only if *c* is *b*. (Weak identity).

.10 $[ab] :: a \square b . \equiv :. [\exists c] . c \in a :. [c] : c \in a . \equiv . c \in b$ (*LR* T26)

i.e., for all *a* and *b*, only every *a* is *b* if and only if for some *c*, *c* is *a*, and for all *c*, *c* is *a* if and only if *c* is *b*. (Strong identity).

Thus far all the functors defined form propositions; now we have one (i.e. 'trm⟨ ⟩') which forms a name from a verb (i.e. from a predicate, a functor which forms a proposition from a name):

.11 $[a\varphi] : a \in \text{trm}\langle\varphi\rangle . \equiv . a \in a . \varphi(a)$

i.e., for all *a* and φ, *a* is a φ-er if and only if *a* is *a* and φ of *a*.

Hence if 'φ' is 'runs', then 'trm⟨φ⟩' amounts to 'runner'. The notation used in .11 is suggested by the expression 'term satisfying…', which is an alternative sometimes used instead of '… er'. Since abstract nouns are sometimes used for the expression of the '$\varphi(a)$' part of the *definiens*, as when we say 'Whiteness is predicated of *a*' instead of '"… is white" is predicated of *a*', it will be found below to be at least convenient to consider abstract nouns as among possible arguments of 'trm⟨ ⟩' (cf. *HLM* 97–8, *HDG* 138–9).

The angular brackets used in .11 indicate that the semantical category of this name-forming functor differs from that appropriate when '( )' is used with proposition-forming functors which take names as their arguments. Brackets of diverse forms should ideally be used at all junctures where such categorial diversity has to be indicated (e.g. .15 below) but the typographical difficulties which would ensue, as well as the informal nature of the present discourse, allow of such brackets being used in only a few cases, as in .11, .12, and .17.

Below, 'trm⟨ ⟩' will, among other uses, serve for the analysis of certain occurrences of nominally construed participles; e.g. if 'φ' is '*lucet*' ⊖ 'shines', then 'trm⟨φ⟩' is '*lucens*' ⊖ 'shiner'. It will also be used in cases where a name or name-like expression is formed from an abstract noun, as when from '*albedo*' ⊖ 'whiteness' we have '*qui habet albedinem*' ⊖ 'that which / he who has whiteness'.

Having just considered a definition which ensures the availability of a name corresponding to every verb or abstract noun, we may now introduce a definition offering a converse guarantee, according to which a verb '$\in[\![\quad]\!]$' corresponds to every noun, i.e.

.12 $[ab]:\in[\![b]\!](a).\equiv.a\in b$

Thus, to take feasible examples from the comparatively small segment of English in which this correlation holds, if '*b*' is 'deputy', then '$\in[\![b]\!]$' is 'deputises'. Correspondingly in Latin, if '*b*' is '*rex*' ⊖ 'king', then '$\in[\![b]\!]$' is '*regnat*' ⊖ 'reigns'.

However '$\in[\![\quad]\!]$' is not the only possible functor which takes a name as its argument in order to form a proposition-forming functor taking, in its turn, a single nominal argument. Of the same semantical category as '$\in[\![\quad]\!]$' are '$\subset[\![\quad]\!]$' and '$\mathrm{Cl}[\![\quad]\!]$', defined as follows:

.13 $[ab]:\subset[\![a]\!](b).\equiv.b\subset a$
.14 $[ab]:\mathrm{Cl}[\![a]\!](b).\equiv.b\bigcirc a$

The functors here defined are chiefly of use as arguments of the higher-order '$\in$' which is the object of the next definition. However, '$\subset[\![\quad]\!]$' may be rendered as '... are included in ...' or 'being included in ...', and '$\mathrm{Cl}[\![\quad]\!]$' as '... form the class of...', of as just 'being...', according to the context in each case. For further discussion of .14, see *n*3.431*a*.

Since verbs (predicates) of various inner structures have now been made available by .12, .13, and .14, it now remains to define a functor which forms propositions out of two such verbs; this was a possibility recognised and used by the medievals in several forms (cf. *n*4.2411*h*, *n*1.000*b*, *n*3.431*a*, *n*3.44*a*, *HLM* 43, 90, 96, *HDG* 131, and *APH* 54, 55, 56, 96). 'Walking is moving' or 'To walk is to move' serve as simple examples of the sort of thing intended. These and more complex problem-sentences will turn out to be capable of resolution in terms of the following higher-order '... $\in$ ...' ('... is ...') which takes verbs (predicates) as arguments:

.15 $$[\varphi\psi]::\varphi\in\psi.\equiv:.[\exists a].\varphi(a).\psi(a):.[bc]:\varphi(b).\varphi(c).\equiv.b\bigcirc c$$

We are now in a position to begin to clarify a factor which often fogs talk about *being*, or talk which involves the verb '... is ...'. For not only can definitions of functors analogous to those already defined in terms of the lower-order '$\in$' now be expressed in terms of the higher-order '$\in$', e.g.

.16 $[\varphi\psi] : \varphi = \psi . \equiv . \varphi \in \psi . \psi \in \varphi$

follows the lines of .8; in addition, all theses which hold at the level of the lower-order '$\in$' hold also in respect of their analogues in terms of higher-order '$\in$'. *LA* may be consulted for further discussion of this higher-order '... is ...'.

Next is defined a functor ('Cl{ }') which exemplifies further semantical complexities, and which will serve in an attempt to give concise co-ordinates to the sense of one of Anselm's results (cf. *n*4.31*a*):

.17 $[a\varphi] : \mathrm{Cl}\{\varphi\}\,(a) . \equiv . \mathrm{Cl}[\![\mathrm{trm}\langle\varphi\rangle]\!]\,(a)$

Some further definitions to which reference may be made are as follows:

.18 $[a] : a \in \vee . \equiv . a \in a$ (*LR* T72)
.19 $[a] : a \in \wedge . \equiv . a \in a . \sim (a \in a)$ (*LR* T73)
.20 $[abc] : a \in b \cap c . \equiv . a \in a . a \in b . a \in c$
.21 $[ab] : a \in \neg\,(b) . \equiv . a \in a . \sim (a \in b)$ (*LR* T74)

In .18 the *definiendum* '$\vee$' may be read as '(an) object'; in .19 '$\wedge$' may be read as '(an) object which does not exist'. The '$\cap$' of .20 is an 'and' forming a name from two names, and the '$\neg$( )' of .21 is a nominal negation, enabling one to distinguish (as is now easily possible, given the unrestricted quantification mentioned above) between such sentences as 'The present King of France is non-bald' and 'It is not that the present King of France is bald', confusion between which has led logicians into endless epicycles since the year 1905 (cf. *n*.4.813*d*, *HLM* 73–4). Examples of the advantages of having available all three of definitions .18, .19, and .21, may be further seen in *HL* §6.6 and *HLM* III §4.

Now it is obviously possible to derive theses of Ontology from the definitions alone, using only considerations derived from Protothetic (i.e. enriched Propositional Calculus) in their support; for example:

.22 $[a] . a \bigcirc a$
.23 $[ab] : a \bigcirc b . \equiv . b \bigcirc a$
.24 $[ab] :. a \bigcirc b . \equiv : [c] : c \bigcirc a . \equiv . b \bigcirc c$
.25 $[ab] : a \bigcirc c . c \bigcirc b . \supset . a \bigcirc b$
.26 $[ab] : a \subset b . c \subset a . \supset . c \subset b$

.27 $[ab] : a \bigcirc b . \supset . a \subset b$

.28 $[abc] : b \subset a . c \bigcirc b . \supset . c \subset a$

.29 $[ab] : a \bigcirc b . \equiv . a \subset b . b \subset a$

.30 $[ab] : \sim (a \triangle b) . \equiv . a \not\subset b$

.31 $[ab] :. \sim (a \bigcirc b) . \equiv : [\exists c] : \sim (c \in a . \equiv c \in b)$

.32 $[ab] :. \sim (a \bigcirc b) . \equiv : [\exists c] : c \in a . \sim (c \in b) . \vee . \sim (c \in a) . c \in b$

However, by invoking the axiom stated above one has theses such as the following, some of which will also of use in the commentary. To each are annexed parenthetical indications of the theses or definitions needed for their proof.

.33 $[a] : \text{ob}(a) . \supset . \text{ex}(a)$ (.3, Ax.)

.34 $[a] : \text{ob}(a) . \supset . \text{sol}(a)$ (.3, Ax., .2)

.35 $[abc] : a \in b . c \in a . \supset . c \in b$ (Ax.)

.36 $[ab] :: b \in a :. [cd] : c \in a . d \in a . \supset . c \in d :. \supset . a \in b$ (Ax.)

.37 $[a] : \text{ex}(a) . \text{sol}(a) . \supset . \text{ob}(a)$ (.2, .1, .36)

.38 $[a] : \text{ob}(a) . \supset . \text{ex}(a) . \text{sol}(a)$ (.33, .34)

.39 $[ab] : a \in b . \equiv . \text{ex}(a) . a \subset b . \text{sol}(a)$ (Ax., .1, .4, .2)

This last thesis elucidates the axiom stated above.

.40 $[ab] : a = b . \supset . a \bigcirc b$ (.8, Ax., .9)

.41 $[abc] : a \in b . b \in c . \supset . b \in a$ (Ax., .36)

.42 $[ab] : a \triangle b . \text{ob}(a) . \text{ob}(b) . \supset . a = b$ (.3, .6, .41, .35, .8)

Now follow theses involving the higher-order '$\in$' (cf. .15) and its arguments:

.43 $[a] . \text{Cl}[\![a]\!](a)$ (.14, .22)

.44 $[abc] : \text{Cl}[\![a]\!](b) . \text{Cl}[\![a]\!](c) . \supset . b \bigcirc c$ (.9, .14, .25)

.45 $[abc] : \text{Cl}[\![a]\!](b) . b \bigcirc c . \supset . \text{Cl}[\![a]\!](c)$ (.9, .14, .25)

.46 $[abc] :. \text{Cl}[\![a]\!](b) . \supset : \text{Cl}[\![a]\!](c) . \equiv . b \bigcirc c$ (.44, .45)

.47 $[ab] : \text{Cl}[\![a]\!] \in \text{Cl}[\![b]\!] . \supset . \text{Cl}[\![b]\!] \in \text{Cl}[\![a]\!]$ (.14, .15, .23, .25)

.48	$[ab]: \mathrm{Cl}[\![a]\!] \in \mathrm{Cl}[\![b]\!] . \supset . \mathrm{Cl}[\![a]\!] = \mathrm{Cl}[\![b]\!]$	(.47, .16)
.49	$[ab]: \mathrm{Cl}[\![a]\!] \in \mathrm{Cl}[\![b]\!] . \equiv . \mathrm{Cl}[\![a]\!] = \mathrm{Cl}[\![b]\!]$	(.47, .48)
.50	$[ab]: \mathrm{Cl}[\![a]\!] \in \mathrm{Cl}[\![b]\!] . \supset . \mathrm{Cl}[\![a]\!] \in \subset[\![b]\!]$	(.15, .14, .27, .13)
.51	$[ab]: a \subset b . \supset . \mathrm{Cl}[\![a]\!] \in \subset[\![b]\!]$	(.13, .14, .22, .15, .24)
.52	$[ab]: \mathrm{Cl}[\![a]\!] \in \subset[\![b]\!] . \supset . a \subset b$	(.15, .23, .13, .28)
.53	$[ab]: \mathrm{Cl}[\![a]\!] \in \subset[\![b]\!] . \equiv . a \subset b$	(.51, .52)
.54	$[ab]: \mathrm{Cl}[\![a]\!] \in \mathrm{Cl}[\![b]\!] . \supset . a \bigcirc b$	(.15, .14, .23, .25)
.55	$[ab]: a \bigcirc b . \supset . \mathrm{Cl}[\![a]\!] \in \mathrm{Cl}[\![b]\!]$	(.14, .15)
.56	$[ab]: \mathrm{Cl}[\![a]\!] \in \mathrm{Cl}[\![b]\!] . \equiv . a \bigcirc b$	(.54, .55)

It has been assumed in respect of theses .47–.56 that the arguments of the higher-order '$\in$' therein involved are of a form sufficiently distinctive to indicate the diversity of semantical category holding between this '$\in$' and the primitive '$\in$' of Ontology. Strictly speaking, as already noted above, a new pattern of bracket enclosing the argument-place should signal this diversity.

Now although it is quite plain that Anselm, like many other medievals, intended his theses based on concrete examples such as '*grammaticus*' ⊖ 'literate' to be taken in a general sense, it will nevertheless make for accuracy of analysis if his actual examples are translated into a language based on Ontology with the help of the following abbreviations of his most-used non-logical constant terms:

.57 '**g**' for '*grammaticus*' ⊖ 'literate'

.58 'γ' for '*grammatica*' ⊖ 'literacy'

.59 '**h**' for '*homo*' ⊖ 'man' (in the sense of 'human being')

.60 'α' for '*rationalitas et mortalitas et animalitas*' ⊖ 'rationality and mortality and animality', i.e. what later came to be regarded as equivalent to '*humanitas*' ⊖ 'humanity'.

.61 '**w**' for '*albus*' ⊖ 'white'

.62 'ω' for '*albedo*' ⊖ 'whiteness'

.63 '**a**' for '*animal*'

.64 '**r**' for '*rationalis*' ⊖ 'rational'

.65 'λ' for '*rationalitas*' ⊖ 'rationality'

.66 '**m**' for '*mortalis*' ⊖ 'mortal'

From what has been said above in connection with 'trm⟨ ⟩ (.11) it may be gathered that abstract nouns such as those abbreviated in .58, .60, .62, and .65, are herein, following the suggestions of *LA*, taken to be more verb-like than name-like, since they are usable as substituends for predicate variables. Aquinas, in his commentary on Boethius' *De Hebdomadibus* lec. 2, n.21, likewise aligns the infinitive form of the verb with the abstract noun as opposed to the concrete noun:

The difference between the meaning of 'to be' and that of 'that which is' is like the difference between 'to run' and 'runner'. For 'to run' and 'to be' signify abstractly, as also does 'whiteness', whereas that which is, i.e. *be-er* and *runn-er* are signified concretely, as in the case of a *white*.	*Aliud significamus per hoc quod dicimus esse, et aliud per hoc quod dicimus id quod est: sicut et aliud significamus cum dicimus currere, et aliud per hoc quod dicitur currens. Nam currere et esse significantur in abstracto, sicut et albedo: sed quod est, id est ens et currens, significantur sicut in concreto, velut album: JN* 126.

Verb-forms (e.g. 'to run') are possible arguments of the higher-order '∊' (.15) as opposed to the concrete names which are possible arguments of the lower-order '∊'. This correlation with Aquinas' text has yielded an interpretation of his discourse concerning *esse* ⊖ to-be and *ens* ⊖ be-er (*HLM* III §6) and may now also be used to clarify the relation between the abstract nouns and the concrete forms which correspond thereto (e.g. the relation between '*albedo*' ⊖ 'whiteness' and '*albus*' ⊖ 'white'). First we need to define 'el⟦ ⟧', i.e. 'element of the class determined by ...', thus:

.67 $[a\varphi] : a \in \mathrm{el}[\![\varphi]\!] \,.\equiv.\, [\exists b] \,.\, \varphi \in \mathrm{Cl}[\![b]\!] \,.\, a \in b$

Assuming the concrete form (e.g. '*albus*' ⊖ 'white') to be less problematical than the abstract (verb-like) form (e.g. '*albedo*' ⊖ 'whiteness') we can now show the relation between the two by means of the following frame:

.68 $[\varphi] :: \varphi \in \mathbf{\Psi} \,.\equiv:.\, \varphi \in \varphi :.\, [a] : a \in \mathrm{el}[\![\varphi]\!] \,.\equiv.\, a \in \mathbf{X}$

Herein, if the concrete form is seen as standing in the place of '**X**' as the argument of the right-hand (lower-order) '∊', then the corresponding abstract form may be viewed as the counterpart of the '**Ψ**' which occurs as the argument of the left-hand (higher-order) '∊'.

§4. BASIC PRESUPPOSITIONS

It is only possible to understand fully the dialogue's central argument in the light of those presuppositions which are traced at full length in the commentary on the text (§ 7). The present section is therefore grounded upon the details of that commentary, and can only yield partial understanding. Neither does it purport to be adequate for the interpretation of the doctrines of all the authors cited in the course of the commentary: only sufficient material for a preliminary appreciation of the central presuppositions and logical status of the discussion in *De Grammatico* has been brought within the scope of the present section. An excellent general appreciation of the logical and grammatical situation of the period is to be found in *JA*, while *JN* may be usefully consulted as a guide to the considerable elaboration of the concepts deployed by Anselm which will have taken place by the time of Aquinas.

It is clear from 4.60 that the dialogue's initial question, i.e. whether *literate* is substance or quality, is a question susceptible of receiving two equivalent answers, one of which is, like the question, expressed in a *de re* ⊖ thing-centred fashion, the other of which is expressed in a *de voce* ⊖ word-centred fashion. It is in the second of these two modes that the central distinctions are first made (4.23). It is also clear (e.g. from 4.24) that the determination of these answers is closely connected in Anselm's mind with a certain view of definition (*n*3.800*b*). This view must hence be investigated and will be found in its turn to be bound up with what is, from a purely logical point of view, a special concept of objecthood (*n*4.2411*d*, *n*4.1201*a*) as well as with the predicables such as *genus*, *species*, and constitutive characteristic, as expounded by Porphyry and commented on by Boethius (*n*4.2411*g*, *n*4.2411*h*, *n*4.22*d*).

The relation between definition and the predicables mentioned can be briefly exemplified in the simple case of the definition of *man* as *rational animal*. This definition is said to hold good because *animal* is a genus (subordinating class) of which *man* is a species (subordinate class), with rationality as the characteristic which serves to separate *man* from other species of *animal*. What we have here is the result of an activity which looks, as it were, in two directions. On the one hand such a definition encapsules truths about objects, these objects being of a sort pre-theoretically recognisable as such. These objects are the unities (in the sense of being unambiguously countable) which figure in ordinary human responses to questions such as 'How many men?'. This is a type of question which can in principle be answered by anybody. In contrast, 'How many whites?', in the absence of any further information as to the sorts of objects which are white (e.g. men, ants, stones) is unanswerable, since one cannot grasp what is to count as a unitary white. (It is to be understood that whitenesses of diverse sorts are *not* in question here: cf. *n*4.2411*d*, *n*4.72*a*, *HL* §3.12231, *AGT* 86–7). Anselm reflects this pre-theoretical basis of his questionings when he advocates, at 3.800, a return to the sure truths which concern *man* and *animal*. Sophistical relapses into falsehood, he says, are unlikely here. On the other hand the definitions themselves are an advance towards the theoretical stage, where one gives an account (*ratio*), involving a definition, of whatever it is that is being discussed. And yet in spite of the eye which is all the time being kept on the obvious (with reference to the pre-theoretical view of things) it may happen that when the account is presented by the theorist, it appears to abrogate that pre-theoretical view. The occurrence of such an apparent abrogation is one of the central themes of the dialogue (1.1, 1.2, 4.10, 4.11, 4.21, 4.62).

In what follows, therefore, it will be convenient to talk in terms of the putative theories which are associated with definitions. This way of talking should be seen as a convention at least suitable for present purposes. If exception is taken to this way of talking, then this is no great matter. It may be relinquished in favour of some of the other possible alternatives. However, it is useful at this present juncture to be able to point out that it is plain from Boethius' language when commenting on the *Categoriae* of Aristotle that there is a feature common to all such theoretical accounts of things, namely that they involve what are technically called predications *de subiecto* ⊖ of a subject (cf. *n*4.101*a*). Hence if some means of characterising such predications can be found, then the result will be what is, in effect, a generalisation concerning the putative theories now in question.

One salient feature of predications *de subiecto* ⊖ of a subject (properly so-called) is already in evidence in Anselm's own text, when he speaks of characteristics in the absence of which an object perishes (4.2411). The attribution of such characteristics is common to all *de subiecto* ⊖ of a subject predications. In respect of temporal objects this is because the names which are predicated *de subiecto* ⊖ of a subject apply to an object during the whole time of its existence. Thus Boethius contrasts the cases of *animal* and *man* (*B*176A, B) with those of fleeting characteristics such as colours, which although they may (in a form of locution which Aristotle and Boethius prefer to eschew in their respect, cf. *n*4.101*a* and *HL* §3.1222) be said to be predicated *de subiecto* ⊖ of a subject, are nevertheless not thus predicated in the technical sense of '*de subiecto*' ⊖ 'of a subject' now in question.

De subiecto ⊖ of a subject predications (in this technical sense) are of two sorts. They may be *in eo quod quid* ⊖ in respect of 'whatness', insofar as they answer the question '*Quid sit?*' ⊖ 'What is it?'. They may also be *in eo quod quale* ⊖ in respect of quality, insofar as they answer the question '*Quale sit?*' ⊖ 'What is it like?'. These two sorts are seen as mutually exclusive (*n*3.501*a*). Those of the first sort are always *de subiecto* ⊖ of a subject, and hence are correlated in an unqualified manner with the existence of the thing in question, in the sense that denial of the predicate is always equivalent to the denial of the existence of the subject (*n*4.2411*d*). In contrast predications *in eo quod quale* ⊖ in respect of quality are not invariably *de subiecto* ⊖ of a subject (in the technical sense). Thus rationality, a constitutive characteristic of *man* (*n*4.22*d*) is predicated both *in eo quod quale* ⊖ in respect of a quality and *de subiecto* ⊖ of a subject, as far as *man* is concerned, whereas the quality warmth, although essential to fire (and hence in relation to fire involving *de subiecto* ⊖ of a subject predication) is not essential to water, and hence is not a *de subiecto* predication as far as water is concerned. When fire is no longer warm it is no longer fire, whereas cessation of the applicability of the predicate 'is warm' to a sample of previously warm water does not amount to a denial of the existence of that water (*B* 192B).

In principle theories of the sort described may have as their subject-matters objects subsumable under any of the Aristotelian categories (cf. *n*3.800*b*) but in order to bring the discussion more immediately to the point most prominently exemplified in Boethius and Anselm, generalisations centred on *de subiecto* ⊖ of a subject predications occurring in theories which have substances (cf. *n*4.1201*a*) as their subject-matter will turn out to be most convenient, especially as objects in categories other than that of substance may be said to be in a sense dependent upon substances. Such substances also correspond most closely to 'objects' in the pre-theoretically grounded sense of the word which is being adumbrated in these preliminaries (cf. *n*4.2411*d*). Hence theories such as those of *man*, *horse*, and *stone* (all of which are drawn upon by Anselm) exemplify the sort now in question.

The type of object-hood described above involves (as has already been pointed out) the two closely interconnected topics of the predicables (*n*4.2411*a*) and the Aristotelian requirements for definition properly so-called (*n*3.800*b*), and may now be partially related to the logical framework described in §3. As regards the first, it is already clear from Lejewski's analysis (*LA* 248–9) and from Boethius' own words (discussed in detail in *n*4.2411*h*, part ii) that assertions involving the vocabulary of the predicables (e.g. '*man* is a species', '*animal* is a genus', and '*man* is *animal*') incorporate an 'is' (or 'is a') of higher semantical category than the primitive '$\in$' of Ontology. They can in fact be interpreted consistently as involving the use of the higher-order '$\in$' defined at §3.15. The consistency of this possible interpretation is illustrated in *HDG* §6, *HLM* III, as well as in the use to be made of the higher-order '$\in$' in the subsequent commentary (§7 below).

This interpretation may next be linked with the definition of *species* if 'genus' ('$\mathbf{\Gamma}$') (cf. *n*4.2411*g*) and '*differentia*' $\ominus$ 'constitutive characteristic' ('$\mathbf{\Delta}$') (*n*4.22*d*) are introduced as undefined constant terms which are proposition-forming functors taking one nominal argument. They should hence be read off as '... form(ing) a genus' and '... stands as a *differentia*' or in some such way which will straddle the diverse ways of talking appropriate when used with a nominal argument (e.g. 'animals form a genus') or when they themselves take on an independent status as arguments of the higher-order 'is'; e.g. '(being an) *animal* is (forming a) genus', cf. *LA* 247–9. In this way one can can elucidate the notion of *species* ($\mathbf{E}$):

.1 $$[a] : \mathrm{Cl}[\![a]\!] \in \mathbf{E} \,.\equiv.\, \mathrm{ex}(a) \,.\, [\exists b\varphi] \,.\, \mathrm{Cl}\,[\![b]\!] \in \mathbf{\Gamma} \,. \\ .\, \mathrm{Cl}\,\{\varphi\} \in \mathbf{\Delta} \,.\, \mathrm{Cl}[\![a]\!] \in \mathrm{Cl}[\![b \cap \mathrm{trm}\langle\varphi\rangle]\!] \qquad (\S 3.1.14.15.11.20)$$

(*n*3.800*b* and *HDG* §6.32 may also be consulted in this connection).

From the foregoing the nature of statements occurring in the context of a discussion involving the predicables is to the relevant extent clarified. '*Man* is a species', '*Animal* is a genus' and '*Man* is *animal*' have the following forms respectively:

.2 $\mathrm{Cl}[\![\mathbf{h}]\!] \in \mathbf{E}$

.3 $\mathrm{Cl}[\![\mathbf{a}]\!] \in \boldsymbol{\Gamma}$

.4 $\mathrm{Cl}[\![\mathbf{h}]\!] \in \subset [\![\mathbf{a}]\!]$

One of Aquinas' comments on the third example is reproduced in *n*3.800*b* and part ii of *n*4.2411*h*. Each of the examples involves what was later to become known as *suppositio simplex* ⊖ simple supposition (cf. *HLM* III §1). Hence it is scarcely true to claim that such *suppositio* 'has little bearing on formal logic' (*DLM* II–I 589).

The close connection of *intelligere* ⊖ to understand and *significatio* ⊖ meaning is discussed in *n*3.101*a*, and the way in which *significatio* ⊖ meaning and definitions are mutually related throughout the dialogue leaps to the eye (e.g. 3.21, 4.240; for fuller details of these relationships see *n*3.101*a*). Now the central point of the dialogue turns on the *significatio* ⊖ meaning or *definitio* ⊖ definition of '*grammaticus*' ⊖ 'literate' (cf. 4.23, 4.24) so that it would be scarcely surprising if much of its discourse turned out to involve the higher-order 'is' also. Quite apart from the internal consistency which will be found to result from this supposition, it receives striking confirmation in the Tutor's words at 4.81. There the question of the meaning of a name (or the *de re* ⊖ thing-centred correlate of such a question) is forcefully distinguished from the question as to whether, in effect, the following is a thesis:

.5 $[a]: a \in \mathbf{w} \,.\supset.\, \mathrm{ob}(a)$

(*utrum omnis qui est albus sit aliquid aut sit qui habet* ⊖ whether everything that is white is something or a haver). In the case of an affirmative answer being given to this question, then the lower-order '∈' of .5 is clearly appropriate. But, says the Tutor, this is not the relevant question: the problem is not whether everything which is white is something, but whether 'is something' can be said to be contained in the meaning of the name 'white' in the way that *man* contains *animal*: *utrum hoc nomen sua significatione contineat hoc quod dicitur aliquid ... sicut homo continet animal*. Now the latter example, that of *man* and *animal*, being *de re* ⊖ thing-centred, is plainly analysable as in .4, with its higher-order '∈'. We may hence infer that higher-order statements such as .4 are the *de re* ⊖ thing-centred correlates of *de voce* ⊖ utterance-centred meaning statements. At least this coheres with the Tutor's conclusion that although of course if something is (lower-order '∈') white, then it is an existing object ('ob( )', *aliquid habens* ⊖ something having ...) this need not have any connection with the meaning of 'white' (cf. *HLM* III §2).

It therefore seems feasible to suppose that the higher-order '∈' will be involved in the statement of the *de re* ⊖ thing-centred equivalent of any statement of the *significatio* ⊖ meaning of 'white'. In the passage which has just been discussed (4.81) as also at 4.4233, the talk about meaning goes on by overt reference to forms of words ('this name ... signifies exactly this phrase ...', 4.4233), yet the admission of *quaestiones de voce* ⊖ word-centred questions and *quaestiones de re* ⊖ thing-centred questions as alternative modes of stating the dialogue's problem (4.601–4.603) is sufficient to show that the offering of *de re* ⊖ thing-centred formulations in terms of the higher-order '∈' as correlates of *de voce* ⊖ word-centred statements in the text of the dialogue is quite in keeping with the spirit of that text. '"Literate" is a word signifying a quality' and '*Literate* is quality' are both stated to be alternative and equally acceptable versions of one result of the discussion (4.601). Similar alternative formulations are to be found elsewhere, e.g. 'In the same way as *man* is made up of animality, rationality and mortality, so that "man" signifies these three things, so also *literate* is made up of *man* and literacy, and therefore the name signifies them both' (4.240). Those parts of this passage which are non-metalinguistic and involve the functor '... is made up of ...' belong to definitional (i.e. predicable-level) talk, for the transcription of which the higher-order '∈' is required. Of course, someone who lacked an analytic language sufficiently rich in parts of speech would be compelled to dismiss such locutions as merely picturesque and misleading ways of expressing the corresponding metalinguistic sentences. On at least one occasion, when at a loss as to how to identify functors at the level now in question, Boethius takes this kind of refuge in the metalinguistic; thus he claims that 'species' in the sentence '*Man* is a species' is the name of a name, *nomen nominis* (*B* 176D, cf. part ii of *n*4.2411*h*).

However, the claims made above as to the dual language levels at which the *de re* ⊖ thing-centred aspects of the discussion move are substantiated further by detailed examination of the development of the argument, and will be pursued throughout the notes. In particular, the logical sections of *n*4.2341*b*, *n*4.230*b*, *n*4.232*b*, *n*4.2341*a*, *n*4.31*a* and *n*4.2411*h* (in that order) constitute a more or less continuous underpinning of these contentions.

§5. SUMMARY OF *DE GRAMMATICO*

For the purposes of this summary only, 'S' and 'T' have been prefixed to the reference numbers in order to indicate which of the two interlocutors (Student and Tutor respectively) is responsible for the material in question.

S1.000 *Introduction.* What account is to be given of things named paronymously? For example, given that 'literate' is a paronym, which of the following is true?

[S1.001] *literate* is a substance

[S1.002] *literate* is a quality.

S1.100 On the one hand, that

S1.101 *literate* is a substance [1.001]

can be proved, since the following are true:

S1.11 Every literate is a man

S1.12 Every man is a substance.

S1.13 For a literate's being a man is all that is required to make *literate* a substance. It having been granted that a literate is a man, the same things follow from *literate* as from *man.*

S1.20 On the other hand, philosophers' treatises contain the assertion that

S1.201 *literate* is a quality. [1.002]

S1.21 And these alternatives [1.001, 1.002] are mutually incompatible.

T2.00 Both alternatives [1.001, 1.002] are valid, and the task is to show how they are not incompatible.

3.00 *First discussion of* 1.11

[S3.100] First disproof of 1.11:

S3.101 No literate can be understood without literacy

S3.102 Every man can be understood without literacy

[3.103 Hence: No literate is a man]
S3.110 Second disproof of 1.11:
S3.111 Every literate is susceptible of degree
S3.112 No man is susceptible of degree
S3.113 Hence: No literate is a man

T3.20 Refutation of 3.10, 3.11, by absurd conclusions from proofs of the same form:
T3.21 *Animal* may be defined as *animated sensitive substance*, so that
T3.221 Every animal can be understood without rationality
T3.222 No man can be understood without rationality
[3.223 Hence: No man is animal.]
T3.231 Further: No animal is necessarily rational
T3.232 Every man is necessarily rational
T3.233 Hence: No man is animal.
S3.234 In 3.22, 3.23, a false conclusion is derived from true premisses by means of valid argument-forms similar to those of 3.10, 3.11. This indicates the necessity for analysis.

T3.30 *Analysis of* 3.10, 3.11:
T3.310 First analysis of 3.10:
T3.311 3.102 = Every man can be understood to be a man without literacy
T3.312 3.101 = No literate can be understood to be literate without literacy.
T3.3121 The two premisses 3.102 and 3.101 as now analysed are shown to have no common term, and hence are incapable of producing a conclusion according to the rules of syllogistic.
S3.320 Analysis of 3.11 by a method similar to that of 3.31 yields:
S3.321 3.112 = No man is susceptible of degree as man
S3.322 3.111 = Every literate is susceptible of degree as literate.
S3.3221 Hence the premisses 3.112 and 3.111 as now analysed are shown to have no common term, and so are incapable of producing a conclusion according to the rules of syllogistic.

T3.33 The capacity of premisses to produce a conclusion by means of a middle term should be decided more by means of analysis of the meanings involved than by attention to the *prima facie* lay-out of terms in comparison with the rules of syllogistic.

T3.40 Hence are possible second versions of 3.311, 3.322, which show that 3.10 was not altogether misguided.

T3.41 3.311 = Being a man does not require literacy

T3.42 3.312 = Being a literate requires literacy.

T3.430 Hence, by means of the common term now revealed, one can infer:

T3.431 Being a literate is not being a man

T3.44 i.e. *literate* and *man* are not identically defined.

T3.450 However, from 3.431 it does not follow that

T3.451 a literate is not a man [3.103, 3.113]

but only

T3.452 a literate is not the same as a man

in the sense of 3.44.

T3.500 *Test question:* how can the following be refuted?

T3.501 Every literate is asserted [so to be] in respect of quality

T3.502 No man is asserted [so to be] in respect of quality

T3.503 Hence: No man is literate.

S3.510 Imitation of method of 3.2 to refute 3.50: the latter is like:

S3.511 Every rational is asserted [so to be] in respect of quality

S3.512 No man is asserted [so to be] in respect of quality

S3.513 Hence: No man is rational (or: *Rational* is predicated of no man).

S3.520 Imitation of the method of 3.31 to refute 3.50: the latter is analysable thus:

S3.521 3.501 = Every literate is asserted [to be] literate in respect of quality

S3.5220 3.502 = No man is asserted [to be] man in respect of quality.

S3.5221 But from these two true premisses it cannot be concluded that *literate* is predicated of no man (3.503), since they now have no common term.

S3.530 But the inference would become a valid one, because of the existence of a common term, were the major premiss (3.521)

to remain as before (3.531) and the new minor premiss shown below (3.532) to become true, thus:

S3.531 Every literate is asserted [to be] literate in respect of quality (3.521)

S3.532 No man is asserted [to be] literate in respect of quality

[3.5321 Hence: *literate* is not predicated of any man.]

S3.5330 Alternatively, a common term would ensue were the minor premiss (3.522) to remain as before (3.5331) and the new major premiss shown below (3.5332) to become true, thus:

S3.5332 Every literate is asserted [to be] man in respect of quality

S3.5331 No man is asserted [to be] man in respect of quality

S3.5333 Hence: *literate* is not predicated of any man.

S3.540 And if the assertion 'a man is not a literate' (cf. 3.451) is understood to assert the non-identity of *man* and *literate* (cf. 3.452) then from the premisses in question here (3.501, 3.502) it does follow that

S3.541 No man is literate (3.503)

S3.542 since what is in a certain sense a common term (cf. 3.53) has been shown to emerge, and this is at least sufficient to prove that

S3.543 The essence of *man* is not the essence of *literate*.

T3.60 Reply to 3.5: [The argument of 3.5 will not do. It contains, among other things, a misguided imitation of 3.31, 3.4. Hence a further analysis of 3.10 now follows.]

T3.610 Consider a case apparently similar to 3.10:

T3.611 No man can be understood without rationality

T3.612 Every stone can be understood without rationality

T3.6121 Hence: No stone is a man

T3.620 Now 3.6121 means

T3.621 a stone is *in no sense* a man

and not just

T3.622 a stone is not the same as a man.

T3.630 How then do 3.611, 3.612 differ from 3.101, 3.102?

S3.631 By the method of 3.31 a refutation of 3.61 could consist in showing that its premisses contained no common term, thus:

S3.6311 3.611 = a man cannot be understood to be a man without rationality

S3.6312 3.612 = a stone can be understood to be a stone without rationality.

S3.6313 But in fact the strong form (3.621) of the conclusion (3.6121) of 3.61 is true. If 3.61 cannot withstand this analysis, then how can 3.10?

T3.6320 The point of introducing 3.61 is that 3.61 and 3.10 are *not* really similar cases, for 3.61 can be analysed thus:

T3.6321 3.611 = No man is in some sense understandable without rationality

T3.6322 3.612 = Every stone is in any sense understandable without rationality.

T3.53221 Hence: No stone is in any sense a man (cf. 3.621).

T3.6330 Whereas 3.10 cannot be similarly analysed as:

T3.6331 3.101 = No literate is in some sense understandable without literacy

T3.6332 3.102 = Every man is in any sense understandable without literacy

For on the contrary, it is the case that:

T3.6333 Every thing which is literate can be understood to be a man without literacy

T3.6334 No man can be understood to be a literate without literacy.

T3.6340 Hence is shown the dissimilarity between 3.611, 3.612 (cf. 3.632) and 3.101, 3.102; for in view of 3.633, the premisses 3.101, 3.102 cannot have as their conclusion:

T3.6341 a literate is in no sense a man.

S3.700 Objection to the analysis of 3.10 given at 3.4:

S3.701 If being a literate is not being a man (3.431) then whatever is essentially literate need not therefore be essentially man.

However,

S3.71 If *man* follows from *literate*, then the essence of *man* follows from the essence of *literate*.

S3.711 But, by 3.701 and 3.431, the consequent consequence of 3.71 is false, hence also the antecedent one, so that

S3.7111 Not every literate is a man.

S3.72 Now either every literate is a man, or none are;

S3.721 But 3.7111 falsifies the first of these alternatives, hence

S3.7211 No literate is a man.

T3.800 Indirect refutation of 3.7 by outline of absurd conclusion from proof of the same form:

T3.8010 If both *man* and *animal* were definable as *rational mortal animal*, then there would be a universal identity of predicates applicable to *rational mortal* and to *animal*.

T3.8011 But the consequent of 3.8010 is false.

T3.8012 Hence also its antecedent is false, i.e. being a man is not being an animal (cf. 3.431, 3.44).

T3.810 Now use of 3.8012 in the same way as 3.431 is used in 3.7 would yield the absurd conclusion:

T3.811 No man is an animal.

T3.900 Direct refutation of 3.7:

T3.901 3.531 = 3.44 = a literate and a man are not altogether identical (cf. 3.41, 3.42, 3.452)

T3.910 Hence 3.701 should read:

T3.911 If being a literate is not being a man and only a man, then whatsoever is essentially literate need not on that account be essentially man and only man.

T3.920 It follows that when 3.71 has its antecedent consequence negated (cf. 3.711) but now in accordance with 3.901, that negation should read:

T3.921 *man* and only *man* does not follow from *literate*

T3.922 i.e. if something is literate it does not follow that it is a man and only a man.

T3.930 Hence the only conclusion from 3.7 is:

T3.931 No literate is a man and only a man.

T3.940 If it can be shown that

T3.9410 Being a literate is not being a man [3.431]

is like

T3.9411 Being a white is not being a man

the sense of the latter being:

T3.9412 a man can be without white, and a white can be without man,

T3.9420 then from 3.941 it follows that
T3.9421 Some literate can be other than a man.
T3.9430 Nevertheless it is now clear that
T3.9431 There is some non-human literate
cannot be shown.

[4.0] *Second discussion of* 1.11
S4.100 Second disproof of 1.11:
S4.101 A literate is in a subject
S4.102 No man is in a subject
S4.103 Hence: No literate is a man.

T4.110 Argument 4.10 involves (in 4.101) a consequence improperly drawn from Aristotle.
T4.1101 When the word *literate* is being used in talk about a literate, then it can be agreed that:
T4.1102 When *literate* is heard, then *man* or literacy is understood, and
T4.1103 When a literate is being talked about, the talk is either about a man or about literacy.
T4.1104 Now *man* is a substance, and not in a subject,
T4.1105 And literacy is a quality, and in a subject.
Under these circumstances (4.110) one might say that
T4.111 a literate is a substance and not in a subject (cf. 4.101) insofar as he is a man (cf. 4.102), and
T4.112 *literate* is a quality and is in a subject (cf. 4.101) insofar as literacy is concerned.

S4.1200 Objections to 4.111:
S4.1201 *Literate* is neither primary nor secondary substance, since
S4.121 *Literate* is in a subject, is asserted of many things, and is therefore not primary substance, and
S4.122 *Literate* is neither genus nor species, nor is it asserted in respect of whatness, and is therefore not secondary substance.

T4.130 Reply to 4.12:
T4.131 Against 4.122: insofar as a literate being is not in a subject, it falls under both genus and species (*animal* and *man*) and to this extent is secondary substance and is asserted in respect of whatness.

T4.132 Against 4.121: insofar as a certain literate being is not in a subject, it is individual and is therefore primary substance.

T4.14 Has it not now been shown that (i) *literate* can be used in speech to refer to men (cf. 4.1103, 4.111) and is to this extent a substance, and (ii) its cognitive content is *literacy*, and it is in this respect a quality (cf. 1.00, 2.00)?

S4.20 How can it be said that *literate* signifies a quality (i.e. literacy)? After all, if one tries to use the word to refer to literacy, then nonsense results.

S4.210 And there is a glaring discrepancy between the assertions involving *literate* which logicians make in their writings, and their use of the word in everyday talk.

S4.211 For they often give *literate* as an example of a word signifying a quality or an accident,

S4.212 Whereas everyone's current manner of utterance shows that *literate* is a substance (man) rather than a quality (literacy) (cf. 4.210).

S4.22 The crux of the matter is this: if we are to say that *literate* is a quality as well as a substance, why should not the same be said of *man*?

T4.230 Substance-signifying words (e.g. *man*) and paronyms (e.g. *literate*) signify in a very dissimilar fashion.

T4.231 Thus *man* signifies principally substance – the unitary completion of the incomplete.

T4.232 Whereas of *literate* one can say that it signifies *literacy* (a quality) in a *per se* ⊖ precisive fashion, and *man* (a substance) only obliquely.

T4.233 *Literate* is, however, appellative (cf. 4.2341) of man, but does not signify (properly or in a *per se* ⊖ precisive sense) *man.*

T4.234 *Literate* in fact signifies in a *per se* fashion only literacy, without at the same time being appellative of literacy.

T4.2341 And a name is *appellative* of that to which it is used to refer in the current course of utterance, [as opposed to that to which logical assertions may appear to make it refer, cf. 4.20, 4.21]. And certainly, in ordinary talk [as opposed to logical writings, cf. 4.5022] one does not say that *literate* is literacy, but that a literate is a man.

S4.240 *Objection:* is not *literate* definable as *man displaying literacy*? How can this be reconciled with 4.233, 4.234?

T4.2410 Five arguments against the definition proposed in 4.240:

T4.2411 (1) If *literate* is defined as *man displaying literacy*, i.e. if *literacy* becomes a constitutive characteristic, then logic is disorganised.

T4.24120 (2) A non-human literate can at least be supposed, hence a possible contradiction can be inferred if the definition of 4.240 is adhered to.

T4.24121 Hence also, *literate* no more signifies *man* than *white* does (cf. 3.941). It just happens to be the case that man alone has literacy (cf. 4.51), but is not the only haver of whiteness.

T4.2413 (3) The assertion *Socrates is an animal man* is inapt because *animal* is already understood when *man* is used; but *Socrates is a literate man* is quite apt, hence *literate* does not include *man*.

T4.2414 (4) Iterated substitutions effected in *Socrates is a literate man* according to the definition of 4.240 leads to an infinite regress.

T4.2415 (5) Generalisation of the synonymy of 4.240 in respect of all paronyms will alter the classification of the paronym *today's* as a part of speech.

T4.30 Thus is confirmed the doctrine of 4.232, 4.233, namely that *literate* does not, strictly speaking, signify *man*.

T4.31 And the sense in which *literate* signifies literacy may be seen by subducting *man* from the *definiens* proposed in 4.2400, so as to truncate it to ... *displaying literacy* (cf. 4.8).

S4.40 Further difficulties arising from 4.23:

S4.411 *Literate* is not appellative of literacy (4.234) but of men (4.233).

S4.412 *Literate* is not significative of *man* (4.233) but of literacy (4.234).

S4.413 Yet *literate* is significative of both literacy (in a *per se* $\ominus$ precisive fashion) (4.234) and of *man* (obliquely), and hence arise the paradoxes:

S4.414 *Literate* is not significative of *man* (4.412) and yet is (4.413);

S4.415 *Literate* is appellative of men (4.411) yet is not significative of *man* (4.412).

[4.420] Reply to 4.4: clarification of terminology by example.

T4.4210 The assertion 'A white is within this building', spoken in respect of an enclosed white horse of which the hearer knows nothing, conveys to the hearer no reference to a horse.

S4.4211 And although the assertion may arouse the empirically-grounded expectation of a body or surface which has the whiteness, yet this expectation reflects something more than just the *per se* signification of *white*.

T4.422 In contrast, the command 'Strike the white!' when addressed to a hearer confronted with a black bull and a white horse, would convey that the horse was in question, even though the word *horse* is not actually used.

T4.4231 The word *horse* signifies the horse precisively, not obliquely.

T4.4232 The word *white* signifies the horse obliquely, *via* the context of utterance, and not in a *per se* or precisive fashion.

T4.4233 The word *white* signifies the phrase ... *having whiteness* and a similar lack of completeness is found in the cognitive content of the word.

T4.4234 This incompleteness is remedied by means of sense-acquaintance with the context of utterance, e.g. by seeing that the whiteness is that of a horse. The word *white* of itself only signifies the horse obliquely, by means of sense-acquaintance. Nevertheless, *white* is in this case appellative of the horse.

S4.424 Thus are solved the difficulties of 4.41:

S4.4241 The paronym *white* signifies a substance not in a *per se* sense, but only obliquely; at the same time it is appellative of substance.

S4.4242 This finding can be extended in like manner to all paronyms.

S4.4243 The distinction between *per se* ⊖ precisive and oblique signification can also be extended to verbs as well as names.

T4.430 *Per se* ⊖ precisive signification pertains essentially to significant utterances as such; oblique signification is only accidentally linked with such utterances (cf. 4.515).

T4.431 When parts of speech are defined as *significant utterances*, precisive (*per se*) signification is then in question (cf. 4.2415).

S4.500 Supposed difficulties following from the proof (4.24, 4.3) that *literate* signifies literacy alone, and not *man* and literacy.

S4.501 How can *literate* be a quality?

S4.5020 How can man alone, i.e. without literacy, be literate?

S4.5021 For either man alone is literate or man along with literacy is literate; but by 4.3, it is false that *man* and literacy are *literate*, hence man alone is literate (cf. 4.24121).

S4.5022 And (cf. 4.501) the answer to the question 'What is *literate*?' can scarcely be '*Literate* is literacy' or '*Literate* is a quality'.

S4.503 Further, to be literate a man must have literacy, i.e. must not be man alone.

T4.510 Reply to 4.502: the word *alone* in 'Man alone is literate' can have two senses:

T4.511 Correct sense: 'Man alone ever possesses literacy (and nothing else ever does possess literacy)'.

T4.5120 Incorrect sense: 'Man alone (deprived of literacy) is literate'.

T4.5121 The correct sense (4.511) corresponds to the case of the first member of a linearly-ordered couple (e.g. a leader); that first member *alone* precedes. The incorrect sense (4.5120) corresponds to the case of that which is *alone*, and hence cannot precede anything else.

T4.5122 Reply to 4.501: the assertion '*Literate* is a quality' must be understood according to the special usage of Aristotle's *Categoriae*.

S4.513 But it would seem to follow from the *Categoriae* that *literate* is a substance, since man alone is literate.

T4.5141 Aristotle's main intention in that treatise was to deal with the signification of words, not the categorisation of things.

T4.5142 He was not primarily concerned with the natures of things, nor with the things of which words happen to be appellative, but with that which the words signify.

T4.5143 This involved, however, assertions in terms of things.

T4.5144 His turn of expression at the opening of the *Categoriae* proves that 4.5142 is the case.

T4.515 Aristotle in fact dealt with words insofar as they are essentially, *per se* $\ominus$ precisively, significative, and not insofar as they are accidentally, obliquely, significative (cf. 4.43).

T4.600 What then is the meaning of the question, 'What is *literate*?' understood in Aristotle's sense?

S4.601 This question can be understood as either *de voce* or *de re*, i.e. as being asked either about a word, or about a thing.

S4.602 If the question is understood in relation to the word, then *literate* is a word signifying a quality (cf. 4.31).

S4.603 If the question is to be understood as having to do with things, then *literate* is a quality.

T4.604 Further. Aristotle's practice was to show things by means of the words significative and not merely appellative of those things.

S4.610 '*Literate* is a quality' can therefore, according to Aristotle's usage, be the answer to a question posed either *de voce* $\ominus$ concerning the word or *de re* $\ominus$ concerning the thing.

S4.611 Nevertheless it still remains true that *literate* is appellative of substance.

T4.620 Thus is solved the difficulty (4.21, 4.5022) about the discrepancy between logicians' spoken usage, and their written assertions about signification: the first involves the use of words to refer (appellation), while the second is concerned with decisions as to *per se* $\ominus$ precisive signification.

T4.621 The results of neglecting this distinction are just as absurd as those which would result from inferring that a stone must be a male object because the Latin word *lapis* $\ominus$ stone is a masculine noun, or that to fear is an action because the verb *timere* $\ominus$ to fear is an active verb, and so on.

S4.700 A further query: can a single circumstance be assigned to diverse categories? For example, can *literate* be said to signify *having* as well as quality?

T4.710 Tentatively, this may be admitted in those cases where a word signifies things of various categories and those things do not form a single whole: *white* can be said to signify a quality and a having, but it is appellative of neither; it is in fact appellative of the thing having whiteness.

T4.711 On the other hand *man* signifies and is appellative of a unity, and hence cannot be assigned to diverse categories.

T4.712 But *white* can be said to signify a quality and a having, because the word is not appellative of quality and having.

S4.713 But (in view of 4.515) in terms of signification alone, can it not be said that *man* signifies a substance and a quality (cf. 4.22)?

T4.714 *Man* signifies predominantly the qualified substantial unity, whereas *white* has no such dominant unifying feature in its meaning.

T4.72 Elucidation of the meaning of "forms a single whole" (cf. 4.710).

S4.800 Final objections:

S4.801 Could it not be said that *white* signifies *something having whiteness* (and not just ... *having whiteness* (4.4233)) but indeterminately?

S4.8020 For everything white is something white,

S4.8021 Also *white* signifies something having whiteness or nothing; but nothing cannot have whiteness, therefore *white* must signify *something having whiteness* (4.801).

T4.810 Whether 4.8020 is true or not is not in question here, where the discourse moves at a level appropriate to that which emerges in a decision as to the signification of forms of words.

T4.811 Thus while it may be true that a white is always something having whiteness, this fact need not affect the account of the signification of *white.*

T4.8120 Indeed, an infinite regress results if *something having whiteness* is assumed to be substitutable for *white.*

T4.8121 A similar regress occurs if *that which has whiteness* is substituted for *white.*

T4.813 And the argument of 4.8021 is a sophism resting upon a misinterpretation of the negation involved in the word *nothing*.

S4.82 Recapitulation of findings in terms of 4.71, with generalisation.

T4.83 Reminder of the provisional nature of the conclusions of the dialogue.

§6. *DE GRAMMATICO:* TEXT AND TRANSLATION

The text is reproduced, with minor modifications and the addition of numbered sub-divisions, from *S* I 145–168, by kind permission of the late F. S. Schmitt, O.S.B. The superscript letters indicate the availability of a note or comment in §7, where the division number and letter are quoted preceded by '*n*', e.g. '*n*1.11*a*'. Cf. §0.

Ch. I

1.000 STUDENT. I'd like you to clear up for me the question as to whether *literate*[a] is[b] substance[c] or quality[d], so that when I've appreciated this example, I'll know how I ought to view other things[e] which like a literate are asserted[g] paronymously[f].

DISCIPULUS. De grammatico[a] peto ut me certum facias utrum sit[b] substantia[c] an qualitas[d], ut hoc cognito, quid de aliis[e] quae similiter denominative[f] dicuntur[g] sentire debeam, agnoscam.

TUTOR. First tell me why you're undecided.

MAGISTER. Dic primum cur dubites.

S. Because it looks as though cogent reasons[h] are available which both prove and disprove either alternative.

D. Ideo quia videtur utrumque posse probari necessariis rationibus[h], esse scilicet et non esse.

T. State them.

M. Proba ergo.

S. Provided you aren't too quick in disagreeing with everything I have to say; let me finish my piece before you concur or correct.

D. Ne ergo festines contradicere quidquid dixero, sed patere me orationem meam ad suam finem perducere, deinde aut approba aut corrige.

T. As you will.

M. Ut vis.

1.100 S. To prove that

1.101 *literate* is substance[a]

one only needs the following premisses:

1.11 Every literate is a man[a]

1.12 Every man is a substance[a].

1.13 For a literate has that from which his substantiality ensues, whatever it may be, only on account of his being a man; so granted that a literate is a man, the same things may be inferred from *literate* as from *man*.

D. Ut quidem

grammaticus probetur esse substantia[a]

sufficit quia

omnis grammaticus homo[a], et

omnis homo subtantia[a].

Quidquid enim habet grammaticus ut sequatur eum substantia, non habet nisi ex eo quia homo est. Quare hoc concesso ut homo sit: quaecumque sequuntur hominem sequuntur grammaticum.

1.20 On the other hand, that

1.201 *literate* is[a] quality

is obviously believed by those philosophers

Quod vero

grammaticus sit[a] qualitas

aperte fatentur philosophi qui de hac re

who have written about this matter[b], and one can hardly disregard their authority[c] on these subjects.

tractaverunt[b]. Quorum auctoritatum[c] de his rebus est impudentia improbare.

1.21 Again, *literate* must be[a] substance or quality in such a fashion that if it is[a] the one of these then it is[a] not the other, and if it is[a] not the one of these then it is necessarily the other[b]; hence correspondingly, whatsoever serves to establish one alternative refutes the other[c], and whatsoever weakens the one strengthens the other. Now as only one of the two can hold, I'd like you to pin-point the falsehood and so clear up the case for me.

Item quoniam necesse est ut grammaticus sit[a] aut substantia aut qualitas, ut quodlibet horum sit[a], alterum non sit[a], et quodlibet non sit[a], alterum necesse sit esse[b]: quidquid valet ad astruendam unam partem, destruit alteram[c], et quidquid unam debilitat, alteram roborat. Cum ergo alterum horum verum sit, alterum falsum: rogo ut falsitatum detegens aperias mihi veritatem.

Ch. II

2.00 T. The points you urge in favour of both alternatives are cogent, but not your assertion that if the one holds the other cannot. So you shouldn't ask me to show the falsity of one or the other of the two – this just can't be done – but rather, if I can manage it, I'll make clear how they can be compatible[a]. However, first of all I'd like to hear what you think might constitute objections to the arguments you brought forward.

M. Argumenta quae ex utraque parte posuisti necessaria sunt, nisi quod dicis: si alterum est, alterum esse non posse. Quare non debes a me exigere ut alteram partem falsam ostendam – quod ab ullo fieri non potest – sed quomodo sibi invicem non repugnent[a] aperiam, si a me fieri potest. Sed vellem ego prius a te ipso audire, quid his probationibus tuis obici posse opineris.

S. You're asking me to take on exactly the task that I was keen that you should perform; but as you assert that the arguments in question are in order, it's up to me, as the doubter, to disclose the qualms I feel about those alternatives, and your job will be to establish the validity and compatibility of each of them.

D. Hoc quod tu a me exigis, ego a te intentus expectabam; sed quoniam tu easdem probationes asseris irreprobabiles: meum est qui dubito aperire quid me sollicitet, tuum vero est utriusque partis firmitatem et convenientiam ostendere.

T. Confide you qualms, then, and I'll try and do as you ask.

M. Dic ergo tu quod sentis, et ego tentabo facere quod poscis.

3.00 S. Well, it seems to me that the premiss[a] [1.11] to the effect that a literate is a man could be disproved thus:

3.101 No literate can be understood[a] [as being] without literacy

3.102 Every man can be understood [as being] without literacy.

3.110 Again,

3.111 Every literate is susceptible of degree[a]

3.112 No man is susceptible of degree.

D. Illam quidem propositionem[a] quae dicit grammaticum esse hominem, hoc modo repelli existimo, quia

nullus grammaticus potest intelligi[a] sine grammatica et
omnis homo potest intelligi sine grammatica

Item:

omnis grammaticus suscipit magis et minus[a], et
nullus homo suscipit magis et minus,

From either of these two sets of premisses an identical conclusion can be drawn, namely:

3.113 No literate is a man.

ex qua utraque contextione binarum propositionum conficitur una conclusio, id est:

nullus grammaticus homo.

Ch. III

3.20 T. It doesn't follow.

M. Non consequitur.

S. Why not?

D. Quare?

3.21 T. Does the name *animal* appear to you to signify[a] anything besides *animated sensitive substance*[b]?

M. An tibi videtur animalis nomen aliquid aliud significare[a] quam substantiam animatam sensibilem[b]?

S. Certainly *animal* is just *animated sensitive substance* and *animated sensitive substance* just *animal*[c].

D. Prorsus nihil aliud est animal quam substantia animata sensibilis, nec substantia animata sensibilis aliud est quam animal[c].

T. Quite so. And now tell me: is it not the case that every being that is just animated sensitive substance can be understood without rationality[d], and is not necessarily rational?

M. Ita est. Sed dic quoque, utrum omne quod non est aliud quam substantia animata sensibilis, possit intelligi praeter rationalitatem[d], nec sit rationale ex necessitate.

S. I can't deny that.

D. Negare non possum.

T. Hence every animal can be understood without rationality, and no animal is necessarily rational.

M. Omne igitur animal potest intelligi praeter rationalitatem, et nullum animal est ex necessitate rationale.

S. There's no knowing what my admissions may not lead to, but I've a shrews notion of what you're aiming at.

D. Nequeo dicere quin ex concessis consequatur, quamquam valde metuam quod te suspicor intendere.

T. On the other hand no man can be understood without rationality, and every man must necessarily be rational.

M. At nullus homo potest intelligi praeter rationalitatem, et omnem hominem necesse est rationalem esse.

S. Now I'm hemmed in on both flanks[e]. For if I admit your last assertion, then you can infer that no man is animal; if, on the other hand, I deny it, you'll say that I'm not merely understandable without rationality, but that I am in fact completely devoid of it.

D. Angustiae mihi sunt utrimque[e]. Nam si concedo, concludis nullum hominem esse animal: si renuo, dices me non tantum posse intelligi, sed vere esse sine rationalitate.

T. Don't worry: the consequences aren't what you think they are.

M. Ne timeas. Non enim sequitur quod putas.

S. If that's a promise, then I freely grant any of your suggestions; otherwise I'm rather reluctant.

D. Si sic est ut promittis, spontaneus concedo quidquid proposuisti; sin autem, invitus.

T. Then construct for yourself two syllogisms from these four premisses of mine.

M. Contexe ergo tu ipse quattuor ultimas propositiones quas feci in duos syllogismos.

S. They can certainly be laid out as follows:

D. Hoc utique ordine digeri possunt:

3.221 Every animal can be understood without rationality[a]

Omne animal potest intelligi praeter rationalitatem[a]

3.222 No man can be understood without rationality[a].

Nullus vero homo potest intelligi praeter rationalitatem[a].

Again:

3.231 No animal is necessarily rational

3.232 Every man is necessarily rational[a].

From this arrangement of the two sets of premisses it seems to follow in either case that

3.233 No man is animal[a].

This is altogether false, although there doesn't seem to be anything wrong with the foregoing premisses.

3.234 The two which have *man* as subject term [3.222, 3.232] are so self-evident that it would be silly to try to prove them, while the two which involve *animal* as subject term [3.221, 3.231] are apparently so sound that to deny them would be mere brashness[a]. However, I notice that the structure of these two syllogisms is wholly similar[b] to that of those two which I put forward a few moments ago [3.10, 3.11]. This makes me suspect that your only motive for producing them[c] is to allow me to sort out the reasons for their obviously false conclusions, so that I may then realise that the same apply to the similar ones which I framed[d] myself.

T. That is so.

S. Then show me how in both cases there can be so serious a mistake that although the premisses are true, and seem to be arranged in conformity with the rules of the syllogism[e], not the least scrap of truth emerges in their conclusions.

Ch. IV

3.30 T. I'll do this for your syllogisms, and then you can analyse mine if you like.

S. Do as you think fit.

3.310 T. Recall and reconstruct the syllogisms you produced before.

3.311 S. 'Every man can be understood without literacy' [3.102]

T. What is it that you assert to be man and to be understandable without literacy?

S. Man.

Item:

Nullum animal rationale est ex necessitate

Omnis autem homo rationalis est ex necessitate[a].

Ex utroque hoc ordine binarum propositionum videtur nasci:

Nullus igitur homo animal est[a], *quo nihil falsius, licet praecedentes propositiones in nullo titubare videam.*

Duae namque quae subiectum terminum habent hominem sic sunt per se notae ut imprudentia sit eas probare; duae vero quae subiciunt animal sic videntur probatae, ut impudentia sit eas negare[a]. *Sed video horum duorum syllogismorum conexionem per omnia similem*[b] *illis duobus quos paulo ante protuli. Quapropter ad nihil aliud suspicor te hos attulisse*[c], *nisi ut cum horum conclusionem aperte falsam cernerem, idem de similibus quos ego feceran decernerem*[d].

M. Sic est.

D. Ostende ergo in quo et hic et ibi tanta sit deceptio, ut cum et verae propositiones et secundum naturam syllogismorum[e] *conexae videantur, nulla tamen eorum conclusiones veritas tueatur.*

M. In tuis syllogismis hoc faciam; meos si vis per te discutito.

D. Fiat tuo iudicio.

M. Repete et contexe syllogismos quos fecisti.

D. Omnis homo potest intelligi sine grammatica.

M. Quid dicis hominem posse intelligi sine grammatica?

D. Hominem.

T. Now include that which you understand within the major premiss[a] itself.

S. Every man can be understood to be man without literacy.

T. Agreed: now state the minor[b].

3.312 S. 'No literate can be understood without literacy' [3.101].

T. What is it that cannot be understood to be literate without literacy?

S. A literate.

T. State in full that which you understand, then.

S. No literate can be understood to be literate without literacy.

3.3121 T. Now combine, as you did before, these two reformulated premisses.

S. Every man can be understood to be man without literacy [3.311]
No literate can be understood to be literate without literacy[a] [3.312].

T. And now check whether they happen to have a common term; otherwise they are useless.

S. I can see that they involve no common term[b], so that nothing follows from them.

T. Reconstruct your other syllogism [3.11].

3.320 S. You needn't bother to analyse it now. I see the fallacy. I should have understood its premisses as if they asserted:

3.321 No man is susceptible of degree as man [3.112]

3.322 Every literate is susceptible of degree as literate [3.111].

3.3221 And as these two propositions have no common term, they prove nothing.

T. So it seems to you that nothing can be inferred from your combination of premisses?

S. That certainly was my impression; but your question makes me suspect that perhaps they still possess some concealed cogency. Yet how can they be used to prove something if they have no common term?

M. Dic ergo in ipsa propositione[a] quod intelligis.

D. Omnis homo potest intelligi homo sine grammatica.

M. Concedo; assume[b].

D. Nullus grammaticus potest intelligi sine grammatica.

M. Quid non potest grammaticus intelligi sine grammatica?

D. Grammaticus.

M. Profer ergo quod intelligis.

D. Nullus grammaticus potest intelligi grammaticus sine grammatica.

M. Iunge has duas propositiones ita integras, sicut eas modo protulisti.

D. Omnis homo potest intelligi homo sine grammatica

Nullus grammaticus potest intelligi grammaticus sine grammatica[a].

M. Vide ergo utrum habeant communem terminum, sine quo nihil efficiunt.

D. Video eas non habere communem terminum[b], et idcirco nihil ex eis consequi.

M. Contexe alterum syllogismum.

D. Non iam opus est ut pro eius ostensione labores. Nam adverto eius fallaciam. Sic enim eius propositiones intelligebam, ac si diceretur quia

nullus homo est magis et minus homo, et

omnis grammaticus est magis vel minus grammaticus.

Et quoniam hae duae propositiones nullum habent communem terminum, nihil conficiunt.

M. Itane tibi videtur his tuis conexionibus nihil concludi posse?

D. Ita utique putabam, sed haec tua interrogatio facit me suspectum, ne forte in illis aliqua lateat efficacia. Sed quomodo efficiunt sine communi termino?

3.33 T. The common term of a syllogism consists not so much in its setting forth as in its meaning; for on the same grounds as those according to which no proof emerges from a merely verbal identity of terms without identical sense, there is nothing wrong with an identity which is understood but not set forth[a]. The meaning of the words is what really binds the syllogism together, and not just the words themselves[b].

M. Communis terminus syllogismi non tam in prolatione quam in sententia est habendus. Sicut enim nihil efficitur, si communis est in voce et non in sensu: ita nihil obest, si est in intellectu et non in prolatione[a]. Sententia quippe ligat syllogismum, non verba[b].

Ch. V

3.40 S. I'm waiting for you to restore cogency to my premisses.

T. You can certainly prove something from them, but not what you are looking for[a].

S. I'll be thankful for anything, whatsoever it be.

T. When it is asserted that

Every man can be understood to be man without literacy [3.102, 3.311],

No literate can be understood to be literate without literacy [3.101, 3.312],

doesn't this mean that

3.41 Being a man[a] does not demand literacy, and

3.42 Being a literate demands literacy[a]?

S. Quite so.

3.430 T. And have these two premisses [3.41, 3.42] which I asserted just now to be equivalent to the other two [3.311, 3.312] a common term[a]?

S. They have.

T. It follows, therefore, that

3.431 Being a literate is not being a man[a],

in the sense that

3.44 *literate* and *man* are not identically defined[a].

S. This is indubitably the case, as well as being logically sound.

3.450 T. But it doesn't hence follow that

3.451 a literate is not a man [3.103, 3.113]

D. Exspecto ut reddas effectum propositionibus meis.

M. Efficiunt vere aliquid, sed non quod exspectas[a].

D. Quidquid illud sit, non ingratus accipio.

M. Qui dicit:

omnis homo potest intelligi homo sine grammatica

et

nullus grammaticus potest intelligi grammaticus sine grammatica,

nonne hoc significat quia

esse hominis[a] non indiget grammatica, et

esse grammatici indiget grammatica[a]?

D. Nihil verius.

M. An habent communem terminum[a] hae duae propositiones quas modo dixi significari in illis aliis duabus?

D. Habent.

M. Conficitur ergo quia

esse grammatici non est esse hominis[a],

id est

non esse eandem definitionem utriusque[a].

D. Procul dubio sic video consequi et esse.

M. Non tamen ideo consequitur

grammaticum non esse hominem,

as you were thinking. If, however, you interpret

a literate is not a man

as asserting:

3.452 a literate is not the same as a man[a]

in the sense that they are not identically defined, then your conclusion is a true one.

sicut tu intelligebas. Sed si ita intelligas

grammaticus non est homo

ac si dicatur

grammaticus non est idem quod homo[a]*,*

id est non habent eandem definitionem, vera est conclusio.

Ch. VI

3.500 S. I understand your point.

T. If, then, you fully understand my point, tell me how you would refute a syllogism composed as follows:

3.501 Every literate is asserted [to be so] in respect of quality[a],

3.502 No man is asserted [to be such] in respect of quality;

3.593 Hence: No man is literate[a].

3.510 S. This seems to me to be like the assertion:

3.511 Every rational [being] is asserted [to be so] in respect of quality,

3.512 No man is asserted [to be such] in respect of quality;

3.513 Hence: No man is rational[a].

But this is not capable of constituting a valid proof that *rational* is predicable of no man.

3.520 Likewise that syllogism which you proposed just now [3.50] doesn't necessarily prove that *literate* is not predicable of man, for if we interpret them in such a way that their truth is preserved[a], we see that its premisses amount to the following assertions:

3.521 Every literate is asserted [to be] literate in respect of quality[a] [3.501]

3.5220 No man is asserted [to be] man in respect of quality[a] [3.503]

3.5221 But from these two propositions it by no means follows that

Literate is predicated of no man,

for it is not the same term which is affirmed of *literate* and denied of *man*[a].

D. Intelligo quod dicis.

M. Si ergo bene intelligis quae dixi: dic quomodo tu dissolveres hunc syllogismum, si quis ita contexeret:

omnis grammaticus dicitur in eo quod quale[a]*,*

nullus homo dicitur in eo quod quale;

nullus igitur homo grammaticus[a]*.*

D. Tale mihi hoc videtur esse, ac si diceretur:

omne rationale dicitur in eo quod quale;

at

nullus homo dicitur in eo quod quale;

nullus igitur homo rationalis[a]*.*

Hoc autem nulla probatio verum efficere valet, ut rationale praedicetur de nullo homine.

Similiter ille syllogismus quem modo protulisti, non necessario concludit grammaticum non praedicari de homine. Hoc enim significant eius propositiones, si secundum veritatem[a] *eas intelligimus, tamquam si diceretur ita:*

omnis grammaticus dicitur grammaticus in eo quod quale[a]*,*

nullus homo dicitur homo in eo quod quale[a]*.*

Ex his autem duabus propositionibus nequaquam consequitir

nullus grammaticus praedicatur de homine,

quoniam non est idem terminus qui affirmatur de grammatico et negatur de homine[a]*.*

3.530 Of course, they would[a] have a common term and be necessary conclusive if *either*

3.531 the major[a] remaining as it is [3.521]

the following minor[b] were to be the case:

3.532 No man is asserted [to be] literate in respect of quality[a]

3.5330 *or*

3.5331 the minor[a] remaining as before [3.5220]

the major could indeed become:

3.5332 Every literate is asserted [to be] man in respect of quality[a],

for then both these combinations [3.531, 3.532; 3.5331, 3.5332] would produce the conclusion that

3.5333 *literate* is not predicable of any man.

3.540 For if one understands the assertion 'A man is not a literate' [3.451] as though it amounted to 'A man is not the same as a literate'[a] in a sense similar to that found in the assertion, 'Either the lightening is the flash or else the lightening is not the flash' – that is to say, 'The lightening either is or else is not identical with[b] the flash' – if, I say, one understands the assertion 'A man is not a literate' in this sense, then it follows from the premisses in question[c], on a careful scrutiny of their import, that

3.541 No man is literate.

3.542 This is because insofar as we are concerned to prove that

3.543 The essence of *man* is not the essence of *literate*[a]

their meaning does involve a common term[b].

Ch. VII

3.60 T. You have understood what I said alright, but perhaps you have not scrutinised it properly.

S. But how could I have understood it fully, and yet not have scrutinised it properly?

3.610 T. Tell me now: what would follow from the assertions:

Esset[a] vero in illis communis terminus et necessariam conclusionen ingererent si aut

manente propositione[a] sicut posita est

sic vera fieret assumptio[b]:

nullus homo dicitur grammaticus in eo quod quale[a]:

aut

manente assumptione[a]

sic vere proponeretur:

omnis grammaticus dicitur homo in eo quod quale[a].

Nam ex utraque hac complexione nasceretur quia

de nullo homine grammaticus praedicaretur.

Si quis vero id quod dicitur: homo non est grammaticus, ita velit intelligere, ac si diceretur: homo non est idem quod grammaticus[a], ut si dicam: fulgor est splendor, aut, fulgor non est splendor, id est, fulgor est idipsum aut non est idipsum quod[b] splendor; si quis, inquam, sic intelligat hoc quod dicitur: homo non est grammaticus: secundum hunc sensum consequitur ex illis propositionibus[c], si earum vis bene consideretur, quia

nullus homo est grammaticus.

Nam ad hoc probandum quia

essentia hominis non est essentia grammatici[a]

habet earum significatio communem terminum[b].

M. Bene intellexisti quid dixi, sed forte non bene considerasti quod dixi.

D. Quomodo bene intellexi, et non bene consideravi?

M. Dic mihi: si quis sic proponeret:

3.611 No man can be understood without rationality[a],

3.612 Every stone can be understood without rationality?

S. Hence,

3.6121 No stone is a man.

What else could follow?

3.620 T. And what do you understand this to assert? Does it mean

3.621 A stone is in no sense[a] a man?

Or does it mean

3.622 A stone is not the same as a man[a]?

S. It means that a stone is in no sense a man.

3.630 T. Tell me then: how does this last syllogism [3.61] differ from that earlier one [3.10] of yours, in which you assert that a literate cannot be understood without literacy, but a man can, and hence a literate is not a man?

3.631 S. As far as the logical cogency is concerned, I fail to see any difference at all between the latter and the former; we saw how the former [3.10] is to be understood as asserting that

A literate cannot be understood to be a literate without literacy [3.312], and that

A man can be understood to be a man without literacy [3.311],

so that the latter [3.61] may likewise be understood to assert:

3.6311 A man cannot be understood to be a man without rationality

3.6312 A stone can be understood to be a stone without rationality[a].

3.6313 Now the conclusion of the syllogism here in question [3.6121] is securely established[a], since no stone is in any sense a man [cf. 3.62]; hence it looks to me as though your skill in analysis overwhelms the conclusion of that exactly similar syllogism [3.10] of mine. So now I understand your saying that I had understood what you said, but without scrutinising it properly: I understood well enough what you might mean verbally,

nullus homo potest intelligi sine rationalitate[a],

omnis autem lapis potest intelligi sine rationalitate; quid consequeretur?

D. Quid nisi:

nullus igitur lapis homo?

M. Quomodo hoc intelligis? An quia

nullo modo[a] *lapis est homo,*

an quia

non est lapis idem quod homo[a]*?*

D. Quia nullo modo lapis est homo.

M. Dic ergo: quid differt iste syllogismus ab illo tuo syllogismo, in quo dicis grammaticum non posse intelligi sine grammatica, hominem vero posse, et ideo grammaticum hominem non esse?

D. Quantum quidem ad vim argumentationis, nihil video hunc ab illo differre. Sicut enim ibi intelligendum est quia

grammaticus non potest intelligi grammaticus sine grammatica, et

homo potest intelligi homo sine grammatica;

ita hic est intelligendum quia

homo non potest intelligi homo sine rationalitate,

et

lapis potest intelligi lapis sine rationalitate[a]*;*

et idcirco cum huius syllogismi sit rata conclusio[a]*, quia nullo modo lapis est homo: videris mihi syllogismi mei, qui omnino similis est isti, conclusionem callidis tuis expositionibus obruisse. Unde iam intelligo quid dixeris quia bene intellexi, sed non bene consideravi. Bene enim intellexi quid loquendo mihi significares, sed idipsum quod significabas non bene consideravi, quia quomodo me deciperet ignoravi*[b].

but I didn't concentrate adequately on the exact point of what you were meaning, since I had no idea how that syllogism might mislead me[b].

3.6320 T. You certainly didn't concentrate adequately; what you didn't realise was the way in which you might *not* have been misled by it.

M. Immo in hoc non bene considerasti, quia quomodo te non deciperet ignorasti.

S. And what way is that?

D. Quomodo?

T. It's true that if this syllogism which I put forward just now [3.61] is expressed in the same way as in the analysis [3.631] of your own [3.101, 3.102] which I gave, so that it asserts:

M. Quippe si iste syllogismus quem modo proposui sic exponatur quemadmodum exposui tuum, ut dicatur

No man can be understood to be a man without rationality [3.6311],

nullus homo potest intelligi homo sine rationalitate

and

Every stone can be understood to be a stone without rationality [3.6312],

omnis autem lapis potest intelligi lapis sine rationalitate,

then it will be no more capable of producing a conclusion that I asserted yours [3.101, 3. 102] to be. Yet because the present one [3.61] can be understood in another way – a way which is not applicable to yours – it *does* produce the conclusion that a stone can in no sense be a man [3.621]. For when I assert that

non habebit aliam vim concludendi quam dixi tuum habere. Sed quoniam iste quodam alio modo potest intelligi quo ille tuus non potest, habet hanc conclusionem, ut nullo modo lapis homo esse possit. Cum enim dico quia

No man can be understood without rationality [3.611],
Every stone can be understood without rationality [3.612],

nullus homo intelligi valet sine rationalitate, et
omnis lapis valet intelligi sine rationalitate,

these propositions can, and indeed ought, to be taken to assert:

sic potest immo debet accipi ac si dicatur:

3.6321 No man is in some sense understandable without rationality[a],

nullus homo potest aliquo modo intelligi sine rationalitate[a];

3.6322 Every stone is in any sense understandable without rationality[a].

omnis vero lapis quolibet modo potest intelligi sine rationalitate[a].

Whence it follows:

Unde conficitur:

3.63221 No stone is in some sense a man[a].

nullus igitur lapis aliquo modo est homo[a].

3.6330 But your own premisses [3.10] are such that the truth is not in the least susceptible of being likewise implicitly conveyed by them; one cannot assert[a] that

In tuis vero propositionibus veritas nequaquam similem admittit subauditionem. Namque non potest dici[a] quia

3.6331 No literate is in some sense

nullus grammaticus intelligi valet

understandable without literacy[a] [cf. 3.6321],

3.6332 Every man is in any sense understandable without literacy[a] [cf. 3.6322],

for not only is it the case that

3.6333 Everything which is literate can be understood to be a man without literacy[a] [cf. 3.6331]

but also that

3.6334 No man can be understood to be a literate without literacy[a] [cf. 3.6332].

3.6340 On this account your premisses cannot produce the conclusion:

3.6341 A literate is in no sense a man[a].

aliquo modo sine grammatica[a],

aut

omnis homo valet quolibet modo intelligi sine grammatica[a].

Nam et

omnis qui grammaticus est, potest intelligi homo sine grammatica[a],

et

nullus homo potest intelligi grammaticus sine grammatica[a].

Quapropter non possunt conficere

grammaticum nequaquam esse hominem[a].

Ch. VIII

3.700 S. I have no objection to raise against your verdict; but since you guide me surreptitiously, so that I don't rest content with understanding what you assert, but concentrate on exactly what it is that you are asserting, it now occurs to me that we should scrutinise the conclusion which you showed to follow from my syllogism [3.1], namely

Being a literate is not being a man [3.431].

3.701 If this [3.431] is granted, then whatsoever is essentially literate need not therefore be essentially man[a]. But

3.71 if *man* follows from *literate* then the essence of man follows from the essence of literate.

3.711 But the second of these two conditionals doesn't hold [3.701], hence neither does the first, so that

3.7111 Not every literate is a man[a].

3.72 Further, every literate has some single feature[a] which makes him susceptible of being a man, so that

Either every literate is a man or none are[b].

3.721 But it has been shown [3.7111] that

Not every[a] literate is a man,

therefore

D. Non habeo quid contra tuam sententiam dicam. Sed quoniam latenter monuisti me ut non sim contentus intelligere quid dicas, sed idipsum quod dicis considerem: videtur mihi consideranda illa conclusio quam ex meo syllogismo confici ostendisti, quia

esse grammatici non est esse hominis.

Si enim hoc est, qui habet essentiam grammatici non ideo necessario habet essentiam hominis[a]. Sed

si homo sequitur grammaticum, essentia hominis sequitur essentiam grammatici.

Sed haec non sequitur hanc. Quare nec ille illum.

Non est igitur omnis grammaticus homo[a].

At cum omnibus grammaticis una sit ratio[a] cur sint homines: profecto

aut omnis grammaticus est homo, aut nullus[b].

Sed constat quia

non omnis[a].

3.7211 No literate is a man[a].
So now it looks as though you have even more ingeniously yielded up[b] for the taking that conclusion which you so cunningly removed from my syllogism [3.10].

Nullus igitur[a].
Videtur itaque quia syllogismo meo conclusionem quam acute abstulisti, auferendo acutius dedisti.[b]

3.800 T. Although I do indeed surreptitiously lead you to concentrate on what you hear, it is not my aim to endow the process with an air of complete futility. And now that you have gone and proved sophistically that no literate is a man [3.7211] by making use of the fact that being a literate is not being a man [3.431], it will nevertheless still be a handy exercise if you can get to the bottom of the fallacy which persists in muddling you with its apparent logicality.

M. Etsi latenter te monui considerare quod audis, non tamen ut apparet inutiliter. Nam etsi sophistice probes nullum grammaticum hominem per hoc quod esse grammatici non est esse hominis; utile tamen tibi erit, cum ipsum sophisma quod te sub pallio verae rationis fallit, in sua fallacia nudum conspicies.

S. Then show me just how and where this proof [3.7] involving *literate* which I put together just now is muddling me.

D. Ostende ergo quod me fallat et ubi me fallat haec quam modo feci de grammatico probatio.

T. Let's go back to the cases of *animal* and *man* – cases in which we as it were so sense the truth that we can't be taken in by any bad proof which might force us into a false opinion[a].

M. Redeamus iterum ad animal et hominem, in quibus ita quasi palpamus veritatem, ut nullum sophisma nobis persuadeat licet cogat credere falsitatem[a].

Tell me: is not what is involved in being so-and-so expressible by definition[b]?

Dic ergo utrum esse uniuscuiusque rei in definitione[b] consistat.

S. That is so.

D. Ita est.

T. Is the definition of *man* also the definition of *animal*?

M. Definitio hominis est definitio animalis?

3.8010 S. Not at all; for if *rational mortal[a] animal*, the definition of *man*, were likewise the definition of *animal*, then to whatsoever *animal* was applicable, *rational mortal* would also apply[b];

D. Minime. Si enim animal rationale mortale[a] quae est definitio hominis, esset definitio animalis: cuicumque conveniret animal conveniret rationale mortale[b],

3.8011 but this is not the case.

quod falsum est.

3.8012 T. Hence being a man is not being an animal[a].

M. Non est igitur esse hominis esse animalis[a].

S. So it follows.

D. Ita consequitur.

3.810 T. Now from this conclusion, by using the same form of reasoning [3.7] as that whereby a moment ago you concluded that no literate is a man [3.7211], you can go on to show that

M. Potest igitur ex hoc probare quia

3.811 No man is an animal[a].
So if it's clear to you in this case that your form of reasoning leads to untruth, you can have no confidence in the supposed

nullus homo animal est[a],
eadem ratione qua probasti modo nullum grammaticum hominem. Quapropter si vides apertam esse falsitatem, quod haec

truth [3.7211] which emerged from your earlier fiddling with the same form[b].

tua ratiocinatio hic concludit: ne credas certam esse veritatem quod ibi ludit[b]

3.900 S. You've shown that it misled me; now show me just where it did so.

D. Iam ostendisti quia me fallit; ostende etiam ubi.

T. Don't you recall that a short while ago [3.4] I asserted, and you agreed, that

M. Non tenes quod paulo ante dixi te concedente quia

Being a literate is not being a man [3.431]

esse grammatici non est esse hominis

means the same as

idem valet ac si diceretur

The definition of *literate* is not the definition of *man* [3.44]?

definitio grammatici non est definitio hominis,

This amounted to saying that

id est

3.901 A literate and a man are not altogether identical [cf. 3.452],

non est idem omnino grammaticus et homo?

for just as *man* shouldn't be defined as possessing literacy, so also *literate* is not definable without literacy [cf. 3.41, 3.42].

Sicut enim homo definiri non debet cum grammatica, ita grammaticus non valet sine grammatica.

3.910 Consequently that contention of yours [3.701] should be understood as follows[a]:

Quare debet intelligi illa tua argumentatio hoc modo[a]*:*

3.911 If being literate is not being man and only[a] man, then whatsoever is essentially literate need not on that account be essentially man and only man [cf. 3.701].

si esse grammatici non est simpliciter[a] *esse hominis: qui habet essentiam grammatici, non ideo consequitur ut habeat simpliciter essentiam hominis*

3.920 Likewise we are to understand that:

Similiter intelligendum est quia

3.921 It is false that from *literate*, *man* and only *man* can be inferred [cf. 3.71, 3.711],

simpliciter homo non sequitur grammaticum,

that is to say:

id est:

3.922 If something is literate, then it does not follow that it is a man and only a man.

si grammaticus est, non consequitur ut sit simpliciter homo.

3.930 So that really the only conclusion is:

Ita vero nihil aliud consequitur nisi:

3.931 No literate is a man and only a man[a].

nullus grammaticus est simpliciter homo[a].

S. Nothing could be more obvious

D. Nihil clarius.

Ch. IX

3.940 T. Were it to be proved true, as I believe could quite easily be done[a], that:

M. Verum si probaretur, quod ut puto facile fieri potest[a]*, quia*

3.9410 Being a literate is not being a man

esse grammatici ita non est esse hominis

is like

sicut

3.9411 Being a white is not being a man[a]

esse albi non est esse hominis[a]

3.9412 (for a man can be without white and white can be without a man)

– potest enim homo esse sine albo et album sine homine –

3.9420 then from this one could indeed draw the consequence that:

3.9421 Some literate can[a] be other than a man.

S. Why do we take all this trouble, then, if this can be proved? Prove it, and the question at issue will be settled.

3.9430 T. That is an improper demand at this point, for in the present investigation we are not trying to find out whether it is *possible* for there to be some non-human literate, but whether

3.9431 there *is* some non-human literate.

And this, as you see, cannot be shown[a].

4.100 S. It's not yet obvious to me, for I still want to raise a point to the contrary.

T. Carry on.

S. Aristotle showed that

4.101 a literate is one of those things which are *in* a subject[a],

but

4.102 No man is in a subject[a],

and from this it follows that

4.103 No literate is a man [cf. 1.11].

4.110 T. Aristotle didn't want this consequence to be drawn from what he said, for this same text of his uses *literate*[a] not only of such and such a man, but also of *man* and *animal.*

S. How then can this syllogism of mine be refuted?

4.1101 T. Tell me now: when you speak[a] to me about a literate, whereof[b] may I understand you to be speaking – of the name, or of the things[c] signified[d] by that name?

S. Of the things[c] signified.

T. What things[c] does it signify[d] then?

S. *Man*[e] and literacy[f].

4.1102 T. On hearing this name, then, I may understand *man* or literacy[a], and

4.1103 when I speak of a literate, my speech may concern *man* or literacy[a].

S. That must be the case.

4.1104 T. Tell me then whether *man* is a substance or in a subject[a].

S. A substance, not in a subject.

4.1105 T. Is literacy a quality and in a subject[a]?

tunc vere consequeretur

aliquem grammaticum posse[a] esse non hominem.

D. Quid ergo laboramus, si hoc probari potest? Proba, et finiatur haec quaestio.

M. Non hoc a me debes hic exigere. Non enim in hac quaestione ventilamus utrum possit esse, sed utrum

sit aliquis grammaticus non homo,

quod vides monstrari non posse[a].

D. Nondum video, quia adhuc habeo dicere contra.

M. Dic.

D. Aristoteles ostendit

grammaticum eorum esse quae sunt in subiecto[a].

Et

nullus homo est in subiecto[a].

Quare

nullus grammaticus homo.

M. Noluit Aristoteles hoc consequi ex suis dictis. Nam idem Aristoteles dicit et quendam hominem, et hominem et animal grammaticum[a].

D. Quomodo ergo dissolvitur iste syllogismus?

M. Responde mihi: cum loqueris[a] mihi de grammatico, unde[b] intelligam te loqui: de hoc nomine, an de rebus[c] quas significat[d]?

D. De rebus[c].

M. Quas ergo res[c] significat[d]?

D. Hominem[e] et grammaticam[f].

M. Audito ergo hoc nomine, intelligam hominem aut grammaticam[a], et loquens de grammatico, loquar de homine aut de grammatica[a].

D. Ita oportet.

M. Dic ergo: homo est substantia, an in subiecto[a]?

D. Non est in subiecto, sed est substantia.

M. Grammatica est qualitas, et in subiecto[a]?

S. It is both.

T. Well then, nothing extraordinary is being asserted if one says that

D. Utrumque est.

M. Quid ergo mirum si quis dicit quia

4.111 insofar as *man* is concerned, *literate* is a substance and not in a subject[a], whereas

grammaticus est substantia et non est in subiecto[a] secundum hominem; et

4.112 insofar as literacy is concerned, *literate* is a quality and in a subject[a].

grammaticus est qualitas et in subiecto[a] secundum grammaticam?

Ch. X

4.1200 S. I can't deny all this; but I might mention one more reason why *literate* is not a substance:

D. Diffiteri non possum. Sed unum adhuc dicam cur grammaticus non sit substantia:

4.1201 every substance[a] is either primary or secondary, whereas *literate* is neither primary nor secondary substance[b].

T. Call to mind that assertion of Aristotle's which I mentioned a little while ago [4.1100] according to which *literate* is both primary and secondary substance, since he invokes the fact that *literate* is used not only of such and such a man, but also of *man* and *animal.* On what grounds, then, can you show *literate* to be neither a primary nor a secondary substance[c]?

quia omnis substantia[a] est prima aut secunda; grammaticus autem nec prima nec secunda[b].

M. Memento dictorum Aristotelis quae paulo ante dixi, quibus dicit grammaticum et primam et secundam substantiam, quia et quendam hominem, et hominem et animal grammaticum dici testatur. Sed tamen unde probas grammaticum non esse primam nec nec secundam substantiam[c]?

4.121 S. Because unlike any substance[a] it is in a subject, also it is asserted of many things, and this is not a mark of primary substance[b].

D. Quia est in subiecto, quod nulla substantia est[a]; et dicitur de pluribus, quod primae non est[b];

4.122 Further it is neither genus nor species[a], nor is it asserted in respect of whatness[b], as secondary substances are[c].

nec est genus aut species[a] nec dicitur in eo quod quid[b], quod est secundae[c].

4.130 T. None of your points, if you bear in mind what has been said, makes *literate* other than a substance.

M. Nihil horum si bene meministi quae iam diximus aufert grammatico substantiam, quia

4.131 For insofar as something literate[a] is not in a subject[b], not only is it both genus and species[c], but it is also asserted in respect of whatness[d]; this is because such a being is both man, i.e. a species, and animal, i.e. a genus[e], and these are asserted in respect of whatness[f] [cf. 4.122].

secundum aliquid grammaticus[a] non est in subiecto[b], et est genus et species[c], et dicitur in eo qiod quid[d]; quia est et homo qui species est, et animal quod est genus[e], et haec dicuntur in eo quod quid[f].

4.132 Further, it is individual[a], like a man or an animal, for some literate is individual in the same way as some man or some animal. For instance Socrates is not only an animal and a man, but also a literate[b].

Est etiam individuus[a], sicut homo et animal, quia quemadmodum quidam homo et quodam animal, ita quidam grammaticus est individuus. Socrates enim et animal et homo est, et grammaticus[b].

S. There's no denying what you say.

D. Non possum negare quod dicis.

Ch. XI

4.14 T. If you have no other grounds on which to base a proof that *literate* is[a] not *man*, now prove that it is[a] not literacy[b].

M. Si alia non habes unde possis probare grammaticum non esse[a] hominem: nunc proba eum non esse[a] grammaticam[b].

S. I could manage to do that more easily by pointing[c] than by argument, now that you have shattered all my contentions by showing the various meanings[d] of *literate*, and how speech and understanding[e] involving *literate*[f] should correspond to those meanings. Yet although perhaps I can't deny all this, my mind is nevertheless not satisfied in such a way that it can settle down[g], so to speak, having discovered the required solution. Indeed, it looks to me as though you are concerned not so much with my enlightenment[h], as with the refutation of my points. But in fact my job was only to make explicit those factors which perplexed me when either of the alternatives in question [cf. 1.1, 1.2] was adopted; yours was either to refute one of those alternatives, or to show how both alternatives are mutually compatible.

D. Facilius hoc possum digito[c] quam argumento. Ibi namque fregisti omnia mea argumenta, ubi aperuisti a grammatico significari diversa[d], et secundum ea loquendum intelligendumque[e] de grammatico[f]. Quod quamvis abnuere non possim, tamen non sic satisfacit animo meo ut velut quod quaerebat invento quiescat[g]. Videris enim mihi quasi non curare ut me doceas[h], sed tantum ut rationes meas obstruas. Sed sicut meum fuit exponere quae me ex utraque parte in ambiguitatem cogunt: ita tuum erat aut unam partem destruere, aut ostendere quomodo non sibi invicem repugnent.

T. Why, in your view, does not the fact that *literate* can be properly spoken of and understood[i] sometimes in respect of man and sometimes in respect of literacy sufficiently bring out the complete absence of incompatibility between the assertions that *literate* is a substance and *literate* is a quality?

M. Cur non satis tibi videtur ostensum quod grammaticum esse substantiam et grammaticum esse qualitatem nequaquam sibi repugnent invicem, in eo quod de grammatico modo secundum hominem, modo secundum grammaticam loqui et intelligere[i] oportet?

4.20 S. Because while it is quite true that no one who understands the name *literate* is unaware that it signifies literacy as well as *man*[a], yet if, on the strength of this, I were to assert at some gathering[b], 'A literate[c] is a useful form of knowledge', or, 'That man displays an adequate literate[d]', not only would this immensely irritate the literates, but even the ignorant would guffaw[e].

D. Quoniam nemo qui intelligit nomen grammatici ignorat grammaticum significare hominem et grammaticam[a], et tamen si hac fiducia loquens in populo[b] dicam: utilis scientia est grammaticus[c], aut: bene scit homo iste grammaticum[d]: non solum stomachabuntur grammatici, sed et ridebunt rustici[e].

4.210 So I just find it impossible to credit that authors of logical works can

Nullatenus itaque credam sine aliqua alia ratione tractatores dialecticae tam saepe et

have no further grounds for so frequently and seriously committing themselves in writing[a] in their books to positions that they would be ashamed to exemplify in conversation[b].

tam studiose in suis libris scripsisse[a], quod idem ipsi colloquentes[b] dicere erubescerent.

4.211 After all, when in their logical discussion they want to show[a] a quality or an accident[b], they most usually add 'such as *literate*', and so on[c].

Saepissime namque cum volunt ostendere[a] qualitatem aut accidens[b], subiungunt: ut grammaticus et similia[c],

4.212 Yet everyone's spoken usage[a] vouches for the fact that *literate* is a substance rather than a quality or accident. But when they want to make a point about substance they never suggest *literate* or anything of that sort[b] as an example.

cum grammaticum magis esse substantiam quam qualitatem aut accidens usus omnium loquentium[a] attestetur. Et cum volunt aliquid docere de substantia, nusquam proferunt: ut grammaticus aut aliquid huiusmodi[b].

4.22 The question boils down to this: if *literate*, because it signifies[a] *man* and literacy, must therefore be said to be quality[b] as well as substance, why is not *man* likewise quality as well as substance[c]? After all, *man* signifies a substance along with all the characteristics[d] of man, such as sensibility and mortality[e], yet when something is laid down in writing concerning some quality or other we never find *man* produced as an example.

Huc accedit, quia si ideo grammaticus quia significat[a] hominem et grammaticam dicendus est substantia et qualitas[b]: cur homo non est similiter qualitas et substantia[c]? Homo namque significat substantiam cum omnibus illis differentiis[d] qiae sunt in homine, ut est sensibilitas et mortalitas[e]. Sed nusquam ubi scriptum sit aliquid de qualitate aliqua, prolatum est ad exemplum: velut homo.

Ch. XII

4.230 T. You reject my argument in favour of regarding *literate* as both substance and quality because it is not equally applicable in the case of the name *man*. You do this, I think, because you don't realise the vast difference between the way in which the name *man* can signify man's make-up[a], and the way in which the name *literate* can signify *man* and literacy[b].

M. Quod illam rationem quam dixi, cur grammaticus scilicet sit substantia et qualitas, idcirco repudias quia non valet in nomine hominis: ideo facis, ut puto, quia non consideras quam dissimiliter significent scilicet nomen hominis ea ex quibus constat[a] homo, et grammaticus hominem et grammaticam[b].

4.231 We may take it that the name *man* signifies precisively and as a single whole[a], the complete make-up[b] of man. Of this, substance[c] is the chief feature, as the ground and possessor of the others, and this not in the sense that it is incomplete without them, but rather that they are incomplete without it. After all, there is no characteristic of substance in the absence of which substance is also

Nempe nomen hominis per se et ut unum[a] significat ea ex quibus constat[b] totus homo. In quibus substantia[c] principalem locum tenet, quoniam est causa aliorum et habens ea, non ut indigens illis, sed ut se indigentia. Nulla enim est differentia substantiae sine qua substantia inveniri non possit, et nulla differentiarum eius sine illa potest existere[d]. Quapropter quamvis omnia simul velut unum totum[e] sub una

absent, whereas in the absence of substance no characteristics can exist[d]. So that although all those characteristics, at the same time, form as it were a single whole[e] covered by a single meaning, and receive as their appellation the single name *man*, nevertheless this name principally signifies[f] and is appellative[g] of substance[h]. Thus it would be correct to assert 'The substance is *man*', and, '*Man* is a substance', while no-one would say, 'The rationality is *man*', or, '*Man* is rationality'; rather, *man* is said to possess rationality[i].

significatione uno nomine appellentur homo, sic tamen principaliter hoc nomen est significativum[f] et appellativum[g] substantiae[h], ut cum recte dicatur: substantia est homo et homo substantia: nullus tamen dicat: rationalitas est homo aut homo rationalitas, sed habens rationalitatem[i].

4.232 On the other hand *literate* does not signify *man* and literacy as a single whole[a]; precisively it signifies only literacy[b], and obliquely it signifies *man*[c].

Grammaticus vero non significat hominem et grammaticam ut unum[a], sed grammaticam per se[b] et hominem per aliud[c] significat.

4.233 Indeed, although the name *literate* is appellative[a] of *man*, it nevertheless may not properly[b] be said to signify *man*[c].

Et hoc nomen quamvis sit appellativum[a] hominis, non tamen proprie[b] dicitur eius significativum[c];

4.234 Further, even though *literate* signifies literacy[a], it is not, however, appellative of literacy[b].

et licet sit significativum grammaticae[a], non tamen est eius appellativum[b].

4.2341 Here I want to stipulate that the name of a thing is appellative of that thing when it is the name by which that very thing is itself called in the customary course of utterance[a]. Thus assertions such as 'Literacy is *literate*', or, '*Literate* is literacy'[b] run counter to such customary usage; we say rather, 'The man is literate', or, 'The literate is a man[c]'.

Appellativum autem nomen cuiuslibet rei nunc dico, quo res ipsa usu loquendi appellatur[a]. Nullo enim usu loquendi dicitur: grammatica est grammaticus, aut: grammaticus est grammatica[b]; sed homo est grammaticus, et grammaticus homo[c].

Ch. XIII

4.240 S. I don't see the point of your saying that *literate* signifies literacy precisively and *man* obliquely, and yet that it only signifies literacy. For just as *man* comprises[a] *animal* along with rationality and mortality, so that *man* signifies[b] all three of these, so also, since *literate* comprises[a] *man* and literacy, the name *literate* must signify[b] both of these[c]; after all, neither a man without literacy nor literacy apart from a man[d] are ever asserted to be literate.

D. Non video quid dicas quia grammaticus significat grammaticam per se, et hominem per aliud, et quomodo grammaticae tantum sit significativum. Sicut enim homo constat[a] ex animali et rationalitate et mortalitate, et idcirco homo significat[b] haec tria: ita grammaticus constat[a] ex homine et grammatica, et ideo nomen hoc significat[b] utrumque[c]. Numquam enim dicitur grammaticus aut homo sine grammatica, aut grammatica sine homine[d].

4.2410 T. Then if you are correct, 'A man displaying literacy[b], would define and

M. Si ergo ita est ut tu dicis, definitio et esse[a] grammatici est: homo sciens

state what is involved in being[a] a literate.

S. It can't be otherwise.

4.2411 T. Therefore as literacy distinguishes[a] the literate man from the illiterate[b], it is the literate's link with being – the constitutive part of that which is its being[c] – the alternative presence and absence of which can only result in the literate's perishing[d].

S. And so what?

T. It would follow, therefore, that literacy is not an accident[e], but a constitutive characteristic[f], *man* being the genus[g], and *literate* the species[h]. And the same would apply to the cases of whiteness and similar accidents. But the treatise on how to deal with wholes shows[i] that this is not so.

S. Though I can't deny your assertions, I'm still not convinced that *literate* may not signify *man*.

4.24120 T. Let it be supposed[a] that there is some rational animal – other than man[b] – which displays literacy in the same way as does men.

S. That's easily supposed.

T. There is thus some non-man displaying literacy.

S. So it follows.

T. And every displayer of literacy[c] is literate.

S. Granted.

T. There is therefore some literate non-man.

S. So it follows.

T. But you persist in asserting that *literate*, according to your understanding, comprises *man*.

S. I do.

T. So that some non-man is man[d], and this is false.

S. This is the outcome of the inference.

4.24121 T. So don't you see that *literate* no more signifies *man* than *white* does? It just happens to be the case that man alone displays literacy, whereas whiteness is found in beings other than men[a].

S. That's what follows from the

grammaticam[b].

D. Non potest aliud esse.

M. Ergo cum grammatica dividit[a] *hominem grammaticum a non-grammatico*[b], *conducit grammaticum ad esse, et est pars eius quod est esse rei*[c], *nec potest adesse et abesse a grammatico praeter subiecti corruptionem*[d].

D. Quid inde?

M. Non est igitur grammatica accidens[e] *sed substantialis differentia*[f], *et est homo genus*[g], *et grammaticus species*[h]. *Nec dissimilis est ratio de albedine et similibus accidentibus. Quod falsum esse totius artis tractatus ostendit*[i].

D. Quamquam non possim negare quod dicis, nondum tamen mihi persuasum est quod grammaticus non significet hominem.

M. Ponamus[a] *quod sit aliquod animal rationale – non tamen homo*[b] *– quod ita sciat grammaticam sicut homo.*

D. Facile est hoc fingere.

M. Est igitur aliquis non-homo sciens grammaticam.

D. Ita sequitur.

M. At omne sciens grammaticam[c] *est grammaticum.*

D. Concedo.

M. Est igitur quidam non-homo grammaticus.

D. Consequitur.

M. Sed tu dicis in grammatico intelligi honinem.

D. Dico.

M. Quidam igitur non-homo est homo[d], *quod falsum est.*

D. Ad hoc ratio deducitur.

M. Nonne ergo vides quia grammaticus non ob aliud magis videtur significare hominem quam albus, nisi quia grammatica soli homini accidit, albedo vero non soli homini[a]*?*

D. Sic sequitur ex eo quod finximus. Sed

supposition adopted, but I'd rather you produced a proof which doesn't depend upon such suppositious cases.

sine figmento volo ut hoc efficias.

4.2413 T. In the same way as *animal* is not predicated along with *man*, since it is comprised in[a] *man*, so also, if *man* is comprised in *literate* the former is not simultaneously predicated along with the latter of some subject. For example, it is inappropriate to say that Socrates is an animal man[b].

M. Si homo est in grammatico, non praedicatur cum eo simul de aliquo, sicut animal non praedicatur cum homine, quia inest[a] in homine. Non enim apte dicitur quia Socrates est homo animal[b].

S. That can't be denied.

D. Non potest contradici.

T. But it is proper to say that Socrates is a literate man[c].

M. Sed convenienter dicitur quia Socrates est homo grammaticus[c].

S. It is proper.

D. Convenienter.

T. Therefore *man* is not comprised in *literate*.

M. Non est igitur homo in grammatico.

S. I grasp that it does so follow.

D. Sic consequi video.

4.2414 T. Again, if *literate* is *man displaying literacy* then wherever *literate* appears the words *man displaying literacy* may be correctly[a] substituted for it.

M. Item si grammaticus est homo sciens grammaticam: ubicumque ponitur grammaticus apte[a] ponitur homo sciens grammaticam.

S. That's right.

D. Ita est.

T. Hence, if it is appropriate[a] to say 'Socrates is a literate man' it is equally appropriate[a] to say 'Socrates is a man displaying literacy man'.

M. Si igitur apte[a] dicitur: Socrates est homo grammaticus, apte[a] quoque dicitur: Socrates est homo homo sciens grammaticam.

S. So it follows.

D. Consequitur.

T. But every man displaying literacy is a literate man.

M. Omnis autem homo sciens grammaticam est homo grammaticus.

S. Yes.

D. Ita est.

T. Thus Socrates, who is a man displaying literacy man, is a literate man man, and since a literate is a man displaying literacy, it follows that Socrates is a man displaying literacy man man, and so on to infinity[b].

M. Socrates igitur qui est homo homo sciens grammaticam, est homo homo grammaticus. Et quoniam grammaticus est homo sciens grammaticam, consequitur ut Socrates sit homo homo homo sciens grammaticam, et sic in infinitum[b].

S. I can't gainsay such obvious inferences.

D. Non possum apertae consequentiae resistere.

4.2415 T. Again, if by *literate* we are to understand *man* as well as literacy, then in all cases of paronymous naming we must understand that which is named paronymously along with that from which it derives its name[a].

M. Item si in grammatico homo intelligendus est cum grammatica, intelligendum est similiter in omnibus similibus denominativis id quod denominatur cum eo a quo denominatur[a].

S. That was my idea.

D. Hoc sentiebam.

T. So that *today's* must signify both that which is called *today's* and, in addition, it must signify today[b].

M. Ergo hodiernum significat id quod vocatur hodiernum et hodie[b].

S. And so what?
T. Thus *today's* signifies something having a temporal side-import[c].
S. It must be so.
T. Under such conditions, then, since *today's* is an incomplex expression[f] having a temporal side-import[e], it must be a verb[d] rather than a name.

D. Quid postea?
M. Hodiernum igitur significat aliquid cum tempore[c].
D. Ita esse necesse est.
M. Igitur hodiernum non est nomen sed verbum,[d] *quia est vox consignificans tempus*[e], *nec est oratio*[f].

Ch. XIV

4.30 S. You have proved to my satisfaction that *literate* does not signify *man*.
T. You see the point, then, of what I said about *literate* not signifying *man*? [4.233]
S. I do see it, and now I'm waiting for you to show that *literate* signifies literacy[a].

D. Satis mihi probasti grammaticum non significare hominem.
M. Vides igitur quid dixerim quia grammaticus non est hominis significativum?
D. Video, et exspecto ut grammaticum ostendas esse significativum grammaticae[a].

4.31 Didn't you assert a few moments ago [4.2410] that *literate* signifies *man displaying literacy*?
S. That was my opinion.
T. But now it has been sufficiently proved that *literate* does not signify *man*?
S. Quite sufficiently.
T. When then is left?
S. *Displaying literacy*[a] is all it can signify.
T. It signifies literacy[b] then.

M. Nonne paulo ante dicebas grammaticum significare hominem scientem grammaticam?
D. Et credebam.
M. Sed iam satis probatum est quia non significat hominem.
D. Satis.
M. Quid ergo restat?
D. Ut non significet aliud quam scientem grammaticam[a].
M. Est igitur significativum grammaticae[b].

4.40 S. It has been amply proved that
4.411 *literate* is appellative of man [4.233] and not of literacy [4.234], and
4.412 that it signifies literacy [4.232] but not *man* [4.233].
4.413 However, since you asserted that *literate* signifies literacy precisively and *man* obliquely [4.232], I'd like you to clearify the distinction between these two types of meaning so that I can understand how:
4.414 *literate* doesn't signify [4.412] that which it in some sense does signify[a] [4.413], and
4.415 how *literate* can be an appellative [4.411] of that which it doesn't signify[a] [4.412].

D. Sufficienter probatum est grammaticum non esse appellativum grammaticae sed hominis;
nec esse significativum hominis sed grammaticae.
Sed quoniam dixisti grammaticum significare grammaticam per se et hominem per aliud, peto ut aperte mihi duas has significationes distinguas ut intelligam
quomodo grammaticus non sit significativum eius quod aliquo modo significat[a], *aut*
quomodo sit appellativum eius cuius significativum non est[a].

4.4210 T. Suppose that unknown to you a white horse were enclosed in some

M. Si est in domo aliqua albus equus te nesciente inclusus, et aliquis tibi dicit: in

building or other, and someone told you, 'A white[a] is in this building'; would that inform you that the horse was inside?

S. No; for whether they speak of a white, or of whiteness, or of that within which the whiteness is enclosed, no definite thing is brought to my mind apart from the essence of this colour.

T. Even though you did happen to understand something over and above the colour, it is at least definite that the name in question conveys to you nothing as to exactly what that something is in which the colour is to be found.

4.4211 S. That is quite definitely so. True, that name brings to mind a body or a surface, but this is simply because experience has shown me that whiteness is usually found in such things[a]. However, of itself the name *white* signifies neither of these, as was shown in the case of *literate*[b]. And now I'm waiting for you to show me what it does in fact signify.

4.422 T. Suppose you were to see a white horse and a black bull standing together, and someone gave the order, 'Give it a thwack!', thereby meaning the horse, but without giving any indication as to which he intended: would you then know that he was referring to the horse?

S. No.

T. But suppose, while still in ignorance, you were to ask 'Which?', and he were to reply, 'The white!'; would you then gather his reference?

S. I would gather from the name *white* that he meant the horse.

T. Thus for you the name *white* would signify the horse.

S. It certainly would.

T. And do you notice that this would be in a fashion other than that proper to the name *horse*?

4.4231 S. I quite see that. I notice that even before I know the horse to be white, the name *horse* signifies to me the substance *horse* precisively, not obliquely[a].

4.4232 On the other hand, the name *white* signifies the substance *horse* not

hac domo est album sive albus[a]; an scis per hoc ibi esse equum?

D. Non. Sive enim dicat album albedinem, sive in quo est albedo: nullius certae rei mente concipio essentiam nisi huius coloris.

M. Etiamsi aliquid aliud intelligis quam colorem istum: illud tamen certum est, quia eius in quo est ipse color essentiam per hoc nomen non intelligis.

D. Certum. Nam etsi occurrat animo corpus aut superficies, quod non ob aliud fit nisi quia expertus sum in his solere esse albedinem[a]; ipsum tamen nomen albi nihil horum significat, sicut probatum est de grammatico[b]. Sed adhuc exspecto ut ostendas quia significat.

M. Quid si vides stantes iuxta se invicem album equum et nigrum bovem, et dicit tibi aliquis de equo: percute illum, non monstrans aliquo signo de quo dicat: an scis quod de equo dicat?

D. Non.

M. Si vero nescienti tibi et interroganti: quem? respondet: album, intelligis de quo dicit?

D. Equum intelligo per nomen albi.

M. Nomen igitur albi significat tibi equum.

D. Significat utique.

M. Nonne vides quia alio modo quam nomen equi?

D. Video. Nempe nomen equi etiam priusquam sciam ipsum equum album esse, significat mihi equi substantiam per se, et non per aliud[a].

Nomen vero albi equi substantiam significat non per se, sed per aliud, id est per hoc

precisively, but only obliquely, that is, thanks to my being aware that the horse is white[a].

quia scio equum esse album[a].

4.4233 Now the name *white* is equisignificant with the phrase *having whiteness*; similarly the precise effect of this phrase is to bring to my mind the understanding of whiteness, but not of the thing which has the whiteness, so that the word *white* has the same effect[a].

Cum enim nihil aliud significet hoc nomen, quod est albus, quam haec oratio, quae est habens albedinem: sicut haec oratio per se constituit mihi intellectum albedinis, et non eius rei quae habet albedinem; ita et nomen[a].

4.4234 However, because I know, otherwise than by means of the name *white* – by sight, for example – that the whiteness is in the horse, when whiteness has been thus conveyed by means of that word, I also gather the reference to the horse because I know that the whiteness is in the horse. Nevertheless this is otherwise than by means of the name *white*, even though that word is an appellative of the horse[a].

Sed quoniam scio albedinem esse in equo, et hoc per aliud quam per nomen albi, velut per visum: intellecta albedine per hoc nomen, intelligo equum per hoc quod albedinem scio esse in equo, id est per aliud quam per nomen albi, quo tamen equus appellatur[a].

Ch. XV

4.424 T. So now you grasp how *white* does not signify what it does in some way signify [4.414] and how it is appellative of what it does not signify[a]? [4.415]

M. Vides ergo quomodo albus non sit significativum eius quod aliquo modo significat, et quomodo sit appellativum eius cuius non est significativum?[a]

S. I now see this further point: *white* signifies yet does not signify the horse;

D. Hoc quoque video. Significat enim equum et non significat,

4.4241 it signifies the horse obliquely, and not precisively, and nevertheless *white* is appellative of the horse.

quia non eum significat per se, sed per aliud, et tamen equus appellatur albus.

4.4242 Further I realise that what I now discern in the case of *white* is applicable to *literate* and all like paronyms[a].

Et quod video in albo, hoc intelligo in grammatico, et in similibus denominativis[a].

4.4243 On these grounds it appears to me that the signification of both names and verbs can be diversely classified: one sort is precisive signification, and the other sort is oblique[a].

Quapropter videtur mihi significatio nominum et verborum sic dividi posse, quod alia sit per se, alia per aliud[a].

4.430 T. Notice also that while the precisive type of signification pertains essentially to significant utterances as such, the other type is only accidental to such utterances[a].

M. Considera etiam, quoniam harum duarum significationum illa quae per se est ipsis vocibus significativis est substantialis, altera vero accidentalis[a].

4.431 Thus, when a noun or a verb is defined as a *significant utterance*, the

Cum enim in definitione nominis vel verbi dicitur quia est vox significativa,

signification in question is to be understood only as being of the precisive sort. Were the oblique sense of signification to be understood in the definition of a noun or of a verb, then *today's* would be a verb, and not a noun, for it signifies some time or other because of its signifying something along with a temporal import, and this, as I remarked before [4.2415] is proper to a verb, not to a noun[a].

intelligendum est non alia significatione quam ea quae per se est. Nam si illa significatio quae est per aliud, in definitione nominis vel verbi intelligenda est, iam non erit hodiernus nomen sed verbum. Significat enim aliquando ea significatione aliquid cum tempore, sicut supra dixi, quod non est nominis sed verbi[a].

Ch. XVI

4.500 S. Obviously it is as you say.

D. Patet quod dicis.

4.501 Nevertheless it is awkward to think of *literate*, although it signifies literacy, as being[a] a quality,

Sed non sine scrupulo accipit animus grammaticum esse[a] qualitatem, quamvis significet grammaticam,

4.5020 or to think of man alone, that is without literacy, as being literate;

aut hominem solum, id est sine grammatica, esse grammaticum,

4.5021 for since man can only be literate alone or with literacy, that man alone is literate[a] follows as a consequence of the proof [4.24] that man along with literacy is not literate.

licet probatum sit hominem simul et grammaticam non esse grammaticum; unde consequitur solum hominem esse grammaticum[a], quoniam non potest esse grammaticus nisi aut solus aut cum grammatica.

4.5022 And although the name *literate* signifies literacy, nevertheless the correct answer to the question 'What is literate?' could scarcely be '*Literate* is literacy' or '*Literate* is a quality'[a].

Quamvis namque grammatici nomen significativum sit grammaticae: non tamen convenienter respondetur quaerenti quid grammaticus sit: grammatica, aut qualitas[a].

4.503 And again, since a literate must participate in literacy, it follows that a man can only be a literate in conjunction with literacy.

Et si nullus est grammaticus nisi participando grammaticam, consequitur ut homo non sit grammaticus nisi cum grammatica.

4.510 T. The assertion that man alone, in the sense of man without literacy, is literate, can be interpreted in two fashions, one correct and the other incorrect, and this is enough to solve your problem.

M. Quod quidem dicitur quia homo solus, id est sine grammatica, est grammaticus, quantum ad tuam quaestionem solvendam sufficit, duobus modis intelligi potest, uno vero, altero falso.

4.511 On the one hand man alone, without literacy, is indeed literate, for he alone ever possesses literacy; literacy itself does not possess literacy, either alone or along with man[a].

Homo quippe solus sine grammatica est grammaticus, quia solus est habens grammaticam. Grammatica namque nec sola nec cum homine[a] habet grammaticam.

4.5120 On the other hand man alone, deprived of literacy, is not literate, for in the absence of literacy no one can be literate[a].

Sed homo solus, id est absque grammatica, non est grammaticus, quia absente grammatica nullus esse grammaticus potest[a].

4.5121 The first case is like that of

Sicut qui praecedendo ducit alium, et solus

someone preceding, leading someone else, and alone being the one who precedes, for that which follows is not a precedent, either separately or in such a way that the two form a single precedent. In the second case, one who is alone is not one who precedes, for unless there is a follower, it's impossible for there to be a precedent[a].

est praevius, quia qui sequitur non est praevius, nec separatim nec sic ut ex illis duobus unus fiat praevius; et solus non est praevius, quia nisi sit qui sequatur, praevius esse non potest[a].

4.5122 And of course, when it is asserted that *literate* is a quality, this assertion is only correct if made in the sense which occurs in Aristotle's treatise *On the Categories*[a].

Cum vero dicitur quia grammaticus est qualitas: non recte nisi secundum tractatum Aristotelis De Categoriis[a] *dicitur.*

Ch. XVII

4.513 S. But doesn't that treatise make the point, 'Everything which is, is one or other of either substance or quantity or quality', and so on[a]? So, if *man* alone is literate, a substance alone is literate. How comes it then that that treatise accounts *literate* a quality rather than a substance[b]?

D. An aliud habet ille tractatus quam: omne quod est aut est substantia aut quantitas aut qualitas et cetera[a]*? Si igitur solus homo est grammaticus, sola substantia est grammaticus. Quomodo ergo secundum illum tractatum magis est grammaticus qualitas quam substantia*[b]*?*

4.5141 T. Although the text in question might be interpreted in the way you claim, since everything which is is some one or other of the things you mention[a], nevertheless Aristotle's main intention in that book was not to show this, but rather to show how every noun or verb signifies one or other of them.

M. Etsi hoc ibi intelligatur quod tu dicis, quia omne quod est aliquid horum est[a]*: non tamen fuit principalis intentio Aristotelis hoc in illo libro ostendere, sed quoniam omne nomen vel verbum aliquid horum significat.*

4.5142 It was not his aim to show the nature of individual things, nor yet of what things individual words can be appellative; rather he wished to show what things they signify[a].

Non enim intendebat ostendere quid sint singulae res, nec quarum rerum sint appellativae singulae voces: sed quarum significativae sint[a].

4.5143 However, since words can only signify things[a], he had, in order to indicate what it is that words signify, to indicate what those things could be.

Sed quoniam voces non significant nisi res[a]*: dicendo quid sit quod voces significant, necesse fuit dicere quid sint res.*

4.5144 For, without going into further detail, the classification which he undertook at the opening of his work on the Categories is enough to bear out what I assert. He doesn't say, 'Each item of whatever is is either a substance or a quantity', and so on, nor yet, 'Each item of whatever is expressed in an incomplex fashion[a] has "substance" or "quantity"

Nam ut alia taceam, sufficienter hoc quod dico divisio quam facit in principio tractatus Categoriarum ostendit. Non enim ait: eorum quae sunt, singulum est aut substantia aut quantitas et cetera; nec ait: eorum quae secundum nullam complexionem dicuntur[a]*, singulum aut substantia appellatur aut quantitas*[b]*, sed ait: eorum quae secundum nullam*

as its appellation[b]', but rather, 'Each item of whatever is expressed in an incomplex fashion *signifies* a substance or a quantity[c]'.

complexionem dicuntur, singulum aut substantiam significat aut quantitatem[c].

S. Your point is persuasive.

D. Persuadet ratio quod dicis.

4.515 T. Now when Aristotle says, 'Each item of whatever is expressed in an incomplex fashion signifies a substance or a quantity', and so on, to which type of signification does it appear to you that he is referring? Is it to that whereby the utterances as such signify precisively[a], and which pertains to them essentially[b], or is it to that other type which is oblique[c] and only accidental[d] to the utterances?

M. Cum ergo Aristoteles ita dicat: eorum quae secundum nullam complexionem dicunter, singulum aut substantiam significat aut quantitatem, et cetera: de qua significatione videtur tibi dicere, de illa qua per se significant[a] ipsae voces et quae illis est substantialis[b], an de altera quae per aliud[c] est et accidentalis[d]?

S. He can only be referring to that sort of signification whereby they signify precisively[e], and which he himself imputes to such utterances when defining the noun and the verb.

D. Non nisi de illa quam idem ipse eisdem vocibus inesse definiendo nomen et verbum assignavit, qua per se significant[e].

T. And do you consider that anywhere in his work he treated the matter otherwise than he did in this classification, or that any of his followers wished to adopt an attitude differing from his own on this topic, when writing on logic?

M. An putas illum aliter prosecutum in tractatu, quam proposuit in divisione, aut aliquem eorum qui eum sequentes de dialectica scripserunt, aliter sentire voluisse de hac re quam ipse sensit?

S. Their writings contain no grounds whatsoever for such an opinion, for at no point does one find any of them proffering an utterance to show[f] something it can signify obliquely; they always proffer an utterance to show what it signifies precisively. Thus, when they want to show a substance, none of them proffers *white* or *literate*; however, *white* and *literate* and so on[g] are advanced as examples when they are dealing with quality.

D. Nullo modo eorum scripta hoc aliquem opinari permittunt, quia nusquam invenitur aliquis eorum posuisse aliquam vocem ad ostendendum[f] aliquid quod significet per aliud, sed semper ad hoc quod per se significat. Nullus enim volens monstrare substantiam ponit album aut grammaticum, sed de qualitate docens album et grammaticum profert, et similia[g].

Ch. XVIII

4.600 T. So that if, given the aforementioned classification, I were to ask you what *literate* is[a] in terms of that classification[b], and in keeping with the opinions of those whose logical writings make appeal to it, what kind of question would I be asking, and what kind of a reply would you give?

M. Si ergo proposita divisione praefata quaero a te quid sit grammaticus[a] secundum hanc divisionem[b] et secundum eos qui illam scribendo de dialectica sequuntur: quid quaero, aut quid mihi respondebis?

4.601 S. This question must concern

D. Procul dubio non hic potest quaeri nisi

either the word or the thing it signifies[a]. Hence since it is agreed that in terms of this classification *literate* signifies[b] literacy and not *man*, I would reply immediately:

aut de voce aut de re quam significat[a]. Quare quia constat grammaticum non significare[b] secundum hanc divisionem hominen sed grammaticam, incunctanter respondebo:

4.602 if your question concerns the word, then it is a word signifying quality[a];

si quaeris de voce; quia est vox significans qualitatem[a];

4.603 if, however, your question is about the thing, then it is a quality[a].

si vero quaeris de re; quia est qualitas[a].

4.604 T. You realise, do you not, that in this same work Aristotle refers to words by the name of the things which those words signify, and not by the name of those of which they are merely appellative? Thus when he says, 'Every substance seems to signify this particular thing'[a], what he means is, 'Every word *signifying* a substance'[b]. It is in this way that he names, or rather *shows* things (as you reminded us just now) by recourse to utterances which only signify them, and which frequently are not appellative of them at all[c].

M. An ignoras quia idem Aristoteles appellat voces nomine rerum quarum sunt significativae, et non quarum tantum sunt appellativae, in eodem libro; ut cum dicit quia omnis substantia videtur significare hoc aliquid[a], id est omnis vox significans substantiam[b]? Sicut nominat vel potius ostendit res – quod tu paulo ante meninisti – solis vocibus earum significativis et saepe non appellativis[c].

4.610 S. I can't help realising this. Hence, whether the question is posed in respect of the word or in respect of the thing, when one asks what *literate* is according to Aristotle's treatise and according to his followers, the correct answer is: a quality[a].

D. Non hoc ignorare possum. Quare sive quaeratur de voce sive de re; cum quaeritur quid sit grammaticus secundum tractatum Aristotelis et secundum sequaces eius, recte respondetur: qualitas[a];

4.611 However, from the point of view of appellation it certainly is a substance[a].

et tamen secundum appellationem vere est substantia[a].

4.620 T. Quite so: we mustn't be disturbed by the fact that logicians make written assertions about words insofar as they signify[a], and yet, in speaking, given the appellative function of those words, use[b] them in a fashion which is at variance with those assertions; for the grammarians also assert one thing about a word considered as an exemplar[c], but quite another when it is considered in relation to the constitution of things[d].

M. Ita est. Non enim movere nos debet quod dialectici aliter scribunt de vocibus secundum quod sunt significativae[a], aliter eis utuntur loquendo secundum quod sunt appellativae[b], si et grammatici aliud dicunt secundum forman vocum[c], aliud secundum rerum naturam[d].

4.621 After all, they tell us that 'stone' is masculine in gender, 'rock' feminine, but 'slave' neuter[a], and that 'to fear' is an active verb whereas 'to be feared' is passive; yet no one asserts that a stone

Dicunt quippe lapidem esse masculini generis, petram feminini, mancipium autem neutri[a], et timere activum, timeri vero passivum, cum nemo dicat esse lapidem masculum aut petram feminam[b],

is male, a rock female, or a slave neither male nor female[b], nor that to fear is to perform an action whereas to be feared is to undergo an action[c].

aut mancipium nec masculum nec feminam, aut timere facere, timeri autem pati[c].

Ch. XIX

4.700 S. Clearly it would be unreasonable of me to question what you have laid down, but there is still another point in connection with this problem which I would like you to clear up for me. Thus if *literate* is a quality because it signifies a quality, I fail to see why *accoutred* is not a substance since it signifies a substance[a]. But if *accoutred* is categorised as a 'having'[b] on account of its signifying a having, I don't see why *literate* is not similarly categorised, since it too signifies a having. For in exactly the same way as *literate* is proved to signify a quality because it signifies having a quality[c], so also *accoutred* signifies a substance since it signifies having substance, namely accoutrements. Again, since *accoutred* quite obviously signifies *having* (for it signifies *having* accoutrements[d]) *literate* must also signify *having* because it signifies *having* learning[e].

D. Aperta ratio nihil me in iis quae dixisti dubitare permittit. Sed adhuc est de hac quaestione quod velim discere. Nam si grammaticus est qualitas quia significat qualitatem; non video cur armatus non sit substantia cum significet substantiam[a]. *Et si armatus ideo est habere*[b] *quia significat habere: ignoro cur grammaticus non sit habere quia significat habere. Omnino enim quemadmodum grammaticus probatur significare qualitatem, quia significat habentem qualitatem*[c], *ita armatus significat substantiam, quia significat habentem substantiam, id est arma. Et sicut armatus convincitur significare habere, quia significat habentem arma*[d]*: sic grammaticus significat habere, quia significat habentem disciplinam*[e].

T. If we are to take these points into account I just can't deny that *accoutred* is substance or *literate* a *having*.

S. Can a single thing be assigned to different categories then? I would like you to settle this for me.

M. Nullatenus hac ratione considerata negare possum aut armatum esse substantiam aut grammaticum habere.

D. Vellem ergo a te doceri utrum unum aliquid possit esse diversorum praedicamentorum.

4.710 T. I do not think that any one and the same thing can properly be assigned to several categories, although in certain cases this may be a matter of opinion[a]; in my view this matter calls for a rather more lengthy discussion that we can undertake in our present brief argument[b]. However, I do not see why one word[c] which signifies several things, but not as a single whole[d], should not at times be variously categorised[e], e.g. if *white* were said to be both a quality and a *having*. In this instance *white* does not signify quality and *having* as a single whole[f] in the same way as *man* does

M. Rem quidem unam eandemque non puto sub diversis aptari posse praedicamentis, licet in quibusdam dubitari possit[a]; *quod maiori et altiori indigere disputatione existimo, quam hac nostra brevi sermocinatione*[b] *assumpsimus. Unam autem vocem*[c] *plura significantem non ut unum*[d], *non video quid prohibeat pluribus aliquando supponi*[e] *praedicamentis, ut si albus dicitur qualitas et habere. Albus enim non ita significat qualitatem et habere ut unum*[f], *quemadmodum homo significat ut unum*[f] *substantiam et qualitates quibus constat*[g] *homo. Res enim quae appellatur homo est unum quiddam*[h] *constans ex iis quae dixi*[i];

signify as a single whole[f] both the substance and the qualities which constitute[g] *man*. This is so because that which receives the appellation *man* is one thing[h] constituted in the way I mentioned[i], whereas the thing which receives the appellation *white* is not just some one thing comprising a having and a quality, for only the thing that has whiteness receives the appellation *white*[j], and such a thing is certainly not composed of a having and a quality[k].

res vero quae appellatur albus non est unum aliquid ex habere et qualitate constans, quia nihil appellatur albus nisi res quae habet albedinem[j], quae nequaquam constat ex habere et qualitate[k].

4.711 In contrast, should it be asserted that *man* is a substance and *man* is a quality, then one and the same thing which this name signifies, and of which it is appellative, would be asserted to be both a substance and a quality, and this seems unacceptable[a].

Quare si dicitur: homo est substantia et homo est qualitas: una eademque res quae significatur et appellatur hoc nomine dicitur substantia esse et qualitas, quod videtur inconveniens[a].

4.712 When, however, we say that *white* is both a quality and a having, we are *not* asserting that that of which this name is appellative is a quality and a having, but that this name signifies both, and nothing improper follows[a].

Cum autem dicimus quia albus est qualitas et habere non dicimus quia quod appellatur hoc nomine est qualitas et habere, sed quia haec duo significantur hoc nomine et nihil inconveniens sequitur[a].

4.713 S. But then why is not *man* a substance and a quality in terms of Aristotle's classification, on account of its signifying both in the same way that *white* is a quality and a having on account of its signifying both?

D. Cur autem non est homo secundum divisionem Aristotelis substantia et qualitas, quia utrumque significat, quemadmodum est albus qualitas et habere propter utriusque significationem?

4.714 T. I think that what I've already said[a] should be enough to settle your query: *man* predominantly signifies a substance; the whole that it signifies is a substance, something qualified[b], rather than a quality. On the other hand *white* has no dominant[c] signification but relates equally to quality and having, nor does any kind of unity[d] result from *white*'s predominantly signifying one or other of them.

M. Aestimo huic interrogationi illud posse sufficere quod supra dixi[a], quia principaliter est significativum substantiae, et quia unum illud quod significat substantia est, et non qualitas sed quale[b]; albus vero nihil principalius[c] sed pariter significat qualitatem et habere, nec fit unum[d] ex his quod magis sit hoc vel illud, cuius sit albus significativum.

Ch. XX

4.72 S. Do you mind explaining more fully how it comes about that something forming a single whole[a] does not result from the things signified by *white*?

D. Planius mihi vellem explicari quomodo non fiat unum aliquid[a] ex iis quae significat albus.

T. If some thing is composed of them,

M. Si aliquid constat ex eis, aut est

then it is either a substance or something in one of the other categories.

S. It must be so.

T. But no category comprises both having and whiteness.

S. I can't deny that.

T. Again, a single whole can only be made up out of a multiplicity[b] either by the composition of parts which are of the same category, in the way that *animal* is made up of body and soul, or by the assemblage of a genus[c] and one or more characteristics[d], as in the cases of *body* and *man*[e], or by the species and collection of properties, as with Plato[f]. Now the things that *white* signifies do not belong to any one category only, neither is one of them related to the other as genus to constitutive characteristic or as species to collection of properties, nor yet again are they characteristics pertaining to one genus; they are in fact accidents of the same subject. Yet *white* does not signify that subject; it signifies only a having and a quality. Therefore no unity[g] result from the things that *white* signifies.

substantia aut aliquid aliorum praedicamentorum.

D. Aliud esse non potest.

M. Sed nihil horum fit ex habere et albedine.

D. Non possum contradicere.

M. Item: unum non fit ex pluribus[b] nisi aut compositione partium quae sunt eiusdem praedicamenti, ut animal constat corpore et anima; aut convenientia generis[c] et differentiae[d] unius vel plurium, ut corpus et homo[e]; aut specie et proprietatum collectione, ut Plato[f]. Illa vero quae albus significat, non sunt unius praedicamenti, nec est alterum alteri genus aut differentia aut species aut collectio proprietatum, nec sunt differentiae unius generis, sed sunt accidentia eiusdem subiecti, quod tamen subiectum albus non significat, quia omnino nihil significat aliud quam habere et qualitatem. Quare non fit unum[g] ex iis quae albus significat.

4.800 S. Your assertion seems to me to be perfectly reasonable. Still, I would like to hear what you would reply should someone object as follows to what you said about *white* signifying only a having and a quality:

D. Quamquam ratio mihi asserere videatur quae disseris, vellem tamen audire quid responderes, si quis ad hoc quod dicis quia nihil omnino significat albus aliud quam habere et qualitatem, sic obiceret:

4.801 as *white* is equivalent to *having whiteness*[a] it does not determinately signify this or that object having whiteness, such as a body[b]; rather it signifies indeterminately some object having whiteness[c].

albus cum sit idem quod habens albedinem[a], non significat determinate hoc vel illud habens, velut corpus[b], sed indeterminate aliquid habens albedinem[c].

4.8020 This is because a white is either that which has whiteness or that which has not whiteness[a]; but that which has not whiteness is not white, so that a white is that which has whiteness[b]. Further since everything which has whiteness must needs be something[c], a white must be something which has whiteness, or something having whiteness.

Albus enim aut est qui habet albedinem aut qui non habet[a]. Sed qui non habet albedinem non est albus. Albus igitur est qui habet albedinem[b]. Quare quoniam omnis qui albedinem habet non nisi aliquid est[c], necesse est ut albus sit aliquid quod habet albedinem, aut aliquid habens albedinem.

4.8021 Finally, *white* signifies either something having whiteness or nothing;

Denique albus aut aliquid significat habens albedinem aut nihil. Sed nihil non potest

but nothing cannot be conceived to have whiteness, hence *white* must signify something having whiteness[a].

intelligi habens albedinem. Necesse est ergo ut albus significet aliquid habens albedinem[a].

Ch. XXI

4.810 T. The question is not whether everything which is white is something, or whether it is that which has[a], but whether the word *white* contains in its signification the expression *something*, or *that which has*[b], in the way that *man* contains[c] *animal*, with the consequence that in the same way as *man* is[d] *rational mortal animal* so also *white* is[e] *something having whiteness* or *that which has whiteness*.

M. Non agitur utrum omnis qui est albus sit aliquid aut sit qui habet[a], sed utrum hoc nomen sua significatione contineat hoc quod dicitur aliquid aut qui habet[b] – sicut homo continet[c] animal – ut quomodo homo est[d] animal rationale mortale, ita albus sit[e] aliquid habens albedinem aut qui habet albedinem.

4.811 Now many things are necessary to the being of anything you care to mention, and yet are not signified by the name of the thing in question. For example, every animal must be coloured as well as either rational or irrational, yet the name *animal* signifies none of these things[a]. Hence, although there is no white which is not something having whiteness or that which has whiteness, nevertheless *white* need not signify these facts[b].

Multa namque necesse est rem quamlibet esse, quae tamen rei eiusdem nomine non significantur. Nam omne animal necesse est coloratum esse et rationale aut irrationale, nomen tamen animalis nihil horum significat[a]. Quare licet albus non sit nisi aliquid habens aut qui habet albedinem, non tamen necesse est ut albus hoc significet[b].

4.8120 Nevertheless, let us suppose that *white* can signify *something having whiteness*. Now *something having whiteness* is the same as *something white*[a].

S. It must be so.

T. *White* therefore always signifies *something white*.

S. Quite so.

T. So that wherever *white* appears it is always correct to substitute *something white* for *white*.

S. That follows.

T. Hence when *something white* is used, the double expression *something something white* is also correct; when the double is correct, so also is the triple, and so on to infinity[b].

S. This is both derivable and absurd.

Ponamus enim quod albus sive album significet aliquid habens albedinem. Sed aliquid habens albedinem non est aliud quam aliquid album[a].

D. Non potest aliud esse.

M. Albus igitur sive album semper significat aliquid album.

D. Ita sit.

M. Ubi ergo ponitur albus vel album, recte semper accipitur pro albo, aliquid album.

D. Consequitur.

M. Ergo ubi dicitur aliquid album, recte quoque dicitur bis: aliquid aliquid album: et ubi bis, ibi et ter, et hoc infinite[b].

D. Consequens et absurdum est hoc.

4.8121 T. Again, let *white* be also identical with *that which has whiteness*. Now *has* is the same as *is having*[a].

S. It can't be otherwise.

M. Sit quoque albus idipsum quod est qui albedinem habet. Sed habet non est aliud quam habens est[a].

D. Nec potest esse.

T. Therefore *white* is the same as *that which is having whiteness*[b].

S. Exactly.

T. But when *having whiteness* is used, this phrase is equisignificant with *white*[c].

S. That is so.

T. Hence *white* is the same as *that which is white*[d].

S. So it follows.

T. Wherever, therefore, *white* appears, *that which is white* may properly be substituted for it.

S. That I can't deny.

T. Then if *white* is the same as *that which is white*, it is also the same as *that which is that which is white*; if it is this, so also is it *that which is that which is that which is white*, and so on to infinity[e].

S. This is just as logical and just as absurd as the case in which the repetition of *something something*[f] ... results.

4.813 And now, when it is asserted[a] that *white* signifies either something having whiteness or nothing, and this is interpreted as asserting that *white* signifies either *something having* or *not-something*[b] *having*, then as *not-something* is an infinite name[c], this disjunction is neither exhaustive nor true, and hence proves nothing. It's like someone asserting, 'The blind man either sees something or he sees not-something'. If, on the other hand, the assertion is interpreted as meaning that the word either signifies or does not signify *something having*, the disjunction is exhaustive and true, and is not incompatible with what has been laid down previously[d].

4.82 S. It's sufficiently obvious that *white* signifies neither *something having whiteness* nor *that which has whiteness*, but only *having whiteness*, that is, a quality and a having, and as these alone do not constitute one thing, *white* is both of them, since it signifies them equally[a]. I see that this reasoning is valid in relation to whatever is expressed in an incomplex fashion[b] and which likewise signifies

M. Albus ergo non est aliud quam qui albedinem habens est[b].

D. Non aliud.

M. Cum autem dicitur albedinem habens, non aliud significat haec oratio quam album[c].

D. Ita est.

M. Idem igitur est albus quod qui albus est[d].

D. Sic sequitur.

M. Ubicumque itaque ponitur albus, recte pro eo accipitur: qui albus est.

D. Non possum negare.

M. Si ergo albus est qui albus est, est etiam qui qui albus est est. Et si hoc est, est etiam qui qui qui albus est est est, et sic in infinitum[e].

D. Nec hoc minus consequens nec minus absurdum est quam ut saepe sit aliquid aliquid[f].

M. Si quis autem dicit[a] *quia albus aut aliquid significat habens albedinem aut nihil: si sic intelligitur, ac si diceretur: albus aut significat aliquid habens aut significat non-aliquid*[b] *habens, ut non-aliquid sit infinitum nomen*[c], *non est integra nec vera divisio, et ideo nihil probat. Veluti si quis diceret: Caecus aut videt aliquid aut videt non-aliquid. Si vero sic intelligitur, quia aut significat aliquid habens aut non significat: integra est divisio et vera, nec repugnat iis quae dicta sunt*[d].

D. Satis apparet quia per album non significatur aliquid habens albedinem nec qui albedinem habet, sed tantum albedinem habens, id est qualitas et habere, ex quibus solis non conficitur unum aliquid, et ideo albus est utrumque, quia pariter utrumque significat[a]. *Quam rationem in omnibus quae sine complexione dicuntur*[b] *et significant quamlibet plura ex quibus non fit unum*[c], *valere video; nec aliquid iis*

some multiplicity which is of such a kind as does not form a single whole[c]. It also seems to me that no valid objection can be made to the theses you have advanced in the course of this discussion.

quae in hac disputatione asseruisti, obici recte posse existimo.

4.83 T. So it seems to me at the moment. You are well aware, however, of the degree to which contemporary logicians[a] are at loggerheads about this problem of yours, so I don't want you to stick to our findings to the extent of stubbornly hanging on to them[b] should someone manage, by the use of better opposing arguments, to demolish our result and establish different ones[c]. Should this occur, at least you can't deny that all this has been handy as an exercise in discussion[d].

M. Nec mihi nunc videtur. Tamen quoniam scis quantum nostris temporibus dialectici[a] *certent de quaestione a te proposita, nolo te sic iis quae diximus inhaerere, ut ea pertinaciter teneas*[b]*, si quis validioribus argumentis haec destruere et diversa valuerit astruere*[c]*. Quod si contingerit: saltem ad exercitationem disputandi*[d] *nobis haec profecisse non negabis.*

§7. COMMENTARY

The numbers shown at the opening of each note are those of the textual subdivisions on which comment is being made. The letters following those numbers are the superscripts given in the translation and text as an indication that the comment is available in connection with the words reproduced at the opening of each note.

*n*1.000*a*: literate ⊖ *grammatico*] The choice of 'literate' as a consistent translation of '*grammaticus*' has already been discussed at some length in *HW* 178–80, *HDG* §4.2 and *HL* §3.132. In the original Latin we have a word which can with equal facility serve both as a noun and as an adjective capable of the adjunctival use exemplified in an expression such as 'white man'. Hence one point is clear: neither 'grammarian' alone nor 'grammatical' alone will serve; the choice of one to the exclusion of the other makes nonsense of certain sections of the text where nonsense is not intended. This difficulty is one of the roots of the puzzlement displayed by Cousin, Maurice, and others who have criticised the dialogue (*CIA* ciii, *HDG* §3.11, *HG* 115). Should *both* 'grammarian' and 'grammatical' be used, then the problems posed by the original example ('*grammaticus*') are not fully reproduced. It is hence necessary to have a single word-form capable of both purely nominal and adjunctive adjectival deployment: 'literate' fulfills both these requirements and in any case probably recalls fairly adequately the spirit of the original word (see *K* IV 186.15–187.2). Although, as pointed out in *CRH*, this translation makes for a loss of the irony of the original at points where grammarians are being criticised, it nevertheless avoids commitment to the translation of '*grammatica*' as 'grammar'. Such a translation would result in the loss, for the modern reader, of the abstract impression conveyed by the original abstract noun '*grammatica*'. On the other hand 'literacy', as the abstract correlate of 'literate', preserves that impression. (cf. *HW* 178).

Another reason for the puzzlement of the critics is far more profound. '*Grammaticus*' ⊖ 'literate' appears to be a name in the present context,

and as this opening question is here posed it is an apparent name which can function as the subject of either of the answering sentences presupposed by that question, i.e. '*Grammaticus est qualitas*' ⊖ '*Literate* is quality' and '*Grammaticus est substantia*' ⊖ *Literate* is substance'. However, should it turn out that '*grammaticus*' ⊖ 'literate' as it figures in such answers has not to be construed as a name, but as a verb-like argument of a novel '... is...', then there remains in ordinary language no means of showing this fact directly. The oddity of '*grammaticus est qualitas*' ⊖ '*literate* is quality' is already a hint that something of this sort may be going on, and in the face of this example all that can be done initially is to give some signal that something unusual is going on by the use of italicisation. Hence the use of italics for 'literate' and other words which are the focus of attention under similar circumstances (cf. *HDG* §2.30, *HL* §3.221).

The historical significance of the use of '*grammaticus*' ⊖ 'literate' as an example by logicians and grammarians is discussed in *n*4.22*c* (cf. *HW* 165–7, *HDG* §4.109). Occurrences of the word in the works of Boethius and Aristotle are traced in *n*1.11*a* and *n*1,201*b*.

*n*1.000*b*: is ⊖ *sit*] So odd-sounding is the latter of the two contrary positions thrown into play by this opening question that it is tempting to take the short-cut beloved of the moderns, and in the light of the distinction between *de voce* ⊖ word-centred and *de re* ⊖ thing-centred interpretation of the question (4.600–4.603) to claim that this troublesome 'is' is just a way of saying 'signifies'. Thus would the contemporary editor's enclosure of '*grammaticus*' in quotation marks be justified up to a point (*S* I 145.4.5). Several cases in which the text of the dialogue makes a transition from 'is' to 'signifies' could also be brought to bear in support of this contention. For example, from '*grammaticus est substantia*' ⊖ 'literate is substance' and '*grammaticus est qualitas*' at the end of 4.14 one passes to '"*grammaticus*" *significat hominem et grammaticam*' ⊖ '"Literate" signifies man and literacy' at the beginning of 4.20. Or again, '*paulo ante dicebas "grammaticum" significare hominem scientem grammaticam*' ⊖ 'not long ago you were claiming that "literate" signifies man displaying literacy' (4.31) is in fact a reference back to '*definitio et esse grammatici est: homo sciens grammaticam*' ⊖ 'the definition and being of *literate* is *man displaying literacy*' (4.2410). And later '*albus est qualitas et habere*' ⊖

'*white* is a quality and a having' is said to mean that '*haec duo* [scil. *qualitas et habere*] *significantur hoc nomine*' ⊖ 'these two [i.e. quality and having] are signified by this name "white"' (4.712)' The presence of '*dicuntur*' ⊖ 'are asserted' in the present opening speech of the Student's would also be explained by this supposition.

However, the dialogue's structure and terminology confirm the taking seriously of the 'is' now in question. It is used repeatedly (1.201, 1.21, 4.14, 4.5022, for example) and the *de voce/de re* (word/thing) distinction of 4.60 *is* a distinction, and not an identification. Were this not the case, then the conundrum about the discrepancy between usage and the written technical declarations of logicians, of which '*grammaticus est qualitas*' ⊖ '*literate* is quality' is one (1.201), raised by the Student (4.20–4.212) would lose much of its point. Yet as we are now realising, the topic of this discrepancy is present from the beginning of the dialogue and leads up to the central distinction on meaning, i.e. that between *per se* signification, and *appellatio* (reference) (4.232–4.2341) which underlines that discrepancy in two ways. (i) *usus loquendi* ⊖ the current course of utterance is mentioned in the definition of *appellatio* (reference); (ii) '*grammaticus est grammatica*' ⊖ '*Literate* is literacy' is given as an example of the way in which declarations about *per se* signification have consequences which trespass against spoken usage (4.20, 4.5022). And even when the logical grammar of 'literate' has led to the conclusion that it signifies literacy (4.31) the Student still has qualms about saying '*Literate* is a quality' or '*Literate* is literacy' (4.501, 4.5022). Anselm, however, believes that the peculiar 'is' accords with the modes of expression occurring in Aristotle's *Categoriae* (4.5122, cf. *HL* §3.121) and shows it to be the counterpart, in some sense, of *per se* meaning (4.515). The *de voce/de re* (word/thing) distinction which then follows (4.600–4.603) is not produced as a means of dissolving away the peculiar 'is'. The distinction issues from the mouth of the Student, and the '*procul dubio*' ⊖ 'doubtless' which precedes it is a sure indication, in accordance with Anselm's constant practice, that it is common property, and not a discovery of the dialogue. Neither is the further remark about Aristotle's linguistic conventions (4.604) intended to show that his *de re* ⊖ thing-centred assertions are merely concealed *de voce* ⊖ thing-centred assertions (cf. the notes annexed to 4.604). The '*est*' ⊖ 'is' of '*grammaticus est qualitas*' ⊖ '*literate* is quality' is to be taken seriously. Indeed, Anselm closes his discussion by pointing out that there

is a parallel here between what obtains in the logical field and in the grammatical one (cf. 4.62) thereby giving an ingenious reply to the grammarian lovers of *usus loquendi* ⊖ the usual course of utterance (cf. *n*4.22*c* and *HL* §3.124) who might complain about the logicians' violation of usage when uttering forth their technical assertions.

It may be concluded, therefore, that the 'is' ('*sit*') is to be accepted and explained in the way outlined. There would, however, be no objection to the use of the *de voce* ⊖ word-centred alternatives (e.g. 'Literate' is a quality-word, cf. 4.602) for the purpose of tidy translation into 'natural' languages, including English. It still remains important, however, that such a choice of the *de voce* ⊖ word-centred mode should not obscure the scandal which plays so important a part in the dialogue's argument. On Boethius' usage in this connection see *n*1.000*g*.

*n*1.000*c*: substance ⊖ *substantia*] On the meaning of this word, see the notes appended to 4.12 and 4.13, in particular *n*4.1201*a*.

*n*1.000*d*: quality ⊖ *qualitas*] '*Grammaticus est qualitas*' ⊖ '*Literate* is a quality' is true if and only if '*Grammaticus dicitur in eo quod quale*' ⊖ '*Literate* is asserted in respect of quality' is also true (cf. 3.501, *n*3.501*a*). It is perhaps worth remarking at this point that '*grammaticus est qualitas*' ⊖ '*literate* is quality' and its *de voce* ⊖ word-centred correlate '"*grammaticus*" *significat qualitatem*' ⊖ '"literate" signifies quality' do not entail or mean that '*grammaticus*' ⊖ 'literate' as used in these sentences names or refers to some object (e.g. literacy) called 'a quality' (4.2341).

*n*1.000*e*: other things ⊖ *aliis*] This reference to other cases shows that '*grammaticus*' ⊖ 'literate' is being considered as an example of a type of word, i.e. of *nomen denominativum* ⊖ paronym (cf. *n*1.000*g*). The findings made in relation to this example may hence be generalised. This possibility of generalisation is underlined at other points in the dialogue, e.g. 4.2415, 4.82.

*n*1.000*f*: paronymously ⊖ *denominative*] The whole phrase '*denominative dicuntur*' ⊖ 'are asserted paronymously' will be examined in *n*1.000*g*. The Migne translation of that sentence of Ch. I of Aristotle's *Categoriae* (1^a 12) which introduces the notion of paronymy reads as follows:

Whatsoever things derive their titles from something else whose name differs from theirs merely in case-termination are said to be paronymously named, as when the literate is so named from 'literacy', and the strong from 'strength'.

Denominativa vero dicuntur quaecunque ab aliquo solo differentia casu secundum nomen habent appellationem, ut a grammatica grammaticus et a fortitudine fortis; B 167D.

The term 'paronym', therefore, applies to the non-abstract members of pairs such as those mentioned by Aristotle.

Boethius comments as follows on the Aristotelian sentence:

Neither is there anything obscure about this definition. For the ancients called 'cases' certain alterations effected upon names, as when from 'justice' we have 'just', from 'strength', 'strong', and so on – such is the sort of change called a 'case' by earlier writers. Hence whenever some thing participates in another, this participation is given in the name as well as in the thing, as when a certain man's participation in justice results in his being called 'just', the name thus reflecting the state of affairs. Hence those names are called 'paronyms' which differ from their root-name only by case-termination, i.e. by alteration only. Thus let the root-name be 'justice'; from this the altered named 'just' is contrived. Hence things are paronymously named whenever they are called by a name which derives from a root-name, and differs from the root-name merely by case-termination, that is, by a name-alteration alone. Thus three things are necessary for the existence of the paronymous situation: first, participation in the thing, second in the name, and finally a certain alteration in the name. For example, when someone is said to be strong on account of his strength, we have here a certain strength-participation on the part of the strong, as well as participation on the part of the name; he is said to be strong, and this is indeed an alteration of the sort intended, since 'strong' and 'strength' do not end in the same syllable. On the other hand, when something does not participate in the thing in question,

Haec quoque definitio nihil habet obscurum. Casus enim antiqui nominabant aliquas nominum transfigurationes, ut a iustitia iustus, a fortitudine fortis, et cetera. Haec igitur nominis transfiguratio casus ab antiquioribus vocabatur. Atque ideo quotiescunque aliqua res alia participat, ipsa participatione sicut rem ita quoque nomen adipiscitur, ut quidam homo, quia iustitia participat et rem quoque inde trahit et nomen, dicitur enim iustus. Ergo denominativa vocantur quaecunque a principali nomine solo casu, id est sola transfiguratione discrepant. Nam cum sit nomen principale iustitia, ab hoc transfiguratum nomen iustus efficitur. Ergo illa sunt denominativa quaecunque a principali nomine solo casu, id est sola nominis discrepantia, secundum principale nomen habent appellationem. Tria autem sunt necessaria, ut denominativa vocabula constituantur: prius ut re participet, post ut nomine, postremo ut sit quaedam nominis transfiguratio, ut cum aliquis dicitur a fortitudine fortis, est enim quaedam fortitudo qua fortis ille participet, habet quoque nominis participationem: fortis enim dicitur. At vero est quaedam transfiguratio, fortis enim et fortitudo non eisdem syllabis terminantur. Si quid vero sit quod re non participet, neque nomine participare potest. Quare quaecunque re non participant, denominativa esse non possunt. Rursus quoque, quae re quidem participant, nomine vero minime, ipsa quoque a denominativorum natura discreta sunt, ut si quis, cum sit virtus, virtute ipsa participet, nullo cum alio

neither can it participate in the name, so that those things lacking in factual participation cannot be paronymously named. Again, those objects are excluded from the paronymous situation which participate in the thing, but not in the name; for example, although we have the name 'virtue', and someone who participates in virtue, we call such a one by no other name than 'wise'; but 'wisdom' and 'virtue' are totally distinct names; in this event, therefore, we have the factual participation without the nominal. It is on this account that the wise man is not said to be paronymously named from 'virtue', but from 'wisdom', in which he also participates, and whence he is named by means of a further name-alteration. Again, one can have an example in which the name-alteration is lacking; thus a lady versed in music participates in the study of *musica* and is herself called *musica*; this title is not paronymous but equivocal, since both the study and the lady are said to be *musica*.

nomine nisi sapientem vocamus. Sed virtus et sapientia nomine ipso disiuncta sunt. Hic ergo re quidem participat, nomine vero minime. Quare sapiens a virtute denominatus esse non dicitur, sed a sapientia, qua scilicet et participat, et nomine iungitur, et transfiguratione diversus est: rursus, si transfiguratio non sit, ut quaedam mulier musica, participat quidem ipsa musicae disciplina, et dicitur musica. Haec igitur appellatio non est denominativa, sed aequivoca, uno enim nomine et disciplina et ipsa mulier musica dicitur. (*B* 167D–168D) (cf. also *B* 281D)

In Priscian '*denominativa*' ⊖ 'paronymous' is used to refer to words, and his usage here is quite wide, covering both names and verbs (*Inst. Gramm.* Bk. IV; cf. also *K* II 140.23.24, 424.28,29, *K* III 479.2.3). As an alternative way of talking about paronyms, Anselm uses the term '*nomen sumptum*' ⊖ 'derived name' (*Ep. de Incarnatione Verbi* 2). Abelard prefers this term to '*nomen denominativum*' ⊖ 'paronym':

Some names are said to be substantives, since they are given to things on account of what they actually *are*; other names are called 'derivative', namely those which are given to things because of the reception by the thing of some quality or other.

Nomina quaedam substantiva dicuntur quae rebus ipsis secundum hoc quod sunt data sunt; quaedam vero sumpta, quae scilicet secundum formae alicuius susceptionem imposita sunt: A 595.32.34; cf. *A* 596.1.

For an account of some Abelardian material on this topic, see *DLM* II–I 200–2. It is there confirmed (as the passage just quoted implies) that paronyms were viewed as contrasting with substantial names (cf. *n*4.1201*a*). The existence of *De Grammatico* illustrates that this contrast was not only 'of much importance in twelfth-century logic' (*DLM* II–I 200) but also in the logic of the eleventh century. It is in pursuance of the same contrast in the present dialogue that Anselm assumes substance-names (e.g. 'man') to differ from paronyms in not having abstract counterparts in the language (cf. *HW* 174, *HDG* §4.1, *HL* §3.131). This assumption is obvious from the fact that he takes it that 'man' is not 'asserted paronymously', whereas (as we are now seeing) 'literate' is thus asserted. Already in Boethius (e.g. *B* 463) the Anselmian supposition does not hold universally, and was soon to be swallowed up in the notoriously widespread abstract-concrete correlations of the medievals. Certainly Petrus Helyas not only correlates '*homo*' with '*humanitas*', but also mentions people who are even committed to '*omnitas*' ⊖ 'allness' and '*nihilitas*' ⊖ 'nothingness' as abstract correlates of '*omnis*' ⊖ 'all' and '*nihil*' ⊖ 'nothing' (*DLM* II–I 231).

The later distinction between *supposita* and *copulata* is an alternative expression of the substantive/paronym contrast (*KSS* 44, *KSL* 107). So while it may be true that Ockham does not mention *copulatio* in his logic (*DLM* II–I 581), his mention of *denominatio* (e.g. in his *Expositio Aurea*) may well amount to the same thing.

The definition of *denominatio* ⊖ paronymy given in the *Rhetorica ad Herennium* (pseudo-Cicero) is of great interest, since Anselm was most probably quite familiar with it (*HSP* 207, *SLB* 36) and also because it incorporates terminology which figures prominently in the present dialogue:

Paronymy occurs when speech draws upon near and neighbouring features of a thing whereby it may be understood [as the object of reference] even though it is not referred to by its own name.	*Denominatio est, quae a propinquis et finitimis rebus trahit orationem, qua possit intelligi res, quae non suo vocabulo sit appellata.* (Lib. IV, 32).

The illustrations which follow in the text of the *Rhetorica* are designed for the production of eloquence, and hence differ in character from those envisaged in the logical texts mentioned above. Nevertheless they contain the '*possit intelligi*' ⊖ 'can be understood' (cf. *n*3.101*a*) and '*appellata*' ⊖ 'things referred to' (cf. *n*4.233*a*) links with the present dialogue which are a feature of the passage just quoted. In addition there is a hint as to the source of the items on Anselm's list (*SN* 34.29.39, *HL* §4.3) of the loose ways in which names and verbs can be used in this same *Rhetorica* when it presents an account of the rhetorical forms. For further general information on paronyms see *HL* §3.123 and *HW*.

*n*1.000*g*: asserted ⊖ *dicuntur*] The expression '*denominative dicuntur*' ⊖ 'are asserted paronymously' occurs in the present text in such a way as to make it appear to the modern eye that the topic of the main clause, i.e. '*grammaticus*' ⊖ 'literate' is to be taken as the name of a name. But if this is so, then the '*sit*' ⊖ 'is' of '*utrum* "*grammaticus*" *sit substantia an qualitas*' ⊖ 'whether "literate" is substance or quality' is either inappropriate or should be replaced by '*significat*' ⊖ 'signifies'. However, as the sentence '*grammaticus est qualitas*' ('*literate* is quality') is taken seriously in the subsequent development (cf. *n*1.000*b*) there seems to be no reason for assuming the '*sit*' ⊖ 'is' to be merely a slack way of expressing "signifies". There is in fact a Boethian passage in which notable use is made of the form of words now in question:

Some of those things which are in a subject (cf. *n*4.101*a*) are such that not even their names are asserted of that subject. Thus virtue is in the soul but virtue is not at all predicated of the soul; sometimes, however, such a thing is predicated paronymously, as when, because literacy is in a man, he is paronymously asserted to be a literate because of his literacy.	*Illorum vero quae sunt in subiecto* (cf. *n*4.101*a*) *aliquoties quidem neque nomen ipsum de subiecto dicitur. Nam virtus in anima est, sed virtus de animo minime praedicatur: aliquoties autem denominative dicitur, ut grammatica, quoniam est in homine, denominative grammaticus a grammatica dicitur; B* 185A.

Here, on one possible interpretation, we have a *grammaticus* ⊖ literate asserted *denominative a grammatica* ⊖ paronymously from literacy (cf. also *B* 253A, *B* 254D). Hence it here appears that for Boethius one could speak of *things* being asserted in a certain fashion (e.g. denominatively, paronymously). Hence the whole sentence with which we are now concerned is perfectly coherent with the Boethian pattern, and the modern compulsion to insert quotation marks around '*grammatico*' ⊖ 'literate' thereby removed. It is in accordance with this realisation that the translation has been constructed. In any case, we have at a later point in the dialogue the sentence '*Nullus homo dicitur in eo quod quale*' (3.502) which can certainly be interpreted as 'No man is asserted [to be so] in respect of quality'; similarly the '*denominative dicuntur*' with which we are now concerned can be understood as 'are asserted [to be what they are said to be] paronymously', i.e. as having *things* (as opposed to words) as its subject-matter.

*n*1.000*h*: reasons ⊖ *rationibus*] From what ensues it is quite clear that

the necessities of the 'reasons' to be given are of two sorts: first we have an inference which purports to be based on a recognised syllogistic form, but which encapsulates within it a statement of the matter of fact, reflected in everyone's spoken usage, that every literate is a human being (1.11). The second involves the '*grammaticus est qualitas*' ⊖ '*literate* is quality' thesis which is continually attributed to the technical declarations of logicians (cf. 4.2, 4.5022, 4.5122, 4.6). It is not until 4.23 that full expression is given to the distinction of status between these two reasons.
but which encapsulates within it a statement of the matter of fact, reflected
*n*1.101*a*: substance ⊖ *substantia*] In the first place one might hold that the proposition '*grammaticus est substantia*' ⊖ '*literate* is a substance' is not at all like '*grammaticus est albus*' ⊖ 'the literate is white', for example. The ways in which the two may differ may be gathered from the close of *n*4.230*b*: the former is analysable in terms of the higher-order '∈' (defined §3.15) while the latter is not. However, even if (as the premisses 1.11 and 1.12 suggest) 'Every literate is a substance' were the conclusion here intended, and even if it were construed in a 'lower-order' sort of way (e.g. §3.4) this truth would still be irrelevant for determining the meaning of 'literate' (cf. *n*1.11*a* and references there given). In Anselm's own terms, his theory will be to the effect that '*grammaticus*' ⊖ 'literate' only signifies '*homo*' ⊖ 'man' in an oblique sense, insofar as the former is merely appellative of *homo* ⊖ man (4.232, 4.233). Only in this secondary sense can '*grammaticus*' ⊖ 'literate', in virtue of 1.12, be brought into relation with substance (i.e. *man*). On substance, see *n*4.1201*a*.

*n*1.11*a*: man ⊖ *homo*] This is of course a true statement, but not one of the sort to be taken into account in determining the meaning of '*grammaticus*' ⊖ 'literate', since if it were allowed to influence the determination of the meaning of 'literate', then a new definition of it and like words (e.g. 'president', 'bachelor') would be necessary every time their application was extended by new uses, and what then could be made of the meaning of the paronym 'white'? (cf. 4.24121).

The dialectical future of the present proposition in the dialogue is as follows. The Student's efforts from 3.00 to 3.7 are mainly devoted to proving its contrary, i.e. 'No literate is man'. The Tutor concludes to a mediate position in 3.9, i.e. 'No literate is just a man' (3.931). However, the Student persists with his thesis ('No literate is man') up to 4.132.

Finally, the merely peripheral manner in which this proposition can contribute to a discussion of the meaning of '*grammaticus*' ⊖ 'literate' is made clear at 4.232 and 4.233. It emerges that while it is quite true, *in point of fact*, that 'literate' has hitherto always been used to refer to (or has been appellative of) men, this truth must, on the grounds noted in the last paragraph, remain extra-theoretical in relation to the theories of both *man* and *literate* (cf. §4). Hence meaning and reference, in respect of paronyms, should not be posited as identical (4.233).

'*Grammaticus*' ⊖ 'literate' and '*homo*' ⊖ 'man' are used throughout Boethius' *Introductio ad Syllogismos Categoricos* as terms of exemplary sentences which include the present one as a true case.

*n*1.12*a*: substance ⊖ *substantia*] Under the guise of this simple categorical form of statement lurks a large complex which the word 'substance' encapsulates (cf. *n*4.1201*a*). In spite of its appearance in what looks like a categorical syllogism, it may be that its logical form is not to be shown as 'Every *a* is *b*' (cf. *n*4.230*b*). Alternatively, even if it is susceptible of a non-complex analysis, it is not relevant to the theory of *literate* (cf. §4 and *n*1.11*a*). The same proposition as the one now in question appears as the conclusion of an example in Boethius' *Commentaria in Topica Ciceronis*, Lib. I, *B* 1050D.

*n*1.201*a*: is ⊖ *sit*] On this special use of 'is' see *n*1.000*b* and the references there made.

*n*1.201*b*: have written about this matter ⊖ *de hac re tractaverunt*] This is the first indication of the source of the statement, '*Literate* is quality': the philosophers are said to be responsible. In 4.21 and 4.22 it is attributed to the *tractatores dialecticae* ⊖ writers on logic, and its incompatibility with spoken usage is illustrated in 4.20, thus leading to the mention of such usage in the definition of *appellatio* ⊖ reference (4.2341). The lack of ease which accompanies this way of talking is stressed throughout 4.5022 to 4.6. Who were the philosophers who insisted on talking in this strange way? At 4.5122 the Tutor refers to the usage of Aristotle's *Categoriae*, and Aristotle's followers are mentioned at 4.600 as adopting that usage. Boethius, one assumes, must be among these followers. '*Grammaticus*' ⊖ 'literate' or its case-variants certainly figure in Boethius' commentary on the *Categoriae*. Thus we have the list of categories which includes *Qualitas, ut album, grammaticum* ⊖ Quality, such as *white, literate*: *B* 180A. '*Grammaticus*' ⊖ 'literate' is also mentioned quite often in the section dealing with Quality (*B* 240C, 252C, 253A, 257B–D, 260D–261A). It is highly probable that the list just quoted is the authoritative root of the paradoxical '*Literate* is quality' and its consequence '*Literate* is literacy'; cf. *n*1.000*b* and *HL* §3.121. Aristotle's classification of *literate* appears to be at variance with Priscian's opinion: cf. *n*3.800*b*, *n*4.22*c*, *n*4.2341*a*, *HDG* §4.109, *HL* §3.124, *HW* 175–6. This disagreement may be one of the background reasons for Anselm's choice of opening question. Certainly this very question of paronyms remained a standard topic of disagreement between logicians and grammarians (cf. for example, *DLM* II–I 182–186). On the other hand Boethius, when commenting on the *Categoriae*, and doubtless guided by the current course of utterance, had already rejected '*Albus est albedo*' ⊖ 'White is whiteness' (which would correspond to Anselm's '*Grammaticus est grammatica*' ⊖ '*Literate* is literacy') in the following terms:

Only that very thing which is susceptible of being possessed in common is named 'quality'. In contrast, the thing that *possesses* the quality is not embraced by the word 'quality'; thus whiteness is indeed a quality, but *white* is not a quality.	*Res enim ipsa quae participari potest sola 'qualitas' nominatur. Res vero quae participat qualitatis vocabulo non tenetur, ut albedo qualitas quidem est, albus vero qualitas non est B* 239C.

Aristotle's original quirks of expression in listing examples of his categories ('Quality, such as *white*') with their implication that the concrete rather than the abstract form is here appropriate, were probably of no logical significance. Not only, however, do they afford Anselm the occasion for his 'nonsense' theses, such as '*Literate* is literacy' (4.2341) but also continue to exercise the ingenuity of medieval commentators (*HL* §3.121).

Although the *Categoriae* in its Boethian version would appear to be an obvious source for the '*grammaticus*' ⊖ 'literate' example used by Anselm, a more varied set of influences centred around this word can also be traced (*n*4.2341*a*).

*n*1.201*c*: authority ⊖ *auctoritatem*] By the time the dialogue has run three-quarters of its course (in 4.6) the Tutor will have convinced the Student of the reasonableness of *prima facie* absurd assertions such as

'*Grammaticus est qualitas*' ⊖ '*Literate* is quality' and '*Grammaticus est grammatica*' ⊖ '*Literate* is literacy', so that these need no longer stand upon the authority of their authors (cf. *n*1.201*b*). Thus he displays ingenuity of the first order in turning to his own account the Aristotelian fashions of talking which of themselves probably concealed no special logical point.

*n*1.21*a*: is ⊖ *sit*] Throughout this paragraph one has once again the special use of '*sit*' ⊖ 'is', on which see *n*1.000*b*.

*n*1.21*b*: necessarily the other ⊖ *necesse sit esse*] On the face of things, substance and quality do not exhaust the possibilities of categorisation; there still remain the other eight accidental categories of the Aristotelian list: quantity, relation, time, place, state, situation, action and passion. It may well be that use is here being made of the convention mentioned by Abelard (*A* 432.25.28) according to which 'quality' could refer in general to categories other than that of substance. Not until 4.70, where the question of alternative categorisation is raised, is this convention dropped.

*n*1.21*c*: other ⊖ *alteram*] The Student is here obviously attempting to express a syllogism having an exclusive disjunction as its major premiss. The vocabulary he uses echoes Boethius' description, in his Commentary on Cicero's *Topica*, of the parts of an argument:

Hence, as every question involves two opposites, one on the affirmative side, the other on the negative, there must always be supporting argument for either side, with the result that one person supports the cause of the affirmation, the other that of the negation, so that as far as is possible one of them seeks arguments for the establishment of the affirmative, the other for its refutation.

Cum igitur omnis quaestio duas habeat partes affirmationis unam, alteram negationis, necesse est ut sit semper ex alterutra parte defensio, ut unus quidem affirmationis partem, negationis alter defendat, et hic quidem ad astruendam affirmationem, ille vero ad destruendam, quae potuerit, argumenta perquirat: *B* 1049B.

De Rijk remarks that Boethius' Commentary on Cicero's *Topica* was not, as far as he knows, commented on by the medievals; here, at any rate, Anselm is displaying what at least may be some acquaintance with the work. The vocabulary of '*propositio*' and '*assumptio*' for major and minor premisses respectively, used by Anselm in 3.53, may also be found in the same source (*B* 1132C, cf. *HL* §9.2). Other disjunctive syllogisms used by Anselm are at 3.72 of *De Grammatico* and in *Cur Deus Homo* I 16.

*n*2.00*a*: can be compatible ⊖ *non repugnent*] The Tutor is in fact to show that both alternatives are in some sense valid when the necessary distinctions in the sense of 'signify' have been made at 4.23. Boethius would classify them as exclusive: he claims that we can assert '*si substantia est, qualitas non est*' ⊖ 'if it is a substance then it is not a quality', since this is '*earum … quaestionem quae ex affirmatione et negatione consistunt*' ⊖ 'one of those questions which are exhausted by the affirmation and the negation only': *B* 1179D.

*n*3.00*a*: premiss ⊖ *propositionem*] The reference is here to 1.11. At this point the word '*propositio*' has the sense of 'proposition' or 'premiss'. It is taken to refer to any simple syllogistic premiss of the type which is supposed to be undergoing discussion:

Every simple proposition has two parts, each made up of a term. Thus a simple proposition is one such as 'Every man is an animal'.

Omnis autem simplex propositio duas habet partes in terminis constitutas. Simplex vero propositio est huiusmodi "Omnis homo animal est": *BTC* 1049D.

However, a more specialised use of the word '*propositio*' occurs in conjunction with '*assumptio*' at 3.5, and is discussed in *n*3.531*a*.

*n*3.101*a*: can be understood ⊖ *potest intelligi*] The origins and associations of '*intelligere*' ⊖ 'to understand' and '*posse intelligi*' ⊖ 'to be able to be understood' are of manifold complexity. Although the use of these words in the present text probably has its immediate basis in Boethius' translation of Porphyry, there are assertions in Priscian and the Herennian Rhetoric which appear to exemplify a kindred notion.

The question as regards the present text is: what logical interpretation is to be given to the phrase '*potest intelligi*' ⊖ 'can be understood'? This problem may be regarded as having two aspects, the one corresponding to '*potest*' ⊖ 'can', the other to '*intelligi*' ⊖ 'be understood'. Does the use of '*potest*' ⊖ 'can' point to the presence of some form of modal or 'intensional' functor, or can the sentences involving this form of words be analysed in such a way as to avoid an interpretation in terms of such a functor? Can any precise sense be given to '*intelligi*' ⊖ '(to) be understood' in this context? It will in fact be found that concentration on the meaning of '*intelligi*' ⊖ '(to) be understood' may provide an answer to the question of the interpretation of '*potest*' ⊖ 'can' as well. Throughout the remainder of the present discussion the truth or falsehood of certain sentences involving 'man', 'animal', 'literate', and so on, will be taken for granted without further discussion. In this the practice of Anselm is being followed, i.e. it is assumed that the reader is in possession of at least the rudiments of the theories which centre round these terms (cf. 3.800, §4, and *n*4.2411*d*).

The first point which may be established is the close connection in Anselm's usage between understanding (*intelligere*, *intellectus*) and meaning or sense (*significatio*, *sententia*). Thus, in the process of bringing out the meaning of a given sentence, as in the series 3.101, 3.312, 3.6321, 3.6322, 3.6331, 3.6333, he refers to the analysis as showing *that which is understood* within the analysandum. Hence, in the course of passing from 3.101 (and its associated assertions) to 3.312 (and its associated assertions) he uses such expressions as 'State, then, what you understand within this major premiss' (3.311) and 'State, then, what you understand' (3.312). Elsewhere, in similar situations, we have 'This syllogism can be understood in a certain other way which that one of yours can't be' (3.6320), and 'In what way do you understand this?' (followed by two alternative analyses) (3.62). Analyses of the meanings thus to be understood are called by Anselm '*expositiones*' (3.6313), and the verb '*exponere*' is used to describe the process of analysis (3.6320). He also states quite explicitly that it is in the sense (*sententia*) which is understood in the course of such analyses that the links between the various parts of inferences are to be found. The fact that he makes this declaration when pointing to the insufficiency of mere verbal conformity with the rules for the setting out of syllogisms amounts to a recognition that the standard syllogistic forms are not sufficient for all types of inference (3.33). Indeed, it is evident from his use in inferences of sentences such as the '*posse intelligi*' ⊖ 'can be understood' ones with which we are now concerned, that although he adheres in a general kind of way to the device of the middle term, the forms which he in practice employs within this framework go well beyond the four proposition-forming functors each having two nominal arguments, which are the special concern of syllogistic (*LAS* §22).

The connection between understanding and meaning may be further and more directly reinforced by the parallelism which Anselm sets up between the explication of the meanings of forms of words by the use of other forms of words, and the process of understanding (4.4233). Indeed, in yet another place in the dialogue, a sentence having the same form as the one at present under scrutiny is developed directly from a definition of *animal* (3.21). The same connection persists in Abelard, an almost identical vocabulary (*intellectus* ⊖ understanding, *sententia* ⊖ sense, *significare* ⊖ to signify, *constituere intellectum* ⊖ to settle the understanding) being employed, e.g. *A* 112.24.32, *A* 147.30, *A* 154.6.29, *A* 562.20.28. In like fashion the pseudo-Abelard says '*significare est idem quod intellectum constituere*' ⊖ 'to signify is the same as to establish (or settle) the understanding': *AO* II 750. Aquinas maintains the same theme: *APH* 67. This common thread has as its source Boethius' translation of Aristotle's *De Intepretatione* (16^b 20):

Therefore these verbs used on their own account are names and signify something in that they establish the understanding of the speaker, and the hearer also is satisfied.	*Ipsa itaque secundum se dicta verba nomina sunt, et significant aliquid. Constituit enim qui dicit intellectum, et qui audit quiescit: BDIL* 309B.

(See also *BDIG* 430C, *n*4.14*g*, *n*4.4233*a*, *n*4.813*b*. For a general account of this sort of connection in Boethius *DLM* II–I 177–182 may usefully be consulted). Of course, community of vocabulary should not be taken to entail complete community of doctrine, especially on the topic of signification. However, enough has been said to show that any analysis of the present problem-sentences involving '*posse intelligi*' ⊖ 'to be able to be understood' may be expected to incorporate some clause which relates to the meanings of the terms involved, or the *de re* ⊖ thing-centred correlate of such a clause (cf. 4.6).

Another and much more promising pointer towards the elucidation of sentences such as the present one is to be found in Anselm's own statement of what two of them signify – a statement in which '*potest intelligi*' ⊖ 'can be understood' has disappeared completely, to be replaced by a formulation which is almost completely unproblematical, at least when considered in relation to the resources of the Ontology outlined in §3. Thus he asserts that

.1 Every man can be understood to be a man without literacy (3.311 cf. 3.40)

.2 No literate can be understood to be a literate without literacy (3.312, cf. 3.40)

respectively signify (*significant*):

.3 To be man does not require literacy (3.41)

.4 To be literate requires literacy (3.42)

From these reformulations (.3 and .4) he concludes:

.5 To be literate is not to be man (3.431)

This last presents no difficulty, and may be rendered as

.6 $\sim(\mathrm{Cl}[\![\mathbf{g}]\!] \in \mathrm{Cl}[\![\mathbf{h}]\!])$ (.5, cf. *n*3.431*a*)

And .3 and .4 in their turn may be expressed as follows:

.7 $\sim(\mathrm{Cl}[\![\mathbf{h}]\!] \in \subset[\![\mathrm{trm}\langle\gamma\rangle]\!])$ (.3)

.8 $\mathrm{Cl}[\![\mathbf{g}]\!] \in \subset[\![\mathrm{trm}\langle\gamma\rangle]\!]$ (.4)

(§3.13, .14, .15, and .22 may be consulted for definitions and discussions of the functors here used). These expressions do have the consequences claimed by Anselm. For example, .5 may indeed be inferred from .3 and .4, since the following (cf. .7 and .8) is a thesis:

.9 $\sim(\mathrm{Cl}[\![\mathbf{h}]\!] \in \subset[\![\mathrm{trm}\langle\gamma\rangle]\!]) \,.\, \mathrm{Cl}[\![\mathbf{g}]\!] \in \subset[\![\mathrm{trm}\langle\gamma\rangle]\!] \,.\supset.\, \sim(\mathrm{Cl}[\![\mathbf{g}]\!] \in \mathrm{Cl}[\![\mathbf{h}]\!])$

This sentence (.9) is a thesis because, by §3.53 and definitions §3.13, .14, and .15, its second conjunct reduces to the truism '$\mathbf{g} \subset \mathbf{g}$' and may be neglected, so that only

.10 $\sim(\mathrm{Cl}[\![\mathbf{h}]\!] \in \subset[\![\mathrm{trm}\langle\gamma\rangle]\!]) \,.\supset.\, \sim(\mathrm{Cl}[\![\mathbf{g}]\!] \in \mathrm{Cl}[\![\mathbf{h}]\!])$

remains to be proved. However, .10 by contraposition and by the equation of '**g**' and '$\mathrm{trm}\langle\gamma\rangle$' resulting from §3.11 becomes the following thesis which is an instance of §3.50:

.11 $\mathrm{Cl}[\![\mathbf{h}]\!] \in \mathrm{Cl}[\![\mathbf{g}]\!] \,.\supset.\, \mathrm{Cl}[\![\mathbf{h}]\!] \in \subset[\![\mathbf{g}]\!]$

Thus the adoption of .7 and .8 as interpretations of .3 and .4 is now shown to be a satisfactory fashion of bringing the present material into contact with the interpretational resources of Ontology. Further elucidation is provided in the general survey of the present set of inferences provided in *n*3.6321*a*.

Thus far it has been taken for granted that '*intelligi*' can properly be translated in this context as 'to be understood' (as opposed, for instance to 'to be thought of'). There are certain pointers in Anselm's reply to Gaunilo which suggest that the translation adopted is justified. Thus Gaunilo defined '*intelligere*' ⊖ 'to understand' as meaning '*scientia comprehendere re ipsa illud existere*' ⊖ 'to have a knowledgeable grasp that the thing in question is so' (S I 125.27–126.1). This definition involves a coupling of intelligibility and truth which Anselm repudiates by pointing out that not only the true is meaningful:

Even things false or doubtful are understood and are in the understanding in the sense that when they are asserted the hearer understand what the speaker intends to mean.	*Falsa et dubia hoc modo intelliguntur et sunt in intellectu quia cum dicuntur audiens intelligit quid dicens significet: S* I 136.8.9.

Again, '*intelligere*' ⊖ 'to understand' and '*cogitare*' ⊖ 'to think (of)' are expressly distinguished by Anselm in the same reply to Gaunilo. Hence, although 'to be thought' may be acceptable as a loose translation of '*intelligi*', it does more justice to Anselm's intentions if 'to be understood' is used, as in the translation adopted.

Apart, however, from the general connection of '*intelligere*' ⊖ 'to understand' with '*significatio*' ⊖ 'meaning' and definition which has been mentioned above, the more particular source of the expression '*posse intelligi*' ⊖ 'to be able to be understood' seems to lie in Boethius' discussion of separable and inseparable accidents: *B* 55D–56C, *B* 133A–134A). There in the course of the discussion as to how the predicable 'accident' should be defined (cf. *n*4.2411*d*, *n*4.2411*e*) it is finally characterised as that which can be present and absent without the perishing of its subject. Boethius and Porphyry also discuss the problem of those accidents which as a matter of fact are never absent from their proper subject, for example, the blackness of a crow or a negro, notwithstanding the non-involvement of these colours in the definition of these beings. In the second of the Dialogues on Porphyry Boethius gets over the problem by distinguishing, as does Anselm in the passage quoted in the last paragraph, between truth and the possibility of understanding:

This definition of 'accident' is itself framed with reference to what may be, not what actually is, and to that which is merely understandable, as opposed to being truly the case.

haec ipsa definitio de accidentibus facta est potestate non actu, et intelligentia non veritate; BDP 56A.

The crow and the negro, he continues, can still be understood to be what they are, regardless of their colour: *sine isto colore ad intelligentiam possunt subsistere* ⊖ even in the absence of this colour they still remain as objects of understanding; *BDP* 56A.

In the Commentary on Porphyry (Bk. IV) Boethius discusses the same examples, and usefully adds an account of a case unlike those which involve the colour *black*. In this case the removal of rationality from the concept of *man* results in one's no longer having a concept of the species *man*:

When it is said [that accidents can] be present and absent, this is to be understood not in respect of reality, but of the mind; things go otherwise as far as substantials (cf. *n*4.1201*a*) are concerned, since these just cannot be split up in any way at all. True, we often analyse in thought or in the mind (as when we take away rationality from *man*) things which in actual fact cannot be split up; nevertheless if we dissociate the elements by the imagination's mental activity, the species *man* immediately is no longer there. But the same thing does not apply to accidents; even though accidents are mentally removed, the species is still there.

quod dictum est 'adesse et abesse' non re sed animo intelligendum est, alioqui et substantialia quae omnino separari non possunt, saepe animo et cogitatione disiungimus, ut si ab homine ratiomabilitem auferamus, quam licet actu separare non possumus, tamen si animi imaginatione disiungimus, statim perit hominis species, quod idem in accidentibus non fit. Sublato enim accidentia cogitatione, species manet: B 134A

The contrast which Boethius is making is now clear, and can be stated in various ways. For example, one might say that *white* is not incorporable, as a constitutive characteristic, into theories of crowhood and manhood, whereas *rational* must be incorporated into the theory of *man*. (*n*4.22*d* contains a discussion of the notion of constitutive characteristic; see also §4). Now this kind of contrast is, in effect, the topic of the whole dialogue; see, for example, 4.241. Anselm's '*Nullus homo potest aliquo modo intelligi sine rationalitate*' ⊖ 'No man can in some way be understood (to be) without rationality' (3.6321) is doubtless ultimately inspired by these words of Boethius. Throughout the assertions of Boethius which have been mentioned, and directly or indirectly throughout most of the present dialogue, the uses of '*posse*' ⊖ 'can' and its negations can usually be traced to theoretical connections of the kind mentioned, or the lack thereof. On this point 3.94, §4, *n*3.21*d*, *DLM II–II* 433 and 511 may be consulted.

In Peter of Spain's work the phrase '*posse intelligi*' ⊖ 'to be able to be understood' seems to be firmly wedded to the discussion of separable and inseparable accidents. Peter's intention seems to be to follow Boethius in this matter. (The text given in Bochenski's edition of Peter's *Summulae Logicales* contains a '*non*' ⊖ 'not' which, in the light of the remarks made above, would appear to be superfluous. Thus, when Peter has said that inseparable accidents such as the crow's or the negro's blackness do not fall outside the definition of 'accident', his text is then shown as:

For, as Porphyry would have it, the crow cannot be understood as white or the Ethiopian as sharing in white without the perishing of the objects undergoing consideration.	*Quia ut vult Porphyrius, corvus non potest intelligi album et Aethiops nitens candore praeter subiecti corruptionem: HSL* 2.16

One should surely read '*corvus potest intelligi*' ⊖ 'the crow can be understood', since otherwise it is difficult to see how the remark agrees with the definition of an accident as that which can come and go without the perishing of its subject).

A remarkable discussion of *intelligere* ⊖ to understand, and one which is closer to Anselm's period, occurs in the *Tractatus de Intellectibus* which Cousin published as Abelard's (*AO* II). A resolution of a paradox of inference involving 'to understand' as a component, and which occurs in this work, may be mentioned here. Thus from the true premisses:

(i) Everyone who understands Socrates to be an ass understands some animal to be an ass	(i) *Omnis qui intelligit Socrates esse asinum, intelligit quoddam animal esse asinum*
(ii) Everyone who understands some animal to be an ass understands a truth	(ii) *Omnis qui intelligit quoddam animal esse asinum, intelligit verum*

it would appear to follow logically that:

(iii) Everyone who understands Socrates to be an ass understands a truth.	(iii) *Omnis qui intelligit Socrates esse asinum intelligit verum.*

This paradox is resolved by taking the 'middle term', i.e. '*intelligit quoddam animal esse asinum*' ⊖ 'understands some animal to be an ass', and distinguishing its senses as follows. If this middle term means '*intelligit de quoddam animali quod sit asinus*' ⊖ 'understands regarding some animal that it is an ass' then (i) is true, but (ii) is false (presumably because the animal in question might not be an ass). If, however, the middle term means '*habet intellectum particularis affirmativae "Quoddam animal est asinus"*' ⊖ 'understands the particular affirmative proposition "Some animal is an ass"' then (i) is false, presumably because '*Socrates est asinus*' ⊖ 'Socrates is an ass' is not the same proposition as '*Quoddam animal est asinus*' ⊖ 'Some animal is an ass', but (ii) is true: *AO* II 749. Another feature of this text is the parallel drawn between the uses of '*intelligere*' ⊖ 'to understand' and '*proponere*' ⊖ 'to assert':

We use 'understand' in the same way as we use 'assert'. Thus the proposition 'Socrates is an irrational animal' does not assert that Socrates is an animal; only a part of it does so. The same applies to the following consequence: 'If Socrates is a pearl then Socrates is a stone'; it does not assert that Socrates is a stone or that Socrates is a pearl. Otherwise this consequence would assert a falsehood, and the aforementioned proposition would be a truth.

Eo quippe modo dicimus 'intelligere' quo dicimus 'proponere'. Tota autem haec propositio 'Socrates est animal irrationale' non proponit Socrates esse animal, sed pars eius; sic nec ista consequentia: 'Si Socrates est margarita, Socrates est lapis' proponit Socratem esse margaritam vel Socratem esse lapidem; alioquin falsum proponeret haec consequentia et illa propositio verum: AO: II 749.

Abelard's discussion (*A*154–5) covers somewhat the same ground.

There is yet another context, namely in the writings of the grammarian Priscian, within which occur locutions very redolent of Anselm's, and which figure in the discussion of a cognate topic. Priscian explains that the attachment of adjectival 'names' to substance-names results in the possibility of comparison (e.g. 'judicious man', 'more judicious man') whereas the substance-names themselves have a meaning which is not susceptible of degree in this way:

For if I say 'man' or 'stone' then I have indicated a substance the signification of which is incapable of being either increased or decreased. But if I mention some accident of a man, then there is room for comparison, as in the case of 'prudent man' and 'more prudent' and of 'black stone' and 'blacker'.

Si enim dicam 'homo' vel 'lapis' substantiam demonstravi, cuius significatio nec augeri potest nec minui, sin aliquid accidens homini vel lapidi proferam tunc habet locum comparatio, ut 'homo prudens' et 'prudentior', 'lapis niger' et 'nigrior': *K* II 83.22–84.2; cf. *n*3.111*a*.

Priscian then adds that although the adjectival additions may really not apply to the substance in question (the man may not in fact be judicious) one still can understand ('*potest* ... *intelligi*') their invariable substantial basis to which they are supposed to apply:

Although he may not be prudent, he may still be understood to be a man, and the stone, although it may not be black, can still be understood to be a stone.	*Quamvis non sit prudens, potest homo intelligi, et lapis, quamvis non sit niger, intelligitur lapis: K* II 84.2.3

In other words, the adjectives will not be involved in the theories of the substances in question (cf. §4): the substance can be understood without the qualities in question.

In *SLB* there is a passage which illustrates the importance of '*intelligere*' ⊖ 'to understand' in the theological affairs of the time. We there learn how, in order to prevent Berengar of Tours from putting 'new interpretations' upon words, his oath of 1079 before the Lateran Council compelled him 'to assent to the eucharistic formula approved by the council and to promise to interpret it in the sense in which it was understood by the council and not otherwise – "sicut in hoc breve continetur et ego legi et vos intelligitis"': *SLB* 46.

For a discussion of the relations between *intelligere* ⊖ to understand and *significatio* ⊖ meaning as seen by Abelard *DLM* II–I 190–199 may be consulted. Again, *DLM* II–I 223–4 shows that William of Conches (1080–1154) uses '*posse intelligi*' ⊖ 'can be understood' in a sense approximating to that of Anselm.

*n*3.111*a*: degree ⊖ *minus*] Verbally, the doctrine behind this and the following premiss is quite easily stated. According to Aristotle's *Categoriae* (Ch. 5) substances do not admit of variation of degree, whereas the having of qualities does so admit. Thus one may be more or less white, but not more or less a man, hence the two premisses now in question (3.111, 3.112). Priscian's remarks quoted in *n*3.101*a* are to the same effect, and Descartes uses this doctrine as an *ad hominem* argument in the first part of the *Discours de la Méthode*.

To make fully intelligible the motives behind this doctrine is, however, a rather more complex matter. Boethius' comment on Aristotle's remark runs as follows:

For a given man is never more of a man either in relation to himself or even in comparison with some other man, as when the two are compared in such a way that both are considered together; hence when some individual man is	*Nam ipse homo a seipso non est plus homo, at vero nec si ad alterum conferatur, ad alterum vero ita, ut sub eadem coniunctione sint, ut quidam homo individuus ad aliquem individuum hominem comparatus, non erit magis et minus homo,*

compared with some other individual man, he will not be found to be more than a man or less than a man. The same applies to the very species *man* was well; it too turns out not to be more or less *man*. This is in fact obvious in the case of substances (cf. *n*4.1201*a*). Yet in the case of qualities a variation of degree is possible. A white (object) can become more white than it now is, and thus be susceptible of degree, so that it can become more white or less white. It can also be more white that some other white (object), even as a lily is more white than is wool. Again, it can be less white than some other white object, as in the case of wool relative to the lily, and the swan in relation to snow. The same applies to other qualities, such as *good* and *hot*. For these can be changed with time, and be transformed in the directions of more or less; thus good can become to some extent better or worse, and heat to some extent hotter or cooler. But a man, in contrast, who is a substance, cannot now be more man than he was earlier, neither can he later become more or less man than he now is.

et ipsa species seipsa non erit magis et minus homo; sed hoc palam est in substantiis, in qualitatibus vero potest esse magis et minus: album enim potest fieri magis album seipso, et suscipere magis et minus, ut sit magis album et minus album; potest et alio albo plus esse album, ut lilium lana; et alio albo minus esse album, ut lana lilio, et cygnus nive, atque idem in aliis qualitatibus, ut bono et calido. Namque haec possunt temporibus permutari, et in plus minusve transduci; fit enim aliquoties bono melius et deterius, et calido ferventius et tepidius: homo vero, quod est substantia, neque nunc plus erit homo quam fuit antea, neque post magis aut minus erit homo quam nunc est: *B* 197B–D.

However, things other than substances are also insusceptible of degree, as for example the qualities which things have when those qualities are considered *per se*. In discussing this point Boethius brings in the example with which 3.111 is concerned, namely that of '*grammaticus*' ⊖ 'literate':

It is Aristotle's opinion that qualities considered in themselves neither increase by any augmentation nor decrease by reduction, whereas the things which participate therein can come under the sway of composition in such a way that they can be said to be more or less so. Thus if health and justice themselves are considered, then one cannot be more or less than the other. Neither would anyone assert that health itself was more than some other health. We can only say that more health is enjoyed, that is, one can be healthier, and more healthy and less healthy. It is on this account that we say

Aristoteles ... ipsas quidem habitudines nulla intentione crescere nec diminutione decrescere putat, sed eorum participantes posse sub examine compositionis venire, ut de his magis minusve dicatur. Sanitatem namque ipsam et iustitiam, alteram altera magis minusve non esse. Neque enim quispiam dicit magis esse sanitatem alia sanitate. Sed hoc solum dicere possumus magis habere sanitatem aliquem, id est esse saniorem, et magis sanum, et minus sanum. Dicimus ergo quod ipsae quidem qualitates non suscipiunt magis et minus. Qui vero secundum eas quales dicuntur, ipsi sub comparatione cadunt, ut iustior, et sanior,

that the qualities in themselves are not susceptible of degree. However, those who in relation to such qualities are asserted to be so and so do indeed come under comparisons, e.g. more just, more healthy, more literate. For literacy in itself is not susceptible of degree, for no one says that one person is more literacy than another; but we do assert that he who participates in literacy is literate; we denominate him so from the abstract noun; being literate does admit of degree, as in the case of the grammarian Donatus who having attained his maturity was more of a grammarian, that is more literate, than he was when he first took up studies of this sort.

et grammaticior. Namque ipsa grammatica, id est litteratura, non suscipit magis et minus, nullus enim dicit alteram altera magis esse grammaticam; sed eum qui grammatica ipsa participat dicimus litteratum quem a litteratura scilicet denominamus; litteratus autem suscipit magis et minus, ut Donatus grammaticus plus erat aetate iam provecta grammaticus, id est litteratus, quam cum primum ad huiusmodi studia devenisset: BC 257C-D.

The parity herein evidenced of the cases of qualities considered in themselves with the case of substances is of interest if considered in the light of the suggestions made in §4 and *n*4.31*a* as to the semantical categories involved in saying that something is a substance (e.g. *homo est substantia* ⊖ man is a substance) and in certain uses of quality-oriented abstract nouns (e.g. the '*Grammaticus est grammatica*' ⊖ '*Literate* is literacy' of 4.2341, 4.5022, which in its *prima facie* interpretation conflicts obviously with the passage just quoted). It was there suggested that the '*est*' ⊖ 'is' in both these cases corresponded to the higher-order '$\in$' of Ontology (cf. §3.15). Can it be that the contrast which Boethius is here making is at bottom a reflection of the diverse semantical categories of 'is' and its arguments? The removal of temporal considerations which Boethius stresses in the passage might point to this. If this were so, it would be indeed ironical that the individualist egalitarianism of political thought in the modern era used as one of its justifications the misunderstanding of a logical distinction: it is *man* insofar as it is a species, not man *qua* individual which is under consideration when the insusceptibility of degree of the qualities which go to make up *man* (e.g. rationality) are in question. As Abelard remarks in his lengthy study of comparison (*A* 424–32), *man* cannot be said to be more or less rational, yet he can nevertheless be said to be more or less of a reasoner (*ratiocinans*) (*A* 425.37–426.1). This is precisely the distinction which is left out of account in the Cartesian discussion in the first part of the *Discours*, already mentioned. Passages close in spirit to Descartes' remarks are also to be found in that chapter of Hobbes' *Leviathan* which describes the 'state of nature'. Gilson's commentary on the *Discours* suggests a common source for both the Cartesian and the Hobbesian remarks.

The association by Abelard of '*intelligere*' ⊖ 'to understand', '*essentia*' ⊖ 'essence', and assertions '*secundum substantiam*' ⊖ 'intra-theoretical', with absence of degree (*A* 425.1.25) appears to accord with the suggestion that this absence of susceptibility of degree reflects a difference of semantical category.

*n*3.21*a*: signify ⊖ *significare*] This is the first occasion on which meaning (*significatio*) is mentioned in the dialogue. Hitherto only the peculiar '*est*' ⊖ 'is' (cf. *n*1.000*b*) and '*intelligi*' ⊖ 'to be understood' (3.1) have been used. One hence gets the impression that talk about meaning is, as it were, a kind of efflorescence supervening on the talk in terms of the functors mentioned. Thus the Student, in his reply, immediately reverts to '*est*' ⊖ 'is' instead of continuing to adhere to the '*significare*' ⊖ 'to mean' used by the Tutor.

*n*3.21*b*: animated sensitive substance ⊖ *substantiam animatam sensibilem*] This is the stock definition of *animal* used by Boethius, e.g.

If you make a declaration as to the definition of *animal* you will say that an animal is that which is an animated sensitive substance.	*Si definitionem reddas animalis, dicas id esse animal quod est substantia animata sensibilis:* *BDP* 22D; cf. e.g. *BD* 16A, *BC* 163D, *BC* 179B, *BDT* 1196C, *BDT* 1187B

*n*3.21*c*: animal] The reason for the emphasis on the reciprocal nature of this definition is plain: 'animated sensitive substance' is truly predicable both of particular men and also of man *qua* species, but the converse does not hold (*BC* 193). It is only when *animal* is equated with this definition that the predication can go both ways. Priscian uses the same example when insisting on the reciprocal possibilities of definitional statements:

It is also customary where definitions are concerned to reply to the question by prefixing the colourless substantives covering all possible definables, and then to add the various common nouns denoting properties. Thus to the question 'What is *animal*?' we have the reply 'A substance which is animated"; conversely one has 'What is a substance which is	*In definitionibus quoque solet ad interrogationem omnium rerum quae definiri possunt, neutrum substantivi praeponi et multa appellativa differentiarum nomina ad id referri, ut 'quid est animal?', 'substantia animata', et per conversionem 'quid est substantia animata?', 'animal' ... idem licet facere per omnes definitiones:* *K* III 135.1.8

animated?' and the reply 'Animal'...
The same performance is proper to all definitions.

The same reciprocity is demanded by Augustine in that part of *De Quantitate Animae* to which attention is called in *CRH*. In the present text it looks as though the Student is trying to give an impression of his acuteness by forestalling the asking of the reciprocal question by the Tutor.

*n*3.21*d*: rationality ⊖ *rationalitatem*] This sentence is a summary of a statement of Boethius' in the Second Dialogue on Porphyry:

For if you take away *animal* neither *rational* nor *irrational* can remain. On the other hand, if you take away *rational*, then *animal* remains. But if you strike out both of the constitutive characteristics (cf. *n*4.22*d*), i.e. *rational* or *irrational*, at least some thing remains to be understood, namely *living sensitive substance*, i.e. *animal*. In this way the removal of the genus (cf. *n*4.2411*g*) removes also all the constitutive characteristics. However, when constitutive characteristics are removed, they do not eliminate the genus along with themselves, since the understanding of the genus remains; that is, *animal* can be understood without further constitutive characteristics, so that you can mentally grasp it definitionally, and assert it to be a substance which is living as well as sensitive.

Nam si abstuleris animal, rationale atque irrationale non remanent. Porro autem si rationale abstuleris, remanet animal. Sed si utrasque interemeris differentias, id est rationale et irrationale, potest tamen quoddam intelligi, quod sit substantia animata sensibilis, id est animal. Ita genus sublatem omnes secum aufert differentias. Sublatae differentiae genus secum non interimunt, quod intelligentia genus remanet, id est quoniam potest animal intelligi praeter differentias, ut eius tantum definitionem animo capias, et esse dicas substantiam animatam atque sensibilem; B 59B-C.

All this is, of course, predicable-level discourse, concerning which *n*4.2411*h* may be consulted.

*n*3.21*e*: on both flanks ⊖ *utrimque*] *S* I 147 points out the parallel with Susanna's words, '*Angustiae sunt mihi undique*' in the Vulgate Dan. 13, 22.

*n*3.221*a*: without rationality ⊖ *praeter rationalitatem*] Aquinas gives what is, in effect, an interesting elucidation of this sort of sentence. He distinguishes between that to which, by definition, an addition *cannot* be made, and that which is theoretically indifferent to addition:

'Something to which an addition is not made' can be understood in two manners.

'Aliquid cui non fit additio' potest intelligi dupliciter. Uno modo, ut de ratione eius

In one way, so that any addition to it is theoretically excluded, as in the case of *irrational animal* which theoretically entails that it should be without reason. In the second way one understands merely something to which an addition happens not to be made; thus *animal* in general does not comprise *rational*, since the having of reason is not comprised in the theory of *animal* in general; at the same time there is no theoretical exclusion of its having reason.

sit quod non fiat ei additio; sicut de ratione animalis irrationalis est, ut sit sine ratione. Alio modo intelligitur aliquid cui non fit additio: sicut animal commune est sine ratione, quia non est de ratione animalis communis ut habeat rationem; sed nec de ratione eius est ut careat ratione: AST I q. 3 art. 4 ad 1.

Plainly Anselm's present sentence is trading on the second situation described by Aquinas, whereas the next (3.222) takes advantage of the impossibility of compounding *irrational* with *man.*

*n*3.222*a*: rationality ⊖ *rationalitatem*] The position of these two premisses (3.221, 3.222) in relation to the main lines of the discussion is such that they receive no further analysis, although 3.222 recurs in another connection at 3.611. However, it is plain from the analyses in 3.3 and 3.4 of premisses having the same form that the Tutor would first of all unravel the pair of them thus:

(3.221) Every animal can be understood to be animal without rationality (cf. 3.311)

(3.222) No man can be understood to be man without rationality (cf. 3.312)

and yet again thus:

(3.221) Being an animal does not demand rationality (cf. 3.41)

(3.222) Being a man demands rationality (cf. 3.42)

From these it follows (cf. 3.43):

Being a man is not being an animal

in the sense that the two are not identically defined (see 3.44). Alternatively the sense may be that a man is not the same thing as an animal (see 3.453) but not in such a way as to exclude a man's being an animal (see 3.451).

The separate analysis of the present premiss (3.222) occurs in connection with another syllogism. Thus at 3.611 the premiss '*nullus homo potest intelligi sine rationalitate*' ⊖ 'no man can be understood as being without rationality' is said to be capable of *expositio* ⊖ analysis in the following form:

> *Nullus homo potest aliquo modo intelligi sine rationalitate* ⊖ No man can in some way be understood as being without rationality (3.6321).

On the same lines as the analyses given at that point, and in particular following the model of 3.6322, the other premiss with which we are at present concerned (3.221) would become:

> *Omne animal quolibet modo potest intelligi sine rationalitate* ⊖ Every animal can in no matter what way be understood as being without rationality.

But this is plainly false, since following the lines whereby 3.6332 is falsified by 3.6334 one has, as a rebuttal of the last premiss:

> *Nullus animal potest intelligi homo sine rationalitate* ⊖ No animal can be understood as being a man without rationality.

These remarks give some indication of the way in which an Anselmian analysis of the present premisses would have been undertaken, had he chosen to pursue such an analysis in the course of the dialogue.

*n*3.232*a*: necessarily rational ⊖ *rationalis est ex necessitate*] The position of the expression of the modality of necessity is, as from its first appearance at the opening of 3.21, perhaps deliberately kept rather ambiguous. In Boethius' translation of Aristotle's *Analytica Priora* the expression of necessity usually appears as applying to the premiss as a whole, e.g. 'a *quidem* b *ex necessitate sumptum est inesse vel non inesse*' ⊖ 'Necessarily *a* must be taken to be in *b* or not to be in *b*' (*B* 648C), or 'a *quidem omni* b *insit ex necessitate*' ⊖ 'Necessarily *a* is in every *b*' (*B* 649A), and '*homo animal est ex necessitate*' ⊖ 'Necessarily man is animal' (*B* 648D). Łukasiewicz translates the original Greek of such assertions as 'It is necessary that man should be an animal' (*LAS* (2nd Edition) p. 148). When the necessity is thus applied to the whole assertion, it is said to be applied *de dicto*, as opposed to the case in which the necessity is asserted of the subject of the assertion, i.e. *de re*. Examples are 'That every man should be rational is necessary' (*de dicto*) and 'Every man is necessarily rational' (*de re*); cf. *HSL* 7.26.

The distinction mentioned originally stems from a passage in *ADSE* (166ᵇ 22–30, cf. *B* 1010D–1011A) where the modal expression '*possibile*' is in question, and a fallacy is there shown to arise if the two senses (*de dicto* and *de re*) are not distinguished (cf. *HSL* 7.26). Can it be that Anselm is here in effect noting a corresponding fallacy in relation to '*ex necessitate*' ⊖ 'necessarily'? One might at first sight make the unorthodox supposition that he was acquainted with Boethius' translation of *ADSE*, since the *potestas scribendi* ⊖ capacity to write mentioned therein reappears in Anselm's passage on *potestas* ⊖ capacity (*SN* 44–5). However, the *potestas scribendi* ⊖ capacity to write figures also in a passage of *BDIG* (*B* 597A, C) with which Anselm was more probably familiar; cf. *n*4.14*g*.

In view of the places of 3.231 and 3.232 in the discussion (e.g. their supposed formal resemblance to 3.112, 3.111 respectively) there can be little doubt that in their final form they are intended as modal assertions *de re*. Indeed, were 3.231 understood as involvfng a modality *de dicto*, i.e. as 'It is necessary that no animal should be rational', this would be so obviously false that the discussion could scarcely continue. On the level of Anselm's modal logic evinced by some of the present arguments, see *HL* §9.50.

*n*3.233*a*: is animal ⊖ *animal est*] The procedure of question and answer, with the answerer being finally forced into the admission of paradox or blatant falsehood, as in this case, is outlined in Bk VIII of Aristotle's *Topica*, a work with which logicians of Anselm's time are supposed to be unacquainted (cf. e.g. *DLM* I 14–15). Thus we have, for instance:

First the consideration of the shape to be taken by the reply is part of the job of the capable respondent, as it is also of the capable questioner. For it is the questioner's job so to steer the conversation as to make the respondent assert untenable propositions to which he is committed by his assumptions; the respondent's job, in contrast, is to make it appear that the untenable

De responsione autem primum quidem determinandum quodnam est opus bene respondentis, quemadmodum bene interrogantis. Est autem interrogantis quidem sic deducere orationem, ut faciat respondentem dicere inopiniabiliora quam ea quae propter positionem sunt necessaria, respondentis vero non propter se apparere, accidere impossibile, aut quod praeter opinionem est, sed propter positionem: *B* 999C.

positions or paradoxes occur not through his own fault, but merely because of the assumptions.

The same procedure is clearly being followed at many of the succeeding phases of the dialogue. An account of the original context of this sort of exercise may be found in *KF* 12.

At this particular point in the dialogue the inadmissible conclusion is in either case (3.22, 3.23) drawn from premisses having somewhat the same form and wording as those belonging to the main stream of the discussion (3.10, 3.11). This acts as a cue for the analysis of the latter – a step which is taken at 3.3. The arguments which provided the cue are not themselves subjected to analysis in detail, although in this present case an Anselmian account of their faults can easily be constructed (*n*3.222*a*).

Yet another manner in which the conclusion 'No man is animal' may be sophistically deduced appears in 3.8. Once again, it is based on faulty deductions effected in connection with definitions.

*n*3.234*a*: to deny them would be mere brashness ⊖ *impudentia sit eas negare*] The word-play which occurs here ('*imprudentia sit eas probare* ... *impudentia sit eas negare*' ⊖ 'imprudent to prove them ... impudent to deny them' is of a type to which Anselm was addicted (cf. *n*3.234*d*, 3.33, 3.7211, 3.811). Such a conceit was known to the Greeks as παρονομασία, and was called *adnominatio* by Latin writers (*CH* IV 21, *QIO* IX, 3, 66). Anselm may well have caught the habit from the writings of St. Augstine of Hippo. Some of the *adnominationes* used by the latter are discussed in *BSA* 292 *et seq*. A near parallel to the present example occurs in *De Civitate Dei*:

Let those who on this account impudently and imprudently scorn the most saving religion take notice of this and be silent...	*Hoc intueantur et taceant, qui saluberrimae religioni hinc impudenter atque imprudenter illudunt ...*: *ADCD* I, 15.

Another occurs in John of Salisbury's *Metalogicon*: *ingratus est et tam impudentis quam imprudentis ingenii* ... ⊖ it is ungrateful and pertains to a mind as impudent as it is imprudent; *SM* 115.4.

The definition of *adnominatio* from the Herennian Rhetoric, with which Anselm was probably familiar, since Lanfranc lectured on the work (*HSP* 207, *SLB* 36), runs as follows:

Adnomination occurs when there comes about a change of one letter or several, of one syllable or several in a word or name which is otherwise the same as another; alternatively it occurs when like words are construed to cover unlike situations. It is engineered for many and various reasons.

Adnominatio est cum ad idem verbum et ad idem nomen acceditur commutatione unius litterae aut litterarum, syllabae aut syllabarum; aut ad res dissimilis similia verba accommodantur. Ea multis et variis rationibus conficitur: CH IV, 21.

*n*3.234*b*: similar ⊖ *similem*] This similarity is in the arrangement and wording of the terms (or supposed terms) only; it does not extent as far as the order in which the premisses are put forward, i.e. the second premiss of each of the Tutor's parallel cases (3.22, 3.23) is of the same general form as the first premiss of each of the Student's corresponding syllogisms (3.10, 3.11) and *vice versa*. Familiarity with Peter of Spain's rules (*HSL* 4.04) and mnemonic rhyme (*HSL* 4.17), versions of which have been current ever since his time, tend to make one suppose that the Tutor's order of premisses is the 'correct' one, since it places the major term in the first of the two premisses. However, as Łukasiewicz reminds us (*LAS* §12) Aristotle himself adopted no fixed order for the proffering of the premisses of categorical syllogisms.

*n*3.234*c*: motive for producing them ⊖ *suspicor te hos attulisse*] The motive here adduced by the Student is in effect an outline of the course described in *n*3.233*a* and systematically adopted by the Tutor here and at 3.8; it is also imitated by the Student at 3.5.

*n*3.234*d*: realise that the same apply to the similar ones which I framed ⊖ *idem de similibus quos ego feceram decernerem*] This is yet another example of an *adnominatio* (*cernerem* ... *decernerem*); cf. *n*3.234*a*.

*n*3.234*e*: of the syllogism ⊖ *syllogismorum*] It being granted that the order of premisses is immaterial (cf. *n*3.234*b*) the syllogisms so far proffered follow the lines of valid syllogisms in a rough sort of way. Thus in the terms of the post-Anselmian Peter of Spain's *Summulae Logicales* syllogisms 3.10 and 3.22 follow the form of *Camestres* (IInd figure) and 3.11 and 3.23 follow the form of *Cesare* (IInd figure). They are not, of course, really categorical syllogisms at all.

The question of the modality of 3.23 has been discussed in *n*3.232*a*.

The absence of a modal functor in the conclusion (3.233) and the facts adduced in *n*3.232*a* make it fairly clear that 3.231 and 2.323 are modal propositions roughly and readily classifiable as *de re*, with 'necessarily rational' considered as the middle term, so that 'necessarily' does not appear in the conclusion.

The two features here mentioned by the Student, namely truth of premisses and formal rectitude, are distinguished by Aristotle at the opening of his *Topica* (*B* 909D). When both are present, then one has a demonstrative syllogism as opposed to a dialectical syllogism in which probabilities are posited in the premisses. Boethius does not directly relate the question of truth to his definition of the syllogism (*BSC* 821A, *BDT* 1183B); the premisses, according to him, are merely '*posita et concessa*' ⊖ 'assumed and granted'; cf. also *B* 641C–D.

The Tutor's central reply to the Student's query at this point has two stages: first (in 3.30–3.32) he shows how the premisses in question (3.221, 3.232) have an interpretation which avoids any conclusion whatsoever being drawn from them; next (3.33) he points out that overt accord or disaccord with syllogistic rules need not always be a guide to validity or invalidity of reasoning, and proceeds (in 3.4) to show that something can in fact be inferred from these premisses.

*n*3.311*a*: major premiss ⊖ *propositione*] The word '*propositio*' must be translated here (in contrast to what obtained at 3.1) as 'major premiss'; see *n*3.531*a*.

*n*3.311*b*: state the minor ⊖ *assume*] The word '*assume*' here means 'State the *assumptio*', where '*assumptio*' is 'minor premiss'; see *n*3.531*a*.

*n*3.3121*a*: literacy ⊖ *grammatica*] These two propositions represent the first of the four successive analyses which 3.101, 3.102 receive in the course of the argument: the others are 3.41.32, 3.6331.6332, and 3.6333.6334. Tabulations of the place of these analyses in the discussion are contained in *n*3.44*a*, *n*3.6321*a*.

*n*3.3121*b*: term ⊖ *terminum*] The expression '*communis terminus*' ⊖ 'common term' receives a lengthy definition related to each of the syllogistic figures in Boethius' *De Syllogismo Categorico* (*B* 798C–D). However, the same author, in his Commentary on Cicero's *Topica* prefers '*medius terminus*' ⊖ 'middle term' to express the same idea.

The technique of showing that the middle term of a categorical syllogism is ambiguous, which is being used here, is the one which was to be systematically exploited in the disputational exercises of the Middle Ages. '*Inventio*' is the science of discovering a suitable middle term whereon to found an argument, according to William of Champeaux (*DLM* II–I 145).

*n*3.33*a*: not made explicit ⊖ *non in prolatione*] The contrast between '*in intellectu*' ⊖ 'in the understanding' and '*in prolatione*' ⊖ 'in the setting forth' which occurs here is directly derived from Boethius' lesser commentary on Ch. 11 of Aristotle's *De Interpretatione.* Here the regresses inferrable by repetition of that which is explicitly or implicitly contained in a complex predicate are under discussion. (Full details are given in *n*4.2414*b*). Boethius' comment runs as follows:

Whenever something is contained in a predicate, and we want to predicate it explicitly, and to join the two repeated predicates into a single one, then an unsuitable predication is generated. Now this can sometimes be seen in the very manner in which the man utters forth his words, sometimes it occurs only in what is implicitly understood according to the content of the term.

Quoties enim inest praedicato aliquid, et nos illud extra volumus praedicare, et in unum rursus duo praedicata coniungere, tunc fit incongrua praedicatio: et haec aliquoties quidem in ipsa hominum prolatione perspicitur, aliquoties vero invenitur in intellectu, atque in termini continentia: BDIL 359B.

Boethius' '*incongrua praedicatio in prolatione*' ⊖ 'unsuitable predication in the manner of uttering forth' and '*incongrua praedicatio in intellectu*' ⊖ 'unsuitable predication in what is understood' correspond respectively to what Caietan calls 'explicit' and 'implicit' nugation when commenting on this same point (*APH* 263). For the use of '*prolatio*' ⊖ 'uttering forth' in a twelfth-century manuscript, see *DLM* II–I 140. Abelard uses the distinction between '*secundum prolationem*' ⊖ 'according to the uttering forth' and '*secundum sententiam*' ⊖ 'according to the sense' (*A* 182.21.27).

*n*3.33*b*: not just the words themselves ⊖ *non verba*] This speech of the Tutor's claims to justify the whole preocedure which is now being carried out, as well as to show the Student that overt agreement or disagreement with the forms of elementary syllogistic is not an invariable sign of cogency or lack of cogency in inference (cf. end of 3.234). The successive analyses further show forth that which is '*in intellectu*' ⊖ 'in the understanding' as opposed to that which is '*in prolatione*' ⊖ 'in the uttering forth'. In the particular case which has occasioned these remarks, the '*prolatio*' ⊖ 'uttering forth' makes the premisses produced at 3.31 look as though they had no common term; however, 3.4 is to show that such a common term is in fact '*in intellectu*' ⊖ 'in the understanding' in respect of those premisses. The present speech expresses, in relation to syllogistic premises, one aspect of Anselm's general policy that analyses of statement should be sought in order to resolve problems. Other examples of declarations on this policy are given in *HL* §2.12. At the same time one may see here a realisation of the inadequacy of attempts to assimilate all premisses which look as though they are suitable for Aristotelian syllogisms to the forms appropriate to the premisses of such syllogisms. In other words, there are occasions on which the simple parts of speech (e.g. sentence-forming functors having two nominal arguments) central to Aristotelian syllogistic proper, will not suffice for the expression of logical theses. This realisation is quite coherent with the central thesis of the dialogue to the effect that violation of *usus loquendi* ⊖ spoken usage may be desirable in order to assert logical truths involving novel parts of speech. It also accords perfectly in principle with the ways in which the Ontology described in §3 is exploited in the present work and in Part III of *HLM*; cf. *n*4.31*a*.

*n*3.40*a*: you are looking for ⊖ *exspectas*] In other words, the premisses 3.102 and 3.101 do not prove that a literate is not a man.

*n*3.41*a*: being a man ⊖ *esse hominis*] The talk about the *esse* ⊖ being of *man* and *literate* which occurs in the dialogue is related to what is stated in the corresponding definitions. This is made clear at 3.44, 3.452, 3.800 ('*esse uniuscuiusque rei in definitione consistat*' ⊖ 'the being of each and every thing is established in a definition'), 3.90, and 4.8, 4.811. For full discussion and references to the logical status of assertions about '*esse*' ⊖ 'being' in this context see *n*3.431*a*, *n*3.44*a*, and *n*3.800*b*.

The '*homo definiri non debet cum grammatica*' ⊖ '*man* should not be defined in terms of literacy' of 3.901 is an alternative expression of the present premiss.

*n*3.42*a*: demands literacy ⊖ *indiget grammatica*] The '*grammaticus non valet sine grammatica*' ⊖ '*literate* is not definable without literacy' of 3.901 is an alternative expression of the present premiss.

*n*3.430*a*: term ⊖ *terminum*] The 'common term' is, of course '*indiget grammatica*' ⊖ 'requires literacy'. Use is here being made of a notion drawn from ordinary syllogistic but applied to premisses which, as the Tutor's speech has just hinted (3.33), are understood to be more complex than their external form might appear to indicate.

*n*3.431*a*: man ⊖ *hominis*] Boethius uses a turn of phrase which is a cross between that of the present conclusion and its alternative expression in 3.452 when he says, in Bk V of his Commentary on Porphyry that *idem est esse homini quod est esse rationale* ⊖ being a man is the same as being rational; *B* 150B. It may be noted that on his assumption that there are rational beings other than men (*B* 137B) Boethius' use of '*idem*' ⊖ 'same as' is not so accurate as is that of Anselm.

We are here concerned with the '*esse*' ⊖ 'being' of such things as men, animals, and literate. Since the text asserts that the '*esse*' ⊖ 'being' of anything is given in its definition (3.800), and that to say that the *esse* ⊖ being of one thing is not the *esse* ⊖ being of another amounts to saying that they are not defined in the same way (3.431, 3.44, cf. 3.901, 4.24), it is clear that to talk about the *esse* ⊖ being of a thing is, for Anselm, to talk about its definitional or quasi-definitional equivalent. Hence, making use of the weak equivalence defined at §3.9 the notion here in question may be expressed in the following fashion: any name or name-like expression may be used to complete the functor-forming functor 'Cl⟦ ⟧', which is defined as follows:

.1 $[ab]: \mathrm{Cl}[\![a]\!](b) \,.\equiv.\, b \bigcirc a$ (§3.9, §3.14)

The functor 'Cl⟦ ⟧' as here defined has as one of its counterparts the infinitive verb-form derived from, or corresponding to, the name in pre-theoretical language; e.g. if '*a*' is 'defendant', then 'Cl⟦*a*⟧' is 'to defend', or if '*a*' is '*dux*' ⊖ 'leader', then 'Cl⟦*a*⟧' is '*ducere*' ⊖ 'to lead', and so on. In a logical language such as that of Ontology, the creation of such an infinitive is effected quite simply in terms of .1, but in non-theoretical language such infinitives are not always available. Hence in the absence of a logical language such as Ontology some medieval logicians and philosophers formed expressions corresponding to the required infinitive by the use of '*esse*' ⊖ 'being' and the genitive of the name in question, as in the examples encountered above. Thus, to use the terms of *BDIL* 348–9 and *APH* 212, 237, all names predicated '*de tertio adiacente*' ⊖ 'as a third component' (as 'white' in 'Jack is white') could be treated in this way. Those verbs predicated '*de secundo adiacente*' ⊖ 'as a second component' (as 'smokes' in 'Jack smokes') and which, being verbs, already have a corresponding pre-systematic infinitive, were nevertheless shown to belong to the same class of case by the equation of that infinitive to '*esse*' and the participial form, as when '*currere*' ⊖ 'to run' is said to mean '*currentem esse*' ⊖ 'to be running'. (Cf. e.g. *AST* I q. 18, art. 2, *sed c.*, *c*; q. 54, art. 1, ob. 2, ad 2; art. 2, ob. 1, ad 1; *AST* II–I q. 3, art. 2, ob. 1, ad 1; q. 56, art. 1, ad 1; *AST* II–II, q. 179, art. 1, ob. 1, ad 1; *AST* III, q. 2, art. 5, ad 3; *ASCG* I, 98, II, 57, III, 104 wherein the well-known adage '*vivere viventibus est esse*' ⊖ 'to live is, for the living, to be' reflects the equation now in question.) Accordingly predications *de secundo adiacante* ⊖ as a second component could be converted into predications *de tertio adiactente* ⊖ as a third component, as when '*homo currit*' ⊖ 'a man runs' and '*homo ambulat*' ⊖ 'a man walks' become '*homo currens est*' ⊖ 'a man is running and '*homo ambulans est*' ⊖ 'a man is walking' respectively; *BDIL* 384D. Again '*lux lucens est*' ⊖ 'the light is lighting' and '*est habens*' ⊖ 'is having' are given by Anselm as respective alternatives for '*lux lucet*' ⊖ 'the light lights' and '*habet*' ⊖ 'has': *S* I 20.14 and 4.8121 of the present text. All these equations are themselves part of a larger complex, involving abstract nouns, by means of which all such types of case were reduced to uniformity; *HDG* §6.3124, *n*4.8121*a*, and *HLM* I §3.

As is well-known, Aquinas's sense of '*esse*' ⊖ 'being' differed from that of his predecessors. For an informal account, see *JN*; an interpretation which relies on Ontology is suggested in *HLM* III §6 and *HEE*.

For the purpose of making available an infinitive corresponding to English names which do not already have one, 'to' also with the termination '-ise' will sometimes serve. Thus 'man' would give 'to man-ise', 'white', 'to white-ise', and so on.

It is plain that the '*est*' ⊖ 'is' which has functor-forming functors of the type of 'Cl⟦ ⟧' as its arguments (as in the present '*esse grammatici non est esse hominis*' ⊖ 'being literate is not being man') is not the same functor as the '*est*' ⊖ 'is' which as names as its arguments (as in '*Socrates est albus*' ⊖ 'Socrates is white'). The first of the two sorts of '*est*' ⊖ 'is' just-mentioned has been defined at §3.14. The difference here in question was noted by Boethius (*BDIL* 309B–310C) and Aquinas (*APH* 96, cf. *APH* 54, 55, 56) when they commented on Aristotle's *De Interpretatione* (16^b 20). In terms of the predicable-level higher-order '*est*' ⊖ 'is' the assertion of Anselm's which is at present under consideration has the form:

.2 $\sim(\mathrm{Cl}\,[\![\mathbf{g}]\!] \in \mathrm{Cl}\,[\![\mathbf{h}]\!])$ (cf. §3.15)

Suggestions as to the logical analyses of the premisses from which it is drawn (3.41, 3.42) will be provided in *n*3.44*a*.

*n*3.44*a*: identically defined ⊖ *definitionem utriusque*] Adding analyses evidently suitable by the thesis already established at §3.52, one may recall that it has earlier been determined that:

.1A *esse hominis non indiget grammatica*

.1B to be man does not require literacy

.1C $\sim(\mathrm{Cl}\,[\![\mathbf{h}]\!] \in \subset [\![\mathrm{trm}\,\langle\gamma\rangle]\!])$ (3.41, cf. §3.13, §3.14)

and that:

.2A *esse grammatici indiget grammatica*

.2B to be literate requires literacy

.2C $\mathrm{Cl}\,[\![\mathbf{g}]\!] \in \subset [\![\mathrm{trm}\,\langle\gamma\rangle]\!]$ (3.42, cf. §3.13, §3.14)

From .1 and .2 there followed:

.3A *esse grammatici non est esse hominis*

.3B to be literate is-not to be man

.3C $\sim(\mathrm{Cl}\,[\![\mathbf{g}]\!] \in \mathrm{Cl}\,[\![\mathbf{h}]\!])$ (3.431, *n*3.431*a*, *n*3.101*a*)

And so we come to the present conclusion which does indeed follow from .3:

.4A *non esse eandem definitionem utriusque*

.4B they (i.e. *man* and *literate*) are not both defined in the same way

.4C $\sim(\mathbf{g} \bigcirc \mathbf{h})$ (3.44, cf. §3.9)

The weak identity used in .4C has been chosen since it is later stated that .4 could be alternatively expressed:

.5A *grammaticus non est idem quod homo*

.5B a literate is not the same as a man

.5C $\sim(\mathbf{g} \bigcirc \mathbf{h})$ (3.452, §3.9)

Note, in view of *n*3.800*b* that the analogous higher-order '○' could really be the functor involved in .5C. In either case, however, the consequence alleged by the Student, i.e. 'no literate is a man' (i.e. 'g ⊄ h') does not follow from .4. The definitions of '○' (§3.9) and '⊄' (§3.5) accord with the Tutor's statement (3.450–3.451) of this non-consequence which will shortly be made (cf. *n*3.452*a*).

*n*3.452*a*: man ⊖ *homo*] We have seen in *n*3.431*a* how 'to be literate is-not to be man' (3.431) may be rendered:

.1 $\sim(\mathrm{Cl}[\![\mathbf{g}]\!] \in \mathrm{Cl}[\![\mathbf{h}]\!])$

The sentence corresponding to .1 is now being said to have as its consequence 'Literate is not the same as man'; this in turn will be said to amount to the non-identity of the definitions of *literate* and *man*. At the same time this non-identity is said not to have the consequence desired by the Student, namely that a literate is not a man (*Non tamen ideo consequitur grammaticum non esse hominis, sicut tu intelligebas*, 3.450, 3.451) in the sense that *no* literate is a man. (The Student has been (3.113). and will continue to be (3.541, 3.3211, 4.103) at pains to defend the latter negatively quantified conclusion). If now 'Literate is not the same as man' is assumed to involve the ontological functor of weak identity (§3.9), i.e. to be of the form:

.2 $\sim(\mathbf{g} \bigcirc \mathbf{h})$

then it is true that

.3 $\mathbf{g} \not\subset \mathbf{h}$

(i.e. 'No literate is man') does not follow from .2, as is evident from the definitions concerned (§3.5, §3.9; cf. *n*3.44*a*). Neither does .3 follow from .1.

Further, .1 does, as the Tutor claims, have .2 as its consequence, for

.4 $\sim (\mathrm{Cl}[\![\mathbf{g}]\!] \in \mathrm{Cl}([\![\mathbf{h}]\!]) . \supset . \sim (\mathbf{g} \bigcirc \mathbf{h})$

which is hence now in question is equivalent to .5 which now follows and is a thesis in view of §3.55:

.5 $\mathbf{g} \bigcirc \mathbf{h} . \supset . \mathrm{Cl}[\![\mathbf{g}]\!] \in \mathrm{Cl}[\![\mathbf{h}]\!]$

Hence the assumption that the occurrence of 'Literate is not the same as man', which is now under discussion, has the form shown in .2 is entirely consonant both with the deductions made in the text and with the definition of the higher-order '∈' adopted at §3.15.

It may be added that 'Literate is not altogether the same as man' which occurs later in the dialogue, does not represent anything other than '$\sim (\mathbf{g} \bigcirc \mathbf{h})$', since it is supported by a reminder of the arguments earlier used to establish 'Literate is not the same as man' (3.901. 3.4).

A definition of '*est idem*' ⊖ 'is the same as' occurs in Aquinas: *quaecumque sunt, et nullo modo different, sunt idem* ⊖ whatsever things exist and in no way differ, are the same; *AST* I q. 90, art. 1, ob. 1. This sounds like a form of strong identity (§ 3.10). Aquinas carries on from this point to the distinction between difference and diversity (ibid. ad 3) on which see *n*4.22*d*.

*n*3.501*a*: in respect of quality ⊖ *in eo quod quale*] The expression '*in eo quod quale*' ⊖ 'in respect of quality' is one of a pair of locutions used to describe two contrasting sorts of predication, and which occur most frequently in Porphyry and Boethius when the predicables are being described (cf. *n*4.2411*h*, *n*4.2411*g*). The other expression of the pair is '*in eo quod quid*' ⊖ 'in respect of "whatness"'. Thus although '*in eo quod quid*' ⊖ 'in respect of "whatness"' does not actually occur until later in the *De Grammatico* (4.122, 4.131) it is impossible to ignore it when dealing with '*in eo quod quale*' ⊖ 'in respect of quality'.

One can, says Victorinus in *Liber de Definitione* ask (among other questions) whether a thing exists (*an sit*), what the thing is (*quid sit*) and what that thing is like (*quale sit*); once it is ascertained that a thing exists one can know what it is like and hence proceed to determine what it is. The fullest statement of what it is (as opposed to what it is like) is given in its definition:

Everything that is indicated by means of speech is shown either *to be* so, or to be of a certain *sort*, or to have certain *qualities*. Granted this, then an expression framed for the purpose of saying whether a thing exists is not a definition. Again, when reasons are given for the qualities of anything, then similarly one does not have a definition. However when *what* a thing is is shown (this being a middle point between the questions of whether it is and what its qualities are) this middle point, this classification which shows exactly what is demanded by the 'What is it?' question, is called a definition. For everything, if it already is now a thing, is there for certain. But now as it certainly is there, and it possesses its qualities whereby it may be simply comprehended, then what it is may also easily be known. For one can never understand *what* a thing is unless its qualities are first understood.

Omne quod demonstratur oratione aut an sit, aut quid sit, aut quale sit, ostenditur, quod cum adhibetur, oratio ad declarationem rei aliciuis an sit non est definitio; item cum quale sit aliquid ratione monstratur, pari modo definitio non erit. Cum vero quid sit ostenditur, quod medium est inter an sit et quale sit ... medium inquam, hoc genus quod ostendit idipsum de quo quaeritur, quid sit definitio nuncupatur ... Omnis enim res si modo iam res est ... certa est. Cum vero iam certa est, et qualitates suas habeat quibus cum facile comprehenditur, facile quid sit agnoscitur. Numquam enim quid sit intelligi potest, nisi quale sit fuerit comprehensum: BDF 892D–893A.

(Quintilian says much the same thing in his discussion of rhetorical questions: *QIO* III).

According to Boethius the '*in eo quod quid*' ⊖ 'in respect of "whatness"' and '*in eo quod quale*' ⊖ 'in respect of quality' determinations are the counterparts of the questions as to *quid sit* ⊖ what it is and *quale sit* ⊖ what it is like respectively: a predicate applied in reply to a question of the form '*Quid sit ...*?' is applied *in eo quod quid* ⊖ in respect of "whatness", e.g.

But since the genus is predicated of the species, we require to know exactly how it is predicated. For if you say 'What is *man*?' and someone replies 'Animal', then he may be seen to have replied well and fully, and rightly so. For when you asked what *man* is, he replied 'Animal', that is to say he predicated the genus of the species in respect of *what* the species is. For you asked what the species might be, and he applied to the species in question in respect of its "whatness" the name 'animal', i.e. the name of the genus.

Sed quoniam praedicatur genus de species, quomodo praedicetur agnoscendum est. Nam si dixeris, 'Quid est homo?' et aliquis responderit 'Animal', bene et integre respondisse videtur, et certe. Nam cum tu quid sit homo interrogaveris, ille respondit 'Animal', genus scilicet de specie in eo quod quid sit species praedicant. Nam tu quid esset species interrogasti: ille vero in eo quod quid sit species de qua interrogasti animalis nomen, id est genus, accomodavit: BDP 260D, cf. *BCP* 94A–C.

Similarly a predicate applied in reply to the question of the form '*Qualis sit* ...?' ⊖ 'What is ... like?' is applied *in eo quod quale* ⊖ in respect of quality, e.g.

For God is said to be rational, but not in respect of *what* he is, but rather in respect of his quality. For if the question of the qualities of someone is raised, then the reply 'Rational' can be given forthwith. If the question as to God's qualities is raised, then 'Rational' is not an absurd reply.

Deus enim rationalis dicitur, sed non in eo quod quid sit, sed in eo quod quale sit. Nam si qualis homo sit interrogetur, 'rationalis' continuo respondetur. Qualis Deus sit, si interroges, 'rationale' non absurde dixeris: BDP 52C–D.

These explanations do not of themselves totally remove the ambiguous nature of the '*Quid sit* ...?' ⊖ 'What is ...?' and '*Quale sit* ...?' ⊖ 'What is ... like?' questions. Only in the light of their use in defining the predicables (genus, species, etc., cf. *n*4.2411g, *n*4.2411*h*) and the systematic framework which those predicables exemplify, can those questions be seen to have a more fully determinate sense.

Yet a certain amount of ambiguity still remains. On Boethius' own admission even *in eo quod quid* ⊖ in respect of "whatness" predications have some qualitative connotation:

When I say 'man' I signify a substance of such a sort that it is predicated in respect of 'whatness' of many numerically diverse things; in so doing I signify, therefore, a quality possessed by the substance... For if *man* is rational, then some substance is rational – and yet *rational* is a quality.

Cum dico 'homo' talem substantiam significo, quae de pluribus numero differentibus in eo quod quid sit praedicatur, qualem ergo quamdam substantiam significo ... Nam si homo est rationalis, et substantia erit rationalis, sed rationalis qualitas est: BC 195A–B.

Again, there is Minto's way of putting the point on which Boethius is commenting in this last-quoted extract: 'When we say "This is a man" do we not declare his Quality? If Aristotle had gone further along this line he would have arrived at the modern point of view that a man is in virtue of his possessing certain attributes, that general names are applied in virtue of their connotation ... But Aristotle did not get out of the difficulty in this way. He solved it by falling back on the differences in common speech. "Man" does not signify a quality simply, as "whiteness" does. "Whiteness" signifies nothing but the quality. That is to say, there is no separate name in common speech for the common attributes of man': *MID* 117–8. Now Boethius used '*humanitas*' ⊖ 'humanity' as a 'separate name for the attributes of a man' (*B* 85D, 93D, 121B, 150D, 463A, 1119A, 1121C) so that the question can clearly be raised as to whether 'man' (a species name, and therefore predicated *in eo quod quid* ⊖ in respect of "whatness", cf. *n*4.2411*h*) is not really predicated *in eo quod quale* ⊖ in respect of quality. Boethius does in fact raise this question:

The species is predicated in respect of 'whatness', whereas the constitutive characteristic (cf. *n*4.22*d*) is predicated in respect of quality. A question can be raised concerning this disparity. For if the humanity in which the species consists is itself a certain quality, why is the species said to be predicated in respect of "whatness" when in fact because of a certain property of its nature it would rather seem to be a certain quality?

Species in eo quod quid sit praedicatur, differentia autem in eo quod quale sit. Huic differentiae poterat quaestio occurrere: nam si humanitas ipsa quae species est, qualitas quaedam est, cur dicatur species in eo quod quid sit praedicari, cum propter quamdam suae naturae proprietatem quaedam qualitas esse videatur? BCP 150D.

Boethius' reply follows the lines of his previously-quoted text. The sole quality-determining aspect of an *in eo quod quid* ⊖ in respect of "whatness" predication is to be found in the constitutive characteristic (*n*4.22*d*, 4.2411) contained in the relevant definition (e.g. 'rational' in the case of *man*):

To this we reply as follows. Only the constitutive characteristic is a quality. Humanity, however, is not a mere quality, but only something that quality completes ... it is in no sense a pure and simple quality, but rather a substance made up of qualities.

Huic respondemus, quia differentia solum qualitas est: humanitas vero non solum est qualitas, sed tantum qualitate perficitur ... qualitas vero ipsa pura simplexque nullo modo est, sed ex qualitatibus effecta substantia: BCP 150D–151A.

A similar question is discussed in *BCP* 97A–B. From these discussions alone it is plain that although an *in eo quod quid* ⊖ in respect of "whatness' predication is always *de subiecto* ⊖ of a subject (cf. *n*4.101*a*) the converse does not hold: certain *in eo quod quale* ⊖ in respect of quality predications, namely those in which the constitutive characteristic is predicated of the appropriate subject, are also *de subiecto* ⊖ of a subject. This is confirmed by the commentary on the Categories (*B* 191C–192C) from which quotations are given in *n*4.101*a*.

The passage in Boethius wherein the two expression in question are most completely and systematically connected with the doctrine of the predicables is to be found at *B* 94B–C (cf. *n*4.2411*h*(ii)). Other samples of their use may be found at *B* 26D, 52C, 91D, 92A–B, 97A–B, 138C, 146C–D. The '*Quid sit* ...?' ⊖ 'What is ...?' and '*Quale sit* ...?' ⊖ 'What is ... like?' questions are also mentioned in *BD* 880B. In Anselm's *Monologion* 16 (*S* I 30.6–31.8) the two are identified in respect of God. The use of '*quale*' ⊖ 'qualified' and '*quid*' ⊖ 'what' in explicating the notions of *genus*, *species*, etc. is described in *n*4.2411*g*, *n*4.2411*h*.

The application of the doctrines described above to Anselm's present assertion is plain enough: '*est grammaticus*' ⊖ 'is literate' is an '*in eo quod quale*' ⊖ 'in respect of quality' predication (3.501), whereas '*est homo*' ⊖ 'is a man' is not (3.502); it is predicated *in eo quod quid* ⊖ in respect of "whatness". 'Is literate' tells what the subject is like; 'is man' tells what the subject is. Similar remarks apply to all the sentences involving '*in eo quod quale*' ⊖ 'in respect of quality' which occur in the present section (3.5). In view the relation of '*in eo quod quid*' ⊖ 'in respect of "whatness"' to '*de subiecto*' ⊖ 'of a subject' which has been outlined above, it is plain (cf. *n*4.101*a*) that the statements of the present section of the dialogue for the most part contrast the types of theory or non-theory (cf. §4) to which the terms in question (i.e. '*homo*' ⊖ 'man' and '*grammaticus*' ⊖ 'literate') should be allocated. This section is largely an interlude devoted to a display of merely formal skill on the part of the Student, who assumes that a mechanical imitation of previous winning moves is the key to correct inference (3.51, 3.52).

*n*3.503*a*: literate ⊖ *grammaticus*] This improperly deduced conclusion is the converse of 3.113. The Student deduces a converse identity (3.540), but one of a sort which is not here really applicable, or which, if it is applicable, does not give the results desired by the Student (cf. *n*3.540*b*).

*n*3.513*a*: rational ⊖ *rationalis*] The Student is here imitating the technique of 3.2 by advancing a syllogism similar to 3.50, but with subject-matter such that the conclusion is clearly false. This procedure then provides a cue for the necessity of analysis (cf. *n*3.233*a*) which follows. Thus 3.521 and 3.522 imitate 3.311 and 3.312 respectively.

*n*3.520*a*: truth is preserved ⊖ *secundum veritatem*] The force of the words '*secundum veritatem*' (literally 'in accordance with the truth') at this point only emerges clearly when it is realised that shortly, in 3.53, purely formal manipulations are to be effected in order to arrive at the desired conclusion (3.5333). In the course of these manipulations the truth-preserving analyses now to be produced (3.521, 3.522) will be deformed into falsehoods (3.532, 3.5332). The English translation suggested has been engineered in order to reflect this contrast.

*n*3.521*a*: quality ⊖ *quale*] A repetitive analysis in imitation of 3.311.

*n*3.5220*a*: quality ⊖ *quale*] In imitation of 3.312.

*n*3.5221*a*: man ⊖ *homine*] In other words, this is the same result as that in 3.3121: there is now no term common to 3.521 and 3.5220.

*n*3.530*a*: would ⊖ *esset*] The mood of the present assertions is important: they are purely subjunctive (cf. '*proponeretur*' ⊖ 'could be asserted' in 3.5331), since 3.532 and 3.5332 are not true, and their falsehood is recognised by the Student.

*n*3.531*a*: major ⊖ *propositione*] It is quite plain from this use of '*propositio*' along with '*assumptio*' (cf. 3.5331) that '*propositio*' must here be translated as 'major premiss', and not just as 'premiss', or 'proposition', as was the case in 3.112. Correspondingly '*assumptio*' means '*minor* premiss'. This vocabulary has already been adumbrated in 3.311 and has various possible sources. It is used by Boethius when speaking of the hypothetical syllogism in Bk. V of his Commentary on Cicero's *Topica*. In Cicero's *De Inventione Rhetorica* the same two terms are used but without any implied restriction to the context of hypothetical syllogistic. However, Boethius himself appears to prefer to speak of major and minor '*propositiones*' when dealing with categorical syllogisms, and this in Bk. I of his same Commentary on Cicero's *Topica* (*BTC* 1051A; cf. *BTC* 1132C and *n*1.21*c*, *HL* §9.2).

*n*3.531*b*: minor ⊖ *assumptio*] See *n*3.531*a* on this use of '*assumptio*'.

*n*3.532*a*: quality ⊖ *quale*] This premiss is false, and presented only conditionally by the Student. It is false either because *man* is in fact asserted to be literate in respect of quality, or because '*grammaticus*' ⊖

'literate' is always asserted *in eo quod quale* ⊖ in respect of quality (cf. 3.501, which is true). Were the terms '*grammaticus*' ⊖ 'literate' and '*homo*' ⊖ 'man' to be reversed, i.e. if the first, instead of the second 'man' of 3.5220, were to be replaced by 'literate', yielding 'No literate is asserted to be man in respect of quality', then this would be a true result, but would not provide the middle term required.

*n*3.5331*a*: minor ⊖ *assumptione*] Cf. *n*3.531*a* on this use of '*assumptio*' with '*propositio*'.

*n*3.5332*a*: quality ⊖ *quale*] Once again, this premiss is false since, for example, '*homo*' ⊖ 'man' is never predicated of anything *in eo quod quale* ⊖ in respect of quality (cf. 3.592, which is true). The arrangement of '*grammaticus*' ⊖ 'literate' and '*homo*' ⊖ 'man' within it is the same as that found in '*Omnis qui grammaticus est potest intelligi homo sine grammatica*' ⊖ 'Everyone who is literate can be understood to be a man without literacy' (3.6332).

*n*3.540*a*: literate ⊖ *grammaticus*] This proposition is a clear imitation of 3.452: the difference is that the terms of the proposition, because of the order adopted in 3.50, occur conversely.

*n*3.540*b*: identical with ⊖ *idipsum quod*] The translation of the '*est idipsum quod*' of the present two alternants as 'is identical with' appears to be dictated by its arguments, i.e. '*fulgor*' ⊖ 'lightning and '*splendor*' ⊖ 'flash'. We have here an occurrence of the converse of the assertion discussed in *n*3.452*a* (i.e. the converse of 'A literate is not the same as a man'). If, says the Student, 'A man is not the same as a literate' constitutes an interpretation of 'Man is not literate' in the same way as '*fulgor* ⊖ lightning is not identical with *splendor* ⊖ flash' constitutes an interpretation of '*fulgor* ⊖ lightning is not *splendor* ⊖ flash', then 'No man is literate' may be deduced, *via* this interpretation, from the various sets of premisses described in 3.53.

Now the general position is clear: the case of *fulgor* ⊖ lightning and *splendor* ⊖ flash is brought in to illustrate a meaning of '*a* is not the same as *b*' such that 'No *a* is *b*' may be inferred from it: the meaning of '*a* is not the same as *b*' so far inspected (cf. *n*3.452*a*) does not permit such an inference. This estimation is confirmed by the Tutor's later reactions to the Student's present assimilation of 'literate' and 'man' to '*fulgor*' ⊖ 'lightning' and '*splendor*' ⊖ 'flash'. He is to propound a case – that of 'man' and 'stone' – in which not only '$\sim(\mathbf{l} \bigcirc \mathbf{h})$', wherein '**l**' stands for '*lapis*' ⊖ 'stone' and '**h**' stands for '*homo*' ⊖ 'man', holds, i.e.

$$.1 \qquad [\exists a]: a \in \mathbf{l} \,.\, \not\equiv .\, a \in \mathbf{h} \qquad (3.61)$$

but also, more strongly:

$$.2 \qquad [a]: a \in \mathbf{l} \,.\supset .\sim(a \in \mathbf{h}) \qquad (3.62)$$

holds.

Next, by means of further comparative analyses (3.632–3.634) of the case of *man* and *stone* with that of *literate* and *man*, the Tutor is able to show that '$\mathbf{g} \not\subset \mathbf{h}$' is not derivable; his previous contention, namely that their case is only like that of .1 (as opposed to .2, cf. *n*3.452*a*) hence still stands.

The nature of the 'man'/'stone' case is sufficient to suggest that the importation of the case of *fulgor* ⊖ lightning and *splendor* ⊖ flash into the discussion represents an attempt on the part of the Student to somehow supplement the meaning of 'is not the same as' in such way that when '$\sim(a \bigcirc b)$' is true (as in .1) then a proposition of the form '$a \not\subset b$' (as in .2) will be derivable from it. (Normally, without some sort of supplementation, this consequence would not, of course, follow). Now although the manner in which he is attempting to perform this supplementation is factually suspect, it is of great logical interest, as it shows an appreciation of the difference between singular identity ('... = ...', cf. §3.8) and weak identity ('... ○ ...', cf. §3.9), the negation of which has hitherto been assumed to be in question. The terms '*fulgor*' ⊖ 'lightning' and '*splendor*' ⊖ 'flash' are, for the purpose of this supplementation, used as the names of pseudo-objects, or essences. It is also assumed that 'literate' and 'man' can, in the present context, be used in the same way, with the result that we now have a supplementation of '$\sim(\mathbf{g} \bigcirc \mathbf{h})$' (the latter already established and agreed) by both 'ob(**g**)' and 'ob(**h**)' (defined §3.3). This supplementation gives the negation of singular identity, i.e. gives '$\sim(\mathbf{g} = \mathbf{h})$', as may now be shown. First it may be noted that the following is a thesis:

.3 $[ab]:. a = b . \supset : a \bigcirc b . \text{ob}(a) . \text{ob}(b)$ (cf. §3.8, §3.9, §3.3)

and since, in general:

$$[pqr]:. p . \supset . q . r : \supset : \sim q . r . \supset . \sim p$$

the following is a consequence of .3:

.4 $[ab]: \sim (a \bigcirc b) . \text{ob}(a) . \text{ob}(b) . \supset . \sim (a = b)$

This last thesis represents exactly the effect of the supposition that the arguments of '$\bigcirc$' each name a single object. That the negation '$\sim$ (**g** = **h**)', which is hence now available thanks to this false supplementation, does in fact give the result required by the Student, namely '**g** $\not\subset$ **h**' (cf. .2), may now be shown. Thus since the following is true:

.5 $[ab]:. a \triangle b . \text{ob}(a) . \text{ob}(b) . \supset : a = b$ (§3.41)

and since, in general,

$$[pqr]:. p . q . \supset . r : \supset : \sim r . q . \supset . \sim p$$

it follows that

.6 $[ab]:. \sim (a = b) . \text{ob}(a) . \text{ob}(b) . \supset . \sim (a \triangle b)$

is also true. But the antecedent of .6, with '**g**' for '*a*' and '**h**' for '*b*', is now assumed to be true, so that the corresponding consequence, i.e. '$\sim$ (**g** $\triangle$ **h**)' also follows. Then this, by the well-known traditional oppositional thesis §3.30 yields '**g** $\not\subset$ **h**', i.e. 'No literate is a man'.

It is of course possible to understand the non-identity here in question as not being the total analogue of the singular identity defined at §3.8, but rather as being constructed in terms of the higher-order '$\in$' (§3.15). This still would not help the Student, since the case would then reduce to that of .4 in *n*3.452*a*, and as that note shows, still will not yield the 'No literate is a man' which the Student requires.

From the above it is evident that the example of the lightning is supposed to convey the notion of something indisputably unitary: the flash is temporally and spatially coextensive with the lightning, and *vice versa.* Hence neither word, in this context, involves that shadow of difference which would diffract that unity into two diverse objects. In what way, then, does the Student claim to have induced such a shadow of difference between the essences of *man* and *literate*? This question points to the probable purpose of his two sets of syllogistic premisses (3.53) each having a false member, and each yielding the conclusion that 'literate' is predicable of no man (3.5333). Their point would appear to be the demonstration that sets of circumstances can at least be specified under which this desired conclusion *could* be inferred, and that this is sufficient to differentiate the essences of *man* and *literate* (3.542). The Student falsely assumes that this non-identity has the diversifying effect mentioned above, and so reaches his desired conclusion (3.541). It may hence be assumed that the case of '*fulgor*' $\ominus$ 'lightning' and '*splendor*' $\ominus$ 'flash' which is now being contrasted with that of 'man' and 'literate' is such that there are no specifiable circumstances under which they would be differentiated.

Quite apart from the commonsense reasons which can be given as to why '*fulgor*' $\ominus$ 'lightning' and '*splendor*' $\ominus$ 'flash' should function in the way described in the last paragraph, one may also consider the rather special status which the earlier medieval tradition assigned to parts of speech having to do with light – a status which was already disappearing in the thirteenth century. The way in which Anselm talks about '*lux*' $\ominus$ 'light' in *Monologion* 6 as being something which is '*per seipsam et ex seipsa*' $\ominus$ 'by itself and from itself', and his analogy between '*lux*' $\ominus$ 'light' and '*essentia*' $\ominus$ 'essence' (*S* I 20.15.16), are sufficient to indicate that '*lux*' $\ominus$ 'light' could be considered as having reference to an essence, a kind of object. The Student is making the assumption, which Anselm does not accept, that '*homo*' $\ominus$ 'man' and '*grammaticus*' $\ominus$ 'literate' can function in the same way as '*lux*' $\ominus$ 'light' was supposed to do. Hence the significance of the Student's words at the close of the present passage:

For the purpose of proving that the *essence of man* is not the *essence of literate* their meaning does indeed have a common term.

Ad hoc probandum quia essentia hominis non est essentia grammatici, habet earum significatio communem terminum (3.542, 3.543).

The Student does imagine that he is dealing with essences, viewed as individual unitary objects. Hence it is that the supplementation, on questionable grounds, of '$\sim (a \bigcirc b)$' by 'ob(a)' and 'ob(b)' as in .4 above, would indeed lead to results precisely in accordance with the Student's misplaced wishes.

Again, the words '*fulgor*' and '*splendor*' tended to be associated with discourse on the heavenly bodies:

He lends brightness to the moon and stars, as also does Christ, shining in his own strength.	*lunae et stellis ... fulgorem praestat, ita et Christus propria virtute splendens.*

These are the words of Raban Maur (*PL* 111, 268A). Lanfranc, in his commentary on St. Paul's second epistle to the Thessalonicans, interjects '*Fulgebant iusti, sicut sol, in regno Patris mei*' ⊖ 'The just shall shine forth their rays as the sun, in the kingdom of my Father' (*PL* 150, 341). One also finds the further association of '*splendor*' with '*essentia*' or '*substantia*' (and the latter '*solet dici essentia*' ⊖ 'is usually said to be substance', says Anselm: *S* I 45.14). Thus on the '*Qui cum sit splendor gloriae*' ⊖ 'He who, as he is the brightness of glory' of the first epistle to the Hebrews, Lanfranc interjects:

proceeding from the Father, as brightness from the sun; not diverse from the Father, but having the same substance.	*procedens a Patre, ut splendor a sole, non tamen diversum, sed eamdem habens substantiam: PL* 150, 375

And St. Ambrose's comment on the same words, given in the same place, runs:

It is indeed rightly that he calls him 'brightness' since he is the light of the world, giving glimpses of the Father. It is by his brightness that he declares the unity of essence, and shows unto us two persons in glory and brightness.	*Merito autem splendorem eum dicit, qui est lux mundi, lumen de lumine, insinuans nobis Patrem. Per splendorem autem unitatem declaravit essentiae, et duas aperuit personas in gloria et splendore.*

These associations, coupled with the notion that light is propagated instantaneously, confirm the interpretation given above of the Student's coupling of '*fulgor*' ⊖ 'lightning', '*splendor*' ⊖ 'flash', and '*essentia*' ⊖ 'essence', and tend to suggest that the case of the lightening and its flash which has been chosen for the translation of his remarks conveys about as near an approximation as can nowadays be given of the situation which they are intended to express.

Anselm's remarks on *splendor* ⊖ brightness and *calor* ⊖ heat in *De Processione Spiritus Sancti* 8 (*S* II 199.25–201.9, and footnotes) extend the scope of kindred notions then current on such matters.

*n*3.540*c*: premisses in question ⊖ *propositionibus*] '*Propositio*' is here being once again used to mean 'premiss' and not in its more specialised sense of 'major premiss' (cf. *n*3.531*a*). To which premisses is reference being made here? If the suggestions made in *n*3.540*b* are correct, it looks as though the reference is complex, in that it is primarily to 3.501 and 3.502, but that these have to be considered as susceptible of the final modifications effected in 3.53, hence the '*si earum vis bene consideretur*' ⊖ 'if their import is carefully scrutinised' which next follows.

*n*3.543*a*: literate ⊖ *grammatici*] As to why this proposition should be supposed to follow from 3.501 and 3.502, as modified in 3.53, see *n*3.540*b*.

The expression

.1 $\sim(\mathrm{Cl}[\![\mathbf{h}]\!] \in \mathrm{Cl}[\![\mathbf{g}]\!])$ (cf. §3.14, §3.15)

might be one way of representing the form of the present assertion, and it is only owing to the Student's mistaken assumption that the assertion is of the type:

.2 $\sim(a = b) \,.\, \mathrm{ob}(a) \,.\, \mathrm{ob}(b)$

that he is able to infer 3.541 ('No man is literate') from it; cf. *n*3.540*b*. This explains the Tutor's next move (3.61), which is to introduce the case of '*homo*' ⊖ 'man' and '*lapis*' ⊖ 'stone', in respect of which an expression like .1 holds, and which is thus far similar to the case of '*homo*' ⊖ 'man' and '*grammaticus*' ⊖ 'literate', yet which also differs from the latter in that a universal negative proposition ('No man is a stone') dissociating the two is in fact true. The introduction of '*aliquo modo*' ⊖ 'in some way' and '*quolibet modo*' ⊖ 'in any way you please' into the sentences undergoing analysis (3.63) is an extremely effective way of bringing out the difference between these cases.

*n*3.543*b*: common term ⊖ *communem terminum*] The 'common term' in question can only be that revealed by the manipulations at 3.531, 3.532, or 3.5331, 3.5332. Now this common term is here stated to be in respect of meaning (*significatio*) only. This is doubtless a conscious contrast with what obtained in 3.52, where the premisses were interpreted '*secundum veritatem*' ⊖ 'with respect to the truth', and did not yield a common term. Only when false premisses were engendered (3.53) could such a common term be found. There is hence here, in the coupling of the common term with *significatio* ⊖ meaning, a presupposed contrast between truth and meaning. There may also be, with the reference to '*essentia*' ⊖ 'essence', '*significatio*' ⊖ 'meaning', and 'common term', an imitation of, and (as the Student thinks) an improvement upon, the Tutor's technique in 3.4, where discussion of the *esse* ⊖ being of *homo* ⊖ man and *grammaticus* ⊖ literate led to the production of a common term.

*n*3.611*a*: rationality ⊖ *rationalitate*] This thesis encapsulates the remark made by Boethius when commenting on Porphyry's definition of the predicable '*accidens*' ⊖ 'accident' (*BCP* 134A) quoted in *n*3.101*a*.

*n*3.621*a*: in no sense ⊖ *nullo modo*] The '*nullo modo*' ⊖ 'in no way' (or 'in no sense') is here an allusion to the possibility of interpositions of the type which occur in 3.6333.6334. A comparison between 3.6331.6332 and 3.6333.6334 makes this quite clear.

The immediate point of calling attention to this strong sense of 3.6121, and contrasting it with 3.622, is to bring out the difference between the present case and that of *man* and *literate*. Were 3.622 ('A stone is not the same as a man') accepted as an interpretation of 3.6121, this would afford no contrast with the results obtained in 3.4, and no further move could be made when, in 3.631, the Student analyses 3.61 in the way that 3.10 was analysed at 3.31.

The cases of '*homo*' ⊖ 'man' and '*lapis*' ⊖ 'stone' are used throughout Boethius' *Introductio ad Syllogismos Categoricos*, e.g. *B* 777C, 779C, 781B, 782B, 783A, 783B, 784A, 784B, 786C, 786D, 787B, 789D, 791A, 791D, 792A, 792D, 793A. Boethius speaks of that which is '*tale quod subiecto nullo modo possit obtingere, ut lapis homini*' ⊖ 'such that it can in no way happen to apply to the subject, as *stone* to *man*'. Again, '*homo*' ⊖ 'man' and '*lapis*' ⊖ 'stone' are said to provide a case in which '*id de subiecto praedicetur quod … numquam subiecto valeat convenire, ut lapis homini*' ⊖ 'that is predicated of the subject which is never able to suit that subject, as *stone* of *man*': *B* 786D. He mentions also things '*quae numquam de subiecto possunt vere praedicari, ut lapis de homine*' ⊖ 'which can never truly be predicated of the subject, as *stone* of *man*': *B* 781B. The '*nullo modo*' ⊖ 'in no way' of the present expression is also to be found in the commentary on the *Categoriae*: *definitio vero albi ad corpus nullo modo dicitur: album namque vel corpus una ratione utraque definiri non possunt* ⊖ In contrast the definition of *white* is in no sense asserted of *body*, for *white* and *body* cannot be defined in terms of a single account: *BC* 185B.

'*Nullus lapis aliquo modo est homo*' ⊖ 'No stone is in some sense a man' is an alternative expression of the present proposition (3.63221). In this connection it is noteworthy that *BSE* 1011D–1012B opposed '*aliquo modo*' ⊖ 'in some sense' to '*simpliciter*' ⊖ 'just/only', an opposition which may be reflected in the relation between the sentences containing '*aliquo modo*' ⊖ 'in some sense' and '*quolibet modo*' ⊖ 'in any sense' of the present part of the dialogue (3.621, 3.632, 3.633) and the later expression of the outcome of the discussion (3.9), where '*simpliciter*' ⊖ 'just / only' occurs (3.911, 3.921, 3.922, 3.931).

*n*3.622*a*: man ⊖ *homo*] This sentence is, of course, true of *lapis* ⊖ stone and *homo* ⊖ man, but is not so strong an expression as 3.621, which is also inferrable from 3.611, 3.612. It corresponds to 3.452 ('*grammaticus non est idem quod homo*' ⊖ 'A literate is not the same as a man') but whereas the latter is all that can be drawn from 3.101 and 3.102 and their analyses at 3.311, 3.312, and 3.4, that stronger expression '*nullo modo lapis est homo*' ⊖ 'A stone is in no sense a man' (3.621) is shown by 3.632 to follow from 3.611, 3.612. In contrast, the corresponding stronger expression '*nullo modo grammaticus est homo*' ⊖ 'A literate is in no sense a man' (or a literary variant thereof as in 3.6341) is shown by 3.633 not to follow from 3.101 and 3.102 or any further analyses thereof.

*n*3.6312*a*: rationality ⊖ *rationalitate*] The quantifiers 'No' and 'Every' are supplied by the Tutor in his restatement of these premisses in 3.632.

*n*3.6313*a*: securely established ⊖ *rata conclusio*] The proposition 'No stone is a man' was used as a stock example by Boethius (cf. *n*3.621*a*). In Anselm's *De Veritate* it is used as an example of a sentence which is not only well-formed, but also is true in such a way that it can never be used to make a false statement; *HL* §8.1.

*n*3.6313*b*: might mislead me ⊖ *me deciperet ignoravi*] The Student imagines that syllogism 3.61 has been introduced as an example of a syllogism of the same form as his (3.10); yet 3.61, in spite of its factually secure conclusion is, he believes, refutable (3.631). How then can his own more dubious syllogism (3.10) stand? This, however, is not the point, as is made clear in 3.632: the distinctions made at 3.621.622 were already a hint that another analysis (3.6321.6322) of 3.61 is possible – an analysis of a sort inapplicable to the Student's original syllogism (3.10), as is shown at 3.633. The general aim is to show that the non-identity of *man* and *literate* is of a sort differing from the non-identity of *man* and *stone*.

*n*3.6321*a*: rationality ⊖ *rationalitate*] As the arguments from this point up to the end of 3.6341 are of considerable interest and complexity, it will be well to comprise them in a unified survey, so that their import may be better understood.

First the steps leading up to the present stage may be noted. After the Student's abortive attempt to obtain the conclusion 'No man is literate' by means of the analogy with the case of the lightning and the flash (3.54) the Tutor replies by bringing forward a case, that of *stone* and *man*, in which 'No stone is a man' (compare 3.113) and not merely 'A stone is not the same as a man' (compare 3.452) does in truth hold. The first enuciation of these *man/stone* premisses, following the pattern of 3.102, 3.101, runs as follows:

.1A	*Omnis lapis potest intelligi sine rationalitate*	
.1B	Every stone can be understood without rationality	(3.612)
.2A	*Nullus homo potest intelligi sine rationalitate*	
.2B	No man can be understood without rationality	(3.611)

From these one should be able to derive:

.3A	*Nullus lapis est homo*	
.3B	No stone is a man	
.3C	$\mathbf{l} \not\subset \mathbf{h}$	(3.6121, §3.5)

The sense of .3 is said to be:

.4A	*Nullo modo lapis est homo*	
.4B	In no way is a stone a man	
.4C	$[a]: a \in \mathbf{l} \,.\supset .\, \sim (a \in \mathbf{h})$	(3.621)

Another way of expressing .4, as it later turns out, is as follows:

.5A	*Nullus lapis aliquo modo est homo*

.5B No stone is in some way a man

.5C $\sim([\exists a] \,.\, a \in \mathbf{l} \,.\, a \in \mathbf{h})$ (3.63221)

However, it is not yet clear how .3, .4, or .5 can be inferred from .1 and .2, since it would appear that use of the repetitive procedure exemplified in 3.311, 3.312, could block any such conclusion (3.631). But now the full purpose of the introduction of .1 and .2 becomes apparent: they *can* be restated in a fashion which results in true sentences, whereas 3.102, 3.101 cannot be thus restated. Hence .1 not only can, but ought (3.6320), to be taken to assert:

.6A *Omnis lapis quolibet modo potest intelligi sine rationalitate*

.6B Every stone can in any way be understood without rationality (3.6322)

Likewise .2 should be expressed:

.7A *Nullus homo potest aliquo modo intelligi sine rationalitate*

.7B No man can in some way be understood without rationality (3.6321)

And from .6 and .7 one can indeed infer .3, .4 or .5 (3.6320–3.63221).

We have now arrived at the material at present undergoing consideration. The first point made is that in contrast to what holds in the case of .6, 3.102 cannot truly be restated (following .6) thus:

.8A *Omnis homo valet quolibet modo intelligi sine grammatica*

.8B Every man can in any way be understood without literacy (3.6332)

Neither can 3.101 be truly restated, after the manner of .7, in the following way:

.9A *Nullus grammaticus intelligi valet aliquo modo sine grammatica*

.9B No literate can in some way be understood without literacy (3.6331)

For in opposition to .8 the following is true:

.10A *Nullus homo potest intelligi grammaticus sine grammatica*

.10B No man can be understood to be literate without literacy (3.6334)

Likewise, in opposition to .9, the following is true:

.11A *Omnis qui grammaticus est potest intelligi homo sine grammatica*

.11B Every literate being can be understood to be a man without literacy (3.6333)

Hence 3.113, or forms corresponding to .3, .4, or .5 cannot be deduced from 3.102 and 3.101.

What now is the relation between *man* and *literate* in .10 and between *literate* and *man* in .11? In particular, what more can be made of the assertion in .11 that every literate *can be understood to be* a man? The connection between 'can be understood' and definition has already been exploited in *n*3.431*a* and *n*3.44*a* by the use of the functor 'Cl⟦ ⟧' defined at §3.14. The same sort of connection, namely that between *understanding* and *signification*, also noted in *n*3.101*a*, can now be brought to bear on .11. For later in the dialogue (4.23) Anselm is to introduce the distinction between precisive (*per se*) and oblique (*per aliud*) signification. In particular he is going to say that 'literate' signifies literacy in the *per se* fashion, but *man* only obliquely. The particular kind of oblique signification in question here, since we are dealing with names, is that of appellation, or reference: 'literate' refers to man, although it cannot properly be said to signify *man* (4.233). Without at this point going further into the meaning of this terminology, it is clear that this distinction immediately gives a sense in which every literate can be understood to be man: 'literate' signifies men obliquely and to be man does not require literacy (3.41). Hence the 'can' of 'can be understood' in .11 merely conveys that there is some mode of signification (*per se* or oblique) according to which 'literate' signifies man, but in view of 3.41, being a man does not demand literacy; hence the truth of .11. However, .10 is a reminder, in view of 3.42, (being literate requires literacy), that once it is granted that a man is literate, then literacy inevitably must be attributed to him. Alternatively, the theories of *man* and *literate* (and hence of literacy) are diverse (4.24, 4.3), hence .11. At the same time the theory of *literate* must involve literacy, hence .10.

This does not, of course, solve all the problems about sentences of the form now being considered. For instance, why will it not do to adduce:

.12 Every man can be understood to be animal without rationality

as an exception to .7 above? The reason probably lies in Anselm's insistence that 'man' is both appellative and significative of its components *as a single whole* (*ut unum*) (4.231), so that the referents of 'man' are not to be notionally dissociated in such a way that .12 holds. In contrast, .11 holds because 'literate' does *not* signify or refer to its significates or referents *ut unum* ⊖ as a single whole, as 4.232 makes clear.

*n*3.6322*a*: rationality ⊖ *rationalitate*] The phraseology of these propositions is redolent of that to be found at certain points in *Monologion*, e.g. Ch. IV: *nullo modo intelligi potest ut quod aliquid est, sit per nihil* ⊖ it can in no way be understood that that which is something has its being by means of nothing (*S* I 19.23.24, see also 20.11.12). For discussion of the present assertion see *n*3.6321*a*.

*n*3.63221*a*: man ⊖ *homo*] From the concluding remarks of 3.6320, and from 3.621, 3.6341, it is clear that this conclusion amounts to the assertion that a stone is in no sense a man, or that a stone can in no sense be a man. Not even in *usus loquendi* ⊖ the common course of utterance does one ever use 'man' as a name by which to call a stone (cf. 4.233, 4.2341, as well as 3.633).

In twelfth-century logic similar examples show that the use of '*nullo modo*' ⊖ 'in no way' often indicated that remote (i.e. incompatible) subject-matter was in question:

That material is remote which involves the predication of that which is in no way in the subject, as in 'Socrates is a stone'.	*remota est illa materia quando id quod predicatur nullo modo inest subiecto, ut 'Socrates est lapis'* (*DLM* II–I 152).
Remote matter is involved in the predication of that which in no way can be in the subject, as in 'A man is a stone'.	*remota est cui predicatum nullo modo potest inesse subiecto, ut 'homo est lapis'* (*DLM* II-II 81).

*n*3.6330*a*: one cannot assert ⊖ *non potest dici*] The '*non potest dici*' ⊖ 'it cannot be said' does not here mean that 3.6331 and 3.6332 are nonsense, as the allusion to truth in the previous sentence shows, and hence amounts to 'it is not true that'. '*Potest dici*' ⊖ 'It can be said' is however used in *Monologion* 8 in connection with meaning, as opposed to truth:

There is another meaning which can indeed be stated, but which cannot be true, however.	*Alio significatio est, quae dici quidem potest, vera tamen esse non potest:* *S* I, 23.13.14

The notion of implicit truth, to be brought out from its hiding place by correct analysis, and which occurs in the present sentences, is also well in evidence in Anselm's statements on the outcome of the use of '*facere*' ⊖ 'to do' as a model for sentence-analysis; these statements are quoted at length in *HL* §2.12.2 and *HL* §4.

*n*3.6331*a*: literacy ⊖ *grammatica*] This falsehood is posited as an analysis of 3.101 so that the exception which falsifies it may be advanced (3.6333). For detailed discussion see *n*3.6321*a*.

*n*3.6332*a*: literacy ⊖ *grammatica*] This second falsehood is posited as an analysis of 3.102 so that the exception which falsifies it may be advanced (3.6334). If these exceptions were not forthcoming, then since 3.6331.6332 would then be true and have a common term, 3.6341 would follow. For discussion see *n*3.6321*a*.

*n*3.6333*a*: literacy ⊖ *grammatica*] In falsification of 3.6331 it is here pointed out, in effect, that the being of which 'literate' is appellative, namely man (cf. 4.233) can be understood without literacy, in the sense not only that *being a man* is not *being a literate* (cf. 3.431) but also that the theories of *man* and *literate* are diverse (4.24, 4.3, cf. §4). For discussion, see *n*3.6321*a*. Note that 'Everything which' has been preferred to 'Everyone who' as the translation of '*Omnis qui*', in accordance with the points made in *n*4.801*c*. See also *n*3.701*a*.

*n*3.6334*a*: literacy ⊖ *grammatica*] This assertion falsifies 3.6332 by showing the circumstances under which a man cannot be understood without literacy, i.e. insofar as he is literate. Man is the being of which 'literate' happens to be appellative (4.233) and *being literate* requires literacy (3.42); alternatively, literacy is involved in the theory of literate (cf. §4). For discussion see *n*3.6321*a*.

*n*3.6341*a*: man ⊖ *hominem*] This sentence could only have followed had the exceptions (3.6333, 3.6334) to 3.6331 and 3.6332 not been forthcoming. As it stands it is a literary variant of the forms exemplified by 3.63221 and 3.621 – a variant designed to express a stronger form of diversity than '*lapis non est idem quod homo*' ⊖ 'A stone is not the same as a man' (3.622) or '*Grammaticus non est idem quod homo*' ⊖ 'A literate is not the same as a man' (3.452). Although Anselm may not have been familiar with Aristotle's *Topica*, nevertheless at least one passage of the latter on the various senses of 'same' and 'different' (*B* 961B–D) may be noted as a statement of some of the problems with which Anselm is here grappling.

*n*3.701*a*: man ⊖ *hominis*] For an analysis and discussion of this sentence, see *n*3.811*a*. The policy adopted in translation accords with that enunciated in *n*4.801*c* (cf. *n*3.6333*a*). The remainder of the assertions made by the Student in the present section of the dialogue (3.7) do not receive detailed treatment in *n*3.811*a* as they represent a by-play in relation to the main discussion. The latter resumes its course in 3.801 with a discussion of the sentence (3.431) on which the assertion now receiving comment (3.701) is itself based. However, comment on the content of some of the points of the remainder of 3.7 is made in the notes which now follow.

*n*3.7111*a*: man ⊖ *homo*] The general form of 3.71 and 3.7111 is that of a valid hypothetical syllogism in *modus tollendo tollens*. The present conclusion is an interpretation of the negation of '*homo sequitur grammaticum*' ⊖ '*man* follows *literate*', and as such a negation appears to be quite in order. Within this generally valid framework, however, the analysis of what is said calls for a great degree of subtlety which may have had some counterpart in Anselm's intuitions, since he regards the argument of 3.7 as invalid (cf. 3.8). Unfortunately he refutes 3.7, not by detailed analysis, but by means of counter-examples drawn from the familiar theories of *man* and *animal* (cf. 3.800), which are directed only against the starting point, and not against the details of 3.7; hence no record of his opinions of those details is presented.

Viewed in isolation, 3.71 would appear to have the form of the true thesis:

.1 $\mathbf{g} \subset \mathbf{h}\,.\supset .\,\mathrm{Cl}[\![\mathrm{trm}\langle\gamma\rangle]\!] \in \subset[\![\mathrm{trm}\langle\alpha\rangle]\!]$ (§3.4.11.12.14.48)

However, since the consequent of 3.71 (and hence of .1) is apparently taken by the Student to be falsifiable by reference back to the '*qui habet essentiam grammatici non ideo necessario habet essentiam hominis*' ⊖ 'Whatsoever is essentially literate need not therefore be essentially man' of 3.701, it looks as though '*essentia hominis*' ⊖ 'essence of man' and '*essentia grammatici*' ⊖ 'essence of literate' in 3.71 are elliptical expressions used instead of '*qui habet essentiam grammatici*' ⊖ 'that which is essentially literate' and '*qui habet essentiam hominis*' ⊖ 'that which is essentially man'. (On the translations here suggested, see *n*4.801*c*). There may also have been a systematic connection between the one form of expression and the other, according to Anselm's way of thinking, and it would not be too difficult to fill in the details of such a connection. However, assuming the ellipsis mentioned, 3.71 becomes (instead of .1):

.2 $$\mathbf{g} \subset \mathbf{h} \,.\supset.\, \mathrm{trm}\langle\gamma\rangle \subset \mathrm{trm}\langle\alpha\rangle \qquad (\S 3.4.11)$$

which once again is true. Given the negation of the consequent of .2, a negation of its antecedent, i.e.

.3 $$\sim(\mathbf{g} \subset \mathbf{h})$$

does indeed follow, as 3.7111 claims (*Non est omnis grammaticus homo* ⊖ it's not that every literate is a man). But 3.7111 is false, and the fault lies in 3.701, i.e.

.4 $$\sim(\mathrm{Cl}[\![\mathbf{g}]\!] \in \mathrm{Cl}[\![\mathbf{h}]\!]) \,.\supset.\, \sim(\mathrm{trm}\langle\gamma\rangle \subset \mathrm{trm}\langle\alpha\rangle) \qquad (\S 3.15.14.11.4)$$

This is plainly not a thesis, since its antecedent is true and its consequent false. In view of this complexity and the various interpretational possibilities here open, the course taken by the Tutor in 3.8, namely a discussion of the consequences drawable from 3.431 is hence the most obvious and economical form of attack on the arguments of 3.7, although, as already mentioned, this form of attack leaves in the dark his opinion as to the details of 3.7. 3.431 itself is represented by the antecedent of .4.

The general form exemplified in 3.71 and 3.711, namely the hypothetical syllogism, to which attention has already been called, was frequently discussed by Boethius, who also wrote a treatise on such syllogisms (*BSH*). In Bk. IV of his commentary on Cicero's *Topica* he discusses the relation between categorial and hypothetical syllogistic premisses (*B* 1128D–1130B). In Bk. V he describes the general form here used (*Modus tollendo tollens*); *B* 1133C, cf. *BTC* 1133D; *BDT* Lib. 1, esp. *B* 1178D–1179D. It is, of course, in *BSH* (*B* 831–876C) that such forms are exhaustively treated. However, the use of hypotheticals as antecedent and consequent of a hypothetical form, as in 3.71, is an added complication representing an advance on the materials thus far mentioned. For examples nearer to Anselm's own time see, for instance, *DLM* II–I 133–9 and Bk. 6 of *G*.

*n*3.72*a*: feature ⊖ *ratio*] The formal purpose of the whole of the present remark is clear enough, and is further discussed in the next note (*n*3.72*b*). However, the way in which '*ratio*' ⊖ 'reason' figures in this remark is far from clear. especially as, in Boethius' terms, '*ratio*' can be used in many ways:

'*Ratio*' has many senses. There is the *ratio* (reason) which pertains to the mind, and there is the *ratio* which pertains to arithmetic; there is the *ratio* (reason) constituted by the nature of a thing, which is, as it were, its origin, and there is the *ratio* (account) which is given in definitions or descriptions.	*Ratio ... multimodo dicitur. Est enim ratio animae, et est ratio computandi: est ratio naturae, ipsa nimirum similitudo nascentium; est ratio quae in definitionibus vel descriptionibus redditur: BC* 166A.

The Student's present assertion could involve a derivative of the penultimate sense mentioned here: the nature of *literate* has some feature (here denoted by '*ratio*') which explains why either all literates are men or none are. This means, in effect, that a satisfactory theory of *literate* will settle the question one way or another. There is, however, a third alternative, i.e. that *literate* may be theoretically indifferent with respect to its referents, as the Tutor is later to claim (cf. 4.24121).

The 'all or nothing' effect claimed by the Student was said by William of Sherwood to be obtainable in propositions involving 'natural matter' (*KSL* 33–4). See also Aquinas' explanation of the way in which 'indefinite' propositions, normally interpreted as sub-contraries, can in fact be contraries (*n*3.800*b*).

*n*3.72*b*: none are ⊖ *nullus*] The first clause of this assertion ('*cum omnibus grammaticis una sit ratio cur sint homines*' ⊖ 'as every literate has some single feature which makes him susceptible of being a man') is an attempt to change the relation which would otherwise hold between contrary propositions such as 'Every literate is a man' and 'No literate is a man'. Clearly both members of such a pair cannot be true together, and they are such that *if* the one is true, the other is false. The conditions under which both may be false, conditions which the Student wishes to exclude, occur when the terms involved are such that some intermediate state of affairs can hold between the extremes represented by such contraries:

Again, if the meaningful utterances are susceptible of a certain intermediate relation, there is no necessity that the one should be true and the other false. For example, consider 'Every man is just' and 'No man is just'. Here the intermediate situation is possible, since it is neither the case that no man is just (since some are) nor that every man is just (since some are not). Hence they can both be false, since a corresponding affirmation and negation are respectively available. Neither is it true that either every man is just or no man is just ... Under these circumstances both the universal affirmative and the universal negative can be false.

Adhuc si ea quae significant habent inter se aliquam medietatem, unam veram, unam falsam esse non est necesse, ut in eo quod est, 'omnis homo iustus est', 'nullus homo iustus est'. Quoniam potest quaedam esse medietas, ut nec nullus homo iustus sit, cum sit quidam, nec omnis homo iustus sit, cum non sit quidam. Et possunt utraeque falsae et affirmatio et negatio reperiri. Neque enim verum est aut omnem hominem iustum esse aut nullum hominem iustum esse ... Sic ergo universalis affirmatio et universalis negatio utraeque falsae esse possunt: BDIG 469C–470A; cf. *BISC* 770D.

Alternatively, and in terms of the description of the situation given in *BISC* 770C–771C, if one can say that there is either an inseparable connection between subject and predicate ('*si a subjecto quod praedicatur non potest segregari*') or a necessary incompatibility between subject and predicate ('*si quod non potest fieri praedicetur*') then only the possibility of one member of a contrary pair's being true while the other is false remains, i.e. they cannot both be false. The Student's remarks are designed to leave only such inseparable connection or necessary incompatibility between 'literate' and 'man', thereby cutting out the possibility of the '*medietas*' ⊖ 'intermediate situation' of which Boethius speaks. Thus is produced the exclusive disjunction contained in the last clause of the assertion (3.72) now being considered. It may be recalled that '*iustus*' ⊖ 'just' which Boethius here uses to exemplify the case which the Student wishes to exclude, i.e. the case in which both contraries can be false, resembles 'literate' in that it too is a paronym.

*n*3.721*a*: not every ⊖ *non omnis*] This is a reference to 3.7111.

*n*3.7211*a*: therefore no literate is a man ⊖ *nullus igitur*] This is the conclusion of a valid disjunctive syllogism in *modus tollendo ponens* having the last sentence of 3.72 as its major and the '*non omnis*' (i.e. 3.7111) of 3.721 as its minor. Its major is, however, false; cf. *n*3.72*b*.

*n*3.7211*b*: yielded up ⊖ *dedisti*] It may be recalled that having, in 3.32, refuted the Student's syllogism (3.10) the Tutor hinted that some conclusion could nevertheless be drawn from its premisses, and then confirmed this hint by inferring '*esse grammatici non est esse hominis*' ⊖ 'being literate is not being a man' from them. However, he gave a very strong demonstration (3.6) that 'No literate is a man' could not be inferred directly from the analyses there given of the Student's premisses. It is to this demonstration that the '*acute abstulisti*' ⊖ 'you cunningly removed' of the present passage refers. The Student now claims to have obtained 'No literate is a man' from 'To be literate is-not to be man' (3.431), and hence, by this indirect route, from his original premisses (3.10). It is to this claim that '*auferendo acutius dedisti*' ⊖ 'you even more ingeniously yielded up for the taking' refers. In other words, the Tutor's hint in 3.32 has now been taken to point to the method just used by the Student to obtain the conclusion he required.

*n*3.800*a*: false opinion ⊖ *falsitatem*] In other words, certain theorems of the theories of *man* and *animal* are sufficiently well-established to act as a check on inferential forms; should one of the latter lead to a thesis incompatible with the theories mentioned, then a verification of the cogency of the form in question is called for (cf. §4).

*n*3.800*b*: by definition ⊖ *definitione*] The words here used, namely '*esse uniuscuisque rei in definitione consistat*' ⊖ 'what is involved in the being of any so-and-so is expressible by definition' are a reproduction of Boethius' statement that '*Definitio est oratio quae uniuscuiusque rei quidem esse designat*' ⊖ 'A definition is an expression pointing to what is really involved in being any given thing'; *BDT* 1196C. The latter formula has been slightly varied by Anselm's borrowing from another of Boethius' statements which occurs a few lines earlier, i.e. '*Totum autem uniuscuiusque rei in definitione constat*' ⊖ 'The whole of any given thing is comprised in its definition'. (The '*constat*' of *BDT* harmonises with the eleventh-century Bodleian MS (Rawlinson A392) of this stretch of Anselm's text which is cited by Schmitt in a footnote (*S* I 152) but not adopted in his edition, wherein '*consistat*' is preferred). Statements which connect '*esse*' ⊖ 'being' and definition are to be found elsewhere in Boethius, e.g.

What, then, is the being of a thing? Only its definition. In answer to the query 'What is it?' posed in respect of any given thing, whoever wants to show what the being in question is, states the definition.	*Quid est autem esse rei? Nihil aliud nisi definitio. Unicuique enim rei interrogatae quid est, si quis quod est esse monstrare voluerit, definitionem dicit: BCP* 129D.

This last extract occurs in close proximity to the sentences on which Anselm draws to express himself in 4.2411.

It is in *De Divisione* as well as in his commentary on Cicero's *Topica* that Boethius treats directly of definition. The work entitled *Liber de Definitione* (*B* 891–910) is a less full treatment now attributed to Victorinus. It nevertheless contains material more or less similar to parts of Boethius' Commentary on Cicero's *Topica* and hence will be referred to below along with genuine Boethian texts.

By 'definition' Boethius usually intends what would nowadays be called the *definiens* (as opposed to the *definiendum*), and Anselm follows him in this, as the next words of our dialogue show: the definition of *man* is *rational mortal animal* and not, according to the text (3.801) the whole equation of *rational mortal animal* with *man*. It is in Boethius's sense, then, that a definition may be said to signify neither truth nor falsehood (*APA* 51), although as Aquinas recognises, it is always possible to use the *definiens* to form a true proposition:

One may say that although a definition taken in itself is not an actual proposition, it is nevertheless virtually a proposition, because once the definition is known it is obvious that the definition can truly be predicated of its subject.	*Potest dici quod licet definitio in se non sit propositio in actu est tamen in virtute propositio quia cognita difinitione, apparet definitionem de subiecto vere praedicari: APA* 52.

In what follows, therefore, the word 'definition' will be used in the commentary to refer to a proposition introducing a *definiendum* by means of a *definiens*, notwithstanding the fact that the authors to whom reference is made use '*definitio*' ⊖ 'definition' in respect of the *definiens* only.

To reconstruct in full the rules of definition, explicit and implicit, presupposed by Boethius, would require a separate work. All that can be given here are fragmentary indications of the material that has to be taken into account, and of the directions in which the central problems lie. The sentences initially quoted above make plain that for Boethius definitions involve a statement of the *esse* ⊖ being of the *definiendum*

(*B* 1196C). This statement is equivalential in form, as is evident from the words of the same author when commenting in Cicero's *Topica*, and describing the effect of the constitutive characteristic (cf. *n*4.22*d*):

In order, therefore, to reduce the extent of *animal* and obtain an equivalent of *man*, we add the constitutive characteristic .... And so I assert that *man* is a *rational animal*. But the latter is not yet the equivalent of *man*, for there can be rational animals which are not men, as in the Platonists' doctrine concerning the stars. I therefore tack on yet another difference, on the assumption that the definition may in some way or another be reduced in extent so as to render the definition coextensive with *man*. I therefore add *mortal*, and assert *man* to be *rational mortal animal*; this yields equality with *man*.

Ut igitur minuatur animal et homini coaequetur, addimus differentiam ... Dico autem hominen esse animal rationale. Sed id nondum coaequatur ad hominem, possunt enim esse animalia rationabilia, sicut Platoni quoque de astris placet, quae homines non sunt. Addo igitur rursus aliam differentiam, si quoquo modo interum definitio contrahatur, ut fiat homini quod definitur aequale; adiungo igitur 'mortale', ac dico hominem esse animal rationale mortale, id aequatur ad hominem: *BTC* 1101C–D; cf. *n*3.8010*a*.

There are, says Boethius, many ways of giving definitions, but only 'substantial' definitions are properly so called:

Definitions can be contrived in various ways. Of these one is the right and complete way of defining and is called 'substantial'; the rest are not properly called definitions.

Multis namque modis fieri definitio potest. Inter quos unus est verus at que integer definitionis modus qui etiam substantialis dicitur; reliqui per abusionem definitiones vocantur: *BTC* 1096B.

Later he enlarges on this statement:

Definitions are such that some are properly so-called, others are only improperly so-called. Now definitions properly so-called are those which are composed of genus and constitutive characteristics, as in the case of the following: *man* is *rational mortal animal*. Here *animal* is the genus, whereas *rational* and *mortal* are the constitutive characteristics. Those definitions which are called 'definitions' not properly, but only improperly, are of two sorts; some only involve a single name, the others an explanatory or elucidatory phrase.

Definitionum enim aliae proprie definitiones sunt, aliae abusivo nuncupantur modo. Ac propriae quidem definitiones sunt quae ex genere differentiisque consistunt, velut haec: Homo est animal rationale mortale, hic enim animal genus est: rationale vero et mortale differentiae. Earum vero definitionum quae non proprie sed abutendo definitiones vocantur, aliae sunt quae singulis nominibus denotantur, aliae vero quas explicat ac depromit oratio: *BTC* 1098D–1099A.

A list of the various types of definition improperly so called, drawn from Victorinus, then follows (*BTC* 1099A–1100B) and need not be reproduced here.

It is most important to note that such 'substantial' definitions need not be definitions of 'substances'; they are, as the last quotation explains, those which have genus and constitutive characteristic as parts: the definitions of accidents can be 'substantial' ones, as is made clear in the preliminary explanation of 'substantial' which is given in the *Liber de Definitione*:

The nature of substantiality is to be explained elsewhere. In the meantime it suffices to note that a determinate and substantial definition is possible wherever a 'What is it?' question is raised in respect of something, insofar as we lay down (as has been said) a genus and annex thereto, in our expression, the constitutive characteristics. It would appear not to be amiss were an example to be given, so as to take us forward to the further obscure points. The question raised is as to what *man* is; in this case, of course, the genus is *animal*. When, then, I utter the word 'animal' in the course of a definition whereby I explain what *man* is, and then add to it the remainder of the definition, one then has a substantial definition. For in saying 'animal' I declared what the substance of *man* is. Again, when I ask what *white* or *black* is, were I to say '*White* is a colour', then once again, since *colour* is a genus relative to what I am asking about, i.e. white or black, one has a substantial definition which begins with the genus and couples it with the rest of the definition. It is this sort of definition which can be said to be substantial, proper, and complete.

Quid autem substantiale sit, alibi explicandum. Ad cognitionem interim illud accedat, quoties de aliquo quaeritur quid sit, tunc posse esse certam et substantialem definitionem, quoties eius rei de qua quaeritur, ut diximus, genus ponimus, et inde caetera per differentias in oratione subingimus. Non alienum videtur exemplum ponere, et sic reliqua quae sunt obscura transire. Quaeritur homo quid sit, huic utique genus est animal. Cum igitur in definitione quae explicabo quid sit homo, 'animal' dixeram, ac deinde reliqua connectam, erit substantialis definitio. Substantiam enim homini declaravi cum dixi 'animal'. Item cum quaero quid sit album aut nigrum, si dixero 'album est color', quia color genus est ad hoc de quo quaero, album vel nigrum, iam substantialis erit definitio quae incipit a genere, et sic caetera connectit. Haec substantialis esse dicetur, et haec propria, et haec integra: BDF 895D–896A.

From this it is evident that there can be substantial theories of accidents as well as of substances; *de subiecto* ⊖ of a subject predications, definitionally based, are possible even when the *subiectum* ⊖ subject is an accident such as a colour (cf. *n*4.101*a*).

This is confirmed in the first of the dialogues on Porphyry, where the genus/species scheme, so important in theory-formation (cf. *n*4.2411*h*) is stated to be applicable to any of the Aristotelian categories:

But in order to show that genera and species do not have to do merely with

Sed ut monstraret non in unis solis substantiis genera speciesque versari, sed

substances, but are related to the explication of all the categories, he gives an example not only of a substance, but also one which has to do with the remaining categories, i.e. those of the accidents. What does he say? 'And *white* is a species of colour'. Here we are dealing with the classification of an accident in the category of quality.

etiam in omnium praedicamentorum nuncupationibus esse connexa, non solius substantiae dedit exemplum sed etiam eius quod reliquum remanserat accidentis. Quid enim ait? 'Et album coloris speciem'. Quae sunt in accidentis divisione qualitatis: BDP 37D.

Again, the definitions of such things as virtues could not be discussed if definitions were of substances only (*BDT* 1188C–D), so that when Boethius remarks:

Only those things which relate to the substance of things are comprised within a definition. For a definition shows forth the substance; a definition is a complete showing of the substance.

Hi vero qui a substantia sunt, in sola definitione consistunt. Definitio enim substantiam monstrat, et substantiae integra demonstratio definitio est: BDT 1187A.

he should not be understood in any exclusive sense.

That 'substantial' definitions have that systematic structure which makes them the key to theory-formation is made very clear in Book II of the Commentary on Cicero's *Topica*, where *definitiones per divisionem* ⊖ divisive definitions and *definitiones per partitionem* ⊖ partitive definitions are distinguished: *aliae definitiones per divisionem, aliae per partitionem fiunt* ⊖ some definitions are effected divisively, other partitively; *BTC* 1094C. The *per divisionem* ⊖ divisive ones are those effected in accordance with the recommendations of the treatise *De Divisione* (cf. *n*4.2411*a*) and are therefore substantial (cf. e.g. *B* 1097C), while the *per partitionem* ⊖ partitive ones are more usually called 'descriptions': *et haec 'descriptio' nuncupatur* ⊖ and this is called a 'description'; *B* 1097A. One systematic difference between the two may be expressed as follows: if '*b*', '*c*', and '*d*' are names involved in the constitution of the *definiens* of a divisive definition, and '*a*' is the name of the *definiendum*, then '*b*', '*c*', and '*d*' each apply to *a*, whereas in the case of a partitive definition this is no so. Thus if *man* is defined as *rational mortal animal*, then 'rational', 'mortal', and 'animal' each apply to man; but if *house* is defined as *foundation, walls, and roof* (and this is a partitive definition, *B* 1097A) one cannot say that either 'foundation', 'wall', or 'roof' apply to the house; this, explains Boethius, is because the parts of a definition of the first kind are 'greater than' ('*maiores*') the *definiendum*, while this does not hold in respect of a definition of the second kind; *BTC* 1097 B–C. The senses of 'greater than', 'whole', and 'part', which occur in this passage require clarification in the light of *De Divisione* (cf. *n*4.2411*a*) for full understanding, and before assuming too quickly that Boethius is victim of an elementary confusion.

The distinction between definition properly so called and mere description is frequently enlarged on by Boethius in terms which once again confirm the systematic character of the first and the accidental nature of the second, e.g.

Definitions differs from description in that a definition involves a genus and differences, whereas a description circumscribes the notion of a thing by fabricating one characterisation either from various accidental features, or even by gathering together various characteristics constitutive of substances out of relation to their appropriate genus.	*Differt autem definitio a descriptione, quod definitio genus ac differentias sumit, descriptio subiecti intelligentiam claudit, quibusdam vel accidentibus efficientibus unam proprietatem, vel substanialibus differentiis praeter conveniens genus aggregatis: BDT* 1187B–C.

Abelard deals with this distinction in some detail; *A* 584–586.

Now although it has been made clear that those things which are categorised by Aristotle as substances and accidents can both be defined in principle, and hence can be the objects of theories, anything more than fragmentary detail on the topic of the definition of accidents seems to have been lacking in Boethius, and this would appear to have given rise to much discussion among logicians of the early middle ages, as is evidenced by the final paragraph of *De Grammatico*. The discussion becomes especially acute when the definition of paronyms is mooted, since these were a point of contention between logicians and grammarians. According to Aristotle, the representative of the logicians, paronyms signify accidents and just accidents: *nihil enim album significat quam qualitatem* ⊖ *white* signifies nothing but a quality, *BC* 194C; *Est igitur qualitas, ut album, quae semper sit in subiecto* ⊖ Thus we have a quality, such as *white*, which is always in a subject, *BC* 195A. In contrast, according to the grammarian Priscian all names (of which paronyms are a sub-class) signify *both* substance and quality (cf. *n*4.22*c*) and he even gives an example which suggests that '*grammaticus*', the problem-paronym of the present dialogue, should be classified as a common noun which signifies substance (cf. *n*4.2341*a*). The *De Grammatico* is itself part of the consequent debate, and Abelard, when dealing with the question of what exactly is being defined when paronyms ('*sumpti*') are the *definienda* (*A* 596–598) begins by recording the prominence of the debate:

I recall that among those who considered universals to be primary among things it was usual for there to be a great controversy concerning those definitions which involve paronyms, and as to exactly what things these should be held to signify.

At vero in his definitionibus quae sumptorum sunt vocabulorum, magna memini, quaestio solet esse ab his qui in rebus universalia primo loco ponunt, quarum significatarum rerum ipsae debeant dici: A 596.2.3.

Abelard, displaying the same consciousness of the distinction between paronyms and non-paronyms which is evinced in *De Grammatico* by Anselm, divides definitions into *definitiones secundum adiacentiam* ⊖ adjectival definitions and *definitions secundum substantiam* ⊖ substantival definitions; the first are concerned with paronyms, the second with substantives; *A* 595.32.39.

It may well be that the recovery by the Latin West of the whole Aristotelian *corpus*, and with it Aristotle's *Metaphysica*, was later to sensibly affect and advance the discussion, since it is from Book E Ch. 1 (1025^{b} 30) of that work that Aquinas apparently draws his typical example of the definition of accidents, and the notion that in such a definition the subject of the accident stands '*quasi genus*' ⊖ 'in the style of a genus' and the accident itself '*quasi differentia*' ⊖ 'in the style of a constitutive characteristic', although in certain other ways of expressing the definition things may go the other way:

As in defining all accidents some subject must be posited, it is hence necessary in the case of those names which signify the accident abstractly that their definitions should involve the accident stated in the nominative case in the style of a genus, but the subject of the accident in some other case, in the style of a characteristic, as when one asserts 'Snubness is a concavity of the nose'. In the case of those names which signify the accident concretely, however, then in the corresponding definitions the subject-matter or subject is posited in the style of a genus, and the accident in the style of a characteristic, as when one asserts '*The snub* is *the nose which is concave*'.

Cum autem in definitione omnium accidentium oporteat poni subiectum, necesse est quod, si qua nomina accidens in abstracto significant quod in eorum definitione ponatur accidens in recto quasi genus, subiectum autem in obliquo, quasi differentia: ut cum dicitur 'simitas est curvitas nasi'. Si qua vero nomina accidens significant in concreto, in eorum definitione ponit materia, vel subiectum, quasi genus, et accidens, quasi differentia; ut cum dicitur 'simum est nasus curvus': APH 40; cf. *APA* 85, *APA* 423–4, and *De Ente et Essentia*, Ch. VII. See also *n*4.31*a*.

Hence not only substances but also accidents are definable, and so are their genera; but supreme genera and individuals are not definable: *BD* 885D–886A; *BDP* 27–8.

Both Boethius and Aquinas require that definition should be of existents:

Now if the definition is that whereby is explained what it is that is being defined, there can be no such explanation of what that thing is which doesn't exist.	*Nam si definitio est qua explicatur id quod defininitur quid sit, eius rei qua omnino non est, nec quid sit explicatio ulla esse potest:* *BTC* 1092C.
As he who defines can either show what the thing being defined is or merely what the name in question means, it is not on the latter account that a definition is taken to be necessarily explicative of what a thing is, this being the proper function of a definition. Otherwise it would follow that a definition which signifies what a given thing is was nothing more than an account having the same meaning as the name; indeed, a definition is just nothing more than such an account, unless it signifies the essence of some thing. Hence if there exists no thing whose essence is signified by the definition, the latter is nothing more or less than an explanatory account of the meaning of some name.	*Cum ille qui definit, possit ostendere vel quid est, vel tantum quid significat nomen, non propter hoc oportebit quod definitio sit manifestiva ipsius quod quid est, quod proprie ad definitionem pertinet: alioquin sequeretur quod definitio significans quod quid est, nihil sit aliud quam ratio significans idem quod nomen; non enim super talem rationem addit aliquid definitio, nisi quia significat essentiam alicuius rei. Unde si non sit aliqua res, cuius essentiam definitio significet, nihil differt definitio a ratione exponente significationem alicuius nominis:* *APA* 465; cf. *APA* 461, 466–7.

Further remarks on these existential requirements will be made below.

The way in which it is desirable that a definition should have a *definiens* consisting of *genus* and constitutive characteristic (*n*4.22*d*) both of which are arrived at in the process of 'division', is well described in Boethius' *De Divisione*, e.g. *BD* 886A–887B, cf. *n*4.2411*a*. The result of this *desideratum* is that every *definiens* ought, according to Boethius, to consist of two terms; however, as he explains, this is not always possible, owing to lack of appropriate names. For example, *rational mortal animal*, the definiens of *man*, involves three terms. He avoids this difficulty by pointing out that this *definiens* can nevertheless be construed as having two parts if one introduces some constant term, such as a single letter, to replace two of the three words:

Every definition and division should be constructed of two terms, did not the lack of names, which often obtains, prevent	*Fieret autem omnis definitio, omnisque divisio duabus terminis, nisi ... indigentia quae saepe existit in nomine prohiberet.*

this. However, a way in which both of the two terms can be constructed may be made obvious as follows. When we say that some animals are rational and other irrational, then the resultant *rational animal* is a step towards the definition of *man*. But since 'rational animal' is not one name, we symbolise it by the letter '*A*'. And now, yet again, of the *A*'s, some are mortal, others immortal. When, therefore, we wish to respond with a definition of *man*, we can assert '*Man* is *mortal A*'. For if the definition of *man* is *rational mortal animal*, and 'rational animal' is signified by the letter '*A*', then 'mortal *A*' is an utterance equivalent to 'rational mortal animal', since '*A*', as pointed out, means 'rational animal'. In this way from the two terms '*A*' and 'mortal', the definition of *man* has been constructed. So if required two terms can always constitute the definition, no matter what the name in question.

Quo autem modo utraeque duobus terminis fierent, erit manifestum hoc modo: cum enim dicimus animalium alia rationalia sunt, alia irrationalia, animal rationale ad hominis definitionem tendit. Sed quoniam animalis rationalis unum nomen non est, ponamus ei nomen 'a' litteram. Rursus 'a' litterae quod est animal rationale, alia mortalia sunt, alia immortalia. Volentes igitur definitionem hominis reddere dicemus 'Homo est "a" littera mortalis'. Nam si hominis definitio est animal rationale mortale, animal vero rationale per 'a' litteram significatur, idem sensit 'a mortale' tamquam si diceretur 'animal rationale mortale'; 'a' enim, ut dictum est, 'animal rationale' significat. Sic ergo 'a' littera et 'mortali' duobus teminis facta est hominis definitio. Quod si reperirentur in omnibus quoque nomina, duobus terminis semper tota fieret definitio: BD 883C–D.

From the information so far gathered, it would appear that the definitional frame (*LR* 173–5) presupposed by Boethius in his definitions properly so-called (*per divisionem*) might in the first place be depicted as follows, using '$\cap$' for 'and' in accordance with §3.20:

.1 $$[a]:.a\in\Phi.\equiv:a\in X\cap\Psi:[\exists b].b\in\Phi$$

wherein 'Φ' is a constant species-name of which species (in any one of the categories) 'X' and 'Ψ' are the genus and constitutive characteristic respectively; cf. *n*4.2411g, *n*4.2411*h* and §4. From .1 it is clear that the general form of a definition of this sort would be a strong identity (defined §3.10). Although the name-forming functor '$\cap$' of the first right-hand clause of .1 is here a conjunction (§3.20), nevertheless further conditions which should be imposed mean that '$X\cap\Psi$' has a total inner structure which amounts to more than a mere conjunction, as is clear from the systematic connection implied in the notions of *genus* and *species*; cf. *n*4.2411*h*. The final clause on the right-hand side of .1 ensures that the existential requirements detected above are fulfilled. It should also be noted that the choice of terms for 'X' and 'Ψ' is governed by the special notion of object-hood discussed in §4 and *n*4.2411*d*. Thus, for example, one particular capacity pertaining solely to man will not serve as a constitutive characteristic of man; it will not do, for instance, to use 'capable of counting' as such a characteristic. What is required is an overriding term such as 'rational':

We assert that man alone has the property of being able to count or learn geometry, so that if this possibility is taken away from man, then man himself would not persist. But these do not directly belong to those sorts of characteristic which are substantially intrinsic. For something is not a man because he can do this sort of thing, but because he is rational and mortal ... whatsoever characteristics are of such a sort that not only do they not occur outside the species, but also are such that the species has its being by them, should be taken up either into the division of the genus or into the definition of the species.	*Dicimus inesse homini ut solus numerare possit, vel geometriam discere; quod si haec possibilitas ab homine sejungitur, homo ipse non permanet. Sed hae non statim earum differentiarum sunt quae in substantia insunt. Nam non idcirco homo est, quoniam haec facere potest, sed quoniam rationalis est, atque mortalis ... quaecumque differentiae huiusmodi sunt, ut non modo praeter has species esse non possit, sed per eas solas sit, hae vel in divisione generis, vel in speciei definitione sumendae sunt:* *BD* 881C.

'Rational', it may be noted, is not the same as '*ratiocinans*' ⊖ 'reasoning', as Abelard explains: *A* 425–6, cf. *n*4.22*d*.

It was suggested above that the general pattern taken by a definition constructed according to the strict Aristotelian rules (as described by Boethius) might well follow the pattern of a strong identity (cf. .1 and §3.10). This conjecture was based to some extent on the existential requirements which appeared to be associated with such a definition. However, the other association also made above, i.e. that of definition with the notions of genus, species, and so on, gives a hint as to the possibility of further conjectures in this matter. Statements involving these notions (e.g. '*Man* is a species') are not only required in definitional discussion, but also involve and 'is' of a higher semantical category than the comparatively more familiar 'is' of which Leśniewski's primitive '$\in$' is the counterpart. Such an 'is', of higher-order type, is defined at §3.15 and further discussed in §4; cf. *n*1.000*a*, *LA* 247–50, *HL* §3.221, *HL* §3.36.4, *HDG* §6.21.15, *HLM* 43. The question arises: is this higher-level 'is' carried forward into the definition itself? It would appear from Anselm's doctrine, as described in *n*4.31*a*, that this carrying forward does occur in the case of paronyms at least. In general, the manner in which definitions and theses linked with them were customarily stated in the Middle Ages without overt quantification, as in '*Homo est animal rationale*' ⊖ '*Man* is *rational animal*' lends colour to the supposition that the higher-order 'is' is being used here, especially as, given the appropriate arguments (viz: 'Cl⟦ ⟧' defined §3.14) such statements are inferentially equivalent to identities (cf. §3.53). In speaking of such theoretical sentences, i.e. those in which quantifiers do not figure ('indefinites') Aquinas asserts:

However they [i.e. indefinites] sometimes can be accounted contraries because of what they signify; this occurs when something is predicated of the universal on account of some universal nature, even though the sign of universality is not prefixed. For example, when one asserts '*Man* is *animal*', '*Man* is not *animal*' these statements, because of what is signified, have the same force as do the statements 'Every man is animal' and 'No man is animal'.	*Contingit autem quandoque ratione significati eas habere contrarietatem, puta, cum attribuitur aliquid universali ratione naturae universalis, quamvis non apponatur signum universale; ut cum dicitur, 'homo est animal', 'homo non est animal'; quia hae enunciationes eamdem habent vim ratione significati, ac si diceretur, 'Omnis homo est animal', 'Nullus homo est animal': APH* 139, cf. *n*4.2411*h*.

Here some realisation of thesis §3.54 appears to be in evidence; if this is so, then theories (including definitions) as viewed by Aquinas are susceptible of being interpreted in terms of the higher-order 'is'. Discourse at this level turns out to be extraordinarily useful in expressing truths involving recondite semantical categories while avoiding the need for variables and quantifiers of a complexity with which the medieval logical and philosophical Latin was ill-equipped to deal; cf. *HLM* 66, 100.

In view of these considerations .1 above could be reconstrued as follows:

.2 $\mathrm{Cl}[\![\Phi]\!] \in \mathrm{Cl}[\![X \cap \Psi]\!]$

Herein there is no counterpart, however, to the final existential clause of .1, although this should of course be inserted where definite existential indications are given, as in the cases of Boethius and Aquinas, discussed above. Anselm himself was working in the dark as far as paronyms were concerned, and did not have available the notion derived from Aristotle's *Metaphysica* and retained by Aquinas, as shown above, to the effect that definitions involving paronyms (accidents) should mimic the form of substantial definitions. But at any rate Anselm's paronymous definitions have in common with .2 the feature of the higher-order 'is' (cf. *n*4.31*a*). It also sometimes appears (e.g. 3.9, 4.8) that for such paronymous definitions he would not require the supposition of the existence of things named by the *definiendum*.

Finally it may be remarked that since the '*Man*' of '*Man* is a (secondary) substance' is the same '*Man*' as that of '*Man* is *rational animal*' or '*Man* is a species', one may also conjecture that the higher-order 'is' is appropriate in such a case (cf. the quotation from *BC* 181D in *n*4.1201*a*).

*n*3.8010*a*: mortal ⊖ *mortale*] The rules according to which this *definiens* of *man* is formed are described in *n*3.800*b*; cf. *BD* 883C–D.

The question may well be asked: why should *mortal* be included in this definition? Would it not be correct merely to divide (cf. *n*4.2411*a*) the genus *animal* by means of the constitutive characteristic (cf. *n*4.22*d*) *rational*, thus obtaining *rational animal* as the *definiens* (cf. *n*3.800*b*) of the species? Boethius often mentions the reasons for the addition of *mortal*: it is because of the supposedly rational animation of the heavenly bodies:

We are operating according to the opinion of those who assert that the sun, the stars, and this whole universe are living, and who even called them by the names of gods.

Secundum eorum opinionem facimus qui solem, stellasque, atque totum hunc mundum animatum esse confirmant, quae etiam deorum nomine ... appellaverunt: BCP 137B.

A characteristic can also be asserted of various species, as in the case of *rational* in respect of man and God as well as of the heavenly bodies which, as the Platonists want to assert, are living and enjoy the power of reason.

Differentia vero ipsa quoque de pluribus speciebus dici potest, ut rationale de homine ac de Deo corporibusque coelestibus, quae (sicut Platoni placet) animata sunt et ratione vigentia: BCP 93A.

Mortality has therefore to be added as the final constitutive characteristic:

As *man* is a species of *animal*, it is circumscribed by the characteristics of rationality and mortality, and thus is separated off both from those animals which are eternal, such as the sun according to the Platonists' belief, and from those animals which lack reason.

Homo cum sit animalis species, differentiis informatur rationabilitatis atque mortalitatis, et seiungitur ab his animalibus quae aeterna sunt, velut sol a Platonicis creditur, et ab iis animalibus quae sunt rationis expertia: BTC 1070C–D.

The passage from *BTC* 1101C–D, quoted in *n*3.800*b*, may also be consulted on this point.

Now although Anselm uses this expanded definition of *man* both at the present point and elsewhere (4.24, 4.810, *Monologion* 10 (*S* I 25.9)) he does nevertheless believe, for reasons given in *Cur Deus Homo* II, 17, that human nature as such does not comprise mortality. Before the fall of man human beings were not mortal, and they will not be mortal after the resurrection:

In my opinion mortality pertains not to pure human nature but only to its corrupt form. Hence if man had never sinned, and his immortality had been changelessly established, he would nevertheless still truly be man; and when mortals rise in their incorruptibility they will be no less truly men. For if mortality belonged to human nature as it truly is, then there could never have existed an immortal human being. Hence neither corruptibility nor the absence of corruptibility pertain to human nature in its purity, since neither of them either makes or unmakes man; rather the former tends to generate his wretchedness, the latter to promote his happiness. But since there is no man who may avoid death, *mortal* is included in the definition of *man* by those philosophers who did not believe man at some time in the past or future to be capable of immortality.

Non puto mortalitatem ad puram, sed ad corruptam hominis naturaliter pertinere. Quippe si numquam peccasset homo, et immortalitas ipsius immutabiliter firmata esset, non tamen minus homo esset verus; et quando mortales in incorruptibilitatem resurgent, non minus erunt veri homines. Nam si pertineret ad veritatem humanae naturae mortalitas, nequaquam posset homo esse, qui esset immortalis. Non ergo pertinet ad sinceritatem humanae naturae corruptibilitas sive incorruptibilitas, quoniam neutra facit aut destruit hominem, sed altera valet ad eius miseriam, altera ad beatitudinem. Sed quoniam nullus est homo qui non moriatur, idcirco mortale ponitur in hominis definitione, a philosophis, qui non crediderunt totum hominem aliquando potuisse aut posse esse immortalem: *S* II 109.8.19.

A similar point is made in Bk. II, Ch. 2 of the same work:

That man is made in such wise that he need not necessarily die is easily proved as follows: as we have already asserted, it would be incompatible with the wisdom and justice of God if that which he created as just and destined for eternal happiness were to be compelled by God to suffer death, even though innocent. It follows, therefore, that had man never sinned, he would never die.

Quod autem talis factus sit, ut necessitate non moreretur, hinc facile probatur quia, ut iam diximus, sapientiae et iustitiae dei repugnat, ut cogeret mortem pati sine culpa, quem iustum ad aeternam fecit beatitudinem. Sequitur ergo quia, si numquam peccasset, numquam moreretur: *S* II 98.8.11.

*n*3.8010*b*: *rational mortal* would also apply ⊖ *conveniret rationale mortale*] Here, as in an earlier portion of the text (3.4), and in view of the connection between *esse* and definition (*n*3.431*a*), it is plain that we are encountering a form of 'is' which has as its arguments not names, but functors formed from names, e.g. *esse hominis* ⊖ being a man. This 'is' is of course of higher semantical category, and use may be made of it in the first phrase of the following thesis which expresses the presupposition of the passage now under inspection:

.1 $\mathrm{Cl}[\![\mathbf{h}]\!] \in \mathrm{Cl}[\![\mathbf{a}]\!] \,.\supset:[b]: b \in \mathbf{a} \,.\supset.\, b \in \mathbf{r} \,.\, b \in \mathbf{m}$ (§3.14.15)

i.e. if to be man is to be animal, then to whatsoever 'animal' applies, 'rational mortal' also applies. The argument of which this is a part is surveyed as a whole in *n*3.811*a*.

On the way in which the present text impinges on Anselm's notion of identity, see *HL* §10.

*n*3.8012*a*: animal ⊖ *animalis*] For an analysis of this assertion, and an account of its setting within the preliminary argument see *n*3.811*a*.

*n*3.811*a*: no man is animal ⊖ *nullus homo animal est*] The Student has been persisting in his attempts to prove that no literate is a man. The details of his pseudo-proof given in 3.7 need not concern us here. However, that proof purports to take the true conclusion 3.431 as its starting point, and thence constructs the following false assertion:

.1A *Si hoc* [*scil. esse grammatici non est esse hominis*] *est, qui habet essentiam grammatici non ideo necessario habet essentiam hominis*

.1B If to be literate is-not to be man, then that which has the essence of literate need not have the essence of man

.1C $\sim(\mathrm{Cl}[\![\mathbf{g}]\!] \in \mathrm{Cl}[\![\mathbf{h}]\!]) \,.\supset.\, \sim(\mathrm{trm}\langle\gamma\rangle \subset \mathrm{trm}\langle\alpha\rangle)$ (3.701))

The argument of 3.8, now undergoing review, counters the Student's arguments in a preliminary kind of way by the device of an inference of the same form as that of the Student's, but involving more familiar terms, and which leads to an openly absurd conclusion. This preliminary counter-demonstration begins with the Tutor's obtaining agreement from the Student that the *esse* ⊖ being of any thing is given in its definition (3.800). The Tutor then asserts:

.2A *Si* animal rationale mortale, *quae est definitio* hominis *esset definitio* animalis; *cuicumque conveniret 'animal' conveniret 'rationale mortale'*

.2B If *rational mortal animal*, which is the definition of *man*, were the definition of *animal*, then to whatsoever 'animal' applied, 'rational mortal' would apply also

.2C $\mathrm{Cl}[\![\mathbf{h}]\!] \in \mathrm{Cl}[\![\mathbf{a}]\!] . \supset : [b] : b \in \mathbf{a} . \supset . b \in \mathbf{r} . b \in \mathbf{m}$ (3.8010, cf. *n*3.8010*b*)

(.2C does not, of course, purport to reproduce precisely the counterfactual mode of .2A and .2B. Neither does it reproduce the metalinguistic expression of their consequents). However, relatively to the theories of the terms now in question (*animal, rational, mortal, man*, cf. §4) the consequent of .2 is false, hence since .2 as a whole is true, its antecedent must be false, i.e.

.3A *non est esse hominis esse animalis*

.3B to be man is-not to be animal

.3C $\sim (\mathrm{Cl}[\![\mathbf{h}]\!] \in \mathrm{Cl}[\![\mathbf{a}]\!])$ (3.8012)

This now constitutes a true starting point of the same type as 3.431, but one would scarcely be prepared to argue from .3 in the way in which the Student has argued in 3.7, using .1, that no man is animal (3.81). Thus ends the preliminary *reductio ad absurdum* counterattack on the Student's argument of 3.7. The more direct attack takes place in 3.9, with the introduction of '*simpliciter*' (cf. *n*3.931*a*).

*n*3.811*b*: fiddling with the same form ⊖ *quod ibi ludit*] Here is yet another example of an *adnominatio* ('*Hic concludit ... ibi ludit*') of the sort discussed in *n*3.234*a*.

*n*3.910*a*: as follows ⊖ *hoc modo*] Analyses and discussion-references for the theses which now follow (3.911–3.931) are given in *n*3.931*a*.

*n*3.911*a*: only ⊖ *simpliciter*] An understanding of the present arguments requires that the effect of this introduction of '*simpliciter*' ⊖ 'only' be accurately assessed.

The final stages of the argument under immediate consideration in this note are occasioned by an attempt on the part of the Student (3.7) to show, by recourse to a conclusion arrived at earlier, that 'No man is literate' is a consequence of this mutually agreed conclusion. It is during the criticism of the opening moves of this attempt that there occur the uses of '*simpliciter*' ⊖ 'only' which are now to be investigated. Thus the Student had asserted that if to be literate is-not to be man (3.431) then that which has the essence of literate need not have the essence of man (3.701). This may be expressed:

.1 $\sim(\mathrm{Cl}[\![\mathbf{g}]\!] \in \mathrm{Cl}[\![\mathbf{h}]\!]) \,.\supset.\, \sim(\mathrm{trm}\langle\gamma\rangle \subset \mathrm{trm}\langle\alpha\rangle)$ (§3.11.14.15.56.57.58.59)

(See §3 and *HDG* §6.312 for further detailed justification of the consequent of this transcription). Now .1 is plainly equivalent to:

.2 $\mathrm{trm}\langle\gamma\rangle \subset \mathrm{trm}\langle\alpha\rangle \,.\supset.\, \mathrm{Cl}[\![\mathbf{g}]\!] \in \mathrm{Cl}[\![\mathbf{h}]\!]$

which in turn can evidently be written:

.3 $\mathbf{g} \subset \mathbf{h} \,.\supset.\, \mathrm{Cl}[\![\mathbf{g}]\!] \in \mathrm{Cl}[\![\mathbf{h}]\!]$

But .3 is not a thesis, since .4, which now follows, is an instance of the thesis §3.54:

.4 $\mathrm{Cl}[\![\mathbf{g}]\!] \in \mathrm{Cl}[\![\mathbf{h}]\!] \,.\supset.\, \mathbf{g} \bigcirc \mathbf{h}$

And .3, together with .4, would yield:

.5 $\mathbf{g} \subset \mathbf{h} \,.\supset.\, \mathbf{g} \bigcirc \mathbf{h}$

which the definitions of weak inclusion and weak identity (§3.4.9) show to be an instance of a non-thesis. Hence .1 is not a thesis either.

Now it is evident that Anselm was aware that .1 was not a thesis, since the present discussion centres round a correction of the Student's assertion which corresponds to it. However, it is not at first sight intuitively evident why it should not be a thesis, especially if considered in the Latin formulation. The delicacy of the task of correction may be made more clear by a consideration of the difference between

.6 $\sim(\mathrm{Cl}[\![\mathbf{g}]\!] \in \mathrm{Cl}[\![\mathbf{h}]\!])$

which is the antecedent of .1, and

.7 $\sim(\mathrm{Cl}[\![\mathbf{g}]\!] \in\subset [\![\mathbf{h}]\!])$ (§3.13)

It can now be shown that although the consequence desired by the Student, namely '$\sim(\mathrm{trm}\langle\gamma\rangle \subset \mathrm{trm}\langle\alpha\rangle)$' does *not* follow from .6, it nevertheless *does* follow from .7. For in view of .8, which is an instance of the thesis §3.51:

.8 $\mathbf{g} \subset \mathbf{h} \,.\supset.\, \mathrm{Cl}[\![\mathbf{g}]\!] \in \subset [\![\mathbf{h}]\!]$

and given the equivalences encapsuled in the theories of the non-logical constant terms in question, it is plain that

.9 $\sim (\mathrm{Cl}[\![\mathbf{g}]\!] \in \subset [\![\mathbf{h}]\!]) \,.\supset.\, \sim (\mathrm{trm}\langle\gamma\rangle \subset \mathrm{trm}\langle\alpha\rangle)$ (§3.11)

is therefore also a thesis. A comparison of .9 with the non-thesis .1 above hence shows that the Tutor must, in terms of the Latin available to him, sufficiently characterise .6 to show that it does *not* have that consequence which .7 does have, as evidenced in .9. It is in order to effect this characterisation that the term '*simpliciter*' ⊖ 'only' is introduced.

Thus, the earlier discussion of .6 and its consequences (3.4) has been recalled and rephrased: to be literate is not to be man (3.431) means that the definition of *literate* is not the definition of *man*, so that a literate and a man are *not altogether* the same (*non est idem* omnino *grammaticus et homo*: 3.901). This is now facilitating a rephrasing of 'to be literate is not to be man' as 'to be literate is not *just* to be man' (*esse grammatici non est* simpliciter *esse hominis*: 3.911). Likewise, a reminder of the argument (3.41, 3.42) which led to the conclusion that to be literate is-not to be man is now being brought to bear in order to reveal the negation of a certain symmetry: *man* should not be defined by literacy, while *literate* should be; hence that which has the essence of literate need not have *just* the essence of man (*qui habet essentiam grammatici, non ideo consequitur ut habeat* simpliciter *essentiam hominis*). Here, as well as in a passage shortly to follow (3.94) wherein Anselm argues against 'to be white is to be man', we are evidently being faced with something very much like the negation of a species of identity.

It may well be, therefore, that the introduction of '*simpliciter*' ⊖ 'only' here expresses a symmetry of the type which occurs in logical identities and equivalences. At any rate, this is precisely what is required in order to bring out the characteristics of .6 as opposed to those of .7. For, characterising an identity having arguments of a semantical category appropriate to the higher-order '∈', thus:

.10 $[\varphi\psi]\colon \varphi = \psi \,.\equiv.\, \varphi \in \psi \,.\, \psi \in \varphi$ (§3.16) not only is it the case that

.11 $[ab]: \mathrm{Cl}[\![a]\!] \in \mathrm{Cl}[\![b]\!] . \equiv . \mathrm{Cl}[\![b]\!] \in \mathrm{Cl}[\![a]\!]$

but also that

.12 $[ab]: \mathrm{Cl}[\![a]\!] \in \mathrm{Cl}[\![b]\!] . \equiv . \mathrm{Cl}[\![a]\!] = \mathrm{Cl}[\![b]\!]$

This is because .11 is an instance of the thesis § 3.47, and .12 an instance of the thesis § 3.49. In contrast, the counterparts of .11 and .12 do *not* hold in respect of '$\mathrm{Cl}[\![a]\!] \in \subset [\![b]\!]$'. Thus it would appear that '*simpliciter*' ⊖ 'only', with its connotation of symmetry, is imported in order to bring out more exactly the special features of '$\sim (\mathrm{Cl}[\![a]\!] \in \mathrm{Cl}[\![b]\!])$'. It has in fact already been shown in *n*3.452*a*.4 that

.13 $\sim (\mathrm{Cl}[\![\mathbf{g}]\!] \in \mathrm{Cl}[\![\mathbf{h}]\!]) . \supset . \sim (\mathbf{g} \bigcirc \mathbf{h})$

is a thesis, and the text at present under discussion is underlining the same point in different terms in order to show that .1 is not a thesis. Thus the sentence, 'If to be literate is not just (*simpliciter*) to be man, then it does not follow that that which has the essence of literate has just (*simpliciter*) the essence of man' is the following equivalent of .13:

.14 $\sim (\mathrm{Cl}[\![\mathbf{g}]\!] \in \mathrm{Cl}[\![\mathbf{h}]\!]) . \supset . \sim (\mathrm{trm}\langle\gamma\rangle \bigcirc \mathrm{trm}\langle\alpha\rangle)$

The '*simpliciter*' ⊖ 'only' may be seen as underlining the symmetry of both sides of .13 and .14, or as an effort to stress .12 in order to better eliminate any faulty intuition which might lead to the assumption of .1. Throughout the remainder of the discussion (3.92, 3.93) '*simpliciter*' ⊖ 'only' may likewise be seen as transforming the Student's asymmetrical functors of inclusion into symmetrical functors of identity (cf. *n*3.931*a*).

The word '*simpliciter*' is used in a similar sense (i.e. as meaning something like 'without qualification') in *Monologion* 15:

He who is not wise is not better in an unqualified sense than he who has wisdom. Nevertheless, everyone who, in an unqualified sense, lacks wisdom, is, insofar as he lacks wisdom, less than the wise.	*Non … est melius simpliciter non sapiens quam sapiens. Omne quippe non sapiens simpliciter, inquantum non sapiens est, minus est quam sapiens:* *S* I 28.33.34.

In *De Sophisticis Elenchis* the term '*simpliciter*' occurs in opposition to '*aliquo modo*' ⊖ 'in some way' (*B* 1011D–1012A, *B* 1014C–D, *B* 1016B, show what is now considered to be a post-Anselmian translation). This opposition is all the more interesting in view of Anselm's use of '*aliquo modo*' ⊖ 'in some way', and '*quolibet modo*' ⊖ 'in no matter what way' in the earlier inferences (3.6321, 3.6332).

*n*3.931*a*: only a man ⊖ *simpliciter homo*] Thus ends, in effect, the first main stage of the argument of the dialogue. After corollaries have been drawn (3.94), a start is made in 4.00 on what proves to be the central theme: the modes of signification. The complexity of the present closing arguments of this first stage is such that a little time must be devoted to their clarification.

After the Tutor's indirect attack (3.8) upon the starting point (3.701) of the Student's last argument, we now have the direct attack which takes the form of a reminder of 3.431, 3.44, the result of which is the introduction of the term '*simpliciter*' ⊖ 'only' into the expression of 3.701. It has been argued in *n*3.911*a* that this is an attempt to characterise the symmetrical nature of 3.431. It may also be added that the Tutor holds that 3.452 may be expressed as:

.1A *non est idem* omnino *grammaticus et homo*

.1B a literate and a man are not *altogether* the same

.1C $\sim(\mathbf{g} \bigcirc \mathbf{h})$ (3.901, cf. §3.9 and *n*3.452*a*)

His aim here is probably to draw a contrast between what has actually been established, i.e. 3.452, and what it has been shown (*n*3.6321*a*) impossible to establish, namely: a literate is *in no way* a man. However, the effect of the introduction of '*simpliciter*' ⊖ 'just' is that 3.701 is corrected to read:

.2A *si esse grammatici non est* simpliciter *esse hominis: qui habet essentiam grammatici non ideo consequitur ut habeat* simpliciter *essentiam hominis*

.2B if to be literate is not *just* to be man, then that which has the essence of literate need not therefore have *just* the essence of man

.2C $\sim(\mathrm{Cl}[\![\mathbf{g}]\!] \in \mathrm{Cl}[\![\mathbf{h}]\!]) \,.\supset.\, \sim(\mathrm{trm}\langle\gamma\rangle \bigcirc \mathrm{trm}\langle\alpha\rangle)$
(3.911, cf. *n*3.911*a*.14)

.2, unlike 3.701, *is* a thesis (cf. *n*3.911*a*). There next follow what are, in effect, re-expressions of the consequent of .2, namely:

.3A *simpliciter homo non sequitur grammaticum*

.3B *literate* does not imply just *man*

.3C $\sim (\mathbf{g} \bigcirc \mathbf{h})$ (3.921)

as well as

.4A *si grammaticus est, non consequitur ut sit simpliciter homo*

.4B if a literate is, it does not follow that it is just a man

.4C $[\exists a]: \sim (a \in \mathbf{g} \,.\equiv.\, a \in \mathbf{h})$ (3.922)

The final re-expression is:

.5A *nullus grammaticus est simpliciter homo*

.5B no literate is just a man

.5C $[\exists a]: \sim (a \in \mathbf{g} \,.\equiv.\, a \in \mathbf{h})$ (3.931)

Each of .3, .4, and .5 represents a corrected restatement of a part of the Student's previous argument (3.7). In this way the asymmetries of inclusion (or its equivalents) are transformed into the symmetries of the identities (with their negations) here suggested.

*n*3.940*a*: easily be done ⊖ *facile fieri potest*] To which possible proofs is the Tutor referring here? Would they rely directly on the foregoing arguments, or would they depend more on the subsequent parts of the dialogue? Two interpretations of the present passage will now be suggested, each corresponding to the alternatives mentioned in the last sentence.

Firstly, it may be noted that the Tutor is to recall the agreed conclusion (3.431), i.e.

.1A *esse grammatici non est esse hominis*

.1*B* to be literate is-not to be man

.1C $\sim (\mathrm{Cl}[\![\mathbf{g}]\!] \in \mathrm{Cl}[\![\mathbf{h}]\!])$ (3.9410)

If, says the Tutor, .1 could be shown to be the same sort of statement as the following:

.2A *esse albi non est esse hominis*

.2B to be white is-not to be man

.2C $\sim (\mathrm{Cl}[\![\mathbf{w}]\!] \in \mathrm{Cl}[\![\mathbf{h}]\!])$ (3.9411) then it *could* be true that

.3A *aliquis grammaticus* [*est*] *non homo*

.3B some literate is not a man

.3C $[\exists a]: a \in \mathbf{g} \,.\, \sim(a \in \mathbf{h})$ (3.9421)

This, he stresses, is a *possible* conclusion: that it is *actually* the case cannot be shown (3.9431). However, any modal sign has been omitted from .3, since the point can in fact be described non-intensionally. Thus, having said that the similarity of .1 and .2 could easily be shown (3.940), the Tutor adds parenthetically that this is because *man* can be without *white*, and *white* without *man* (3.9412). Now this statement, apart from its 'can' mode, offers exactly the two alternatives which would be needed to negate an identity or equivalence. The first suggestion for the interpretation of the Tutor's remarks, therefore, is that he is here stating '$\sim(\mathbf{w} \bigcirc \mathbf{h})$', (compare '$\sim(\mathbf{g} \bigcirc \mathbf{h})$' in *n*3.931*a*.3 above), but instead of expounding this expression after the fashion of *n*3.931*a*.4.5, he intends to assert the following:

.4 $[\exists a]: a \in \mathbf{h} \,.\, \sim(a \in \mathbf{w}) \,.\vee.\, \sim(a \in \mathbf{h}) \,.\, a \in \mathbf{w}$

.4 is, by §3.32 and §3.54, logically equivalent to '$\sim(\mathbf{w} \bigcirc \mathbf{h})$', as well as to .2. The 'can' which occurs in the statement '*man* can be without *white* and *white* and *white* without *man*' may then be interpreted as the correlate of the particular quantifier in .4, and the statement's global purpose seen as being to draw attention to these alternatives and to the result of producing similar ones in respect of *man* and *literate*. For if '$\sim(\mathbf{g} \bigcirc \mathbf{h})$' (cf. *n*3.931*a*.3.4.5) is now subjected to this same alternative interpretation, i.e. as

.5 $[\exists a]: a \in \mathbf{h} \,.\, \sim(a \in \mathbf{g}) \,.\vee.\, \sim(a \in \mathbf{h}) \,.\, a \in \mathbf{g}$

then the point of the modalisation of .3 becomes clear: .3 is a statement of the second alternative of .5, and the modalisations is a way of expressing this fact. And of course it is quite true that it is not possible to prove .3 categorically from the conclusions stated in *n*3.931*a*.3.4.5.

The whole corollary may therefore in the first place be construed as a statement that both .1 and .2 yield the non-equivalences shown in .4 and .5, and that as .3 is only one of the alternatives of the non-equivalence .5, it cannot be inferred from the findings of the discussion whose course we have been following. Thus there exists a contrast between the cases just considered and that of 'man' and 'stone' in which it *did* turn out to be possible to deduce 'No stone is a man' or some equivalent conclusion (*n*3.6321*a*.3.4.5).

Secondly let us approach the matter in another not altogether alien light. The Tutor asserts that if

.6 to be literate is-not to be man (3.9410)

could be shown to be like

.7 to be white is-not to be man

then it would follow that

.8 some literate may be non-man (3.9421)

This may plainly be connected with the Tutor's later statement that 'literate' really no more signifies man than does 'white'; the former only seems to signify man because men alone happen to be literate: in contrast, other things than men happen to be white, but this does not really make a distinction between the two cases (4.24121). The position of the last-cited case within the text suggests the alternative way in which the one under consideration may be interpreted. A passage (4.2411) has been shortly before devoted to showing, in effect, that literacy is not a characteristic constitutive of some species of man, whereas rationality nevertheless is such a characterist and constitutes the species *man* (cf. *n*4.22*d* for discussion). In the light of this context .6 and .7 could be taken merely to assert that neither 'literate' nor 'white' were terms signifying characteristics constitutive of sub-species of man. Then, given the reminder that other things than men happen to be white (4.24121), .8 would represent the result of an inference based on the parity of *literate* and *white*: both are equally extra-theoretical in respect of anthropology so that there is no theoretical reason why beings other than men should not be literate in the same way as there is no reason why beings other than men should not be white. The 'may be' ('*posse*') of .8 may hence be taken to reflect the extra-theoretical status of 'literate' relative to the theory of *man* – a status which could hence be the basis of the '*fictio*' argument at 4.2412.

*n*3.9411*a*: being a man ⊖ *esse hominis*] A sense in which this statement is true is given at 4.24121: cf. *n*3.940*a*.

*n*3.9421*a*: can ⊖ *posse*] It is suggested in *n*3.940*a* that this '*posse*' ⊖ 'can' may represent the extra-theoretical status of *literate* in respect of anthropology or may be an elliptical expression of what can be represented by means of quantifiers. According to Boethius ('*Introductio ad Syllogismos Categoricos*') the unmodalised version of the present thesis is false: *falsum est dicere quemdam grammaticum hominem non esse* ⊖ it is false to say that some literate is not a man, *B* 786C. Whether he would agree with Anselm in admitting its possibility is unclear.

*n*3.9431*a*: cannot be shown ⊖ *monstrari non posse*] This impossibility is a reflection of the theoretical indifference of *literate* in relation to its *appellata*, an indifference common to all paronyms in view of the elasticity of their applications: cf. 4.24121, *n*3.940*a*.

Of course, one of the most interesting features of the present passage is the way in which it demonstrates Anselm's awareness of the question as to whether, from conceptual analysis (which in effect has been the concern of much of the preliminary argument) existential conclusions can emerge. As the author of the so-called 'ontological' argument for the existence of God (*Proslogion* 2, 3) he has often been charged with drawing such a conclusion from the analysis of the concept of God. If this charge is well-founded, then in view of the care with which the present point is made one would at least expect Anselm to show how the case of God differed from these other cases with which he is here concerned. Yet he does no such thing, unless *Proslogion* 3 were considered to constitute such a showing, which seems doubtful: cf. *HL* §5.5.

*n*4.101*a*: in a subject ⊖ *in subiecto*] The origin of this remark is traceable with moderate ease; the senses which are to be attached to the 'in', and to its counterpart '*de*' ⊖ 'of' (as in '*de subiecto*' ⊖ 'of a subject') may however all too easily give rise to misunderstanding, and must therefore be discussed in some detail below, especially as they have important connections with the general presuppositions of the dialogue's doctrine; cf. §4.

Schmitt (*S* I 154 *n* 1) suggests that the particular remark to which the Student is here alluding is that of Aristotle's in chapter 2 of the *Categoriae*; this remark is translated as:

Some of the things which exist are *in a subject* and are not asserted *of* any *subject*	*Eorum quae sunt ... alia in subiecto quidem sunt, de subiecto autem nullo*

whatsoever .... For example, a certain literacy is *in* a subject, to wit,.the soul, but is not asserted of any subject whatsoever.

dicuntur ... ut quaedam grammatica in subiecto quidem est, in anima, de subiecto autem nullo dicitur: BC 169B.

However, if this *is* the origin of the allusion then it is immediately evident that the Student is straining the text: it is '*quaedam grammatica*' – a particilar literacy, the literacy of some individual person – which is there in question, and not, as the Student claims, a (or the) literate. Alternatively, as the Tutor implies in his reply (4.110) the Student is using a way of speaking which represents an unwarranted consequence of Aristotle's text: *Noluit Aristoteles hoc consequi ex suis dictis.* And indeed, the Student's way of speaking could be based on Boethius' commentary on part of Ch. 5 of the *Categoriae* (2^a 29–34, *BC* 184C) from which one might infer that since '*grammaticus*' ⊖ 'literate' is used to predicate *grammatica* ⊖ literacy (which is 'in a subject') paronymously, the former can also in some sense be loosely said to be 'in a subject'. The following are Boethius' words:

Of those things which are *in* a subject, some are such that not even the mere name is asserted of the subject. Thus virtue is *in* the soul, but virtue just cannot be predicated *of* the soul. Others, however, are asserted paronymously, as in the case of literacy: since the latter is *in* a man, he is asserted to be literate paronymously from literacy.

Illorum vero quae sunt in subiecto aliquoties quidem neque nomen ipsum de subiecto dicitur. Nam virtus in anima est, sed virtus de animo minime praedicatur: aliquoties autem denominative dicitur, ut grammatica, quoniam est in homine, denominative grammaticus a grammatica dicitur: BC 185A.

The background to the pair of expressions '*de subiecto*' ⊖ 'of a subject' and '*in subiecto*' ⊖ 'in a subject' is quite complex. Of course, if one scans chapter 2 of Aristotle's *Categoriae* in the light of subsequent interpretations one may obtain the impression that the salient feature of the '*in*' of '*in subiecto*' is the 'in' of 'inherence in' at which the seventeenth-century Locke was prepared to mock. The text then becomes a collection of obsolete theories about accidents inhering in a substance-substratum underprop, having the alleged consequence that substance is unknowable and not predicable of anything, thus outlawing 'Socrates is Socrates' and like locutions. This is not, however, an adequate representation of the doctrine which Boethius transmitted to the medievals. In fact the central point of the *de subiecto* and *in subiecto* expressions is to underline the distinction between theoretical statements (i.e. definitionally-founded theses concerning those things which *qua* definables in the strict Aristotelian sense (cf. *n*3.800*b*) can be the objects of theories) and non-theoretical statements or non-theses: *BC* 170D–171A, *BC* 163–7. Realisation of this fact at least enlarges the field of interpretational possibilities for statements such as the one which asserts that neither the individual man nor the individual horse is *in subiecto* nor are they asserted *de subiecto* (*alia neque in subiecto sunt neque de subiecto dicuntur, ut aliquis homo vel aliquis equus; nullum horum neque in subiecto est, neque de subiecto dicitur*: *BC* 169C). This need not now be interpreted as Aristotle's outlawing of expressions such as 'Socrates is Socrates'. He may well just be saying that these sentences are not theses. However, he cannot here admit his usual locution for non-theses (i.e. he cannot, in terms of Boethius' translation, say that they are *in subiecto*) since he has already attached to this locution the note, more usually useful from his point of view, of dependence for existence upon definables:

I use the expression 'to be *in* a subject' in such a way that although the item described by it is *in* something without being some part thereof, it is impossible for that item to exist in the absence of that in which it is.

In subiecto autem esse dico, quod cum in aliquo non sicut quaedam pars sit, impossibile est sine eo esse in quo est: *BC* 196B, 1^{a} 23.

After all, 'Socrates is Socrates' occurs both in the text (*B* 356D) and commentary (*BDIL* 358A). John of Salisbury discusses this problem (as well as others covered in the present note) in his *Metalogicon* Bk. II, Ch. XX (*SM* 113.13–115.8).

We are hence here considering a context in which the authors concerned would refuse to use the expression 'predicated of a subject' to describe non-thetic predications. Thus 'Socrates is white' would not, for them, involve the predication of whiteness 'of a subject' in the technical sense of this latter locution; strictly, for them, 'Socrates is white' is a statement to the effect that whiteness is 'in a subject'. Boethius senses the artificiality of these technical conventions, and tries to make clear their import in two fashions. First he distinguishes between (i) *secundum accidens* ⊖ accidental predication *de subiecto* ⊖ of a subject, and (ii) predication *de subiecto* ⊖ of a subject and *in eo quod quid* ⊖ in respect of whatness (cf. *n*3.502*a*). He plainly regards (ii) as the proper sense of '*de* *subiecto*' ⊖ 'of a subject': *BC* 175D–176A, cf. *HL* §3.1222.1). Secondly he will say (as in the quotation from *BC* 185A given above) that if the '*de subiecto*' ⊖ 'of a subject' form of description is insisted on for cases such as those wherein *literate* (or other paronyms) are predicated of a subject (e.g. 'Socrates is literate'), then we must here be said to have a denominative (or paronymous) *de subiecto* ⊖ of a subject predication only, thereby making plain its non-thesishood. This line is followed in the twelfth-century *Dialectica Monacensis*: *DLM* II–II 508. A *de subiecto* ⊖ of a subject predication in the full sense only occurs when a single definition embraces both subject and predicate of the assertion in question: *BC* 185A–C; cf. *BC* 167 B–C, *BC* 191A–B; for a fuller discussion see *HL* §3.1222.

It follows, therefore, that the decision as to which true sentences form part of a theory, i.e. are properly said to involve predications *de subiecto* ⊖ of a subject, depends upon what objects of definition (in the Aristotelian sense, cf. §4, *n*3.800*b*, *n*4.2411*h*) are available. Only such objects, in effect, constitute the ranges of the universal quantifiers of such theories cf. *n*4.72*a*. The *Categoriae* could perhaps be construed as an attempt to divide definable objects into groups such that the functors which may be introduced into the theories of a given group are homogeneous as to their arguments, and so avoid the nonsense to which the use of certain functors without regard to this grouping could give rise. Alternatively, although the non-substance categories circumscribe areas across which the 'What is the something else ...?' question (cf. *n*4,1201*a*) may lead one to pass, all have a substantial aspect, in that they can, for appropriate purposes, represent the outer boundary of a series of such questions. It follows that when the expression '*de subiecto*' ⊖ 'of a subject' occurs, the 'subject' in question need not be a substance in any of the various senses of the word. It can in fact be an object (in a describable variation of the sense of 'ob' (§3.3) given in Ontology; cf. §4) subsumable under any of the categories (quantity, quality, state, etc., cf. *BC* 180A–B and *n*3.800*b*).

From Aristotle's point of view there is no logical necessity that the *de subiecto/in subiecto* ⊖ of a subject/in a subject distinction should tend to be wedded to talk about substances; it just so happens that a fragmentary anthropology, a theory of *man*, was at Aristotle's disposal, and he therefore illustrated his point by using familiar examples from this field. In any case, Aristotle also uses 'this literacy' as an instance of a *subiectum*, and says that knowledge is predicable of it *de subiecto*: here he is obviously stating a thesis of what might be called 'Noology': *ut scientia ... de subiecto autem dicitur, ut de hac grammatica* ⊖ Knowledge is asserted *of* a subject; for instance it is asserted of this particular literacy: *BC* 169B. The part omitted from the last-quoted sentence says that knowledge is also *in subiecto* ⊖ in a subject, in the soul (*in subiecto quidem est in anima* ⊖ it is also, of course, *in* a subject, namely the soul) but the mention here of something which is both asserted *of* a subject and *in* a subject (and hence involving allusion to both thesis and non-thesis) is not an exception to the technical use of these terms described above. The knowledge is *in subiecto* ⊖ in a subject as far as the mind is concerned, but predicated *de subiecto* ⊖ of a subject insofar as literacy is in question.

As already indicated '*in subiecto*' ⊖ 'in a subject' also carried with it the sense of existential dependence: *BC* 172B–D. But this is by no means incompatible with the doctrine described. The same applies to other apparent exceptions (cf. *HL* §3.1222).

Nevertheless the account so far given is still susceptible of clarification and further investigation on a number of points, e.g. might it not be that the availability (in the case of paronyms) and the non-availability (in the case of concrete names) of corresponding abstract names is at the bottom of the 'in' and 'of' distinction? (cf. *HL* §3.1222, *HG* §4.1, *HW* §2). Might this not be also at the bottom of the Aristotle-Boethius distinguishing criterion according to which one can predicate definitions when concrete names are in question, but not when paronyms are involved (*BC* 185A–B). This would be rather a poor contention, however, given that constitutive characteristics (*n*4.22*d*), usually expressed by abstract names (e.g. 'rationality') are nevertheless said to give rise to *de subiecto* predications in the full sense (*BC* 129A). In any case the distinction did not disappear when abstract names became universally available for all names, including the concrete ones, in technical medieval Latin. Again, the possibility of defining accidents either *in abstracto* ⊖ abstractly or *in concreto* ⊖ concretely (*APH* 40, *APH* 85) also appears to put this contention out of court.

The general situation is clear enough: the decision as to what is to be an object of theory rests on notions of object drawn ultimately from the pre-theoretical, especially in the case of 'substance' (cf. §4, *n*3.800*b*, *n*4.72*a*, *n*4.22*d*, *n*4.1201*a* and e.g. *B* 191A) and hence so also does the technical use of '*de subiecto*' ⊖ 'of a subject' and '*in subiecto*' ⊖ 'in a subject'. Some further details are also clarified in *n*3.52*a* and *n*4.2411*h*.

Although the textual occurrence of the actual words '*in subiecto*' ⊖ 'in a subject' and '*de subiecto*' ⊖ 'of a subject' is limited in *De Grammatico* to the few lines of the present sections (4.10, 4.11) and to a passing allusion in 4.12, 4.13, the presuppositions underlying them are of great importance in the whole substructure of the dialogue. The word '*grammaticus*' ⊖ 'literate' itself receives a place in the logical scheme: it is a word used to express paronymously that literacy (*grammatica*) is in a subject (*B* 185A, quoted above) and is hence not a term used in the theory of the 'subject' (man) in question. Again, those parts of the *Categoriae* and its commentary which have been scrutinised contain many examples of theses of definitionally-founded theory of the sort presupposed by the dialogue (cf. *n*3.800*b*). Indeed, it is on the availability or non-availability of such theses that the argument of the whole dialogue, and especially the complex '*intelligi*' ⊖ 'to be understood' reasoning of its first half, turns.

Throughout the present note it has been assumed that the 'subjects' *of* which predicates are affirmed and the 'subjects' *in* which accidents are, are both extra-linguistic entities. There is little doubt about this in the second case. It would also be very difficult to make any sense of much of Boethius' commentary on the *Categoriae* if the distinction between extra-linguistic object and sentence-subject were assumed to be entailed by the '*in subiecto est*' ⊖ 'is in a subject' and '*de subiecto praedicatur*' ⊖ is predicated of a subject' locutions respectively: cf. *HL* §3.12233.

*n*4.102*a*: in a subject ⊖ *in subiecto*] The import of this assertion is made clear by the preceding note (*n*4.101*a*).

*n*4.110*a*: literate ⊖ *grammaticum*] A Latin translation of the relevant passage from chapter 5 of Aristotle's *Categoriae* runs as follows:

Principal substances are properly so called because they are the foundation of all the others, and all the others are either predicated *of* them or are *in* them (cf. *n*4.101*a*). In the same way as first substances are related to all the others, so also are the genera and species of principal substances related to all the others. Of them are all these others

Amplius principales substantiae eo quod aliis omnibus subiaceant, et alia omnia de ipsis praedicantur aut in ipsis sunt, idcirco propriae substantiae dicuntur. Sicut autem primae substantiae ad omnia alia sese habent, ita principalium substantiarum genera et species ad omnia reliqua sese habent. De his enim omnia reliqua praedicantur, aliquem enim hominem dicis

predicated, as when from the assertion that some man is literate it follows that both a man and an animal can be said so to be literate, and so on in other cases.

grammaticum esse, ergo et hominem et animal grammaticum dicis, similiter autem et in aliis: B 189B.

The last sentence is the one paraphrased by the Tutor here, and is commented on by Boethius thus:

In the same way as all primary substances stand under all accidents, so also do secondary substances. For because some man is the foundation of some accident, so also *man* and *animal* take on the accident; thus since a certain man (e.g. Aristarchus) is literate not only is it the case that a man is literate, but also that an animal is literate.

Et sicut primea substantiae cunctis subiacent accidentibus, sic etiam secundae. Nam quoniam aliquis homo accidentibus subiacet, et homo et animal accidenti supponitur, et quoniam est quidam homo grammaticus, id est Aristarchus, est homo grammaticus, est etiam animal grammaticum: BC 189C.

Clearly the Student's conclusion (4.103) cannot stand in the face of these declarations. The Tutor is here not attacking the Student's syllogism directly, but showing that its conclusion is incompatible with other Aristotelian doctrines, and hence that Aristotle cannot have intended that conclusion to be drawn from other assertions of his to which the Student claims to appeal. Boethius' text shows very well how the relation between *man* and *literate* to which the Tutor is appealing, is an extra-theoretical matter, since it depends on the assumption that there is some literate man, such as the Aristarchus mentioned (cf. 4.233 and the absence of theoretical interconnection there implied by *appellatio*).

*n*4.1101*a*: you speak ⊖ *loqueris*] The mention of speaking at this point is highly significant in view of the contrast which the Student is shortly to draw (4.210) between the logicians' current speech, in which the word '*grammaticus*' ⊖ 'literate' occurs, and the scandalous technical assertions of the same logicians when writing about *grammaticus* ⊖ literate (cf. *n*1.000*b*). These technical assertions are such that were they to be taken as a guide to the current course of utterance in ordinary company (*loquens in populo*) would just result in nonsense (4.20). The conclusion at which the Tutor is here aiming (4.111, 4.112) is such that both the indications of *usus loquendi* ⊖ spoken usage (4.111) and the assertions of logicians (4.112) can already be adumbrated, hence the express mention of a concrete speaker-hearer situation at this point.

*n*4.1101*b*: whereof ⊖ *unde*] In view of the distinctions later to be drawn (4.23) it seems highly likely that '*unde*' is here chosen for its ambiguity. Its use helps to avoid the impression that both *man* and literacy, which emerge from the present questioning, are the referents of 'literate'; 'literate' will be shown to be appellative, but not strictly speaking significative, of *man* (4.233), and to be significative of literacy but not appellative thereof (4.2340). The ambiguity of '*unde*' is dealt with by Anselm in *Monologion* 8:

When one asks, concerning someone who is silent, whereof he is speaking, then the answer is 'Of nothing', i.e. he is not speaking. It is in this style that one may reply to someone who poses the question 'Whereof is it made?' concerning the supreme being; one can rightly reply 'Of nothing' and this amounts to saying that it is not made at all.

Cum quarenti de tacente unde loquatur, respondetur: de nihilo; id est non loquitur. Secundum quem modum de ipsa summa essentia ... quaerenti unde factum sit, recte responderi potest: de nihilo, id est: nequaquam factum est: S I 23.8.12.

For a similar use, see also *Epistola de Incarnatione Verbi: nescit unde loquitur* ⊖ he knows not whereof he is speaking: *S* II 30.12.

*n*4.1101*c*: things ⊖ *rebus*] The expression '*de rebus*' ⊖ 'concerning things' is opposed to '*de nomine*' ⊖ 'concerning the name' not merely to express the contrast between extra-linguistic objects and names, but rather that between the different kinds of discourse distinguished at 4.601, 4.602, 4.603, i.e. assertions *de re* ⊖ about things and assertions *de voce* ⊖ concerning words. The latter concern the meaning of words, and the former are the correlates of such meaning-statements, but need not necessarily be literally *about* existing objects. An example of such a *de re* statement is '*grammaticus est grammatica*' ⊖ '*literate* is literacy' (cf. *n*1.000*b* and the references there made). It should be noted that the '*est*' ⊖ 'is' of this last statement is definable (§3.15) ultimately in terms of the '*est*' ⊖ 'is' of '*Socrates est philosophus*' ⊖ 'Socrates is a philosopher' and like sentences, i.e. in terms of an 'is' which is more like a familiar, everyday, 'is' in that it does require the existence of objects for the truth of sentences which turn upon it.

*n*4.1101*d*: signify ⊖ *significat*] 'Signifies' is here used in a loose sense, since the distinctions of 4.23 have not yet been brought to bear: in fact at this point 'signifies' may mean 'signifies *per se*' or 'signifies obliquely'

(4.232). It may on the other hand be an inferentially equivalent substitute for the '*est*' ⊖ 'is' in '*grammaticus est substantia*' ⊖ '*literate* is substance' and '*grammaticus est qualitas*' ⊖ '*literate* is quality', both of which figure in the conclusion to the present passage.

*n*4.1101*e*: man ⊖ *hominem*] More precisely, 'literate' signifies *man*, but only *per aliud* ⊖ obliquely (4.232) in that 'literate' is appellative of men (4.233).

*n*4.1101*f*: literacy ⊖ *grammatica*] More precisely, 'literate' signifies literacy, but in a *per se* fashion, and not merely obliquely (4.232).

*n*4.1102*a*: literacy ⊖ *grammaticam*] The use of '*aut*' ⊖ 'or' between '*hominem*' ⊖ 'man' and '*grammaticam*' ⊖ 'literacy' is particularly important, since the present statement would not be strictly true were '*et*' ⊖ 'and' to be substituted, although in relation to the immediately preceding discourse there appears to be no reason why '*et*' ⊖ 'and' should not appear here. However, in relation to the doctrines which are to follow, '*aut*' ⊖ 'or' is exactly right, since in the strict sense only one of the two alternatives shown actually holds. Thus if the verb '*intelligere*' ⊖ 'to understand' is being used in the strict sense (i.e. as correlated with *per se* signification (4.232)) then the *man* member of this disjunction is out of place. Of course, in a loose sense of 'signify', 'literate' can be said to signify *man* (4.233), and '*intelligere*' ⊖ 'to understand' can embrace this loose sense, as it appears to do in the earlier '*intelligi*' ⊖ 'to be understood' arguments of the dialogue (cf. also *n*4.1101*d*).

For another similar link-up of the speaker-hearer situation indicated by the '*audito*' ⊖ 'on hearing' of the present passage and the '*loqueris*' ⊖ 'you speak' of 4.1101, the reply to Gaunilo (*S* I 136.8.10) may also be consulted.

*n*4.1103*a*: literacy ⊖ *grammatica*] As in the case of 4.1102 (cf. *n*4.1102*a*) the use of '*aut*' ⊖ 'or' (as opposed to '*et*' ⊖ 'and') is essential to the truth of this assertion if it is presupposed that *significatio* ⊖ meaning in its strict sense is in question here. The mention of speaking which is here made (*loquens de grammatico* ⊖ talking of a literate) shows that *usus loquendi* ⊖ the current course of utterance, and hence *appellatio* ⊖ refer-

ence is in the Tutor's mind (cf. 4.210, 4.234). 'Literate' is as a matter of fact appellative only of men and not of literacy (4.233). In other words the two latter do not, so to speak, stand on the same level, as might be misguidedly inferred from the present conclusion.

*n*4.1104*a*: in a subject ⊖ *in subiecto*] The alternatives mentioned here, i.e. substance or *in subiecto* ⊖ of a subject, are exclusive, as is evident from *n*4.101*a*, *n*4.1201*a*.

*n*4.1105*a*: in a subject ⊖ *in subiecto*] As the Student's response correctly states, literacy is both a quality and is *in subiecto* ⊖ in a subject. It would appear that this and like statements are implicitly relativised to a substance-theory such as that of *man* (cf. *n*4.101*a*).

*n*4.111*a*: in a subject ⊖ *in subiecto*] Here the '*significat*' ⊖ 'signifies' of 4.1101 has been replaced by the higher-order '*est*' ⊖ 'is' (cf. *n*1.000*b* and references there given). Later (4.232, 4.233) the present findings will be refined insofar as 'literate' will be said to be appellative, but not (*per se*) significative, of *man*. It is only in this sense that '*literate* is substance' is true.

*n*4.112*a*: in a subject ⊖ *in subiecto*] Once again (cf. *n*4.111*a*) the '*significat*' ⊖ 'signifies' of 4.1101 has been replaced by the higher-order '*est*' ⊖ 'is' (cf. *n*1.000*b* and the references there given). Later (4.232, 4.234) a more exact statement of the present result will be made available: 'literate' signifies (*per se*) literacy, but is not appellative of literacy.

*n*4.1201*a*: substance ⊖ *substantia*] In terms of a Latin translation of the *Categoriae*:

In the proper and fundamental sense, that which is neither asserted of a subject nor is in a subject, e.g. a given man or a given horse, is most adequately said to be substance. The species which embrace those things which are substances in the most fundamental sense are said to be second substances. The same title applies not only to these, but also to the genera of the species; for example, a given man is

Substantia autem quae proprie et principaliter et maxime dicitur est quae neque de subiecto dicitur neque in subiecto est, ut aliquis homo vel aliquis equus. Secundae autem substantiae dicunter species, in quibus illae quae principaliter substantiae dicunter insunt. Et hae quidem et harum specierum genera, ut aliquis homo, in specie quidem est in homine, genus vero speciei animal est. Secundae

a member of the species *man*, and the genus of this species is *animal*. Hence both *man* and *animal* are said to be second substances.

ergo substantiae hae dicuntur, ut est homo atque animal: BC 181D.

(For an explanation of 'in a subject' and 'of a subject' as they occur in this passage, see *n*4.101*a*).

If the suggestions contained in *n*4.101*a* and §4 are accepted, then it becomes evident that the notion of 'substance' inherited by Anselm is a complex involving several strands. It is common knowledge that the division into 'primary' and 'secondary' substances represents a distinction between individuals and what are sometimes vaguely described as the generic or specific 'natures' which embrace those individuals. This much is clear from the passage just quoted. Yet an individual colour, such as a particular patch of whiteness, is not a primary substance; neither are species of colour secondary substances: *B* 183B. Consider first, therefore, the notion of secondary substance. This is encountered in statements such as '*Man* is a substance' or '*Man* is *animal*', and Boethius' words support the contention of §4 and *n*3.800*b* that the 'is' of such statements belongs to the same level of language as does the 'is' of '*Man* is a species', i.e. saying that *man* is a substance is not like saying that Socrates is white (cf. *n*3.800*b*).

On the assumption that not only may there be theories centred round certain terms (§4), but also that there is, so to speak, a lower limit below which it is no longer proper to pursue such theories, it is possible to define such a lower limit as *species specialissima* (*n*4.2411*h*). Now secondary substances are *species specialissimae* or the genera thereof, but there are some *species specialissimae* and their genera, as in the case of colours, which are not secondary substances (*B* 183B). Can this distinction of cases be given expression? The distinction appears to turn on the difference between *de subjecto* ⊖ of a subject and *in subiecto* ⊖ in a subject (cf. *n*4.101*a*). As was pointed out in *n*4.101*a*, the 'in' carries with it the note of existential dependence (cf. *BC* 169B therein quoted). Thus at the level of first substances (e.g. the man Socrates) and particular instances of non-substantial *species specialissimae* (e.g. this particular whiteness occurring in Socrates) one would tend to feel that the existence of the whiteness was dependent upon the existence of Socrates rather than that the existence of Socrates was dependent upon the existence of the whiteness. True, the existence of the white spatio-temporal segment of

Socrates is dependent upon the existence of the particular whiteness in question, but our usual ways of talking tend to avoid the segmentation of Socrates in this manner, and so to work the other way round: of this we have a clear reminder in 4.231.

Again, in respect of a term such as 'white' (which when predicated is said, in Boethius' terms, to show that whiteness is *in subiecto* ⊖ in a subject) one can always ask, for example, 'What is it that is white?', or, more circuitously, 'Of what is the whiteness the whiteness?', especially if such a term occurs as the subject of an assertion (e.g. 'Some whites are coming down the road') and the context of utterance leaves room for doubt as to the referents of that subject-term. Thus in the example given the whites in question could be men, horses, ants, and so on. But when substance-terms such as 'man' or 'horse' are used as sentence-subjects, then since these are names which are predicated *de subiecto* as well as being substance-names, one does not seek information as to the something else *in* which they are (in the sense of existential dependence outlined above) or *of* which they are (in some relative sense of 'of'). For Boethius denies that substances can be said to be 'of' anything in the sense in which an accident can be said to be 'of' and hence 'in' something (*BC* 234B–D).

Aquinas also often contrasts the case of a name such as a paronym which presupposes an *in subjecto* ⊖ of a subject state of affairs with that of a substance-name which can occur in a *de subiecto* ⊖ of a subject predication. When the former is used as a sentence-subject then a 'something else' in which the accident is can sensibly be asked about. When, however, a substance name is a sentence-subject, such a query is not apt (*APA* 285, cf. *HL* §3.12230).

Thus far the contrast in question could be described as that which holds between *in subiecto* ⊖ in a subject shared names and substance names which are predicated *de subiecto* ⊖ of a subject. In other words the contrast is between two sorts of shared names. That the contrast also holds between *in subiecto* ⊖ in a subject names and names of primary substances (individuals) is also made clear by Aquinas: in the case of the former (as we have already seen) an enquiry as to a 'something else' (*aliquid aliud*) is appropriate; in the latter case it is not (*APA* 87; cf. *HL* §3.12230).

In all, therefore, there are three possibilities, of which the following three sentences are examples:

Some whites are coming down the road
Some men are coming down the road
Socrates is coming down the road.

In the absence of other indications (e.g. sight or general contextual knowledge, cf. 4.42) only the first of these three leaves place for a question about what the 'something else' is which is white and is coming down the road. No such 'something else' question arises in the last two cases. This 'something else', like men or Socrates, must ultimately be an unambiguously countable object (cf. the '*unum aliquid*' ⊖ 'single object' of 4.72 and *HL* §3.12231).

From the foregoing, incidentally, it is amply clear that Locke's theory of substance is, at the crucial points, quite different from the concept here described. According to the medievals, substances are things you see about the place (man, horses, and stones, for example) and when a substance-name occurs as a sentence-subject it is, as we have seen, inappropriate to ask for information about the 'something else besides' the observable then in question. For Locke, however, it is *always* appropriate, no matter what the sentence-subject, to ask for such information, until at last the only acceptable final answer is the indescribable and unobservable '*something* besides'. As he puts it: 'the substance is supposed always *something besides* the extension, figure, solidity, motion, thinking, or other observable ideas, although we know not what it is' *LE* II, XXIII, §3; cf. *HL* §3.12230, *HAN* 51–4.

Other details of the doctrine of substance, with appropriate texts, are given in the notes which comment on further occurrences of the term 'substance' and other associated terms in the present dialogue, e.g. *n*3.800*b*, *n*4.2411*h*. In *HL* §3.1221 may be found a unified account.

*n*4.1201*b*: secondary substance ⊖ *secunda*] Here is the first move of a series in which the dual senses in which 'literate' may signify (4.23) are exploited. First, the Student here states that *literate* is neither primary nor secondary substance. This is true, insofar as *literate* is not a substance at all: *being a literate* is not *being a man* (cf. *n*3.44*a*, *n*3.431*a*, *n*4.230*b*). However, 'literate' is appellative of man, and hence of substance (4.233).

*n*4.1201*c*: substance ⊖ *substantiam*] In accordance with the point made in the last sentence of the last note, the Tutor reverts to the Aristotelian statement (cf. 4.1100) which is based on factors extra-theoretical in respect of *literate*: in point of fact 'literate' refers to primary substances (individual men) and statements derivative from this fact might involve *man* at the level of the higher-order 'is' (§3.15) and hence at the level of secondary substance. In these senses *literate* can loosely be said to 'be' both primary and secondary substance.

*n*4.121*a*: unlike any substance ⊖ *nulla substantia est*] The Tutor's loosely stated results (4.112) enable the Student to maintain here his erroneous thesis of 4.101: this immediately allows him to distinguish *literate* from both primary and secondary substance. Compare Boethius:

In the same way as primary substances are not in a subject, so also secondary substances likewise lack a subject. Hence a feature common to all substances, be they primary or secondary, is not to be in a subject.	*Quemadmodum primae substantiae in subiecto non sunt, sic secundae subiecto carebunt. Commune est igitur omnibus substantiis, et secundis et primis in subiecto non esse: BC* 191B.

*n*4.121*b*: is not a mark of primary substance ⊖ *primae non est*] First substances, or individuals (cf. *n*4.1201*a*) in terms of chapter 7 of Aristotle's *De Interpretatione* are (unlike universals) not predicable of many things:

One has on the one hand universals of things, and on the other hand singulars. I use the word 'universal' in the sense of that which is suited to be predicated of many things, as opposed to the singular, which is not thus suited.	*Quoniam autem sunt haec quidem rerum universalia, illa vero singillatim. Dico autem universale, quod in pluribus natum est praedicari, singulare vero quod non: BDIL* 318, cf. *BDIG* 462B.

(On the problem as to whether the existence of many men called 'Plato', for example, invalidates this distinction, see *BDIG* 464A–D, *APH* 124). Although this leaves us with *literate* as something which is predicated *of* something (and hence *de subiecto* ⊖ of a subject) this is not *in eo quod quid* ⊖ in respect of whatness: cf. *n*4.101*a*, *n*3.501*a*, and 4.122.

*n*4.122*a*: species] See *n*4.2411*g* (on genus) and *n*4.2411*h* (on species). It is in effect being said here that *literate* lies below the level of theoretical objecthood appropriate to *species specialissimae* of substances: cf. §4 and *n*4.2411*h*.

*n*4.122*b*: in respect of whatness ⊖ *in eo quod quid*] This expression is to be understood as opposed to 'in respect of quality' *(in eo quod quale)* on which see *n*3.501*a*.

*n*4.122*c*: as secondary substances are ⊖ *quod est secundae*] Secondary substances *are* identifiable with genera or species, and are hence asserted *in eo quod quid* ⊖ in respect of whatness: cf. *n*4.1201*a*, *n*4.2411*g*, *n*4.2411*h*. The Student's assertion is therefore quite correct.

That technical logical terminology is here being used to show that *literate* is not a substance is, of course, highly significant. It is only according to *usus loquendi* ⊖ the current course of utterace, and not according to the doctrines of logicians (cf. 4.21, 4.23) that *literate* and *man* are associated; only because of its factual application to human beings can *literate* be said to be substance. In order to bring out to the full the confusion which results from lack of distinction between the intra-theoretical and the extra-theoretical, the Tutor's immediate reaction (4.13) is to appeal, in effect, to the extra-theoretical facts of *usus loquendi* ⊖ the current course of utterance in order to rebut the Student's theoretically correct assertions. The means of avoiding these confusions are given in 4.23, where meaning and application are distinguished. For a general view of such dialectical oscillation from theoretical to extra-theoretical, see *HL* §3.133, §3.21, §3.22.

*n*4.131*a*: something literate ⊖ *aliquid grammaticus*] The introduction of *'aliquid'* ⊖ 'something' into the Tutor's contentions here, like the introduction of 'a certain' *('quidam')* into 4.132, is designed to ensure that his counter arguments (as forecast at the close of *n*4.122*c*) are based on the extra-theoretical facts of the application of 'literate' and not on the theory of *man* or *literate*. He reaps the advantage of this basis by identifying the referents of 'literate' (i.e. the *aliquid grammaticus* ⊖ something literate) as human beings (*'est ... homo'* ⊖ 'is ... a man') and then carrying on to give the logical characterisation of *homo* ⊖ man, a characterisation which is, of course, entirely opposed to that of *grammaticus* ⊖ literate which the Student has correctly recounted in 4.122.

*n*4.131*b*: is not in a subject ⊖ *non est in subiecto*] This is in reply to part of 4.121, and is true insofar as literates are men, as the Tutor goes on to point out. See *n*4.1201*a* and *n*4.101*a* on the meaning of *'in subiecto'* ⊖ 'in a subject'.

*n*4.131*c*: species] Part of 4.122 is countered by this remark, and again, as the Tutor goes on to point out, is true insofar as *literate* has (accidentally, extra-theoretically) to do with *man*. See *n*4.2411*g* and *n*4.2411*h* on the meanings of 'genus' and 'species'.

*n*4.131*d*: in respect of whatness ⊖ *in eo quod quid*] This counters part of 4.122, and is, strictly speaking, redundant, since being asserted *in eo quod quid* ⊖ in respect of whatness (cf. *n*3.501*a*) is part of the notions of genus and species which have just been mentioned: cf. *n*4.2411*g* and *n*4.2411*h*.

*n*4.131*e*: genus] See *n*4.131*c*.

*n*4.131*f*: in respect of whatness ⊖ *in eo quod quid*] See *n*4.131*d*.

*n*4.132*a*: individual ⊖ *individuus*] That part of 4.121 which claims that *literate* is not primary substance is countered by this remark. The present assertion, in accordance with the forecast of *n*4.122*c*, continues with the programme of reliance on the application, as opposed to the general theoretical specification, of *literate*. Thus the individual, such as the Socrates mentioned in the next sentence, is one of the beings to which 'literate' *applies* – a purely accidental, extra-theoretical fact – and it is on this fact that the Tutor is now basing his assertion. This is, of course, part of his design to confuse the Student.

*n*4.132*b*: literate ⊖ *grammaticus*] Given that Socrates is literate, it follows (as stated in the Tutor's previous sentence) that some literate is an individual. But it by no means follows from this that the theoretical statement '*Literate* is a primary substance' is true, since literacy is insufficient to determine that sort of objecthood entailed by substantiality (cf. §4 and 4.2411 and notes appended thereto).

Thus ends the series of exchanges which began at 4.1200, and which were designed to throw into relief the confusions which can arise in this context; paronyms which apply to human beings alone can best bring out such confusions as occur when theory and non-theory are not properly distinguished (cf. *n*4.122*c*). The closeness of the vocabulary used by Anselm to express these exchanges to that used by Boethius when distinguishing primary and secondary substances may be seen by consulting the quotations given in *n*4.110*a*.

*n*4.14*a*: is ⊖ *esse*] Here is yet another case of the use of that 'is' which Anselm employs alternatively with 'signifies', and to which attention was first drawn in *n*1.000*b*. Thus, in 4.1101, 'signifies' was used, then in 4.1105 and 4.1200 the discourse reverted to the 'is' now being maintained. Yet in the speech which is to follow the Student will return to the use of 'signifies' when he speaks of the various things that can be signified by 'literate'. The use of 'is' in the way described does not represent a careless indifference on the part of Anselm; the maintenance of its use is vital to the full maintenance of the rift between *usus loquendi* ⊖ the common course of utterance and the ways in which logicians express themselves; this rift has been in the air ever since the first words of the dialogue (cf. *n*1.000*b*) and will shortly be brought well into the open (4.20, 4.21, 4.23). Only after yet another reminder of its existence (4.5022, 4.5122) will its character finally be settled in 4.6. The logical status of this 'is', which corresponds to the higher-order '$\in$' as defined in Ontology (§3.15) is discussed in §4. It is made clear at 4.601–4.603 that the 'is' and 'signifies' which alternate in the manner depicted above can in fact indicate inferentially equivalent *de re* ⊖ thing-centred and *de voce* ⊖ word-centred statements respectively.

*n*4.14*b*: literacy ⊖ *grammaticam*] This remark presupposes a recollection of the Student's assertion (1.21) that an exclusive disjunction holds between '*literate* is substance' and '*literate* is quality'. Now that he has failed to show that 'a literate is a man' is false (which he thinks would have allowed '*literate* is quality' to be true) he is now being invited to show that '*Literate* is literacy' (cf. *n*1.000*b* and 4.2341) is false (which would allow '*Literate* is substance' to be true).

*n*4.14*c*: by pointing ⊖ *digito*] To resort to ostensive definition, as the Student now suggests, in order to show that '*Literate* is literacy' is false, is exactly the wrong procedure. Such definition might be used in connection with *usus loquendi* ⊖ the common course of utterance in order to show of which objects a name is appellative (cf. 4.4234), but is quite irrelevant as a disproof of the statement mentioned, since that statement is a technical assertion propounded by logicians, and hence involves parts of speech other than those resorted to in the current course of utterance. In particular, as a statement indicating *per se* signification, it does not involve the simple name/object-called-by-the-name relation which the reference to pointing here implies. Of course, if the Student wanted to show that of which the name 'literate' is appellative (4.23) the pointing procedure would be helpful and appropriate, but he would then be pointing to a human being; the pointing would thus answer one question, namely, 'What is it that is called "literate"?', but would get one no further towards answering the question 'What is involved in being a literate?'. There still hence appears to be place left for a question about the signification of 'literate' as opposed to its reference.

At one point Wittgenstein appears to hold that pointing is sufficient to 'define' a name:

> in giving an ostensive definition, we often point to the object named and say the name ... it is precisely characteristic of a name that it is defined by means of the demonstrative expression 'That is *N*' (or 'That is called "N"'): (*W* 19).

Here, as the use of 'is called' shows, pointing to a sample of that of which the name is appellative (cf. 4.23) is equated with defining. But Anselm's procedure alone is quite enough to show that there is more to the matter than this. Indeed, Wittgenstein himself appears to realise that there is more when dealing with the familiar paronym 'green', which is exactly the kind of case which Anselm has chosen in the present dialogue to bring out what more there is to be said in this matter of meaning:

> As yourself: what *shape* must the sample of the colour green be? Should it be rectangular? Or would it then be the sample of a green rectangle? – So should it be 'irregular' in shape? And what is to prevent us from regarding it – that is, from using it – only as a sample of irregularity of shape? (*W* 35).

That the word '*ostentatio*' as used by Anselm may involve a notion which is in many respects opposed to that which revolves around the modern 'ostensive definition' will be suggested in *n*4.604*c*.

*n*4.14*d*: various meanings ⊖ *significari diversa*] Here, as the words which immediately follow show, the reference is to 4.11, where *literate* was shown to be both substance and quality. The different senses in which it is these two was not there brought out; however, this will be effected in 4.23.

*n*4.14*e*: and understanding ⊖ *intelligendumque*] Here recurs the contrast between speech and understanding which was adumbrated, although in a concealed manner, by the use of '*aut*' ⊖ 'or' in 4.11 (cf. *n*4.1102*a*, *n*4.1103*a*). For the present, owing to this earlier use of '*aut*' ⊖ 'or', the Student does not see the full force of the contrast, and so here merely juxtaposes speech and understanding. However, once the relation between '*intelligere*' ⊖ 'to understand' and '*significatio*' ⊖ 'meaning' is realised (cf. *n*3.101*a* and the references there given) it is plain that the central distinction between *appellatio* ⊖ reference (defined in terms of *usus loquendi* ⊖ the current course of utterance) and *per se* meaning (4.23) is here being approached. That central distinction finally emerges from a long complaint made by the Student (4.20, 4.21, 4.22) on the way in which common usage and the assertions of logicians appear to be at cross-purposes. Here once again, as we are later to realise, *per se* meaning and *appellatio* ⊖ reference are being opposed. The subtle way in which the contrast is thus built up and resolved betrays the very great concern for logical precision which underlies the whole structure of the dialogue.

*n*4.14*f*: literate ⊖ *grammatico*] In view of the preceding words ('*loquendum intelligendumque*' ⊖ 'speech and understanding') it follows that the word '*grammaticus*' ⊖ 'literate' as it occurs in the resultant context, can be understood in two manners. In relation to the '*loquendum*' conjunct it is nominal ('**g**' or 'trm⟨γ⟩' (§3.11)), but in relation to the '*intelligendum*' ⊖ 'understanding' conjunct it is verb-like (e.g. 'Cl⟦trm⟨γ⟩⟧' (§3.14)); cf. *n*4.31*a*. The Student does not, of course, realise this, but Anselm has clearly taken great care to make the sentence as ambiguous as possible while at the same time not losing touch with the points which he desires to develop: cf. *n*4.14*e*.

*n*4.14*g*: settle down ⊖ *quiescat*] Two points are of interest here. The mention of the settling down or resting of the mind has its origin in

Boethius' translation of Aristotle's *De Interpretatione: constituit enim qui dicit intellectum, et qui audit quiescit* ⊖ the speaker has a determinate understanding, and the hearer also rests: *BDIL* 309C, *BDIG* 429C. Anselm uses the '*constituere intellectum*' ⊖ 'to establish the understanding' type of expression at 4.4233 of the present dialogue, and elsewhere (*n*4.813*b*); this in fact becomes a common medieval form of logical expression. The mention of the hearer's *mind* rather than the hearer's *intellect* suggests that Anselm was echoing Boethius' greater commentary on *De Interpretatione*, rather than the lesser: compare *B* 310 and *B* 430, and see also *HL* § 1.4.

*n*4.14*h*: with my enlightenment ⊖ *ut me doceas*] The Student is of course correct in his suspicions that the Tutor has not really made clear what is at the bottom of the trouble. Indeed, the Tutor has not only, by his subtle use of '*aut*' ⊖ 'or' in 4.110 (cf. *n*4.1102*a*, *n*4.1103*a*) been at pains to conceal the central contrast (4.23) without at the same time asserting falsehood, but has also ensured the production of a carefully worked-out set of assertions exemplifying some of the talk at cross-purposes which goes on if that contrast is ignored (4.12, 4.13). Yet all this is part of a teaching process whereby the Student is plunged, in true Socratic style, into a full experience of the confusions inherent in the situation. He will then be in a proper position to appreciate the solution.

*n*4.14*i*: understood ⊖ *intelligere*] The Tutor, by his use of the loose '*modo*' ⊖ 'sometimes' and the juxtaposition of '*loqui*' ⊖ 'to speak' and '*intelligere*' ⊖ 'to understand', is still underplaying the radical division between *usus loquendi* ⊖ spoken usage and *per se* signification (cf. *n*4.14*e*). The same concealment was effected by the '*aut*' ⊖ 'or' of 4.1102 and 4.1103 (cf. the respective notes). However, the Student himself will now bring that division into the open in the form of the contrast between logicians' personal current spoken usage and their technical logical assertions (4.21, 4.22).

*n*4.20*a*: literacy as well as *man* ⊖ *hominem et grammaticam*] The Student is here using 'to signify' instead of the correlated 'is' (cf. e.g. *n*4.14*a*) which occurred in the Tutor's results (4.111, 4.112) to which reference is now being made. However, those results are shortly (4.23) to be refined in terms of distinctions between ways of signifying, as a consequence of the Student's present speech. The scandal against spoken usage now to be brought to light is caused by the apparent use of 'literate' to *refer* to literacy (since it is now agreed that 'literate' signifies the latter as well as man). The Tutor will rectify this mistaken impression that *reference* to literacy is here intended by his clarification at 4.2340.

*n*4.20*b*: at some gathering ⊖ *in populo*] The setting of the examples in a situation in which only the rules of grammar founded on spoken usage and not on the rules of logical grammar, are assumed to be operative, is quite deliberate. It leads up to the mention of *usus loquendi* ⊖ the current course of utterance in the definition of *appellatio* ⊖ reference (4.2341).

*n*4.20*c*: literate ⊖ *grammaticus*] The Student will shortly blame this nonsense on the dialecticians who insist that *literate* is a quality (4.211), an insistence which has the ungrammatical consequence that *grammaticus est grammatica* ⊖ *literate* is literacy (cf. 4.2341, 4.5022). It is, strictly speaking, on the strength of the latter that the present nonsensical assertion is made, i.e. it is taken to authorise the substitution of '*grammaticus*' ⊖ 'literate' for '*grammatica*' ⊖ 'literacy' in the sentence '*Utilis scientia est grammatica*' ⊖ 'Literacy is a useful form of knowledge'. At any rate, '*grammaticus est grammatica*' ⊖ '*literate* is literacy' is the sentence recognised as stating a logical truth while trespassing against *usus loquendi* ⊖ the current course of utterance, in the Tutor's response to the present difficulty (4.234, cf. 4.5022). In particular it will be pointed out that '*grammaticus*' ⊖ 'literate' is not appellative of *grammatica* ⊖ literacy (4.2340), i.e. is not usable in the course of *usus loquendi* ⊖ spoken usage to refer to *grammatica* ⊖ literacy (4.2341). This, however, is precisely the kind of reference which the Student supposes himself to be making in his present grammatical experiment. The example which he uses may have been suggested by Cicero's specimen conclusion '*Utilis ... est iuris civilis scientia*' ⊖ 'Civil law is a useful form of knowledge': *BTC* 1058D.

*n*4.20*d*: literate ⊖ *grammaticus*] The mistaken assumption underlying the substitution of '*grammaticus*' ⊖ 'literate' for '*grammatica*' ⊖ 'literacy' here is the same as in the previous case (cf. *n*4.20c). The English version of the present sentence has had to be arranged to accord with the adoption of 'literacy' as the translation of '*grammatica*' and hence loses some of the original effect (cf. the next note).

*n*4.20*e*: the ignorant would guffaw ⊖ *ridebunt rustici*] In the original Latin this clause might at first sight appear somewhat incongruous, since taken literally it means that the peasants ('*rustici*') will appreciate the ungrammatical nature of a Latin sentence. After all, peasants could hardly be supposed to speak Latin at this date. One is hence initially tempted to construe this remark as one construes the account of some *rustica puella* ⊖ peasant lass in the *Carmina Burana*; when she espies the scholar on the greensward she must not be supposed literally to say to him in Latin '*Veni mecum ludere!*' ⊖ 'Come and sport with me!'. On the contrary, the quoted remarks in such contexts have to be understood as the translation of some current vernacular. However, an interesting sidelight on the use of '*rusticus*' ⊖ 'peasant' at the monastery of Bec, where the dialogue was written, occurs in the works of the chronicler Orderic Vitalis, according to whom the less literate of the monks of Bec were called '*rustici*' ⊖ 'peasants', and yet were in fact well able to appreciate Latin grammar, for he says: 'From their conversation, even of those who seem illiterate among them, and are called peasants (*rustici*), even pompous men of letters (*spumantes grammatici*) may learn something worth knowing'. This being understood, we find ourselves admitted to a monastic private joke of the 11th century: cf. *HL* §1.1, *HR* 131–2.

The reason why the *grammatici* ⊖ grammarians would be annoyed at the senseless sentences is rather more obvious. It is not merely that queer things appear to be asserted about *grammatici* ⊖ grammarians in those sentences, but – and this is much more serious – the rules laid down by *grammatici* ⊖ grammarians, the rules governing *usus loquendi* ⊖ spoken usage are therein being violated. And Anselm himself is going to assert that logic demands such violation, although not the ones here perpetrated by the Student (4.2341). Anselm's picture of the annoyance of the *grammaticus* ⊖ grammarian on such an occasion is paralleled by John of Salisbury's description of the behaviour of the *grammaticus* ⊖ grammarian on a similar occasion (*SM* 39.11.26, quoted *n*4.2341*a*). Later in the dialogue Anselm is finally to deny the consequences for ordinary speech here drawn by pointing (in 4.62) to the very procedures which are adopted by the grammarians. On the conflict between logicians and grammarians of which *De Grammatico* is itself a reflection, see *HL* §3.124.

*n*4.210*a*: in writing ⊖ *scripsisse*] In view to 4.5122 – 4.6 it would appear that the '*tractatores dialecticae*' ⊖ 'writers on logic' whose modes of expression Anselm is most concerned to explain must be Aristotle, Boethius, and any other authors on logic who write in their style. The written words in the books of such writers are the correlate of the '*intelligere*' ⊖ 'to understand' which has hitherto been mentioned along with, and as an alternative to, '*loqui*' ⊖ 'to speak; cf. e.g. *n*4.14*e*. Such books are concerned with meaning in the strict (*per se*) sense of the word, to which *intelligere* ⊖ understanding in its strict sense is linked: cf. *n*3.101*a* and references there given. '*Grammaticus est grammatica*' ⊖ '*Literate* is literacy' is used as an example of one of the logicians' statements which sins against *usus loquendi* ⊖ spoken usage (4.212, 4.2341, 4.5022). Thus '*intelligere*' ⊖ 'to understand' and '*loqui*' ⊖ 'to speak' are now no longer to be seen as alternatives on the same level, so to speak, but as separated by distinctions as to logical type.

Whether Boethius' logical writings contain such sins against usage, or whether Anselm is only entitled to say that such sins may be inferred as consequences of what Boethius writes, is a matter that might be worthy of further investigation. In point of fact, for instance, Boethius himself feels impelled to rectify such potential sins, as when he overtly denies the propriety of '*White* is a quality' (*BC* 239C, cf. *n*4.2341*b* and *HL* §3.121).

*n*4.210*b*: in conversation ⊖ *colloquentes*] This word is, of course, a link with '*loquens in populo*' ⊖ 'uttering at some gathering' of 4.20, as well as with the previous contrast of *loqui* ⊖ speaking with *intelligere* ⊖ understanding which will be carried forward into the *appellatio/significatio* ⊖ calling/meaning distinction of 4.23. The present assertion hence refers to the non-technical conversation of logicians, and not, of course, to their written or spoken words in technical discussion; in the latter, as in the present dialogue (cf. *n*1.000*b*) their speech as well as their writings may well involve breaches of *usus loquendi* ⊖ spoken usage, and the Student betrays a continued uneasiness on just this point (4.5022).

*n*4.211*a*: to show ⊖ *ostendere*] This verb, although the origin of the English 'ostensive', should not be taken to indicate anything resembling the 'ostensive definition' of the moderns; cf. *n*4.14*c* and *n*4.604*c*.

*n*4.211*b*: accident ⊖ *accidens*] Strictly speaking, this second alternative is superfluous, since a quality is a particular case of an accident. Of course, the intention might be to mean 'or some *other* accident'.

*n*4.211*c*: and so on ⊖ *similia*] '*Grammaticus*' ⊖ 'literate' is, as the Student here says, constantly used throughout Boethius' translations and commentaries as a quality-word. It is prominent in the *Categoriae* and its commentary, particularly in that section which treats of quality (*BC* 239–261, cf. *n*1.201*b*).

*n*4.212*a*: everyone's spoken usage ⊖ *usus omnium loquentium*] Here we have a continuation of the *loqui*/*intelligere* ⊖ speaking/understanding contrast (cf. *n*4.14*i*, *n*4.20*b*, *n*4.210*b*) which now brings into play almost the same expression which the Tutor is to employ when defining *appellatio* (4.2341), i.e. the expression '*usus loquendi*' ⊖ 'spoken usage'.

*n*4.212*b*: of that sort ⊖ *huiusmodi*] It is easy to specify other names of the same sort as 'literate' which will not serve to 'show' substances: such names are the paronyms which are the general topic of the dialogue (cf. *n*1.000*e*). The logical reason why such names will not serve is that they are extra-theoretical in respect of their *appellata* ⊖ referents (cf. 4.23 and §4), the range of such *appellata* ⊖ referents lying within *species specialissimae* of substances (cf. *n*4.2341*a*). 'Literate' is appellative of man; it does not signify man *per se* (4.23). The practical counterparts of these logical reasons are the difficulties of ostensive definition of paronyms (cf. *n*4.14*c*) and the possibility of asking the 'What is the something else ...?' question which the use of paronyms leaves open (cf. *n*4.1201*a*, *n*4.31*a*).

*n*4.22*a*: signifies ⊖ *significat*] The Student is still using '*significat*' ⊖ 'signifies' as he did at the beginning of his speech (4.20) in preference to the scandalous 'is' (cf. *n*1.000*b*, *n*4.14*a*), and here seems to be implying that that 'is' is a consequence of facts of signification. Thus he is here saying that 'literate' signifies man and literacy, and that therefore *literate* is substance and quality.

*n*4.22*b*: quality ⊖ *qualitas*] The Student's juxtaposition of 'substance' and 'quality' at this point brings out how cleverly the Tutor, while making only true statements (e.g. 4.1102, 4.1103, 4.111, 4.112, 4.14, cf. *n*4.1102, *n*4.1103*a*, *n*4.14*i*) has allowed the Student to think that the results so far obtained mean that the 'substance' and 'quality' aspects of '*grammaticus*' ⊖ 'literate' stand on the same level, so to speak. In fact, as the Tutor will shortly show (4.23) the ways in which '*grammaticus*' ⊖ 'literate' signifies quality and substance are vastly discrepant, and it is therefore misleading to juxtapose them in this manner.

*n*4.22*c*: substance ⊖ *substantia*] It has been suggested that one of the factors which gave rise to the topic of the dialogue was a difference of opinion between grammarians and logicians on the function of paronyms like '*grammaticus*' ⊖ 'literate' (*n*1.201*b*, *n*3.800*b*, *n*4.2341*a*). It may also very well be that the position which the Student is now putting forward, namely that both paronyms and concrete non-paronymous names (which are assumed to be substance-names) signify substance and quality on the same level, is itself a representation of a position held by grammarians. Priscian appears at some points to have maintained such a doctrine: *Proprium est nominis substantiam et qualitatem significare* ⊖ the special property of the name is that it signifies substance and quality; *K* II 55.6. This doctrine, without the necessary qualifications suggested by Anselm in 4.23, is plainly at variance with the logicians' thesis that paronyms, strictly speaking, signify only quality. Even the admission, on the part of logicians, that 'man' signifies substance and quality, must be understood in such a way that 'man' cannot be profered as an example of a quality-word (4.23). It was in *HW* that I first suggested that here we have the roots of a controversy between logicians and grammarians. The supposition that Anselm is in fact putting a grammatical thesis into the mouth of the Student is confirmed in the first place by Abelard's discussion of what is, in effect, part of the same question as that of the present dialogue. In the treatise on meaning in his *Dialectica* Abelard refers to controversy among certain masters, as to whether the referents of a name should be included in an account of its meaning ('*utrum omnis impositio in significatione ducatur*'). Reference is there made to the grammatical doctrine, as well as to a development of it which in some ways resembles Anselm's position;

Those who channel all reference into meaning claim to have the authority to say that whatsoever the name applies to is signified by it; thus for them 'animal' signifies also *man*, 'man' signifies Socrates, and the relevant physical object is signified by 'white' and 'coloured' (cf. 4.4211). They are led to demonstrate this by recourse not only to the logical art, but also to the authority of Grammar. Grammar (they say) lays it down that every name signifies both substance and quality, so that 'white' which both names the relevant substance and delineates its quality, signifies both. However, the quality is signified primarily, since it is the justification for the reference, and the object secondarily.	*His vero qui omnem vocum impositionem in significationem deducunt, auctoritatem praetendunt ut ea quoque significari dicant a voce quibuscumque ipsa est imposita, ut ipsum quoque hominem ab 'animali' vel Socratem ab 'homine', vel subiectum corpus ab 'albo' vel 'colorato'; nec solum ex arte, verum etiam ex autoritate grammaticae, id conantur ostendere. Cum enim tradat grammatica omne nomen substantiam cum qualitate significare, 'album' quoque quod subiectam nominat substantiam et qualitatem determinat circa eam, utrumque dicitur significare; sed qualitatem quidem principaliter causa cuius impositum est, subiectum vero secundario: A* 113.15.24

The '*principaliter*' ⊖ 'primarily' and '*secundario* ⊖ 'secondarily' recur in a 12th century gloss (*DLM* II–I 258) and correspond exactly to the distinction between *per se* meaning and oblique meaning made by Anselm, insofar as these apply to names (4.232).

The whole passage of Abelard's from which the above is an extract is an account of a controversy centred round the grammarian's definition of a name, in which Anselm is an earlier participant, as is further amply confirmed at numerous points in *DLM*, e.g. II–I 98, 183–6, 222–3, 225–6, 232–2, 222–3, 241–3, 259–60, 521–3. For a general account of the development of medieval grammar see also *DLM* II–I, Ch. II.

*n*4.22*d*: characteristics ⊖ *differentiis*] It would be misleading to translate '*differentia*' as 'difference'; the word rather conveys *that by which* the relation of difference is constituted. Thus 'differentiator' would be an adequate coining, but the word 'characteristic' has been used as the minimum translation in the present work.

The prime text available to Anselm and dealing with the various kinds of *differentia* ⊖ characteristics centres around Boethius' works on Porphyry, in particular the second dialogue on Porphyry (*BDP* 47–54) and Bk. IV of the commentary on Porphyry (*BCP* 115–130). These embody an apparent optimism as to the objectivity of human capacities for the classification of things, an optimism not shared, for instance, by Aquinas. The present note, therefore, falls roughly into two parts, the first consisting of largely uncritical exposition, and the second of qualifications.

Following Porphyry, Boethius distinguishes three types of characteristics; they may be either common (*communes*), individual (*propriae*) or overriding (*magis propriae*): *BDP* 48C, *BCP* 115C–116D. Common characteristics are those attributable to various individuals, and more particularly, to a single individual at different times: thus you may now stand while I sit, whereas a few moments ago you sat while I stood: further, I who now sit was a short while ago standing. Here *standing* and *sitting* are examples of common characteristics; such characteristics are not attributable to the individual during the whole of its existence, and are attributable to other individuals (*BCP* 117A–B). Individual characteristics (*differentiae propriae*) are, generally speaking, those which endure during the whole span of the individual's existence, such as blue-grey eyes, curly hair (*BCP* 48C–D) or a snub nose, and are in some sense inseparable from the individual (*BCP* 117B). Overriding characteristics (*differentiae magis propriae*) are those which will be encountered later in the dialogue (4.2411) under the title of "constitutive" (or 'substantial') characteristics; they are those whereby one species of existents is distinguished from another, in the way that rationality or mortality specify *man* (*BDP* 48D, *BCP* 117C–D). The reason for the '*propriae*' and '*magis propriae*' terminology is said to be grounded in the fact that common characteristics are separable (*separabiles*) from the individuals to which they are attributed, i.e. they may be found elsewhere than in those individuals, whereas individual differences (*propriae*) are not so separable. Nevertheless, both represent merely accidental, extra-theoretical characteristics: a man does not cease to be a man because he happens to have or not to have some one or other of them. Constitutive characteristics such as rationality, however, are not merely inseparable from individual men (as are the *propriae*) but are also inseparable from man *qua* species, hence the '*magis propriae*': *BCP* 117D. It is in this sense that Boethius is able to define a characteristic (*differentia*) as that which is predicated in respect of quality of various things of different species: *differentia est quae ad plurimas res specie distantes in eo quod quale praedicatur; BDP* 52D. (See *n*3.521*a* on '*in eo quod quale*' ⊖ 'in respect of quality').

From a logical point of view the third type of characteristic, the *differentia magis propriae* ⊖ characteristic in the fullest sense, or as we may also call it, the overriding characteristic, is the most important, and the examples quoted suggest that reference is usally being made to these in

Anselm's dialogue when the word *differentia* appears without further qualification; thus '*sensibilitas*' ⊖ 'sensibility', '*mortalitas*' ⊖ 'mortality' (4.22) and '*rationalitas*' ⊖ 'rationality' (4.231) are mentioned without qualification.

Is it possible to further specify the way in which *differentiae magis propriae* ⊖ overriding characteristics are distinguishable from others? For the fact that they are inseparable from the species (cf. *n*4.2411*h*) does not suffice to distinguish them totally from individual accidents, which are also incapable, though in a different sense, of separation. Well, they are in the first place responsible for the essential distinctions of things from things, whereas the other sorts of characteristic establish accidental distinctions only. This diversification of types of characteristic is expressed in various ways by Boethius and others. In the second dialogue on Porphyry common and individual characteristics are said to be '*alteratum facientes*' ⊖ 'otherwise-making', while overriding characteristics are '*alterum facientes*' ⊖ 'other-making'. The first merely differentiate between various states of the same changing individual or individuaals, the second represent the deeper and more permanent division of one kind of thing from another, as in the case of *rational* which separates *man* out from all other animals: *BDP* 49A–C. Thus the same man may at various times be curly-haired or bald, but no single object is ever at once or at various times a man and a horse. Boethius appears to be inconsistent when he says, without qualification, that both common and individual characteristics give rise to numerical disparity: *ex communibus et propriis secundum numerum distantiae nascuntur; BCP* 117D. Common ones at any rate *need* not do so, since they can cause us, for example, to differ only from our former selves: *communes sunt quibus omnes aut ab aliis differimus, aut a nobis ipsis; BDP* 48C.

In the commentary on Porphyry a kindred distinction is made between '*alteratum*' ⊖ 'otherwise' and '*aliud*' ⊖ 'other-sorted'. According to this distinction accidental (i.e. common and individual) characteristics merely make a thing *otherwise than (alteratum)* its fellow existents, while constitutive or overriding characteristics make a thing to be of a different sort *(aliud)* from other things:

Common and proper characteristics are accidents which only make a thing otherwise, ... whereas characteristics in the

Communes et propriae differentiae ... accidentium sunt quae solum efficiunt alteratum ... magis autem propriae, quoniam

fullest sense, since they fix the substance and are predicated as features of its structure, make things not merely otherwise, but also of other sorts.

substantiam tenent et in subiecti forma praedicantur, non modo alteratum ... sed etiam aliud faciunt: BCP 118B–C.

Aquinas uses a similar terminology:

Even as an accidental characteristic makes a thing otherwise, so also an essential characteristic is the reason for other-sortedness.

Sicut accidentalis differentia facit alterum, ita differentia essentialis facit aliud: AST III q.2, art 3, ad 1.

One thus has *alteritas* ⊖ otherwiseness, which comes from accidental characteristics, and does not necessarily give rise to numerical plurality, and essential distinction, which does:

Otherwiseness, which arises from accidental characteristics, may have reference to the same substance or subject as far as created things are concerned, in that the same individual can be the bearer of various accidental characteristics. However, in created things the same individual's being the bearer of various essences or natures does not occur.

Alteritas, quae provenit ex differentia accidentali, potest ad eandem hypostasim vel suppositum pertinere in rebus creatis, eo quod idem numero potest diversis accidentibus subesse. Non autem contingit in rebus creatis quod idem numero subsistere possit diversis essentiis vel naturis: AST III q. 2, art. 3, ad 1; cf. *APA* 544.

However, unless the meanings of '*alterum*' and '*aliud*' are firmly fixed, and *APA* 544 alone suffices to suggest that they are not, then they are of little use in making more precise the notion of overriding characteristics.

Nevertheless, overriding characteristics insofar as they are diversifiers of genera into species, i.e. insofar as they are *differentiae substantiales* ⊖ constitutive characteristics, can, according to Boethius, be distinguished from common and individual characteristics by the fact that the two latter are both susceptible of degree, while the former are not:

Inseparable characteristics which are merely individual can vary by way of increase or decrease. However, overriding (or constitutive) characteristics neither increase by the gathering of intensity nor decrease by fading away.

Inseparabiles propriae possunt alicui plus minusve contingere. Inseparabiles magis propriae nec cumulis intentionis augentur, nec imminutione decrescunt: BDP 50A.

Constitutive characteristics are susceptible neither of increase nor decrease.

Substantiales differentiae neque intentionem, neque remissionem suscipiunt: BCP 121C, cf. *A* 424–432.

Thus *literate* and *white* are common characteristics, both susceptible of degree (cf. 3.111, 3.112) whereas *rational* (like *man* in 3.112) is not thus susceptible:

The constitutive characteristic *rational* does not admit of degree. All men, insofar as they are men, are equally rational and mortal.

At vero magis propria, id est rationale, neque plus neque minus admittit. Omnes enim homines in eo quod homines sunt, aequaliter sunt rationales atque mortales: BDP 50B, cf. *BCP* 121D.

This, explains Boethius, is because the definition created by the addition of the overriding characteristic to the genus is equally applicable to all men.

To the objection that it appears sensible to say that one man is more rational than another, Abelard replies that when this comparison is made then '*rationcinans*' ⊖ 'reasoning' probably represent better the sense of 'rational' here: *nec hic homo magis rationalis, sed fortasse magis rationcinans* ⊖ it's not that this man is more rational, but rather, as the case may be, more reasoning: *A* 425–6. (On this question of susceptibility of degree, see *n*3.111*a*).

That definitions (cf. *n*3.800*b*) comprising *differentiae substantiales* ⊖ constitutive characteristics are not detached from matters of fact is shown by another feature of them which figures in *De Grammatico* itself (4.2411): they must be such that their presence or absence affects the existence of what is being defined (cf. *n*4.2411*d*). Thus one might suggest that man is the only literate animal, or the only animal capable of navigating (*BDP* 54C), calculating, or doing geometry (*BD* 881B) and hence that some one or other of these notes would suffice as a characteristic constitutive of the species *man*. Yet in fact there are no beings who exist just as long as they can navigate, or rhetoricise, or possess a literate capacity (*BDP* 54C). Hence such characteristics will not serve to differentiate species from their genera; man is not just *animal navigabile* ⊖ an animal capable of sailing (*BDP* 54C, cf. *BCP* 129B–130B). These remarks of Boethius appear to convey that the *esse* ⊖ being of a thing is bound up with its definition, a position which he adopts elsewhere, and which Anselm takes up from him (cf. *n*3.800*b*). The same idea is underlined in *BCP* 129B–130B.

For Aquinas the statement of what something is *(quod quid est)* does not constitute an account of the *esse* of that thing:

What is involved in being a man and *being a man* are diverse. In the first Principle of being only, which is essentially being, are *being* itself and *whatness* to be identified. In all other things, which are beings by

Aliud est quod quid est homo et esse hominem: in solo enim primo essendi Principio, quod est essentialiter ens, ipsum esse et quidditas eius est unum et idem: in omnibus autem aliis, quae sunt entia per

participation, the *being* and *whatness* of the thing must be diverse.	*participationem, oportet quod sit aliud esse et quidditas entis: APA* 463.

An important change has plainly taken place here in relation to the earlier doctrine taken for granted by Anselm. For the study of some of its details I have found *JN* an excellent aid. In *HEE* and *HLM* III §6 a tentative suggestion as to the formulation of Aquinas' position in terms of Leśniewski's Ontology is made.

It may also be noted that according to Aquinas, while the fact that one thing *differs* from another (because of characteristics of the types described above) entails that those things are *diverse*, the converse is not true, i.e. it does not always follow that because one thing is *diverse* from another those things must also be *different*. For difference presupposes a certain community – likeness in some respects, unlikeness in others – and hence also a certain compositeness. But two (alleged) simples, such as overriding characteristics, cannot evince such a presupposed community, and hence are not merely different from each other, but should rather be said to be *diverse* from each other: AST I q. 90, art. 1 ad 3. Similarly, God does not *differ* from *materia prima* ⊖ prime matter, yet one cannot conclude from this that God is the same as *materia prima* ⊖ prime matter: the two are in fact *diverse: AST* I, q. 3, art. 8, ad 3.

Since the notion of constitutive or overriding characteristic is closely connected with the rules of definition presupposed by the Aristotelians, and since these rules in turn imply a certain conception of unity, the following notes should also be consulted for further clarifications of the context within which such characteristics are brought into play: *n*3.800*b*, *n*4.2411*h*, *n*4.2414*b*, *n*4.72*a*. For a thirteenth-century account see *KSL* 55–6.

As we have already seen, Boethius' account of characteristics, and in particular of what I have termed 'overriding' or 'constitutive' characteristics *(differentiae magis propriae, differentiae substantiales)* appears to be most optimistic as to human powers of discerning exactly what is or is not part of the essential constitution of things. From the point of view of a totally presuppositionless general account of how things are there seems to be no obvious reason why even *differentiae communes* ⊖ common or shared characteristics should not be held to be constitutive of species, e.g. why should not bald men be considered to be a species of men? For while it is quite true that a man does not cease to be a man on becoming (or ceasing to be) bald, he does nevertheless cease to be a *bald-man* on ceasing to be bald: 'bald' is a constitutive characteristic, then, of *bald-men*. Similar points could be urged as regards 'literate', 'navigating' and 'rhetorical', which are mentioned by Boethius as accidental characteristics (*BDP* 54C, *BCP* 130A). The same goes for colour-names too. It is easy to urge the view that the whole apparatus outlined is in fact purely relative to the pragmatically-grounded structure of a particular kind of natural language. Thus, given our form of life it would be highly inconvenient if one had separate single names for white men, black men, tall men, short men, bald men, curly-haired men, and so on, but not the single name 'man', since we more frequently find ourselves wanting to talk about men insofar as they are men, without any necessary commitment as to further differentiating characteristics. Contrast, for example, the Eskimo's variety of names each descriptive of a different type of snow.

Aquinas is in fact prepared to admit that the essential constitutive characteristics of natural objects are, generally speaking, unknown to us, and in any case we lack names for them:

It sometimes happens that that which is most obvious to us is not most obvious absolutely speaking; this discrepancy is exemplified in physical things where essences and capacities are hidden from us since they pertain to matter, and yet they become apparent to us from the surface phenomena available to us.

Quandoque id quod est notius quoad nos, non est notius simpliciter, sicut accidit in naturalibus, in quibus essentiae et virtutes rerum, propter hoc quod in materia sunt, sunt occultae, sed innotescunt nobis per ea quae exterius de ipsis apparent: APA 43 bis.

Constitutive characteristics are not known to us, and we even have no names for them.

substantiales differentiae non sunt nobis notae, vel etiam nominatae non sunt: AST I q. 29, art. 1, ad 3.

In some cases, he says, one must resort to the customary course of utterance in order to make a distinction in this field:

In order to prove this distinction [Aristotle] drew upon the usual fashion of speaking.

ad huius distinctionis probationem [Aristoteles] inducit communem loquendi consuetudinem: AST I–II q. 49, art. 2, ad 3.

He adds that accidental characteristics frequently have to be used instead of substantial ones:

In the category of substance accidental characteristics are frequently taken into account instead of constitutive ones.

In genere substantiae frequenter accipiuntur differentiae accidentales loco substantialium: loc. cit.

These remarks do not, of course, apply to the definition of such things as the objects of mathematics:

Sometimes however, that which is most obvious to us is most obvious absolutely speaking and in accordance with reality: this occurs in mathematics, wherein, thanks to the abstraction from material conditions, demonstrations are only effected by recourse to purely structural principles.	*Quandoque autem id quod est magis notum quoad nos est etiam magis notum simpliciter et secundum naturam: sicut accidit in mathematicis, in quibus, propter abstractionem a materia, non fiunt demonstrationes nisi ex principiis formalibus: APA* 43 bis.

One has thus, on the one hand, an apparently highly naïve spinning out, even to the extent of great tediousness in the case of Boethius, of merely relative distinctions grounded in natural language, and on the other, a just suspicion that such distinctions are comparatively unfounded except when the theoretical language of mathematics is in question. Behind this apparently paradoxical position lies the assumption, among the Aristotelians at least, that metaphysics has to do with being, becoming perishing, one-ness, many-ness, difference and otherness, and all these in senses which are at least initially proportioned to, mean something to, human beings, as opposed to senses which render human beings helpless before the remote fictions of philosophical terminology having no such concern for connection with human intelligibility. Hence one has no alternative, if one's discourse is to have any humanly intelligible relation to how things are, as opposed to how one may remotely guess or conjecture that they may be, to start by considering cases of perishing, for instance, which are recognisable as such before any new theoretical, technical, descriptions have intruded. Otherwise philosophising becomes primarily poetic – a work of construction – tremendously exhilerating for its undertaker, a linguistic *divertissement* of the first order, but carrying with it the threat of alienation from the pre--theoretical ground, with its hopes and fears, achievements and evaluations, from out of which (since all philosophers are men) the enterprise originally grew; 'Where am I, or what? From what causese do I derive my existence, and to what condition shall I return? Whose favour shall I court, and whose anger must I dread? What beings surround me? And on whom have I any influence, or who have any influence on me? I am confounded with all these questions, and begin to fancy myself in the most deplorable condition imaginable, inviron'd with the deepest darkness, and utterly deprived of the use of every member and faculty. Most fortunately it happens, that since reason is incapable of dispelling these clouds, nature herself suffices to that purpose, and cures me of this philosophical melancholy and delirium, either by relaxing this bent of mind, or by some avocation and lively impression of my senses, which obliterate all these chimeras. I dine, I play a game of back-gammon, I converse, and am merry with my friends: and when after three or four hours' amusement, I wou'd return to these speculations, they appear so cold, and strain'd and ridiculous, that I cannot find it in my heart to enter into them any further'; *HT* I Part iv, sec. vii.

The history of modern philosophy is, for the most part, the history of such alienation, usually as a result of pressure and influence from the side of the outlooks and theories involved in the rise of modern science, technology, and invention. Hume's particular alienation, of which the account has just been reproduced, could with some show of justice be described as the consequence of an attempt to portray experience in terms of the *minimum corruptibile* – the 'impression', the 'sense-datum'. Seen in this light the preparedness of Boethius and Aquinas to start at a level of tedious naïveté turns out to be not so naïve; their '*corruptio*' ⊖ 'perishing' is at least a recognisable perishing, not to be abrogated as mere 'appearance' in the light of those theoretical perishings (such as, for instance, the perishing of the *minimum corruptibile*, or of the blushing Socrates when Socrates ceases to blush) which no matter how remote from their pre-theoretical originals, must have some intelligible connection with those originals. The recognition of this primacy of the pre-theoretical has as its counterpart the explanation of primitive terms prior to the advance into an interpreted logical system (cf. §3).

For a discussion of this same point from another aspect see *n*4.72*a*.

*n*4.22*e*: mortality ⊖ *mortalitas*] The Student is, of course, assuming *rational mortal animal* to be the *definiens* of *man*: cf. *n*3.8010*a*.

*n*4.230*a*: make-up ⊖ *ea ex quibus constat*] A similar use of '*constat*' ⊖ 'comprises' occurs in 4.231, 4.240. It has been suggested in §4 that the use of such a verb need not be construed as a crude, material-sounding metaphor referring to the parts of a definition, but as a sign that some functor such as the higher-order 'is' (§3.15) or its arguments are in question.

*n*4.230*b*: literacy ⊖ *grammaticam*] Here are forecast the central distinctions to be made in the dialogue and which are to turn on the diverse ways in which 'man' and 'literate' signify (4.23, 4.71). On the assumption that in accordance with the suggestions of *n*4.2341*b* the *de voce* ⊖ word-centred statements concerning meaning are inferentially equivalent to *de re* ⊖ thing-centred statements in terms of the higher-order 'is' (§3.15), it may first of all be noted that 'man' and 'literate' both figure in sets of terms which satisfy, i.e. make true, the following situation-function:

.1 $[\exists abc] . \mathrm{Cl}[\![a]\!] \in \mathrm{Cl}[\![b \cap c]\!]$

For if, in general, the substitution of some term 'β' for a term 'α' in a given formula is represented by 'α/β', then both the sets of substitutions now listed make .1 true:

.2 $a/\mathbf{h}$ $b/\mathbf{a}$, $c/\mathbf{r}$ (cf. §3)

.3 $a/\mathbf{g}$ $b/\mathbf{h}$, $c/\mathrm{trm}\langle\gamma\rangle$ (cf. §3)

It is to such a factor of community that the Student is drawing attention at 4.240: *homo constat ex animali et rationalitate et mortalitate ... grammatica constat ex homine et grammatica* ⊖ *man* comprises *animal* and rationality and mortality ... *literate* comprises *man* and literacy. Further, .1 with the .3 substitutions not only constitutes the background to many of the '*intelligi*' ⊖ 'to be understood' sentences which occur earlier in the dialogue, but also represents the starting point for the discussions which succeed them. Thus, from the assumption of .1 and .3 not only does it follow that

.4 $\mathrm{Cl}[\![\mathbf{g}]\!] \in \subset [\![\mathbf{h}]\!]$ (§3.13.14.15)

but also that

.5 $\mathrm{Cl}[\![\mathbf{g}]\!] \in \subset [\![\mathrm{trm}\langle\gamma\rangle]\!]$ (§3.11)

and by §3.53 expressions .4 and .5 are respectively inferentially equivalent to the two following:

.6 $\mathbf{g} \subset \mathbf{h}$ (§3.4)

.7 $\mathbf{g} \subset \mathrm{trm}\langle\gamma\rangle$

Now in the discussion at 4.11 we learn that the name 'literate' can convey the sense of *man* or literacy, or can be used to speak of a man or his literacy: *Audito ergo hoc homine* [scil. '*grammaticus*'] *intelligam hominen aut grammaticam; et loquens de grammatico, loquar de homine aut de grammatica* (4.1102, 4.1103) ⊖ On hearing this name ['literate'] then, I may understand *man* or literacy, and when I speak of a literate, my speech concerns a man or literacy. But since *intelligere* ⊖ understanding falls over on the side of *significatio* ⊖ meaning and *definitio* which are the counterparts of the higher-order 'is' (§3.15), the first pair of alternatives just mentioned (i.e. *man* or literacy) corresponds to .4 and .5 and the second pair (a man or (his) literacy) to .6 and .7; (cf. the close of *n*4.2341*b*). The preliminary conclusion which is then drawn, namely that insofar as *man* enters into the situation *literate* is a substance and not *in subiecto* ⊖ in a subject (and is therefore predicated *de subiecto* ⊖ of a subject), but that insofar as literacy is involved, *literate* is a quality and *in subiecto* ⊖ in a subject (and therefore is not predicated *de subiecto* ⊖ of a subject) can also be drawn from .1 with the .3 substitutions. (On *in subiecto/de subiecto* ⊖ in/of a subject see *n*4.101*a*). For given the rules of definition (*n*3.800*b*) here in question, it is clear that *man* is a species of substance, but *literate* is not, hence the possibility of literacy's being a constitutive characteristic is plainly out of court at this juncture (cf. *n*4.22*d*).

However, it is primarily the fact that .2 and .3 *both* provide true instances of .1 which calls forth the central distinction now being forecast, i.e. the distinction between *per se* ⊖ precisive signification and oblique (*per aliud*) signification (i.e. *appellatio* ⊖ reference, in the case of names). For the .3 substitutions yield the *prima facie* paradoxical result that *literate* is both substance and quality: why then cannot the .2 substitutions, which also verify .1, be said to allow the inference that *man* is both substance and quality? This is the question raised at 4.22 to which the Tutor is now giving a reply. It later turns out (4.2411) that part of the difference lies in the sort of factor mentioned in the last paragraph, in that where *literate* is concerned literacy is not a constitutive characteristic, whereas in the case of *man* rationality is such a characteristic (cf. *n*4.22*d*).

Comment on the central distinctions here forecast, and which appear at 4.231–4.2341 is provided in *n*4.232*b* and *n*4.2341*a*.

*n*4.231*a*: as a single whole ⊖ *ut unum*] The point of the locution *'per se et ut unum'* ⊖ 'precisively and as a single whole' in relation to at least the verbal development of Anselm's theme is easy enough to determine: it is posed here in contrast to what holds in the case of *literate* which at

4.232 is said not to signify *man* and literacy *'ut unum'* ⊖ 'as a single whole' but literacy *per se* ⊖ precisively and *man per aliud* ⊖ obliquely. Other occurrences of *'ut unum'* are in 4.71, and the meaning of this qualification is discussed in the note to *'unum totum'* ⊖ 'one whole' (*n*4.231*e*) as well as in *n*4.72*a* and *n*4.31*a*. *Per se* ⊖ precisive signification is discussed in *n*4.232*b*, i.e. in connection with the application of the present qualifications to the paronym *'literate'*.

*n*4.231*b*: make-up ⊖ *ea ex quibus constat*] See *n*4.230*a*, *n*4.240*a* and §4.

*n*4.231*c*: substance ⊖ *substantia*] See *n*4.1201*a* and the references there given.

*n*4.231*d*: exist ⊖ *existere*] It should be clear from *n*4.1201*a* and the material there cited that this way of speaking does not entail that a human being is made up of a central nucleus of an unknown something called substance around which his qualities cling. Anselm is here saying, in effect, that the theory of *man* is such that men have that sort of theoretical object-hood typified by the sentence '*man* is a substance', wherein the 'is' is of a higher type than the 'is' of 'This man is pale' (cf. §4, §3.15, and the close of *n*3.800*b*).

The end of the last sentence (*quoniam est causa* ... *indigentia* ⊖ as the ground .. without it) reflects the position of substance-words as stop-words, as marks of a completeness such that in ordinary discourse it is inappropriate to continue with the 'What is the something else ...?' question: cf. *n*4.1201*a*. The present sentence, as the '*enim*' ⊖ 'for' towards its opening shows, is an expression of the foregoing fact in the technical terminology of substance and characteristic; on the latter see *n*4.22*d*. These considerations are also reflected in the requirements of the theory of definition (*n*3.800*b*) by means of genus (*n*4.2411g) and constitutive characteristic (*n*4.22*d*).

The '*indigens*' ('incomplete', 'lacking', or 'needful') of the present passage may have been inspired by the *Liber de Persona et Duabus Naturis* which uses a similar turn of speech with regard to substance and accident:

That thing *subsists* which is not in need of accidents in order that it may exist.	*Subsistit enim, quod ipsum accidentibus, ut possit esse, non indiget; substat autem id*

That thing *substands* which supplies to other accidental things a certain subject, relative to which they may exist. Individuals not only subsist but also substand, for to exist they do not need accidents.

quod aliis accidentibus subiectum quoddam, ut esse valeant, subministrat ... Individua vero non modo subsistunt, verum etiam substant; nam neque ipsa indigent accidentibus, ut sint: BPDN 1344B.

Further, Anselm's *'Nulla est differentia substantiae sine qua substantia inveniri non possit'* ⊖ 'There is no characteristic of substance in the absence of which substance is also absent' of the present passage is a direct expression of Boethius' *'Idem ait substantiam ad alia substantiam, in eo quod substantia sit, nulla differentia disgregari'* ⊖ 'He said that *qua* substance no substance has characteristics which separate it off from any other': *BDP* 16C.

In the light of what is said on 'substance' in *n*4.1201*a* it would not be too difficult for a sympathetic reader to give an unexceptionable sense to statements such as these. In the absence of such sympathy, however, we are plainly launched in the direction of a Lockeian 'featureless somewhat' interpretation of the theory of substance.

*n*4.231*e*: as a single whole ⊖ *velut unum totum*] This is an alternative expression of the '*ut unum*' ⊖ 'as one thing' which has occurred shortly before (cf. *n*4.231*a*) and which will recur in 4.232 and 4.710. The general intention is clear: the scission between *man* and literacy which is effected in 4.232 in respect of *grammaticus* ⊖ literate must be avoided in the case of *man*, if the Student's contention of 4.22 is to be rebutted (cf. *n*4.230*b*). This insistence of the unity of man's make-up is the way in which the scission is avoided. However, that this insistence is not a mere debating point, brought forward for the local purposes of the dialogue, is made clear by the background to '*unum aliquid*' ⊖ 'one thing': *n*4.72*a*, *n*4.2411*h* (ii), *n*4.2414*b*. This in its turn is linked with the theory of definition: *n*3.800*b*. These points reflect the possibility of unambiguous countability and the inappropriateness of the 'What is the something else...?' question expressed by the use of the word 'substance': n4.1201*a*.

*n*4.231*f*: principally signifies ⊖ *principaliter ... significativum*] cf. *n*4.232*b* on *significatio per se* ⊖ precisive signification.

*n*4.231*g*: appellative ⊖ *appellativum*] See *n*4.233*a* on *appellatio* ⊖ reference. In his misguided and unsympathetic discussion of *De Grammatico* Prantl (*PG* II 92 et seq.) blames Gerberon for having omitted in his edition of Anselm a '*non*' ⊖ 'not' before the word '*appellativum*' ⊖ 'appellative' at his point. Hence according to Prantl the text should read: '*Hoc nomen est significativum et non appellativum substantiae*' ⊖ 'This name signifies but is not appellative of substance'. However, Dom Schmitt in his edition mentions no variant MS which would authorise this emendation; the latter is in fact only suggested because its absence damages Prantl's own interpretation of the dialogue. Quite apart from the interpretation suggested in the present study, this emendations seems unjustified on account of its inconsistency with 4.710 and 4.711, where 'man' is said to be both significative and appellative of the '*unum quiddam*' ⊖ 'one object', the '*res*' ⊖ 'thing', which is a man.

*n*4.231*h*: of substance ⊖ *substantiae*] The foregoing statement has the effect of guaranteeing the theoretical unity of *man* and expressing the unity *in re* of each individual man (cf. *n*4.1201*a* and §4). The theoretical unity represented by '*hoc nomen est significativum substantiae*' ⊖ 'this name signifies substance' eliminates any possibility of future *usus loquendi* ⊖ spoken usage extending the use of the word 'man', whereas the lack of any such theoretical unity between *man* and literacy (4.232) leaves open the possibility of extension in the case of *literate*. According to this thesis, Anselm could never call a 'thinking machine' a 'man', although he might be prepared to call such a machine 'literate' provided it displayed the necessary aptitudes. In other words, a new theory, in respect of this new extension of 'literate' would not be necessary: cf. *n*4.31*a*. In the case of *man* the elimination of any such further extension has as a consequence the automatic coincidence of accounts of *appellatio* ⊖ 'calling' (cf. *n*4.234*b*) and *per se* ⊖ precisive signification (cf. *n*4.232*b*), at least in the unrefined accounts of the two available in unmodified natural language.

*n*4.231*i*: rationality ⊖ *rationalitatem*] It may well be asked: what is the point of this procedure at this juncture? Why, in confirmation of his earlier statements (as the exemplary '*ut*' ⊖ 'as in the case of' indicates) should the Tutor bring to bear this contrast between what may be rightly or correctly asserted (*recte dicatur*) and that which no-one would say?

From 4.2341 it is evident that this contrast is intended as a confirmation of his previous assertion according to which 'man' is principally appellative of substance. The sentences '*substantia est homo*' ⊖ 'the substance is a man' and '*homo est substantia*' ⊖ '*man* is a substance' both accord with, or at least serve to underpin, *usus loquendi* ⊖ spoken usage, and hence may be used as an index of '*appellatio*' ⊖ 'calling'. In contrast, there is no such object as *rationalitas* ⊖ rationality of which 'man' is appellative since, as has also been previously asserted: '*nulla differentiarum eius* [scil. *substantiae*] *sine illa* [scil. *substantia*] *potest existere*' ⊖ 'none of its [i.e. substance's] characteristics can exist without it [i.e. substance]'.

The whole of this passage may be significantly compared with Aquinas' remarks in *AST* III q.2, art.2, *c.*:

Hence it comes about that in such things [i.e. composites of matter and form] the nature and its bearer differ as far as things are concerned; not that they are as it were altogether separate objects; rather, because the bearer comprises the specific nature to which are added certain other things which do not enter into its specification [cf. 4.811] the bearer is therefore signified as a whole *having* a nature which is its formal and constitutive part. It is because of this that in composites of matter and form the nature is not predicated of its bearer: thus we do not assert that this man *is* his humanity.

*Et ideo in talibus [*scil. *in his quae sunt ex materia et forma composita] secundum rem differt natura et suppositum; non quasi omnio aliqua separata, sed quia in supposito includitur ipsa natura speciei, et superadduntur quaedam alia quae sunt praeter rationem speciei: unde suppositum significatur ut totum habens naturam sicut partem formalem et perfectivam sui: et propter hoc in compositis ex materia et forma natura non praedicatur de supposito; non enim dicimus quod hic homo sit sua humanitas.*

Had Anselm been prepared, as he apparently was not (see *HL* 67–8, *HW* 172–3, *HDG* 85–7) to accept '*homo*' ⊖ 'man' as the cognate denominative from '*humanitas*' ⊖ 'humanity', then his example might well have been the same as Aquinas'. Both are insisting that the specification and the thing specified are distinct, but that that thing may be said to *have* whatever is so specified ('*habens naturam*' ⊖ 'having the nature', '*habens rationalitatem*' ⊖ 'having rationality'). Compare also a Latin translation of the *Categoriae*:

If blindness and *blind* were the same, then they would both be predicable of the same thing. But although a man is said to be

Si idem esset caecitas et caecum esse, utrumque de eodem praedicaretur. Sed caecus dicitur homo, caecitas vero nullo

blind, a man cannot sensibly be said to be blindness.	*modo homo dicitur: B* 271A.

Abelard also discusses this passage from the *Categoriae*: *A* 386–7.

*n*3.232*a*: as a single whole ⊖ *ut unum*] This expresses the contrast between the case of 'literate' and that of 'man'; in the case of the latter the components of its meaning are signified '*ut unum*' ⊖ 'as a single whole' (4.231, cf. *n*4.231*e*).

*n*4.232*b*: precisively ... literacy ⊖ *grammaticam per se*] Literacy is here said to be signified in a *per se* (or precisive) fashion by 'literate'. The immediate result of this declaration is to create a fissure between *man* and literacy, a fissure which cannot be created within the components of *man*. This has the consequence that *grammaticus* ⊖ literate has to be defined according to rules which differentiate its case from that of *homo* ⊖ man (4.24–4.3, cf. *n*4.230*b* and *n*3.800*b*). Precisive signification (*significatio per se*) is that which is understood (4.4233, cf. *n*3.101*a*) and defined (*n*3.800*b*); it can be expressed in two ways: (i) in terms of the functor '... *significat* ...' ⊖ '... signifies ...', which has the name of a name as its first argument (e.g. 'literate') and a name or quasi-name as its second argument (e.g. literacy, *sciens grammaticam* ⊖ displaying literacy); (ii) in terms of the functor '... *est* ...' ⊖ '... is ...' having names or quasi-names as both its arguments, as in '*grammaticus est grammatica*' ⊖ '*literate* is literacy', '*grammaticus est sciens grammaticam*'; on the translation of the latter see *n*4.31*a*. Case (i) involves assertion *de voce* ⊖ concerning words, and (ii) is said to be an assertion *de re* ⊖ concerning things (4.601–4.603). It is the second, *de re* ⊖ thing-centred, type of expression, with its parts of speech which in the case of '*grammaticus est grammatica*' ⊖ '*literate* is literacy' are plainly not those of ordinary grammar, that gives rise to the contrast constantly drawn in the course of the dialogue between *usus loquendi* ⊖ spoken usage (4.2341) and statements made for logical purposes (4.20–4.22, 4.2341, 4.5022, 4.62, cf. *n*1.000*b*). The manner in which Anselm allows the discourse to alternate between the two forms of expression (i) and (ii) described above already suggests that they are inferentially equivalent, and this appears to be confirmed by 4.601–4.603.

Per se (precisive) signification and the violation of *usus loquendi* ⊖

spoken usage which may go with it (or which may result from confusing it with *appellatio* ⊖ reference (4.2341)) relates to that which is intra-theoretical in respect of the theory of the term in question: *illa* [*significatio*] *quae per se est, ipsis vocibus est substantialis* (4.43), and as such may be contrasted with *significatio per aliud* ⊖ oblique signification (cf. *n*4.232*c*). The latter is the accidental, i.e. extra-theoretical, aspect of the term in question: *altera* [scil. *significatio per aliud*] *vero accidentalis* (4.43). The same contrast is reiterated later in the dialogue: 4.515. It is on such contrasts that the falsehood of 3.6331, 3.6332, and the truth of 3.6333, 3.6334, are grounded.

The distinction between precisive signification and oblique signification applies to both names and verbs (4.4243–4.431). *Appellatio* ⊖ reference is that form of oblique signification proper to names. Only precisive signification is *significatio* properly so-called (4.233) and only it has *de re* ⊖ thing-centred correlates requiring for their analysis the special logical use of 'is' mentioned above and which is at odds with *usus loquendi* ⊖ spoken usage (cf. *n*4.2341*b*). The contrast of logical forms with spoken usage in also made outside *De Grammatico*; indeed, the contrast pervades much of Anselm's literary output, and is surveyed in detail in *HL*, especially in §4, §5, and §6 thereof.

The Aristotelian background to these distinctions insofar as they concern names lies ultimately in the distinction between that which is predicated *de subiecto* ⊖ of a subject and that which is *in subiecto* ⊖ in a subject (*n*4.101*a*, §4). Some suggestions as to the origins of the terminology of *per se* ⊖ precisive and *per aliud* ⊖ oblique are made in *n*4.232*c*.

In the present dialogue, not only is '*grammaticus*' ⊖ 'literate' said to signify in a *per se* ⊖ precisive fashion *grammatica* ⊖ literacy; 'man' signifies in the same *per se* ⊖ precisive way the single whole constituted by man's make-up (4.231), 'horse' signifies the 'substance' of horse *per se* ⊖ precisively, and 'white' signifies *having whiteness* (4.4231, 4.4233). The sense of 'having whiteness', as here used, receives clarification at 4.8. This clarification is most important, since '*grammaticus*' ⊖ 'literate' is also said, in a corresponding fashion (4.31) to signify *displaying literacy*. See *n*4.31*a* for a full discussion of this point.

Let us now attempt a general review of the situation before advancing to an attempt to characterise in more detail the notion of *per se* signification in respect of names. We have seen that that particular type of oblique signification proper to names is *appellatio*, i.e. appellation, reference, calling or naming. 'Literate' signifies literacy precisively, but refers to man without signifying man (4.232, 4.233). Although this name signifies literacy, it does not refer to literacy (4.2340). In short, 'literate' signifies a quality, i.e. literacy, but refers to substance, i.e. *man*. On the other hand the substance-word 'man' is both significative precisively of, and is appellative of, everything indicated by the definition of man, and principally of the substantiality thereby implied (4.231). This, as we have seen at least verbally, is the manner in which a wedge is driven between the cases of *man* and *literate* (and hence between the manners of signification of all substance-words and paronyms) notwithstanding their common participation in the situation delineated in *n*4.230*b*.1.

A more detailed understanding of the situation involves six main considerations: (i) the already-extablished Anselmian parallelism between assertions *de re* ⊖ concerning things and assertions *de voce* ⊖ concerning words, and the use of the higher-order 'is' in connection with the former (cf. §4 as well as *n*4.234*b*); (ii) the preliminary decisions on the signification of 'literate' (*n*4.230*b*); (iii) descriptions given in the dialogue of the various types of signification (e.g. 4.23); (iv) examples used to illustrate the main distinction (e.g. 4.4); (v) the theory of definition, dependent upon the predicables, and the presupposition of putative theories of certain sorts of objects, which lies behind that theory of definition (§4, *n*4.22*d*, *n*4.2411*d*); (vi) the problems posed by the '*intelligi*' ⊖ 'to be understood' texts (*n*3.101*a*).

Our present concern is with a slight amplification of problem (iii), in particular with the notion of the precisive signification (*significatio per se*) of a name. An account of such signification must clearly involve some kind of equation. The latter will in fact be a definition at the level of discourse appropriate to the predicables (*n*4.22*d*). This definition will be one of the axioms of the theory of the term defined (§4) and hence will state something substantial (i.e. intra-theoretical) and not accidental (i.e. extra-theoretical) in respect of the *definiendum* (4.430, 4.515). Precisive signification is part of logical theory; it is made explicit in logic books (4.620, 4.21) and is not gleaned from the current course of utterance (4.620). In general, given the predicable-level of discourse here involved (cf. §4), when '*a*' is said to signify precisively, an equation of the form

.1 $\mathrm{Cl}[\![a]\!] \in \mathrm{Cl}[\![\ \ ]\!]$ (§3.14.15)

will at least be part of the *de re* equivalent of that statement. Conversely, when it is stated that '*a*' does not signify something precisively, the negation of .1, i.e.

.2 $\sim(\mathrm{Cl}[\![a]\!] \in \mathrm{Cl}[\![\ \ ]\!])$

will be at least part of the *de re* ⊖ thing-centred equivalent of that statement (cf. 4.603). It may be noted that .1 and .2, because of their use of the higher-order '∈' (in contradistinction to what holds in the case of the lower-order '∈') are particularly suited to the assertion of the correlates of pure statements of meaning, since with the arguments shown, and in the absence of other assumptions regarding *a*, the existence ('ex') or object-hood ('ob') (cf. §3) of *a* or of anything else cannot be inferred from either; this accords very well with the Tutor's separation off of questions of meaning from questions about existence (3.9, 4.810). Forms such as the above will therefore be used for the further analysis of Anselm's results concerning precisive signification in *n*4.31*a*.

It may be noted that a contrast between *per se* signification and actual usage which runs parallel to that with which are are now involved (cf. 4.2341) also occurs in an 11th century manuscript: *DLM* II–I 114–5.

*n*4.232*c*: obliquely ... man ⊖ *hominem per aliud*] The previous note has stressed the sense in which the oblique signification (*significatio per aliud*) is the accidental (4.43, 4.515) component of the signification of an utterance, and as such is to be contrasted with signification in the proper sense, i.e. signification *per se*, precisive signification.

It may now be noted that this accidental nature of *per aliud* ⊖ oblique signification arises, in terms of the dialogue's examples, on two principal counts. Thus, restricting attention to the case of paronyms, such names may in the first place only apply temporarily or permanently, to individuals of *various* species, as in the case of 'white' (cf. the case of the white horse, 4.42). In such cases the theories incorporating such species-names will not embrace or be embraced by the theory of *white*. On the other hand, as in the case of 'literate', the application may be constantly to individuals of the *same* species only, but since such application is neither to all the members of such a species, nor does it hold throughout the whole duration of any such individual's existence, it cannot be part of the substantial being of such individuals (4.2411). The rules of substantial definition (*n*3.800*b*) cannot hence be directly applied in such cases. We have seen Aquinas' views on this modification in *n*3.800*b*. However, Anselm, lacking the influence of Aristotle's *Metaphysica* appears to have evolved an alternative modification. For Anselm what is needed in the case of paronyms is an open, truncated, definition (4.31), expressive of incompleteness (*indigentia*), as spoken of in 4.231. Thanks to this openness, redefinition for each new application of the name becomes unnecessary (cf. *n*4.31*a*). So that whether, in fact, the paronym applies to members of one species only (as in the case of 'literate'), or whether it applies to individuals of various species (as in the case of 'white'), all paronyms may be defined in this open way which ensures that they are equally extra-theoretical in respect of the species concerned (4.24121). In those cases in which a constancy of application to one species occurs (as when 'literate' applies always to human beings, or 'white' to things insofar as they are surface-havers, or bodies) the mistaken impression that a theoretical connection may be said to hold can arise from an experientially-founded disposition which is set up in the mind of the language-user, so that on the occasion of the utterance of this sort of paronym the oblique and accidental component of its signification is habitually brought to mind (4.4211).

Appellatio ⊖ referring, calling, is the particular form of oblique signification proper to names (4.233) and is elucidated in *n*4.233*a*.

The origins of the present contrast made by Anselm between *per se* (precisive) and oblique (*per aliud*) appears to lie in Book II of Boethius' commentary on the *Categoriae*, wherein *per aliud* ⊖ oblique is related to *secundum accidens* ⊖ extra-theoretical, and the latter then in its turn contrasted with *per se* ⊖ precisive:

A thing is chiefly said to be that which it *is* when it is shown to be so in a *per se* manner. The extra-theoretical is that which *is* such as it is asserted to be, not *per se*, but only obliquely. For example, whiteness is said to be a colour in the *per se* fashion, since it is of the very nature of the white that its colour should be said to be whiteness. However, when a man is said to be coloured, this is not asserted

Principaliter aliquid esse dicitur, quod per se tale est quale esse demonstratur. Secundum accidens vero illud quod non per se, sed per aliud tale est quale esse dicitur, ut albedini per se inest color: secundum naturam enim albi color esse dicitur albedo; cum vero homo dicitur coloratus, non per se dicitur, idcirco quod homo in eo quod homo est, color non est, sed quoniam habet colorem, idcirco dicitur coloratus.

in a *per se* fashion, since a man insofar as he is a man, is not a colour, but since he *has* a colour, is merely said to be coloured. Hence in the same fashion as *white* is a colour in the *per se* sense, since colour is a certain genus by nature, and a man, in contrast, is said to be coloured because he *has* a colour, so also *white* is said to be principally and *per se* colour, whereas in contrast man is coloured only in an extra-theoretical sense.

Ergo quemadmodum album idcirco color est per se quoniam color naturale quoddam est genus, homo vero idcirco coloratus dicitur quoniam habet colorem; et dicitur album quidem per se et principaliter color, homo vero secundum accidens coloratus: *BC* 209B.

(On the ambiguity of '*album*' ⊖ 'white' in Latin, which parallels that of 'evil' in English, see *HL* 44).

Certainly this possible origin of the distinction is wholly coherent with the interpretation of *per se* signification as having to do with that which is intra-theoretical in respect of the term in question and *significatio per aliud* ⊖ oblique signification (and hence *appellatio* ⊖ reference) as extra-theoretical in the same respect.

*n*4.233*a*: appellative ⊖ *appellativum*] See 4.2341 for Anselm's definition of '*nomen appellativum*' ⊖ 'appellative name'. *Appellatio* ⊖ reference, is that sort of oblique signification (*n*4.232*c*) proper to names, and is by that definition connected with *usus loquendi* ⊖ spoken usage, as opposed to the apparently ungrammatical assertions to which the doctrines of logicians appear to commit one (4.21, 4.2341, 4.5022, cf. *n*1.000*b*). Further discussion of the notion of *appellatio* ⊖ reference is undertaken in *n*4.2341*a*.

*n*4.233*b*: properly ⊖ *proprie*] For other examples of Anselm's use of '*proprie*' ⊖ 'properly' the references listed under 'propriety and impropriety of word use' in the index of *HL* may be consulted.

*n*4.233*c*: signify man ⊖ *eius significativum*] *Man* is the *per aliud* ⊖ oblique signification of 'literate' according to 4.232. As in the case of *appellatio* ⊖ reference (cf. *n*4.2341*a*) no theoretical connection, but at the most a factual, extra-theoretical (4.423) or psychological (4.4211) connection is implied by *per aliud* signification, one result of *appellatio* ⊖ reference is the present denial of 'propriety' to it as a sense of signification (cf. *n*4.232*c*). Henceforward, and especially when contrasted with '*appellatio*'

⊖ 'reference' (e.g. 4.62) the word '*significatio*' ⊖ 'signification' when used without qualification by the Tutor must be understood in the *per se* ⊖ precisive sense, as is evident from 4.515.

The contrast between *appellatio* ⊖ calling and *significatio* ⊖ meaning which is laid down both here and in 4.2340 appears to be akin to the doctrine to which John of Salisbury refers as a common one in Bk. II Ch. 20 of his *Metalogicon*:

Nor are these points incompatible with what is vastly well-known and mouthed by everybody, namely that what is signified by a common noun is different from what that common noun names.	*Nec istis preiudicat quod fere in omnium ore celebre est, aliud scilicet esse quod appellativa significant et aliud esse quod nominant: SM* 104.5.8.

The origin of the contrast may well lie in Bk. I of Boethius' commentary on the *Categoriae*:

Every thing is indicated either by its name or by its definition, for we either call the thing in question by its appropriate name, or we show what it is by means of its definition. For example we call a certain substance by the name 'man', and we provide its definition when we say that *man* is *rational mortal animal.*	*Omnis res aut nomine aut definitione monstratur: namque subiectam rem aut proprio nomine vocamus, aut definitione quid sit ostendimus. Ut verbi gratia quandam substantiam vocamus hominis nomine, et eiusdem definitionem damus dicentes esse hominem animal rationale mortale: BC* 163D.

From the foregoing it is by now quite plain that the distinction between the broad and strict sense of '*significatio*' ⊖ 'meaning' as well as the distinction between this strict sense and *appellatio* ⊖ calling (or *nominatio* ⊖ naming) which have been attributed to the twelfth century (*DLM* II–I 561) are well in evidence in the eleventh-century *De Grammatico*.

*n*4.234*a*: literacy ⊖ *grammaticae*] That is to say that 'literate' is precisively significative of literacy (cf. 4.232 and *n*4.232*b*, *n*4.31*a*).

*n*4.234*b*: appellative of literacy ⊖ *eius appellativum*] Although '*grammaticus est grammatica*' ⊖ '*literate* is literacy' is true, and is indeed one of the occasions of the present distinctions (cf. 4.21, 4.5022, *n*1.000*b*) yet by the definition of *appellatio* ⊖ reference which is now to follow (4.2341) it cannot be said that '*grammaticus*' ⊖ 'literate' is appellative of, i.e. names or refers to, *grammatica* ⊖ literacy. In that definition *usus loquendi* ⊖ spoken usage is taken as a guide to reference, as opposed to signification properly so-called. Such usage has already been exemplified, without explanation, in 4.231, where the contrast between '*homo est substantia*' ⊖ '*man* is a substance' and '*rationalitas est homo*' ⊖ 'rationality is man' was made; cf. *n*4.231*i*. At the same time *appellatio* ⊖ referring (and hence *usus loquendi* ⊖ spoken usage) appears to be regarded at 4.710–4.712 as a kind of pre-theoretical guide to the kind of unitary objecthood required for theory. In spite of this, however, the pervasive and present contrast between *significatio* ⊖ meaning and *appellatio* ⊖ reference must be taken as forceful evidence that Anselm by no means equated 'meaning' and 'naming' (cf. *Q* 9, *Q* 21).

Fredegisus, against whom Anselm appears to be arguing in *De Casu Diaboli* 11, held, in effect, that the only sense of 'meaning' was that subordinate sense distinguished by Anselm as '*appellatio*' ⊖ 'reference', so that for him *to have meaning* meant to *stand for* or *to name* some object. This point of view was also envisaged in the *De Magistro* of St. Augustine of Hippo: *PL* 32, 1196. A crucial problem arises for those who hold such a theory when they further assume that 'nothing' is a name, and then have to give an account of its meaning. Anselm's corrections of the sophisms which then occur will be recounted in *n*4.813*b*.

Further discussion of the sense of the present *denial* of reference must be postponed until immediately after the argument in favour of the Tutor's thesis, and may hence be found at the close of *n*4.31*a*.

*n*4.2341*a*: called in the customary course of utterance ⊖ *usu loquendi appellatur*] The contrast between *usus loquendi* ⊖ the current course of utterance and logical assertions such as '*grammaticus est qualitas*' ⊖ '*Literate* is quality' and '*grammaticus est grammatica*' ⊖ '*Literate* is literacy' (cf. 4.5022) forcibly brought out by the Student in 4.21 will be further prolonged (4.5022, 4.620). At present, thanks to this definition of *appellatio* ⊖ reference, a place is being assigned to *usus loquendi* ⊖ the current course of utterance. The latter is, in respect of paronyms, a guide to reference, not meaning: it is extra-theoretical, contingent, and accidental (cf. 4.515, §4).

However, although logical sense (*signifiatio per se*) and reference (*appellatio*) are thus differentiated by Anselm, we find at 4.71 that *appellatio* ⊖ reference, and hence *usus loquendi* ⊖ the current course of utterance, are used in order to determine what constitutes *unum aliquid* ⊖ one thing, i.e. a unitary unambigously countable object of the sort which is fit to become an object of theory (cf. §4, *n*4.72*a*). Hence, although itself extra-theoretical, *usus loquendi* ⊖ spoken usage is in certain respect a junction between fact and theory. *Usus loquendi* ⊖ spoken usage is also embraced by, and is the foundation of, the grammar produced by the grammarians (cf. *n*4.22*c*). Such grammar does not, however, account for the parts of speech required for logical assertions (cf. the examples which folllow, and 4.5022, 4.8, *n*1.000*b*, *n*4.31*a*).

In general the extra-theoretical facts of *appellatio* ⊖ reference stand in contrast to the intra-theoretical theses of *significatio per se* (*n*4.232*b*). All the arguments in which it is (wrongly) maintained that 'literate' signifies *man* or that *literate* is *man* (1.11, 4.13, 4.2, 4.240, 4.502, 4.513) as well as the exceptive *intelligi*-sentences (3.6333, 3.6334) ultimately rely on the extra-theoretical fact that 'literate' is appellative of man.

The insistence that *appellatio* ⊖ reference is conserned with *res* ⊖ things (4.2341, 4.710), and that here is something accidental to the theory of the term (4.430, 4.515) indicates that although a statement of the conditions of *appellatio* ⊖ reference may be possible, such a statement will not be part of the theory of the type of objects referred to, and will involve the recognition of the existence of those objects. That the objects in question will be of a type circumscribed by the theory of some term, i.e. determined by *de subiecto* ⊖ of a subject predications which are *in eo quod quid* ⊖ in respect of "whatness" (cf. §4) must be taken for granted. The concrete cases which Anselm provides are those of 'literate' and 'white', which are said to be respectively appellative of man (4.233) and of a particular horse (4.42). The extra-theoretical truths which are involved in these situations (e.g. that the whiteness in 'in' the horse) are dependent upon particular sense-experiences, those of sight, for example: *velut per visum* (4.4234). The examples suggest that the theoretical objecthood whose recognition is implied by *appellatio* ⊖ reference will have to be described at the level of *species specialissimae* (*n*4.2411*h*) and not at a generic (*n*4.2411*g*) level. The *species specialissima* name '*homo*' ⊖ 'man' occurs in Anselm's cryptic exemplary segments of that *usus loquendi* ⊖ spoken usage which is the medium wherein *appellatio* ⊖ reference functions, i.e. '*homo est grammaticus*' ⊖ 'A man is literate' and '*grammaticus est homo*' ⊖ 'A literate is a man' (4.2341, cf. *n*4.2341*b*).

The amount of discussion devoted by John of Salisbury in this *Metalogicon*, especially in chapters 15 and 16 of Book I, to the topic of grammatical nonsense as opposed to *usus loquendi* ⊖ spoken usage, suggests that he may have encountered the kind of contrast which Anselm is here propounding. For instance, in bringing out the diverse concerns of the logician and the grammarian, John shows the first as being concerned with truth and falsehood, and the second as being the champion of grammatical congruity alone:

As things are at the moment '*Man* is rational' is in some sense necessary. '*Man* is capable of laughing' is probable. 'A man is white' is possible but doubtable, since it is equally capable of being true or false. But '*Man* is capable of braying' is indeed impossible and just cannot be true. The grammarian will balk at none of these sentences, since in every case he finds his rules adhered to. The logician, however, pounces on the fourth sentence and argues against it, since his allotted task is the sorting out of the true from the false, and hence says that to lend an ear to it would be absurd. But now suppose a fifth sentence to be brought along, namely, '*Man* is categorical'. Forthwith the grammarian, who has shown hospitality not merely to the doubtable, not merely to the false, but even to the impossible, condemns this last sentence as absurd. Why so? Just because it doesn't follow his rules; he has announced an everlasting veto on the combination of these adjectives with these subjects.	*'Homo est rationalis': rebus existentibus ut nunc sunt, hec quodammodo necessaria est. 'Homo est risibilis'; hec probabilis est. 'Homo est albus': hec quidem possibilis, dubia tamen, eo quod eque uera potest esse et falsa. 'Homo est rudibilis': hec quidem impossibilis est, ut omnino uera esse non possit. Nullam istarum gramaticus abhorret, quia ubique inuenit legem suam ... Quartam corripit et redarguit logicus, eo quod sibi ueri falsique commissa est examinatio. Et ob hoc quidem, ei prebere aurem dicit absurdum. Modo premissis quintam adice. 'Homo cathegoricus est': hanc utique absurditatis damnat gramaticus, qui non modo dubiam, non modo falsam, sed etiam impossibilem admittebat. Quare, inquit? nisi quia non sequitur leges suas; perpetua enim dicebat inhibitum hec adiectiua illis copulari subiectis:* *SM* 39.11.26.

Further examples of John's discussion of the violation of *usus loquendi* ⊖ spoken usage are given in *n*4.5122*a*.

The terms '*appellativum*' and '*nomen appellativum*' ⊖ 'shared name' which we are encountering in Anselm's present text were already well-established in grammatical use. Thus for Priscian these terms apply both to what would nowadays be termed common nouns and to adjectives. It is by contrast with proper names that he (as well as Donatus: *K* IV 373.5.6) emphasises the essentially shared nature of the appellative:

Proper and appellative names differ in that the appellative is by nature shared among many.	*Hoc autem interest inter proprium et appellativum, quod appellativum naturaliter commune est multorum:* *K* II 58.14.15.

The '*adiectivum*' ⊖ 'adjective' is a sub-class of the appellative:

Adjectives are so called because it is customary for them to be adjoined to other appellatives which signify substance, or even to proper names: this joining is effected to make clear the quality or quantity, which can increase or decrease without the perishing of the substance involved: for example 'good animal', 'great man', 'wise grammarian', 'the great Homer'.	*Adiectiva autem ideo vocantur, quod aliis appellativis, quae substantiam significant, vel etiam propriis adici solent ad manifestandum eorum qualitatem vel quantitatem, quae augeri vel minui sine substantiae consumptione possunt, ut 'bonum animal' 'magnus homo', 'sapiens grammaticus', 'magnus Homerus'.* K II 58.20.24.

From this last-quoted passage it would appear that according to Priscian '*grammaticus*' ⊖ 'literate' (or 'grammarian') is an 'appellative which signifies substance' to which '*sapiens*' ⊖ 'wise' has been prefixed as an adjective. The conclusion which hence emerges, namely that '*grammaticus*' ⊖ 'literate' signifies substance, may be one of the factors which made the opening question of the dialogue the topical one which the Tutor later describes it as being (4.83; cf. *n*3.800*b*, *n*4.22*c*). This is because that conclusion it completely at odds with the declarations of logicians that *literate* is a quality (cf. *n*1.201*b*). At the same time Priscian's own principle that all names signify substance *and* quality coheres with that conclusion: cf. *n*4.22*c*. Thus 'literate' figures not only in Aristotle and Boethius, but also in Priscian, and this at the point of contention which is the subject of the present dialogue. It has also been pointed out in *CR* that St. Augustine uses '*grammaticus*' ⊖ 'literate' when discussing definition in *De Quantitate Animae* 25. Altogether, therefore, the word from which the present dialogue takes its title encapsulates a confluence of considerations from diverse sources in distinct centuries.

The term '*appellatio*' ⊖ 'calling' is often used by Boethius. Thus Book III of his commentary on the *Categoriae*, especially *B* 253–4, shows it as an alternative to '*nomen*' ⊖ 'name', and it is brought into direct contact with the word '*grammaticus*' ⊖ 'literate':

Literates are so called from literacy, and it happens in lots of cases that given the requisite name, whatever is said to be 'qualified' because it has certain qualities can then have its appellation governed by its possession of those qualities.	*Grammatici a grammatica nominantur, atque hoc est in pluribus, ut posito nomine si quid secundum ipsas qualitates quale dicitur, ex his ipsis qualitatibus appellatio derivetur: BC* 253A.

It may be added that a most useful collection of references to *appellatio* in early medieval logic and grammar is to be found in *DLM* II–II 797–8. For a historical survey, see *DLM* II–I 560–4.

Gilbert de la Porrée refers to the grammarians' use of the term '*appellatio*' (*B* 1372B) without, however, creating a distinctive logical use thereof. On the other hand Peter of Spain (*HSL* 10) appears to use '*appellatio*' in a sense differing from that found in Priscian, since singular terms can, according to Peter, be appellative, as well as general terms (*HSL* 10.02). His definition runs: *Appellatio est acceptio termini pro re existente* ⊖ Appellation is the acceptance of a term in place of an existing thing. Thus 'Caesar' and 'Antichrist' are not appellative of anything, whereas '*homo*' ⊖ 'man' is appellative of existing men (*HSL* 10.01).

Anselm's definition of *appellatio*, with its mention of *res ipsa* ⊖ things themselves, might be regarded as approaching that of Peter's. However, in *Epistola de Incarnatione Verbi* 11 Anselm appears to prefer '*designatio*' in respect of singular reference. But he retains '*appellatio*' in discussing the state of affairs in which the individual white horse is the referent of '*album*' ⊖ 'white' (4.422, 4.423).

The relation of the term '*usus loquendi*' ⊖ 'the common course of utterance' to the parts of the dialogue which have preceded is now being made plain by the text: *usus loquendi* ⊖ spoken usage has already been brought on to the scene with the Student's mention of '*loquens in populo*' ⊖ 'speaking in ordinary company' and '*colloquentes*' ⊖ 'in conversation' (4.210), and will be adverted to yet again at the conclusion of the central phase of the work (4.620). Again, cognate expressions are to be found throughout Anselm's works; some indication of these may be found in the references given under 'usage' in the index to *HL*.

In Bk. II of Boethius' commentary on Porphyry the term '*usus loquendi*' ⊖ 'spoken usage' occurs thus:

But this is not the primitive way of speaking, but arises from human speech-customs. Thus first of all (he says) the meaning of *genus* referred to a generator, but as the ages went by the name 'genus' was by spoken usage extended to cover cases wherein many things stood in some relation to one thing ... and so it came about later that spoken usage allowed it to be said that a genus involved some sort of interrelation between many things and some one thing.

Sed hic non de se loquitur, sed de humani consuetudine sermonis, in quo prius eam significationem generis fuisse dicit, quae a procreante sit tracta, accedente vero aetate usu loquendi nomen generis etiam ad multitudinem habentem se quodammodo ad aliquen fuisse translatum ... post autem factum est ut per loquendi usum etiam multitudinis ad aliquem quodammodo se habentis genus diceretur: *BCP* 90A–B.

The same term is also to be found in Ch. III of *Liber de Persona et Duabus Naturis*:

Were it not for the fact that the spoken usage of the church excluded the assertion of three substances in God ...

Nisi enim tres in Deo substantias ecclesiasticus loquendi usus excluderet; BDPN 1345B.

Although in the first of these last two quotations the contrast between logically primitive modes of expression and *usus loquendi* ⊖ the current course of utterance might be said to be in question, the contrast is scarcely of the sort which Anselm delineates. John of Salisbury, however, in the course of his discussion to which allusion has been made above, speaks of custom as the arbiter in the face of which grammatically scandalous combinations of technical terms, including those of logic, must yield, and gives a quotation from Horace within which the words '*usus loquendi*' ⊖ 'spoken usage' can be traced:

A proposition is rightly said to be 'hypothetical' and a name 'patronymic'. But if you switch things round so that 'hypothetical name' or 'patronymic proposition' are the resultant utterances, then according to the grammarian you are just saying nothing at all, or you are speaking incongruously. Besides, to usage belongs the supreme authority for the testing of speech, nor can that which usage condemns be restored save by usage. Hence the poet says:

> Many words that now are fallen from use will be restored, and many now highly regarded will fall, should such be the will of usage, which is the judge, the law, and the standard of speech.

For in the same way as the lawyers hold that custom is the best interpretation of the law, so also the usage prevailing among those who speak rightly is the most powerful interpreter of the rules.

Siquidem propositio recte dicitur 'ypothetica', nomen 'patronomicum'. Si uicissim uertas, ut dicatur 'ypotheticum nomen', 'propositio patronomica' aut nichil utique dices, gramatico iudice, aut inepte loqueris. Preterea penes usum est summa examinandi sermonis auctoritas, neque eo non restituente convalescet quod ipse condemnat.

Hinc est illud:

Multa renascentur que iam cecidere, cadentque,
que nunc sunt in honore uocabula, si uolet usus,
quem penes arbitrium est et ius et norma loquendi.

Sicut enim in iure dicitur quod consuetudo optima legum interpres est: sic et usus recte loquentium est potentissimus interpres regularum: SM 41.26–42.8

Such opinions and the further material to be quoted in *n*4.5122*a* show that John has encountered innovations of the sort which Anselm claims to find in Aristotle's *Categoriae* (4.5122, 4.6) and that he was unsympathetic towards them, owing perhaps to his not having realised the advantages of nonsense when the current course of utterance fails in its resources.

Communis usus loquentium ⊖ the common usage of speakers is said in the *Tractatus Anagnini*, edited by De Rijk, to be the cause of the various modes of signification of terms (*DLM* II–I 541, II–II 260.16). This assertion is repeated when, on pp. 274–282 of *DLM* II–II, those modes are described in detail.

*n*4.2341*b*: literacy ⊖ *grammatica*] That these two ungrammatical examples are given in order to show that '*grammaticus*' ⊖ 'literate' is not appellative of *grammatica* ⊖ literacy is evident from the preceding sentence. What is perhaps not immediately evident is that at least the second of the two is for the Tutor a thesis inferentially equivalent to the positive thesis of 4.234 (cf. *n*4.232*b*), and has not only been in the discussion since the first sentence of the dialogue (cf. *n*1.000*b*) but will also remain an object of disquiet to the Student (4.5022) until the end of the central phase of the dialogue (4.62). The present context, however, is the first occasion on which it has been openly stated, and not merely implied. To Anselm's contemporaries it may have been so obvious an accompaniment of the '*grammaticus est qualitas*' ⊖ '*literate* is a quality' alternative of the dialogue's first sentence as not to need overt statement.

Although '*grammaticus est qualitas*' ⊖ '*literate* is a quality' and '*grammaticus est grammatica*' ⊖ '*literate* is literacy' are theses for the Tutor, and have been shown by the Student to be entailed by the works of the '*tractatores dialectici*' ⊖ 'writers on logic' (4.21) there are passages in Boethius' commentary on the *Categoriae* which appear to be opposed to any formulations of this sort:

The thing that possesses the quality is not embraced by the word 'quality'; thus whiteness is indeed a quality, but a white is not a quality In every case of paronymy, the thing denominated is not identical with that from which it draws its name; for example a literate is not the same as the lireracy from which he draws his name.	*Res ... quae participat, qualitatis vocabulo non tenetur, ut albedo qualitas quidem est, albus vero qualitas non est: BC* 239C. *Omnis autem denominatio non est id quod est ea res de qua nominatur, ut grammaticus, non enim idem est quod grammatica de qua nominatus est:* *BC* 220B, cf. *HL* §3.121.

True, '*idem est quod*' ⊖ 'is the same as', and not merely '*est*' ⊖ 'is' is in the second of these two passages the functor of the sentence declared by Boethius to be false. In the text of *De Grammatico* it is not made clear whether the Tutor is supposed to accept as true both of the two sentences now being considered. If he does accept them, then the two together would yield the identity indicated by Boethius' '*est idem quod*' ⊖ 'is the same as'. Certainly both these sentences count as theses if the elucidations suggested in *n*4.31*a* are accepted. Now at the close of the dialogue mention is made of the extent to which contemporary logicians were at loggerheads on the question raised by the Student: *nostris temporibus dialectici certent de quaestione a te proposita* ⊖ our contemporary logicians are in dispute as to the question brought up by you (4.83). Can it be that in addition to the incompatibility between logical and grammatical doctrines which can be represented as one of the seeds of the discussion (*n*4.22*c*) there was also some dispute which arose from the incompatibility between various assertions within Boethius' work on the *Categoriae*? The denial of the sameness of '*caecitas*' ⊖ 'blindness' and '*caecum*' ⊖ 'the blind', quoted in *n*4.231*i* might also be brought in to underpin the quotations from Boethius given above. (cf. also *A* 386–7). The prominence given by Anselm to the claim that the Tutor is uncovering a mode of expression proper to the *Categoriae* suggests that this logical dispute may also be in question. Abelard displays a like concern in the '*caecitas*' ⊖ 'blindness' case to uncover the correct Aristotelian position: *Sed haec quidem sententia nec rationi nec verbis aristotelicis congruit* ⊖ But this opinion coheres neither with reason nor with the Aristotelian text; *A* 386.34.35.

The use of reciprocal sentence-forms such as the present ones and those of 4.231 so as to show that the relation of appellation holds also figures in Priscian in the same connection:

The philosophers mentioned above [i.e. the Stoics] also used to call participles 'reciprocal appellations' ... as in the cases of 'He who reads is a reader' and 'The reader is he who reads', 'The runner is he who runs' and 'He who runs is a runner'. 'The lover is he who loves' and 'He who loves is is a lover'

*Supra dicti philosophi [*sc. *Stoici] etiam participium aiebant appellationem esse reciprocam ... hoc modo: 'legens est lector' et 'lector legens', 'cursor est currens' et 'currens cursor', 'amator est amans' et 'amans amator': K* II 548.14.17.

A like association between *appellatio* ⊖ calling and reciprocity is to be found in Boethius;

On the other hand the specific property, since it applies equally only and always to a single species can be treated on the same level, and the names in question can replace one another, e.g. 'What is man?' 'Capable of laughter'; 'What is capable of laughter?', 'Man'.

At vero proprium, quoniam aequaliter et ad unam speciem semper aptatur, aeque appellatione convertitur. Dicitur enim, 'Quid est homo?', 'Risibile'; 'Quid est risibile?', 'Homo': BDP 66D (cf. *BCP* 158A–B).

The present nonsensical sentences constitute the most striking proof that Anselm clearly realises the need for new semantical categories in order to express his thought. They are the extremest examples of his contrast between *usus loquendi* ⊖ the current course of utterance and the kind of statement to which the expression of logical truths can commit one. The *de re* ⊖ thing-centred formulation of the dialogue's outcome is '*Literate* is a quality' (4.603), but if one asks, 'Which quality?' the reply can only be 'literacy', so that one is left with '*Literate* is literacy' as a conclusion (4.5022), and this is nonsense from the point of view of *usus loquendi* ⊖ the current course of utterance. The words which are grammatically classified as names in *usus loquendi* ⊖ the current course of utterance are usually construed as being used to refer to objects (*res ipsae* ⊖ things themselves), hence Anselm's coupling of *usus loquendi* ⊖ the common course of utterance with reference (*appellatio*) (4.2341). It *is* in accord with *usus loquendi* ⊖ the common course of utterance to say '*homo est grammaticus*' ⊖ 'A man is literate' or '*grammaticus est homo*' ⊖ 'A literate is a man', for here '*grammaticus*' ⊖ 'literate' is being used to 'call' some man or other, and the '*est*' ⊖ 'is' represents some functor at the comparatively familiar level of the lower-order '∈' of Ontology (§3). However, the present peculiar statement to which the *de re* ⊖ thing-centred formulation of the dialogue's outcome commits us, namely '*grammaticus est grammatica*' ⊖ '*Literate* is literacy' or '*grammatica est grammaticus*' ⊖ 'Literacy is literate', go clean against *usus loquendi* ⊖ the current course of utterance, as is now asserted in the passage undergoing examination; cf. also 4.5022.

This disparity arises because '*grammaticus*' ⊖ 'literate' in '*grammaticus est homo*' ⊖ 'A literate is a man' is of a semantical category differing from that of '*grammaticus*' as it occurs in '*grammaticus est grammatica*' ⊖ '*Literate* is literacy', with corresponding categorial differences between the '*est*' ⊖ 'is' of each sentence. Hence, as Anselm properly implies in the Student's objection at 4.20 which first brings *usus loquendi* ⊖ the common course of utterance to the fore in the dialogue, nonsense can result if one supposes that consequences drawn from logicians' statements can be deployed in ordinary talk (*loquens in populo*) and its primitive grammar which tends to apply its classifications as to parts of speech immutably to words of a given shape. The *grammatici* mentioned at 4.20 would take offence, not only because the Student would appear to be saying strange things about them, but also because he would be violating their grammatical norms. It is from the logicians' need for novel parts of speech, undistinguished by the grammarians of *usus loquendi* ⊖ spoken usage, that there arises what the Student describes as the incredible disparity between the conclusions of their writings and their ordinary speech habits.

However, by the time the discussion is drawing to its close, the Tutor has made use of new semantical categories, such as those which occur in the *de re* ⊖ thing-centred correlates of statements about meaning (*de voce*), and has shown this use to be reasonable. The logicians' writings are concerned with words insofar as they signify, and hence those words which would be classified as names by ordinary grammar, and which would therefore be said to have an appellative, referring, function when used in non-technical speech, do in fact perform a quite different function, i.e. are to be ascribed to a novel semantical category, in those writings. The same kind of disparity, he continues, is quite familiar in the case of the grammarians' own classification of names according to gender, or of verbs according to voice (4.62). Ontology, with its unlimited capacity for generating semantical categories which are either totally absent from non-technical speech, or which if they do occur, are quite unrecognised by ordinary grammar, supplies exactly the need which Anselm has so actutely sensed.

Thus, given that the scandal of the statement '*grammaticus est grammatica*' ⊖ '*Literate* is literacy' (4.2341, cf. 4.5022) is in fact an indication of the presence of parts of speech not recognised by ordinary grammar, and given also that it will turn out that '*grammatica*' at this new level is to be interpreted as '... *habens grammaticam*' ⊖ '... having literacy' (4.31), then in accordance with the suggestions of the last paragraph, and as will appear in more detail later (*n*4.31*a*) that statement can be given the expression:

.1 $\mathrm{Cl}[\![\mathbf{g}]\!] \in \mathrm{Cl}[\![\mathrm{trm}\langle\gamma\rangle]\!]$ (§3.11.14.15)

In contrast, that statement which from the point of view of *usus loquendi* ⊖ the common course of utterance is totally unoffending, involving as it does familiar semantical categories, i.e. '*homo est grammaticus*' ⊖ 'A man is literate' (4.2341) could be expressed:

.2 $[\exists a] \,.\, a \in \mathbf{h} \,.\, a \in \mathbf{g}$

or as its equivalent:

.3 **h**$\triangle$**g** (§3.6)

Whatever interpretation of '*homo est grammaticus*' ⊖ 'A man is literate' be adopted (and its article-free Latin leaves some latitude) the important point is that the interpretation should involve semantical categories which have their counterparts in the familiar grammar of *usus loquendi* ⊖ spoken usage. It would, however, be more difficult to reduce .1 to such a formulation. In this situation, and with only the Latin language at his disposal, Anselm calls attention to the out-of-the-way functors involved in .1 by resorting to the shock of the violation of the rules of *usus loquendi* ⊖ spoken usage. The locutions resulting from this violation ('*grammaticus est qualitas*' ⊖ 'Literate is quality', '*grammaticus est grammatica*' ⊖ '*Literate* is literacy') are described by Anselm as *de re* ⊖ thing-centred alternatives to the *de voce* ⊖ word-centred statements '"*grammaticus*" *est vox significans qualitatem*' ⊖ '"Literate is a word signifying a quality' (4.602) and '"*grammaticus*" *significat grammaticam*' ⊖ '"Literate" signifies literacy' (4.232) respectively: cf. 4.6.

In conclusion, therefore, Anselm's consideration of names suggests that for him there are at least three aspects of language: (i) *usus loquendi* ⊖ the current course of utterance, according to which names can be used as prescribed by ordinary grammar, and may refer to extra-linguistic objects (ii) the *de re* ⊖ thing-centred formulations of logical discussions and their conclusions, both of which may require the violation of the rules of *usus loquendi* ⊖ the common course of utterance on account of the grammar of the latter not having a sufficient range of appropriate parts of speech; logical analysis of this aspect can sometimes involve appeal to what is in effect the higher-order 'is' (§3.15) of Ontology; (iii) the *de voce* expressions of the *de re* ⊖ thing-centred statements mentioned under (ii), expressions which reflect the discontinuity of (i) and (ii). It may be noted that (ii) may comprise the sort of case in which the logical statement overtly accords with *usus loquendi* ⊖ spoken usage, and yet for logical purposes has not to be interpreted in one of the more obvious ways permitted by ordinary grammar. Such as case arises with the '... *sciens grammaticam*' ⊖ 'displaying literacy' result of 4.31. It is made plain in 4.8 that this expression is not, for certain logical purposes, to be interpreted in one of the ways which have been approved by Priscian: cf. *n*4.31*a*.

It looks very much as though Abelard was not prepared to tolerate *de re* formulations of type (ii) in connection with paronyms (*DLM* II–I 201) although on other counts his solution to the problem runs on lines somewhat similar to those adopted by Anselm. Adam of Balsham, however, is very conscious of the equivocations which may occur when a term is employed on the one hand according to *usus loquendi* ⊖ the common course of utterance, and on the other for technical logical purposes; *cum alterius in usu loquendi, alterius ad artem docendam fit eadem appellatio* ⊖ The same name can be used in one way according to spoken usage, but in another for the purpose of putting over a technical point: (*DLM* I 65).

*n*4.2341*c*: man ⊖ *homo*] That these sentences conform to *usus loquendi* ⊖ the current course of utterance is taken as evidence of the fact that '*grammaticus*' ⊖ 'literate' is appellative of *homo* ⊖ man. It is important, if the spirit of Anselm's thesis is to be reproduced, that these sentence should be capable of being understood in such a way as to avoid the necessity for recourse to special logical semantical categories for their analysis: cf. *n*4.2341*b*.

*n*4.240*a*: comprises ⊖ *constat*] See §4, where it is suggested that this functor corresponds to the higher-order '∈' of Ontology (§3.15), and is not to be dismissed as a mere picturesque metaphor. It is in fact the *de re* ⊖ thing-centred correlate of the *de voce* ⊖ word-centred statement which now follows (cf. 4.601–4.603).

The present remark runs quite close to that of Boethius on the same topic:

As *man* comprises these constitutive characteristics (cf. *n*4. 22*d*) the positing of *rational* and *mortal* alone yields a part of the substance of *man*	*Cum homo ex his differentiis constet, id est ex rationali et mortali, rationale et mortale solum positum pars est substantiae hominis: BDP* 54B.

*n*4.240*b*: signifies ⊖ *significat*] This is the *de voce* ⊖ word-centred correlate of the *de re* ⊖ thing-centred sentence which has just preceded; cf. *n*4.240*a*.

*n*4.240*c*: both of these ⊖ *utrumque*] The Student is still insisting on the accidental element of the meaning of 'literate' (cf. *n*4.232*c*). To insist that *literate* should include *man* in its definition will, however, leave one with a word having no application to any unitary object, in the Aristotelian sense of 'unitary' (4.2411). Further, no contradiction is involved in the supposition of a non-human literate any more than one is involved in the supposition of a non-human white object (4.2412). Again, predicational practice shows that this definition is at fault (4.2413), and an infinite regress can be generated from it (4.2414). Finally, generalised adoption of its principle will affect existing and established grammatical classification (4.2415).

*n*4.240*d*: apart from a man ⊖ *sine homine*] Yet another of the elegantly designed symmetries of the dialogue is now becoming apparent. At 4.20 the Student tried out the supposition, which in fact represents the logicians' technical verdict, that 'literate' signifies literacy. He found that supposition wanting when tested against the measure of spoken usage (*usus loquendi*), subsequently embraced by *appellatio* ⊖ reference (4.23). Now, conversely, he is insisting on the factual universal conjunction of literacy and man which is evidenced by spoken usage, and his insistence will in its turn be rebutted, as *n*4.240*c* has made clear, by a series of technical objections drawn from theoretical considerations.

*n*4.2410*a*: being ⊖ *esse*] The connection between *esse* ⊖ being and definition is established at 3.800 (cf. *n*3.800*b*).

*n*4.2410*b*: man displaying literacy ⊖ *homo sciens grammaticam*] This proposed definition will be truncated to '... *sciens grammaticam*' ⊖ '... displaying literacy' at 4.31, after a series of technical (cf. *n*4.240*d*) objections to the presence of '*homo*' ⊖ 'man' within it. This procedure, and the theory which lies behind it, is discussed in *n*4.31*d*. The main reason for the truncation in fact immediately follows the present remark: *grammaticus* ⊖ literate, although factually co-extensional with *homo sciens grammaticam* ⊖ man displaying literacy, cannot be defined as though it were a full-blown unitary theoretical object. The reasons why *homo sciens grammaticam* ⊖ man displaying literacy does not constitute such an object are naturally quite closely connected with the arguments used by the Tutor in the present part of the dialogue (4.24), as the notes will show.

In general, the problem as to the unitary objecthood of *homo sciens grammaticam* ⊖ man displaying literacy arises out of questions which Aristotle left unclear. Thus a close examination of that part of chapter 11 of *De Interpretatione* which is concerned with the combination of predicates previous divided shows that of the three consequences used as examples of such combinations, only two are later expressly discussed, and it is hard to see how the neglected third one is covered by the rule for composition which Aristotle provides, and which is discussed in *n*4.72*a*. Thus three pairs of divided predicates are put forward as potential compounds, the third of which, says Aristotle, plainly will not stand compounding: these are, (i) 'is animal', 'is two-footed', (ii) 'is man', 'is white', and (iii) 'is a harpist', 'is good':

Of a man it is true to say not only *animal*, but *two-footed* as well, and these comprise one thing. Or again, *man* and *white* may be taken as one thing. But one cannot say that if he is both a *harpist* and *good*, then he also is a *good harpist*.	*De homine enim verum est dicere et extra animal et extra bipes, et ut unum; et hominem et album, et haec ut unum. Sed non si citharoedus et bonus, et iam citharoedus bonus: B* 573A.

At first sight it looks very much as though Aristotle is putting forward the first two pairs as examples of valid potential compoundings, with the third as obviously invalid, since from the truth of 'Socrates is a harpist' and 'Socrates is good' one clearly cannot infer the consequence 'Socrates is a good harpist', whereas a similar process using the first two pairs would appear to be unexceptionable. But when summing up the results of his rule for such compoundings, Aristotle only mentions pairs (i) and (iii): the first, he says, yields a valid consequence in combination, the third does not:

Hence while *good harpist* is not unexceptionable, nevertheless *two-footed animal* is, since its components are not theoretically disparate.	*Quocirca nec citharoedus bonus simpliciter, sed animal bipes; non enim secundum accidens: B* 575A.

Thus not only is pair (ii) ignored, but it is hard to see how *homo albus* constitutes a unity of the sort demanded by the rules of definition which form the basis for Aristotle's decision on such compoundings (cf. §4, *n*4.72*a*, *n*3.800*b*).

Caietan sums the situation up in the following manner:

The following facts should not be lost sight of: he brings forward three consequences when initiating the investigation of the matter, namely: 'He is animal and two-footed, hence he is a two-footed animal', 'He is a man and white, hence he is a white man', and 'He is a harpist and good, therefore he is a good harpist'. The two first he supposes to be valid, but the third not. Now how does it come about that wishing to discover the reason for this difference he only recalls the first and third consequences when settling the problem, and does not at all mention the second one? For he leaves unexamined the question of whether that consequence is valid or invalid.

Nec praetereundum est quod cum tres consequentias adduxit quaestionem praeponendo, scilicet: est animal et bipes, ergo est animal bipes, et: est homo et albus, ergo est homo albus, et: est citharoedus et bonus, ergo est bonus citharoedus; et duas primas posuerat esse bonas, tertiam vero non; huius diversitatis causam inquirere volens, cur solvendo quaestionem nullo modo meminerit secundae consequentiae, sed tantum primae et tertiae. Indiscussum namque reliquit an illa consequentia sit bona an mala: APH 269. (Note that the extra words *'ergo est homo albus; et est citharoedus et bonus'* of the manual Leonine are clearly superfluous).

Caietan here supposes that pairs (i) and (ii) were put forward as apparently yielding valid combinations, but (iii) as not, and that the discussion and rule confirm the supposition regarding the validity of (i) and the invalidity of (iii), leaving (ii) not explicitly settled. Notwithstanding the fact, therefore, that Caietan is able to record a way in which (ii) resembles (i), and hence might be settled by the decision regarding (i), the fact still remains that the case of (ii) is not overtly settled, and it must be admitted that Caietan's solution (discussed in *n*4.2414*b*) still appears to fall outside the scope of the rule given by Aristotle, i.e. *quaecumque secundum accidens dicuntur ... haec non erunt unum* ⊖ whatever things lacking a theoretical connection are asserted ... such things will not constitute a unity: *BDIG* 575A.

It would in fact appear that '*homo albus*' ⊖ 'white man' does not form a strictly definable or defining unity in the sense of '*unum*' ⊖ 'one' envisaged in this last-quoted sentence of Aristotle's. Anselm is, in effect, taking this standpoint in the present section (4.24): '*homo sciens grammaticam*' ⊖ 'man displaying literacy', (i.e. '*homo grammaticus*' ⊖ 'literate man') exactly corresponds to Aristotle's problematical compound '*homo albus*' ⊖ 'white man'. Significantly, he provides examples (4.2414) of exactly the regresses which Aristotle used in connection with the problem of the compounding of predicates in chapter 11 of *De Interpretatione*, and also (4.2411) attacks the use in definition of the

Student's compound. Anselm's regresses are compared in detail with those of Aristotle in *n*4.2414*b*.

*n*4.2411*a*: distinguishes ⊖ *dividit*] The notion of 'division' here presupposed is one of several technical meanings of the word '*divisio*' which are elaborated by Boethius in his *Liber de Divisione* (*B* 875–892A). The particular sort of division which enters into the present question is that of a genus (cf. *n*4.2411*g*) into its species (cf. *n*4.2411*h*) by means of a constitutive characteristic (cf. *n*4.22*d*).

Boethius' treatment of the present topic commences at *BD* 880A, and presupposes acquaintance with the predicables (cf. *n*4.2411*h*(ii)). The constitutive characteristics properly used for the division of a genus are the same as those needed for definition in its strict sense (cf. *n*3.800*b*):

Everything that is capable of subdividing a genus can also quite correctly be assimilated within definitions.	*Omne ... quod ad divisionem generis aptum est, idem ad definitiones rectissime congregamus: BD* 881A.

Starting from the idea that the division must be exhaustive of the genus, one has the rule that only pairs of terms which are contraries, such as 'rational' and 'non-rational', and which are appropriate to the genus, shall be used for the division of that genus. Miscellaneous divisions by other than contraries of the sort described, are barred:

There are some things which differ but which should not be opposed to eachother to form sub-divisions, as in the cases of *rational* and *biped* in the subdivision of *animal*. For no one asserts that animals can be exhaustively subdivided into those which are rational and those which are two-footed. Hence *rational* and *biped*, although they differ, do not form an exhaustive pair of opposites. Only whatever things differ from eachother on account of their being exhaustive opposites can properly be used to split the genus itself by being used as its subdivisions.	*Quoniam vero quaedam sunt quae differunt, quae contra se in divisionibus poni non debent, ut in animali rationale et bipes: nullus enim dicit animalium alia sunt rationalia, alia duos pedes habentia, idcirco quod rationale et bipes, licet differant, nulla tamen a se oppositione seiunguntur. Constat quaecunque a se aliqua oppositione differunt, eas solas differentias sub genere positas genus ipsum posse disiungere: BD* 881C–D.

The general framework of this system of classification by exhaustive division contains nothing logically obscure. The obscurity lies rather over on the side of the decisions in choosing constitutive characteristics (cf. *n*4.22*d*), and these decisions in their turn rely on presuppositions as to what is meant by *unum aliquid* ⊖ one thing (cf. *n*4.2414*b*, *n*4.72*a*). As these points are dealt with in the notes cited, it will suffice here to quote Boethius' own description of the way in which the division of a genus is effected in order to arrive at the definition of a given species:

Given, therefore, that we are dealing with that sort of species which does have a genus, and which is predicated of something further, I first take the genus, add a difference to the genus, and then inspect whether that difference combined with the genus happens to be the equivalent of that species which we have undertaken to delineate by means of a definition. If it turns out that the species to be defined is smaller than this result, then we consider again that difference which we had earlier combined with the genus, look on it as a genus, and split it up in turn into its opposed differences and again make a combination of these two differences with the original genus: if then we have equality with the species which has to be defined then the result is said to be a definition of that species. If that species is still less, then we take yet a further difference and split it up. We join together all the differences we now have and again inspect to see whether they all, when combined with the original genus, are equal to the species to be defined. In the end we gather together as many differences with other differences as are required up to the point where their combination with the genus yields a definitionally equal species.

Data igitur huiusmodi specie quae et genus habeat, et de posterioribus praedicetur, primo eius sumo genus, et illius generis differentias divido, et adiungo differentiam generi, et video num illa differentia iuncta cum genere aequalis possit esse cum ea specie quam circumscribendam definitione suscepi: quod si minor fuerit species, illam rursus differentiam quam dudum cum genere posueramus quasi genus ponimus, eamque in alias suas differentias separamus, et rursus has duas differentias superiori generi coniungimus; et si aequavit speciem, definitio speciei esse dicetur; sin minus fuerit, secundam differentiam rursus in alia separamus. Quas omnes coniungimus cum genere, et rursus speculamur si omnes differentiae cum genere illi aequales sint speciei quae definitur, et postremo toties differentias differentiis distribuimus usque dum omnes iunctae generi speciem aequali definitione describant: BD 886A–B.

For a concrete example of this process of division in action *n*4.2411*h* (ii) may be consulted. There is quoted that passage from book II of the commentary on Porphyry (*BCP* 94A–C) in which Boethius attempts to give a unified and systematic description of the predicables by using this system.

Boethius' treatise *De Divisione* contains, as has already been noted, a discussion of all types of division, of which division of the genus is only one. This treatise has what is probably the most elegantly systematic opening of all Boethius' logical works, although it soon tails off into his customary prolixity. In all, Boethius lists and treats of four kinds of division, namely of the genus into species, of the whole into its parts, of the word into its meanings, and of division which is *secundum accidens* ⊖ extra-theoretical. The latter, in turn, is of three sorts:

The word 'division' is used in many ways. There is the division of a genus into its species, and there is the sort of division which occurs when a whole is divided into its own parts. Yet another occurs when a word having many meanings undergoes a separation out of its various meanings. Besides these three there is another type of division which is said to be effected extra-theoretically. This in turn has three modes: one when we divide a subject into its accidents; one when we divide an accident among its subjects, and thirdly when we divide an accident into its accidents.	*Divisio namque multis modis dicitur. Est enim divisio generis in species. Est rursus divisio cum totum in proprias dividitur partes. Est alia cum vox multa significans in significationes proprias recipit sectionem. Praeter has tres, est alia divisio quae secundum accidens fieri dicitur. Huius autem est triplex modus, unus cum subiectum in accidentia separamus, alius cum accidens in subiecta dividimus, tertius cum accidens in accidentia secamus: BD* 877B.

The first of the four main types of division is covered at length from *BD* 880A to 887D, the second from *BD* 887D to 888D, the third from *BD* 888D to 890D, and the last from *BD* 890D to 892A. The preliminary discussion (*BD* 887B–880A), in which the existence of the varieties of division is established is succinct, to the point, and makes rewarding reading, especially when the distinction between genus/species and part/whole divisions is being argued, the subject-matter here approximating to certain segments of Leśniewski's Ontology and Mereology respectively.

The extremely lengthy section of Abelard's *Dialectica* which deals with division (*A* 535–581) is an interesting demonstration of the lively treatment which this topic was receiving in the twelfth century.

*n*4.2411*b*: illiterate ⊖ *non-grammatico*] Here division of what is falsely supposed to be a genus (*homo* ⊖ man) is being effected exhaustively by means of contraries (presence or absence of literacy) in accordance with the canons of division mentioned in *n*4.2411*a*.

*n*4.2411*c*: its being ⊖ *esse rei*] The previous sections of the dialogue in which the '*esse*' ⊖ 'being' of something or other is discussed (e.g. 3.4, 3.8) and the connection with definition which is there set up, are sufficient of themselves to show that '*pars eius quod est esse rei*' means, in effect 'part of what is comprised in the definition of the things'. This does not, of course, mean that defining is purely a verbal matter. On definition in the strict Aristotelian sense here intended, see *n*3.800*b*. On the identification of the argument-type composed of '*esse*' ⊖ 'to be' and a genitive, as in this case, see *n*3.431*a*.

The Tutor is here mocking an alert Student who knows his texts by quoting the exact words of Porphyry for the purpose of following through the Student's contention. For in Bk. IV of the commentary on Porphyry we find the latter quoted as saying that a constitutive characteristic (*differantia*) has to be 'That which endows a thing with being, and which is a part of that which is the being of the thing' ('*quod ad esse conducit et quod est eius quod esse rei pars est*': *BB* 272.3.4, *BCP* 129B). These words are practically identical with those of the text.

*n*4.2411*d*: perishing ⊖ *corruptionem*] Given the theory of definition (cf. *n*3.800*b*) and the notion of what constitutes one thing (*unum aliquid*) (cf. §4, *n*4.2414*b*, *n*4.72*a*) which together lie behind this remark, its point is obvious enough: 'literate' is a separable accident (cf. *n*3.101*a*) of man; it is at one time true of a given man that he is not literate and at another time true that he is literate. Indeed, according to Anselm, 'literate' may for the present purposes be regarded as on the same level as 'white' or any other similarly transient characteristic of physical objects (4.2421).

The Tutor of the dialogue is therefore at this point drawing out what he holds, given the presuppositions mentioned, to be the absurd consequences of the Student's wishing to define *literate* as *man displaying literacy*. Definition is of the being of an object, and involves those names which never fail to apply to objects of the sort undergoing definition. From a pretheoretical point of view we would find it quite absurd to say that there was such an object as a literate which came into existence only when literacy was present in it, and went out of existence when literacy was absent. Likewise the blushing and the unblushing Socrates would not ordinarily be distinguished as two diverse objects. However, given the theory of definition on which the Tutor is relying for his argument, these are exactly the absurdities to which the Student is committing himself, and to which the Tutor's remarks are intended to call attention.

It is plain, therefore, that a conception of 'object' is here in question which represents a restriction upon the more general notion made available in Ontology. Thus reading 'ob ( )' as '... is an object', it is evident that 'that of which there is exactly one' might be said to be the most general specification of 'object', as is evidenced by the definition:

.1 $[a]:\mathrm{ob}(a).\equiv.[\exists b].a\varepsilon b$ (§3.3, *LR* T16)

But this definition still allows the very widest latitude in the choice of objects; for example any spatio-temporal segment of the physical world, no matter how fancifully selected, as well as purely notional constructs such as spatio-temporal minimals may count as objects according to .1, provided that they exist. Conversely, looking at the matter from the point of view of *a*'s *non*-objecthood, there is no name (apart from '*a*' itself and '*V*', defined §3.18) which if denied of *a* would amount to denial of its existing objecthood.

The remarks of Anselm at present undergoing comment make it plain that neither he nor Boethius, from whom the vocabulary of these remarks is directly drawn (see below), are working with this very general notion of 'object' in mind. The reason for this is quite plain: they are accustomed to work in terms not of Ontology, but of the theories of those particular types of object (men, animals, rocks, plants, colours) which lie within the field of their ultra-empiricism. Within such theories, or within the fragmentary sketches of such theories, theses involving non-Ontological constant terms (e.g. 'man', 'animal', etc.) are available which are such that denial of certain predicates amounts to denial of the existence of an object comprised by the theory in question. For example, it follows from the theses of Anthropology, the theory of *man*, that to say that Socrates is not an animal is to say that Socrates does not exist. Conversely, it is only to the extent that such predicates are true of him that Socrates is an object subsumable under the terms deployed in Anthropology. What we have here, then, is not so much an abrogation of Ontology, the most general theory of objects, as a set of limitations imposed for the purposes of theories of particular types of object. The truth of the theses of Ontology is not, of course, impugned: 'Socrates' is still a possible substituend for the '*a*' in .1 above. But these other theories, and generalisations thereon, even though one may to some extent be able to clothe them in the language of Ontology, as is attempted herein, are not Ontology, in virtue of their involving or presupposing constant terms which lie outside the purview of Ontology.

One may enlarge on the position in the following way: it is plain from the discussion of '*unum aliquid*' ⊖ 'one thing' (cf. *n*4.2414*b*, *n*4.72*a*) that Anselm and his predecessors, working in terms of natural language, were haunted by the fear that given an unlimited substitution-range in generalisations involving names, they might find themselves committed, e.g. by equivocal names, to a breakdown of the universality of certain logical principles such as that of the Excluded Middle. It is their desire for concretely-guided qualification in this matter of what is to count as being an object which separates them off from those modern logicians who are content to run briefly through quantificational theory with few, if any, explicit thoughts on the nature of objecthood. Quantification and systems of the Leśniewskian type at least hold open the possibility of specifying such notions.

Provisionally, however, the limitations on the scope of objecthood mentioned above could be given a logical representation quite simply by imposing appropriate restrictions on the quantifiers used in theory-exposition. (On quantification-restriction in general, see §3, *HLM* II and *LLE*).

The historical origin of the first set of expressions used by Anselm in the text now undergoing scrutiny, and which presupposes the Aristotelian notion of objecthood, is quite obvious: it lies in that text of Porphyry's which is reproduced in Bk. IV of Boethius' commentary on Porphyry. Here it is being pointed out that in accordance with the rules of division (cf. *n*4.2411*a*) not just *any* differentiating characteristic can be the characteristic constitutive (cf. *n*4.22*d*) of a species:

However, they who look more exactly at the matter assert that a difference is not just any feature which splits up the things that come under the same genus, but rather whatever contributes to the being of the thing, and which is part of the being of the thing.

Interium autem perscrutantes de differentia dicunt non quodlibet eorem quae sub eodem sunt genere dividentium esse differentiam, sed quod ad esse conducit, et quod eius quod est esse rei pars est: BCP 129B, *BB* 272.1.4.

The Tutor is hence reminding the Student that he is taking literacy to be a characteristic constitutive of a certain species, and this, as the Tutor points out a few lines later, is false (cf. *n*4.2411*i*). The reasons for this falsehood have been outlined above. Boethius more or less reproduces Porphyry's words in his commentary (*BCP* 129D) and confirms that connection between definition and *esse* ⊖ being which was remarked on at the opening of this note; this confirmatory passage (*BCP* 129D–130A) is reproduced in *n*3.800*b*.

The second set of expressions on which Anselm is here drawing when he uses the phrase '*nec potest adesse et abesse praeter subiecti corruptionem*' ⊖ 'the alternative presence and absence of which can only result in the subject's perishing' occurs towards the same book of Boethius' commentary. Porphyry's own words are: '*Accidens est quod adest et abest, praeter subiecti corruptionem*' ⊖ 'An accident is that which comes and goes without the subject's perishing': *BCP* 132C. Boethius adds, in his commentary, that modality ('can') which Anselm reproduces: *quae accidentaliter dicuntur, quoniam substantiam minime informant, et adesse et abesse possint praeter subiecti corruptionem* ⊖ those things which are asserted extra-theoretically, since they do not constitute the substance, can be present and absent without the perishing of the subject: *BCP* 133A. (This is, of course, part of the discussion of the predicable accident. The '*adesse et abesse*' ⊖ 'present and absent' does not indicate simultaneous presence and absence, but is intended to cover the idea that the presence or absence of the accident does not affect the identity of the subject). The Tutor, therefore, is pointing out to the Student that the latter is assuming literacy not to be an accident, and hence to be possibly suitable for use as a constitutive characteristic. In short, the Student is regarding 'is literate' as a *de subiecto* ⊖ of a subject (cf. *n*4.101*a*) predication, which it is not. Boethius himself goes on to make this contrast, which lies behind the Tutor's words, by stating what applies in the case of the constitutive characteristic 'rational', as opposed to an accident: *BCP* 134A, cf. *n*4.2411*e*. However, Boethius' discussion has by then moved on to the topic of separable and inseparable accidents, and this is more fully dealt with in the course of *n*3.101*a*. The distinction between 'rationality' and accidental characteristics is also made in the first of the Dialogues on Porphyry: *BDP* 31A–B.

The commentary on the *Categoriae* stresses the same point in other terms, namely that denial of an accident does not affect the integrity of its subject, whereas denial of a *de subiecto* ⊖ of a subject predicate amounts to a denial of the appropriate subject's existence. Thus, when speaking of constitutive characteristics (cf. *n*4.22*d*) Boethius observes:

But this same heat is in the fire, yet when the heat is not present, that is necessarily

Idem tamen calor est in igne, sed perempto calore, ignem interire necesse est. Quare

the end of the fire. Hence this quality *heat* pertains substantially to the fire, and is a characteristic intrinsic to it, i.e. a substantial characteristic.	*haec qualitas caloris substantialiter inest igni, et est propria differentia, id est substantialis: BC* 192B.

Finally, there are Boethius' express denials that *grammaticus* ⊖ literate, *navigabile* ⊖ capable of sailing, *rhetoricus* ⊖ rhetorical, and the like, can serve as constitutive characteristics: *BDP* 44B–C, *BDP* 54C, quoted in *n*4.2411*i*.

Porphyry's description of an accident as '*quod adest et abest praeter subiecti corruptionem*' ⊖ 'that which comes and goes without the perishing of the subject', which Anselm is here adopting with Boethius' modification, is used as a stock phrase by later logicians. Abelard (*A* 579.17.18), William of Sherwood (*KSL* 56), Peter of Spain (*HSL* 2.15) and Aquinas (*ASCG* II 81) all employ it, for example. See also *DLM* II–II 433.17 and 511.14.15.

*n*4.2411*e*: accident ⊖ *accidens*] Here we have a reference to the predicable 'accident' (cf. *n*4.2411*h* (ii)) which is variously defined by Porphyry (*BDP* 55C–56D, *BCP* 132C–134B; cf. *KSL* 56). The central idea is that of being extra-theoretical (cf. §4), which sometimes has as its counterpart the non-continuousness of application of a predicate to a definable object. Anselm has in fact just recalled the conventional definition of an accident as that which can come and go without the 'corruption' of such an object (cf. the previous note). Porphyry not only describes an accident as *quod adest et abest praeter subiecti corruptionem* ⊖ that which comes and goes without the perishing of the subject (*BCP* 123C) as described in the last note, but also as '*quod infertur et aufertur sine eius in quo est interitu*' ⊖ 'that which is added or removed without the cessation of that in which it is' (*BDP* 55C). This presupposes a '*subiectum*' ⊖ 'subject' which is not constituted by temporary and fleeting *in subiecto* ⊖ in a subiect characteristics (cf. *n*4.101*a*), i.e. a subject not merely notional, but recognisable as an object by criteria implicit in pre-theoretical judgements (cf. §4 and e.g. *n*4.22*d*). Hence accidents do not enter into definitions: *accidens vero ad definitiones nihil prodesse non dubium est* ⊖ there is no doubt that accidental characteristics are of no service in the work of definition: *BDP* 17A. However, the position is complicated by the distinction between separable and inseparable accidents, the discussion of which is so bound up with the '*intelligi*' ⊖ 'to be understood' vocabulary that it has been relegated to *n*3.101*a*.

The relation of '*accidens*' ⊖ 'accident' to other predicables is clarified in *n*4.2411*h*.

The thesis urged in the text, namely that '*grammaticus*' ⊖ 'literate' is not an accident is, of course, false from Boethius' and Anselm's point of view: cf. *n*4.2411*i*.

*n*4.2411*f*: characteristic ⊖ *differentia*] The particular sort of *differentia* ⊖ characteristic here in question, namely the constitutive characteristic, is treated in detail in the note which deals with *differentiae* ⊖ characteristics in general, i.e. *n*4.22*d*.

*n*4.2411*g*: genus] 'Genus' is one of the predicables (cf. *n*4.2411*h*) and is defined by Porphyry as 'that which is predicable *in eo quod quid* ⊖ in respect of "whatness" (cf. *n*3.501*a*) of diverse things which are specifically diverse": *Genus est quod ad plurimas differentias specie distantes in eo quod quid sit praedicetur*; *BDP* 25C, *BCP* 91A, cf. *KSL* 52. The clause '*specie distantes*' ⊖ 'diverse in species' serves to distinguish genus from species: both are predicated of many things *in eo quod quid* ⊖ in respect of "whatness" but while the genus is predicable of various species as well as of numerically distinct individuals, the species (in the strongest sense of the word 'species', cf. *n*4.2411*h*) is *only* predicable of numerically distinct individuals:

Genus and species are alike insofar as both are predicated in respect of whatness ... They are alike again insofar as both are predicable of many things. They are alike yet again insofar as both are predicable of numerically differing things ... But the genus differs from the species insofar as the genus is predicated of many things which are specifically diverse, whereas this does not apply to the species.

Congruunt namque genera speciebus, quod utraque in eo quod quid sit praedicantur ... Congruit item et genus et species quod utraque ad res plurimas praedicantur. Congruit item genus ad species, quod utraque ad res numero differentes praedicantur ... vero distat ab specie genus, quod genus de pluribus rebus specie differentibus praedicatur, quod species non habet: BDP 32C–D.

The main discussions of *genus* in Boethius are at *BDP* 22B–37B, *BCP* 87–98C. The position of *genus* in relation to the rest of the predicables is sketched in *n*4.2411*h*(ii).

The suggestion made in the text under scrutiny is, of course, false.

According to Porphyry and Boethius *man* is not a genus, since there are no constitutive characteristics (*n*4.22*d*) available to diversify the species; only accidental characteristics remain:

But if it happened that Socrates should be seated, and Plato happened to walk, there would be the diversifying characteristic of *being seated* or of *walking*, but these are not intra-theoretical ... the one only differs from the other in theoretically irrelevant ways.	*Quod si Socrates sedeat, Plato vero ambulet, erit differentia sessio vel ambulatio, quae substantialis non est ... nullo autem alio modo distare nisi accidentibus potest: BCP* 129A–B.

*n*4.2411*h*: species] This present note will be divided into two parts; (i) will deal with Boethius' use of the word 'species', and (ii) with the logical status of the predicables in general.

(i) 'Species' is one of the predicables (see part (ii) of this note) and is defined as that which is predicated *in eo quod quid* ⊖ in respect of "whatness" (cf. *n*3.501*a*) of many numerically diverse objects: *quae ad plurima numero differentia in eo quod quid sit praedicatur*; *BDP* 38B, cf. *KSL* 52-3. This definition must be understood as stating the equivalent of 'species' in the strong sense of the word *species*, namely as *species specialissima* ⊖ most subordinate species, which cannot be regarded as genus of further subordinate species:

Whoever wants to indicate definitionally that sort of species which is fully species, that is, the most subordinate species which is species only and can never be a genus, will do so in the following manner ...	*Si quis vero illam speciem definitione monstrare velit quae vere species est, id est specialissimam speciem quae tantum species numquam et genus sit, hoc modo definiet ...: BDP* 39B.
This is the definition of that sort of species which most properly is said to be a species ...	*Haec definitio eius speciei est, quae magis species dicitur ...: BDP* 39C.

In general, that genus is most properly genus which is never species, and that species most properly species which is never genus: *Magis genus esse dicitur quod genus semper sit, numquam species, et quo superius nullum genus sit. Rursus magis species est, quae species semper sit, numquam genus: BDP* 42A. The *genera generalissima* ⊖ most general genera are, for example, the Aristotelian categories, says Boethius; *BDP* 43A–C. The *species specialissimae* ⊖ most specific species are, so to speak, the minimum definables, given the theory of definition here presupposed;

cf. *n*3.800*b*, *n*4.22*d*, and *BDP* 44B–D. It is this theory of definition, and the notion of '*unum aliquid*' ⊖ 'one thing' which goes with it (*n*4.72*a*) that makes the scheme of genus and species less totally arbitrary and relative than may at first sight appear.

The assumption proposed in the text, namely that *grammaticus* ⊖ literate is a species of man, so that *man* is a genus, is plainly at variance with Boethius' doctrine. For him *man* is never a genus (*BC* 176D) and *rhetorica* ⊖ rhetoric (a case parallel to that of '*grammatica*' ⊖ 'literacy') never a constitutive characteristic; *BDP* 44B–C.

(ii) It now remains to give some review of the predicables in general, as well as to attempt some assessment of their logical status.

Boethius sums up his account of the predicables in a passage which at the same time illustrates the use of '*in eo quod quid*' ⊖ 'In respect of "whatness"' and '*in eo quod quale*' ⊖ 'in respect of quality' (cf. *n*3.501*a*):

Of those things which are asserted, some are predicated of one thing, others of many. Of those things which are predicated of many things, some are predicated intra-theoretically, others extra-theoretically. Of those which are predicated intra-theoretically, some are asserted in respect of whatness, others in respect of quality. Genus and species are asserted in respect of whatness, constitutive characteristics in respect of quality. Again, of those things which are predicated in respect of whatness, some are predicated of many species, others are not so predicated. Thus genera are predicated of many different species, whereas species are not thus predicated. Of those which are predicated extra-theoretically, there are some which are predicated of many things, as in the case of accidental characteristics, others of only one thing, as in the case of properties. One can also give a classification in the following form: of those things which are predicated, some are predicated of individual things, others of many things. Of those whings which are predicated of many things, some are predicated in respect of whatness, others

Eorum quae dicuntur, alia quidem ad singularitatem praedicantur, alia ad pluralitatem; eorem vero quae de pluribus praedicantur, alia secondum substantiam praedicantur alia secundum accidens: eorum quae secundum substantiam praedicantur alia in eo quod quid sit dicuntur, alia in eo quod quale sit: in eo quod quid sit quidem genus et species, in eo quod quale sit differentia. Item eorum quae in eo quod quid sit praedicantur, alia de speciebus praedicantur pluribus alia minime: de speciebus pluribus praedicantur genera, de nullis vero species. Eorum autem quae secundum accidens praedicantur, alia quidem sunt quae de pluribus praedicantur, ut accidentia, alia quae de uno tantum, ut propria. Posset autem fieri etiam huiusmodi divisio: eorum quae praedicantur, alia de singulis praedicantur, alia de pluribus; eorum quae de pluribus, alia in eo quod quid sit, alia in eo quod quale sit, praedicantur. Eorum quae in eo quod quid sit, alia de differentibus speciebus dicuntur, ut genera, alia minime, ut species; eorum autem quae in eo quod quale sit de pluribus praedicantur, alia quidem de differentibus specie praedicantur, ut differentiae et accidentia communiter, alia

in respect of quality. Of those things predicated in respect of whatness, some are asserted of many things specifically diverse, as are genera, others are not so predicated, and these are species. Of those things which are predicated in respect of quality of many things, some are specifically diverse (as in the cases of both characteristics and accidental qualities) others are predicated of one species only, as in the case of properties. Of those things which are predicated in respect of quality of many things specifically diverse, some are predicated intra-theoretically, as in the case of constitutive characteristics, others relate to the ordinary course of happenings, as in the case of accidental qualities. It is from this classification that the definitions of these five things can be assembled as follows. A genus is that which is predicated in respect of whatness of many things specifically diverse. A species is that which is predicated in respect of whatness of many things not specifically diverse. A constitutive characteristic is that which is predicated intra-theoretically and in respect of quality of many things specifically diverse. A property is that which is predicated in respect of quality and extra-theoretically of one species only. An accident is that which is predicated in respect of quality and extra-theoretically of many things specifically diverse.

de una tantum specie, ut propria: eorum vero quae de pluribus differentibus specie in eo quod quale sit praedicantur, alia quidem in substantia praedicantur, ut differentiae, alia in communiter evenientibus, ut accidentia. Et per hanc divisionem quinque harum rerum definitiones colligi possunt hoc modo: genus est quod de pluribus specie differentibus in eo quod quid sit praedicatur. Species est quod de pluribus minime specie differentibus in eo quod quid sit praedicatur. Differentia est quod de pluribus specie differentibus in eo quod quale sit in substantia praedicatur. Proprium est quod de una tantum specie in eo quod quale sit non in substantia praedicatur. Accidens est quod de pluribus specie differentibus in eo quod quale sit non in substantia praedicatur: *BC* 94A–C.

This list gives details of all the predicables so far covered by these notes, i.e. genus, species, and constitutive characteristic, as well as one more which has not received special mention, i.e. accident, some account of which is given in *n*4.24121*a*.

Although, in the quotation given, Boethius articulates his thought by means of a process of 'division' (cf. *n*4.2411*a*) he would not claim to have defined the predicables in the strict sense of the word 'definition' (cf. *n*3.800*b*) since definition properly so-called presupposes acquaintance with the predicables. As in the case of *genera generalissima* ⊖ most generic genus, only a '*ratio subscriptiva*' ⊖ 'descriptive account' can be given in such a case (*BDP* 27A–28A). Thus, in respect of the description of genus, Boethius concludes:

This definition of genus which has been constructed is not based on the notion of genus; only a sort of descriptive, ostensive, or designative account of genus has been given.	*Haec definitio generis quae facta est, non a genere tracta est, sed subscriptiva ratio et demonstrativa et designativa quodammodo generis est reddita: BDP* 28A.

This point itself indicates an obvious use of the predicables, namely in definition strictly so-called:

Knowledge of these five things can be brought to bear in definitions, so that neither are those things which are requisite omitted by you, nor are those things which contribute nought of any utility added by you.	*Prodest ergo in definitionibus harum quinque rerum cognitio, ut nec ea quae sunt utilia praetermittas, nec ea quae nihil praestant commoditatis, adiungas: BDP* 13A.

The process of division (*n*4.2411*a*) also, if it is to be properly carried out, calls for a knowledge of the predicables:

In the process of division such knowledge is useful to such an extent that in its absence nothing can be rightly allocated and divided. For how can there be a correct allocation and division when we are not guided by an acquaintance with the theory of those very things in terms of which the division is being effected?	*In divisione vero tantum prodest, ut nisi per horum scientiam nulla res recte distibui secarique possit. Nam quae generum vel specierum recta distributio divisione erit, ubi ipsarum per quas dividuntur rerum nulla scientiae cognitione dirigimur? BDP* 13A, cf. *BDP* 18A–B.

Boethius likewise considers that the study of the predicables is essential to the understanding of Aristotle's *Categoriae: Est namque ad categorias Aristotelis introitus, et quaedam quasi ianua venientes admittat* ⊖ It is the entrance to Aristotle's *Categoriae* and admits those who approach them after the manner of a gate: *BDP* 14C. Their usefulness in this connection is plain from the identification of 'secondary substances' (cf. *n*4.1201*b*) with certain species and genera:

He calls certain species 'secondary substances' as in the case of *man*, likewise the genera of which these species are sub-classes, as in the case of *animal*. Hence these cannot be known, except through a presupposed acquaintance with genus and species.	*Secundas vero substantias species appellavit, ut est homo, vel genera in quibus ipsae species continentur, ut est animal. Hae igitur nisi praelibata generis specieique cognitione sciri non possunt: BDP* 16B.

It should be noted that this identification is not complete: there are genera and species which are not secondary substances:

This statement appears to have been made lest anyone should think that colour (a genus) and *white* (a species) are secondary substances; for these do not contain primary substances as their instances.	*Hoc autem idcirco dictum videtur ne quis colorem quod genus est vel album, quod est species, secundas putet esse substantias; ista enim primas sub se non continent:* *BC* 183B.

Further, the discernment of univocals and equivocals, and the corresponding thesishood or lack thereof (*BC* 167B, *BC* 191A–B, *HL* §3.1222) would be impossible, says Boethius, without knowledge of the predicables:

Hence it is evident that none of those things predicated equivocally are ever contained under the same genus. The point of this would forever be lost to you, were you to lack prior knowledge of, and acquaintance with, genera, species, properties, and characteristics.	*Quare constat quoniam numquam sub eisdem generibus continentur quaecunque aequivoce praedicantur. Quam vim, nisi prius de generibus, speciebus, propriis et differentiis notitiam scientiamque perceperis, nullo numquam tempore discernis:* *BDP* 16B.

The same points are made in the commentary on Porphyry: *BCP* 75–82.

The identification of certain species with 'secondary substances' (cf. *n*4.1201*b*) i.e. with that which is predicated *de subiecto* ⊖ of a subject (*n*4.101*a*) and *in eo quod quid* ⊖ in respect of 'whatness'' (*n*3.501*a*) by means of a shared name has been mentioned above, and already suggests that the predicables revolve round an 'is' if higher semantical category than the primitive 'is' of Ontology, i.e. the higher-order 'is' defined at §3.15. This suspicion is strongly confirmed by an important passage at the close of Bk. I of Boethius' commentary on the *Categoriae*. Here he reminds the reader that *man* and *animal* can be viewed in two ways: they can be considered insofar as they are predicable of many things, or alternatively insofar as they have reference to (primary, individual) substances:

Man and *animal* can be viewed in two fashions, firstly insofar as they are predicable of many things, secondarily insofar as they are substances.	*Duobus modis animal atque homo spectentur, uno quod de pluribus praedicentur, altero quod substantiae sint:* *BC* 201A–202A.

This is an immediate link with the predicables, as evidenced by the '*de pluribus praedicentur*' ⊖ 'can be predicated of many things', so prominent in Boethius' discussion of the predicables. Indeed, Boethius goes on to speak of *animal* insofar as it is a genus, namely, insofar as it is predicated of various species (cf. the definition of genus *n*4.2411*g*) and *man* insofar as it is predicated of various individuals, i.e. *qua* species (cf. part (i) of the present note). Taken in this sense, says Boethius, *animal* and *man* cannot be said to be e.g. healthy or unhealthy, or wise or stupid; it is only insofar as individuals are concerned that such assertions can be made:

Animal insofar as it has reference to the species is neither wise nor stupid, and *man* insofar as its predicability of individuals is concerned, is neither healthy nor sick. However, insofar as they are substances, and point to individual substances, they *are* susceptible of such contraties.

Animal in eo quod de speciebus dicitur neque sapiens est, neque insipiens, et homo in eo quod de individuis dicitur, neque sanus est neque aeger; in eo vero quod substantiae sunt, et quod individuis substantiis praesunt, contrariorum susceptibiles sunt: BC 202A.

Leaving aside the complications which are being caused here by the lack of articles in the Latin, it is evident that Boethius is here in effect, distinguishing between the lower and higher-order '$\in$', as described in §3, by pointing out the differing types of term which they can take as their arguments. The 'is' if 'Cicero is ill', or of 'The man is ill', is of a semantical category differing from that of the 'is' of '*man* is *animal*' or '*man* is a species', as is evidenced by the impossibility of predicating 'is ill' or 'is not ill' of *man* as used in the last two sentences. Whence doubtless is derived the sophism (having a long subsequent history) mentioned by John of Salisbury:

Hence if a horse is promised in a general sort of way, and the beneficiary asserts, 'The horse you promised to me is either well or ill, since every horse is either well or ill' then he is arguing in vain, because there is no horse which is promised to him.

Unde si equus promittatur in genere, et dicat stipulator, 'Equus qui mihi promissus est, sanus aut eger est, cum omnis equus sit aut sanus aut eger', arguit nugari, eo quod non est equus qui sit ei promissus: SM 102.18.21.

A genial account of one of the later developments of this sophism (in Buridan) may be found in *MB*.

Boethius develops this same line of thought earlier in Book I of the *Categoriae*; because Socrates is a man, and man is a species, one cannot thence infer that Socrates is a species; again, from '*man* is *animal*' and '*animal* is a genus' one cannot infer that *man* is a genus:

But perhaps someone is going to deny totally the truth of what has been asserted, for although 'man' is predicable of Socrates (since Socrates is a man), and 'species' of *man* (since *man* is a species),

Sed fortasse quisquam dicat minime verum esse quod dictum est, nam cum 'homo' de Socrate praediceter (Socrates enim homo est) de homine vero 'species' (homo enim species est), Socrates species esse non

Socrates is nevertheless not asserted to be a species. Again, although 'animal' is predicable of *man*, and 'genus' of *animal* (since *animal* is a genus) the word 'genus' does not apply to *man*; *man* is not a genus but only a species.

dicitur. Et rursus cum 'animal' de homine praedicetur, de animali vero 'genus' (animal enim genus est) homo generis vocabulo caret, non enim dicitur homo esse genus; homo enim genus non est, sed tantum species: BC 176C–D.

Strictly speaking, only the first of these two examples comes within the scope of the point now being made (for '*man* is a genus' involves no confusion of semantical categories, but is merely false), and part of Boethius' resolution of the sophisms turns upon the meaning of '*in eo quod quid*' ⊖ 'in respect of "whatness"' (cf. *n*3.501*a*) which need not be considered here. Nevertheless his description of the status of 'genus' and 'species' in assertions such as '*man* is a species' and '*animal* is a genus' makes it appear that he understands the semantical category of 'genus' and 'species' to be quite diverse from that of, say, 'man' in 'Socrates is a man' (and hence also the 'is' of the latter assertion differs from that of the two former). The first assertion, he says, involves the use of the name 'species' to tell us that the name 'man' is predicated of various individuals only, and the name 'genus' in the second assertion tells us that the name 'animal' is predicated of various species. The words 'genus' and 'species' are hence in some sense, he continues, 'names of names':

Nor is it the case that in giving the definition of *man* one names the species itself. 'Species' is in fact only a name and indicative of whether the name 'man' is predicated of many things specifically diverse, or whether it is restricted to the naming of individuals only. Thus because 'man' is predicated of individuals only it is hence said to be a species. And because 'animal' is asserted of things specifically diverse, we therefore call 'animal' by the name 'genus'. They are thus in a certain fashion *names of names* ... they indicate the manner in which 'man' and 'animal' are predicable of their appropriate subjects.

Neque enim si quis hominis definitionem reddat speciem nominavit, sed designativum nomen est tantum, utrum de pluribus specie differentibus praedicatur hoc nomen quod est homo, an certe tantum de solis individuis. Nam quoniam de individuis solis 'homo' praedicatur, idcirco species dicitur, et quoniam de specie differentibus 'animal' dicitur, idcirco 'animal' 'genus' vocamus. Et sunt quodammodo nominum nomina ... designant quomodo 'homo' et 'animal' de subiectis ... propriis praedicentur: BC 176D–177A.

Of course, as still often happens when explanations are being given in a natural language comparatively poor in available parts of speech, Boethius has taken refuge in the metalinguistic attic on being faced with a situation which can be resolved without the necessity of such a flight when a language sufficiently rich in semantical categories is brought to bear. Nevertheless, he does recognise a difference here, and in §4, following the key suggestion of *LA* 248–9, a parsing of the kind of assertion which occurs in a discussion of the predicables in terms of the higher-order '∈' (defined §3.15) has already been suggested (cf. *n*3.800*b*). Appropriate definitions of the arguments suitable to the higher-order '∈' are also available in §3. In this way some of the consequences enumerated at tedious length by Porphyry and Boethius can be reproduced, as well as the relation, so prominently mentioned by Boethius, of the predicables to definition. It may be noted that the expression 'names of names' used by Boethius in the passage quoted has a long and interesting subsequent history which would be well worthy of further investigation. It stretches forward through Ockham into Hobbes.

The interpretation of '*man* is *animal*' at the level of the predicables suggested at §4.4 ran as follows:

.1 $\mathrm{Cl}[\![\mathbf{h}]\!] \in \subset [\![\mathbf{a}]\!]$ (cf. §3.13.14.15)

This turns out to be quite consonant with the observations of Aquinas when dealing with the way in which such expressions can enter into logical relations such as that of contrariety, notwithstanding the lack of those quantifiers which are the usual mark of such relations:

However, they sometimes can be accounted contraries because of what they signify; this occurs when something is predicated of the universal on account of some universal nature, even though the sign of universality is not prefixed. For example, when one asserts '*man* is *animal*', '*Man* is not *animal*' these statements, because of what is signified, have the same force as the statements, 'Every man is animal', 'No man is animal'.

Contingit autem quandoque ratione significati eas habere contrarietatem, puta, cum attribuitur aliquid universali ratione naturae universalis, quamvis non apponatur signum universale; ut cum dicitur 'homo est animal', 'homo non est animal': quia hae enunciationes eamdem habent vim ratione significati ac si diceretur, 'Omnis homo est animal', Nullus homo est animal': *APH* 139, cf. *n*3,800*b*.

If '*ratione naturae universalis*' ⊖ 'on account of a universal nature' is here taken to express the predicative, predicable-level nature of the arguments of Aquinas' 'is' in '*man* is animal', for instance, then that 'is' may already be seen to correspond to the higher-order '∈' of .1. When, further, it is realised that we have also in his words complete agreement with theorem §3.52, then the accord with the interpretation in terms of the higher-order '∈' is complete. These terms also serve to give a logical elucidation of the later *suppositio simplex* ⊖ simple supposition, at least in non-Ockhamist writers (cf. *HLM* III §1 and *HL* §3.4).

Boethius' sophism involving 'Socrates is a species', as described above, occurs again along with a variant of the same sophism, but based on '*White* is a colour', in the late twelfth-century *Summa Sophisticorum Elencorum* (*DLM* I 357–8). This juxtaposition is exactly right, since both the problem-sentences involved are susceptible of interpretation in terms of the higher-order '∈'. The only trouble is that this passage of the *Summa* speaks of the '*White*' of '*White* is a colour' as *referring* to the colour whiteness ('*appellat albedinem sive colorem*'), whereas Anselm, perhaps a century earlier, had been at pains to avoid any confusion between *significatio* ⊖ meaning and *appellatio* ⊖ reference, in such cases (cf. *n*4.2341*a*).

Adoption of interpretations in terms of the higher-order '∈' for 'indefinite' propositions of the sort discussed by Aquinas can clearly obviate the puzzlement evinced in note 36 (pp. 30–1) of *KSL* over the classification of '*homo currit*' ⊖ 'a man runs' as particular (i.e. as equivalent to 'some man runs') and '*homo est animal*' ⊖ '*man* is *animal*' as universal (i.e. as equivalent to 'All men are animals', as in Aquinas' passage just quoted). Aquinas has dealt with the second, and the first does not involve the higher-order '∈'. The first is extra-theoretical, the second intra-theoretical (cf. §4). Compare also the dual interpretation possible of '*sciens grammaticam*' ⊖ 'displaying literacy' (cf. *n*4.31*a* and *HL* 79–86).

*n*4.2411*i*: shows ⊖ *ostendit*] It is pointed out in several of the preceding notes that the Student's assumption is certainly incorrect, provided that the rules of definition presupposed by the Tutor's remarks are adhered to. In terms of those rules, a constitutive characteristic is needed in order to divide a genus into its species (cf. *n*4.2411*a*); yet not only is *man* not a genus, but also *literate* is not a constitutive characteristic; it is, as the text implies, an accident, and so of the same status as a transient characteristic which occurs in all sorts of objects, such as the characteristic *white*. Of course, it may be questioned whether the rules of definition which apply in the case of *literate* need be the same as those which apply in the case of the substance *man*, for example, to which the Student has compared it (4.240). And, in effect, that *literate* cannot be defined like *man* is the result at which Anselm arrives, thanks to the distinction between *per se* ⊖ precisive and *per aliud* ⊖ oblique signification. (It is clearly assumed that to give the signification is at the same time to give the definition, cf. 4.240). The finding ultimately approved by the Tutor, namely that '*grammaticus*' ⊖ 'literate' signifies in a *per se* manner *sciens grammaticam* ⊖ displaying literacy, and signifies *man* obliquely, shows that Anselm in fact does wish to distinguish between the rules of definition applicable in the differing cases of *literate* and *man*. For a further discussion of this point cf. *n*4.31*a* as well as *A* 596–598.

To which treatise is the Tutor referring here when he claims that '*totius artis tracatus*' shows the falsehood of the Student's assumption? This Latin expression has two possible interpretations. The '*ars*' ⊖ 'art' here in question may just be logic in general (cf. *A* 113.29, *JA* 14 *n*. 2). The reference would then be to a treatise on the whole of the logical art. On the other hand we could have a parallel with '*Liber musicae artis*' ⊖ 'Book of the musical art' (*A* 71.6) which would yield 'Treatise on the art of the whole' or 'treatise on how to operate on wholes' as a more feasible and relevant translation. In support of this second alternative, which has been adopted for the translation presented in §6, one may note that the present drawing out of the consequences of the Student's assumption (4.2411) began with a reference to the process of division (cf. *n*4.2411*a*) which, in effect, the Student is carrying out in an improper fashion. Secondly, there has been a reference to literacy as a constitutive *part* of the literate. Hence it may well be that the mention of 'whole' here points to Boethius' *Liber de Divisione*. Further, the Tutor has stressed the way in which the Student's position would involve the use of colour-words such as 'white' to signify constitutive characteristics of supposed sub-species of men. Now for the refutation of this particular consequence one need look no further than the first pages of *De Divisione*, where such a use of colour-words in respect of *man* is condemned, inasmuch as it is expressly denied that man is generic in respect of variously coloured sub-species:

The division of the subject into its accidents is among those cases where extra-theoretical classification is being

Eorem autem quae secundum accidens dividuntur, subiecti in accidentia divisio est, ut cum dicimus omnium hominum alii sunt

effected, as when we say in respect of all men that some are black, some white, and others of an intermediate colour. These are accidents of *man*, not sub-species of *man*. In relation to them *man* is their subject, not their genus.

nigri, alii candidi, alii medii coloris. Haec enim accidentia sunt hominibus, non hominum species, et homo his subiectum, non horum genus est: BD 878A–B.

There is also at least one place, namely in the second dialogue on Porphyry, in which *literate* itself is explicitly mentioned as not constituting a species of *animal*:

If a man sails, he can be said to be an animal capable of sailing. But sailing does not enter into the theory of *man* ... It is not the case that man exists because he sails ... (cf. *n*4.2411*d*). The same applies to being rhetorical or literate. These differences which do not contribute to the being of the thing ... are not counted as specific ones.

Si homo navigat, potest dici animal navigabile. Sed navigare in substantiam hominis non convertitur. Neque enim homo inde subsistit, quia navigat ... Eodem modo et esse rhetorem vel grammaticum. Has igitur differentias quas ad esse non prosunt ... non ponimus specificas esse: BDP 54C.

Although Porphyry is here dealing with the division of *animal* (as opposed to the *man* which is in question in the Student's assumption) he at least makes clear that literacy is not a constitutive characteristic. Again, *rhetoricus* ⊖ rhetorical, which is here coupled with *literate*, is declared not to be a species in the first dialogue on Porphyry: *BDP* 44B–C.

The contrast between what is here being expressed by Porphry (e.g. 'it is not the case that a man exists because he sails') and the sort of thing which Descartes was prepared to concede in his discussion of the *Cogito ergo sum* might prove to be instructive.

*n*4.24120*a*: let it be supposed ⊖ *ponamus*] This supposition is only feasible because of the extra-theoretical status of *literate* in relation to *man*. The Tutor has, after all, already spoken of the possibility of showing that '*aliquis grammaticus potest esse non-homo*' ⊖ 'some literate can be other than a man' (3.94) and it has been suggested in *n*3.6321*a* that the '*potest*' ⊖ 'can' here reflects that extra-theoretical status. The present argument (4.24120) may in any case be taken to be a consequence of 3.94.

The Tutor is about to show, in effect, that if *man* is taken to be intra-theoretical in respect of *literate*, then new uses of 'literate' become impossible.

*n*4.24120*b*: other than man ⊖ *non tamen homo*] This supposition does not, of course, amount to the contradiction that some man is not a man, since strictly speaking 'mortal' has to be added to 'rational animal' in order to complete Boethius' definition of *man*. The reasons for this addition are discussed in *n*3.8010*a*.

If one is to take seriously what Boethius says in *Introductio ad Syllogismos Categoricos*, and not regard his words as having to do with a merely formal example, then it appears that he would not agree that the present supposition is a possible one:

'Some man is not literate' is true, but falsehood results if I say, 'Some non-man is not non-literate'. The former is the more true since that which is not a man cannot be literate.

'Quidam homo grammaticus non est' vera est, sed falsa est si dicam, 'quidam non-homo non grammaticus non est'. Cum illud sit verius, quoniam qui homo non fuerit, non potest esse grammaticus *BSC* 781B.

Thus 3.9 must also be at variance with what might appear to be Boethius' opinion. Anselm's position for the purpose of the present dialogue is that some non-man *may be* literate, but that in fact men alone *are* literate. The sense of the latter proposition is discussed in 4.500–4.512.

*n*4.24120*c*: displayer of literacy ⊖ *sciens grammaticam*] It will be pointed out in *n*4.31*a* that this occurrence of '*sciens grammaticam*' must be interpreted as 'trm $\langle \gamma \rangle$' (§3.11), and is thereby distinguishable from the '*sciens grammaticam*' of 4.31 which emerges from the present discussion as the meaning of '*grammaticus*' ⊖ 'literate'. The '*sciens grammaticam*' of 4.31 belongs in fact to a semantical category which makes it a suitable argument for the higher-order '*est*' ⊖ 'is' appropriate to logical assertions and which contrasts with the '*est*' ⊖ 'is' of *usus loquendi* ⊖ the current course of utterance (cf. n1.000*b*). In contrast, 'trm $\langle \gamma \rangle$' is not usable as an argument for the higher-order '$\in$'.

Quite apart from this proposed interpretation, however, there is sufficient material in the text of the dialogue to demonstrate Anselm's consciousness of the distinction proposed in these notes between the two senses of '*sciens grammaticam*'. Most notably we have the discussion at 4.8 which is designed to show that in the cognate case where '*albus*' ⊖ 'white' is said to signify *habens albedinem*, the latter must not be interpreted as '*aliquid habens albedinem*' ⊖ 'something having whiteness' or as '*qui habet albedinem*' ⊖ 'that which (he who) has whiteness', i.e. must not be taken to have the nominal character which 'trm $\langle \gamma \rangle$' also has. This doctrine plainly excludes the present, plainly nominal, occurrence of '*sciens grammaticam*' from any assimilation to that of 4.31 (cf. *n*4.31*a*).

English translations of the Latin participial '... *ens*' followed by an abstract noun have had to be eschewed in the present note on account of the ambiguity of sense described.

*n*4.24120*d*: man ⊖ *homo*] Since this is the conclusion of a supposition (cf. *n*4.2412*a*) the modal functor 'possibly' is to be understood as figuring in it. This addition does not, of course, make its assertoric version any less false. When the 'possibly' is supplied in this way, however, then the resemblance of the whole argument (4.24120) to the following one suggested by A. Church is quite close: 'Let "*b*", "*f*" and "*m*" mean respectively the class of bipeds, the class of naturally featherless creatures, and the class of man. Then the sentence is true (9) "$fb = m \,.\, \Diamond fb \neq m$" [*featherless biped* is identical with *man* and it is possible that *featherless biped* is not identical with *man*] – the non-existence of featherless bipeds other than men being man being a zoological accident. But where "α" is a class variable, the inference from (9) of the sentence "$(\exists\alpha); \alpha = m \,.\, \Diamond\, \alpha \neq m$" [there is a class α such that α is identical with *m*, and it is possible that α is non-identical with *m*] must be in error, since having "$\alpha \neq m$" we could substitute "*m*" for "α" and infer further the false sentence "$\Diamond\, m \neq m$" [it is possible that *man* is not *man*]': *CR*.

*n*4.24121*a*: other than men ⊖ *non soli homini*] This corollary, deriving as it does from a series of logical reasons, is a repetition of the thesis of 3.94 (cf. *n*4.241*a* and the references there given).

For Anselm's own analysis of the sentence 'Man alone displays literacy', which occurs in this corollary, see 4.5 and the notes thereto annexed.

The total theoretical diversity of *man* and *literate* which the present statement implies is exceedingly strong in comparison with the kind of doctrine later to be found in Aquinas' *De Ente et Essentia* (Ch. 7). The latter contains the distinction between *accidentia quae consequunter materiam* ⊖ accidents which are consequential upon matter and the *accidentia quae consequuntur formam* ⊖ accidents consequential upon form, the two being respectively *accidentia individui* ⊖ accidents of the individual and *propriae passiones vel generis vel speciei* ⊖ qualities proper to the genus or species. In the case of the second there is a certain intelligible connection between the nature of the species and the accident in question:

It [i.e. such an accident] is to be found in all those things which share in the nature of the genus or species, as when the capacity for laughter is consequential upon the form of *man*, since laughter occurs from some mental perception on the part of man	*Invenitur in omnibus participantibus naturam generis vel speciei, sicut risibile consequitur in homine formam, quia risus contingit ex aliqua apprehensione animae hominis.*

According to Aquinas therefore, there would be some difference of status between *albus* ⊖ white and *grammaticus* ⊖ literate, in that the first would be *accidens individui* ⊖ an accident of the individual and the second *propria passio speciei* ⊖ quality proper to the species, since *grammaticus* ⊖ literate, like *risibile* ⊖ capable of laughter, is a *proprium* ⊖ property of *man* (*BDP* 54D).

*n*4.2413*a*: comprised in ⊖ *inest*] In view of what immediately follows (cf. *n*4.2413*b*) this material appears to emanate from *De Interpretatione* 11: *Amplius nec quaecumque insunt in alio ... insunt enim in homine animal et bipes* ⊖ Also to be excluded are those things which are already contained in another thing ... thus both *animal* and *two-footed* are already contained in *man*: *BDIG* 575A. Boethius gives '*continentur*' ⊖ 'are contained in' as an alternative to '*insunt*' ⊖ 'are contained in': *insunt in alio, id est continentur* ⊖ they are 'in' something else, that is, they are contained in: *BDIG* 576D.

*n*4.2413*b*: animal man ⊖ *homo animal*] In order to avoid the infinite regresses resulting from the compounding of previously divided predicates, Aristotle expressly bars the inferring of such combinations as '*homo animal*' ⊖ 'animal man' or '*homo bipes*' ⊖ 'two-footed man'. Caietan (*AHP* 263) describes them as involving 'implicit nugation' (cf. *n*4.2414*b*). Abelard adds that '*corpus coloratum*' ⊖ 'coloured physical object' is not nugatory, and so is unlike 'animal man' and 'two-footed man' (*A* 162.28.32). In so saying he is in agreement with Anselm's point made at 4.4211 of the present dialogue (cf. also *A* 334.31–335.2).

*n*4.2413*c*: literate man ⊖ *homo grammaticus*] By the definition of *literate* proposed by the Student, the combination '*homo grammaticus*' ⊖ 'literate man' will, in 4.2414, be shown to be just as nugatory as '*homo animal*' ⊖ 'animal man' and '*homo bipes*' ⊖ 'two-footed man'. For the moment, however, the Tutor is content to obtain an admission of the 'aptness' of '*homo grammaticus*' ⊖ 'literate man' and argues from that alone that '*homo*' ⊖ 'man' should not be contained in the definition of *grammaticus* ⊖ literate.

*n*4.2414*a*: correctly ⊖ *apte*] Throughout the passage which now follows, and in which a regress is generated, Anselm keeps the discussion on the plane of '*apte*' ⊖ 'aptly' rather than on that of '*vere*' ⊖ 'truly'. Whether the former is supposed to ential more than the latter, or less than it, is not obvious. As will become clear in *n*4.2414*b*, something more than mere truth-preservation is demanded by Aristotle for inferences resulting in compound predicates such as '*homo grammaticus*' ⊖ 'literate man'. However, 'aptly' is a suitably ambiguous word for a situation which even after Aristotle's original has been inspected, is itself ambiguous. Are the regresses supposed to exemplify some logically significant fault, or are they merely a sign that implicit nugation (cf. *n*4.2414*b*) is occurring? Boethius uses '*incongruus*' ⊖ 'incongruous', a similarly obscure epithet, in a similar connection: *tunc fit incongrua praedicatio* ⊖ then is brought about an incongruous predication: *BDIL* 359B; cf. *BDIL* 360B.

*n*4.2414*b*: to infinity ⊖ *in infinitum*] Both the argument of 4.2413 and the regresses of the present passage (4.2414) are derived from Ch. 11 of Aristotle's *De Interpretatione*. The primary aim of that chapter is to determine what is meant by saying that an affirmation or negation is *one*; the answer to this question turns on what is meant by '*unum aliquid*' ⊖ 'one thing', and the details of this discussion are given in *n*4.72*a*: Thus, given an inference in which divided predicates are combined, as when from 'Socrates is a man' and 'Socrates is white' one infers 'Socrates is a white man', does the combined predicate of 'is a white man' make the conclusion one conclusion?

In order to show exactly how these regresses of Aristotle are generated it will be necessary to make a survey of all the inferences which he uses as examples. From the at times immensely compressed text of *De Inter-*

pretatione 11 it is possible to extract inferences which presuppose the truth of the following hypotheticals. It should be stressed that the inferences, not the truth of these hypotheticals, are the object of the discussion. It is however more convenient to list the cases in hypothetical form, thus:

(1) If the man is animal and the man is two-footed, then the man is a two-footed animal.

(2) If Socrates is a man and Socrates is white, then Socrates is a white man.

(3) If Socrates is a harpist and Socrates is good, then Socrates is a good harpist.

(4a) If Socrates is a white man and Socrates is white, then Socrates is a white white man.

(4b) If Socrates is a white white man and Socrates is white, then Socrates is a white white white man.

(5a) If Socrates is white and Socrates is musical and Socrates is walking, then Socrates is a musical walking white.

(5b) If Socrates is a musical walking white and Socrates is musical, then Socrates is a musical musical walking white.

(6a) If Socrates is Socrates and Socrates is man, then Socrates is a Socrates man.

(6b) If Socrates is a Socrates man and Socrates is Socrates, then Socrates is a Socrates Socrates man.

(6c) If Socrates is a Socrates Socrates man and Socrates is two-footed, then Socrates is a Socrates Socrates two-footed man: (*BDIG* 574C–D).

(6d) If Socrates is a Socrates Socrates two-footed man and Socrates is two-footed, then Socrates is a Socrates Socrates two-footed two-footed man: *BDIG* 574D.

(7a) If the man is white and the man is musical, then the man is a musical white.

(7b) If the man is white and the man is musical, and the white is musical, then the man is a musical white (cf. *APH* 265).

(8a) If Socrates is a man and Socrates is animal, then Socrates is an animal man

(8b) If Socrates is a man and Socrates is two-footed, then Socrates is a two-footed man.

(9) If Socrates is a white man then Socrates is white and Socrates is a man.

(10) If Socrates is a dead man, then Socrates is dead and Socrates is a man (cf. *APH* 273).

(11) If Homer is a poet, then Homer is.

(Cases (9)–(11), unlike the rest, are instances in which the compound predicate is divided, not combined). Of the cases listed above, it is plain that 4a, 4b, 5b, 6a, 6b, and 6d exemplify the kind of thing that Anselm is taking over in the present text, but apart from this, very little of the real purpose of the exercise is apparent to the modern reader. A similar obscurity veils Aristotle's corresponding moves. At first it would appear, as in the cases of 1 and 2, that we are faced with a simple truth-functional matter. But then the important exception, i.e. 3, appears. Next the regresses are introduced (4–7) which are, from a purely truth-functional point of view, capable of interpretation in terms of quite impeccable theses, notwithstanding the fact that Aristotle uses them as a kind of *reductio ad absurdum*. Among the divisive inferences (corresponding to 9–11) there is once again the non-trivial case of 10, akin to 3 in some ways, and finally there is 11, which some might tend to separate off from the rest as pertaining to a different question. Very many things, therefore, are *prima facie* unclear.

However, once can at least follow Caietan (*APH* 263) in saying that two reasons for the regresses, namely explicit and implicit nugation, are to be found here: *nugatio duobus modis committitur, scilicet explicite et implicite* (loc. cit.): 4a–6b represent the regresses arising from the first of these two causes, and only in 6c and 6d does the second actually figure, although it arises in the first place from combinations such as those effected in the consequents of 8a, 8b. Caietan, in the last paragraph of *APH* 263, may have toned down Aristotle's intentions in order to present a neater division of the inferences, and I have followed Boethius' interpretation (*BDIG* 574–D) in drawing up the list.

A specimen generation of nugation runs as follows: starting from the assumptions

(i) Socrates is a man,

and

(ii) Socrates is white,

one can, by 2, conclude that

(iii) Socrates is a white man.

But then, by (iii), (ii), and 4a, one has

(iv) Socrates is a white white man.

Then again, by (iv), (ii) and 4b, one can infer

(v) Socrates is a white white white man.

A similar procedure is possible in the cases covered by 5a and 5b. All of these involve Caietan's 'explicit nugation'.

Caietan's comment on all this is as follows:

It is true to say separately of some man, namely Socrates, that he is a man, and again that he is white. 'And so on with all the rest' [Aristotle's words on which he is commenting] that is, we can also assert jointly 'Socrates is a white man'. But yet again of the same Socrates we can say separately that he is a white man and that he is white – 'and so on with all the rest' – that is, we can therefore assert jointly 'Socrates is a white white man', wherein the vain repetition is obvious. Again, if in respect of the same Socrates you again have the separate assertion to the effect that he is a white white man, you can also properly and truly say of the latter that he is white, and if in accordance with this you again have a separate repetitive assertion, you likewise still preserve truth, and so the process may be carried on to infinity: we have 'Socrates is a white white white ... man' to infinity. The same applies to the other example.

De aliquo enim homine, puta Socrate, verum est separatim dicere quod homo est et albus est: 'quare et omne', id est et coniunctim dicetur, Socrates est homo albus. Rursus de eodem Socrate potest dici separatim quod est homo albus et quod est albus; quare et omne, idest, igitur coniunctim dicetur, Socrates est homo albus albus, ubi manifesta est nugatio. Rursus si de eodem Socrate iterum dicas separatim quod est homo albus albus, verum dices et congrue quod est albus, et secundum hoc, si iterum hoc repetes separatim, a veritati simili non discedes, et sic in infintum sequeretur, Socrates est homo albus albus albus in infinitum. Simile quod ostenditur in alio examplo: APH 263.

Boethius claims to detect a case corresponding to 6b above in Aristotle's text, but Caietan does not mention it; this too involves the same explicit nugation.

However, the case covered by 6c has a new feature, thanks to the presence of 'two-footed man', namely, what Caietan calls 'implicit nugation'; thus

(vi) Socrates is a Socrates Socrates man

is assumed, and in addition it is also assumed inexplicitly that by some definition of man,

(vii) If Socrates is a man then Socrates is two-footed,

with the result that from (vi) (which comprises within it the antecedent of (vii)) supplemented by (vii), one can by 6c infer

(viii) Socrates is a Socrates Socrates two-footed man.

Again, from (viii), (vii) and 6d, one has:

(ix) Socrates is a Socrates Socrates two-footed two-footed man,

and this process can similarly be continued on the assumption of a general thesis as to the validity of such conjunctions. Here, because of the necessity of using (vii), which makes explicit something deducible, by definition, from *man*, in order to continue the process, one has 'implicit nugation' in a combination such as 'two-footed man'. In 8a 'animal man' is likewise an implicit nugation, since by the definition of 'man' one can infer 'animal animal man', and so on.

Boethius' commentary at this point runs as follows:

Again, Socrates is also Socrates as well as man, so that Socrates is the man Socrates. But he is also two-footed, so that Socrates is the two-footed man Socrates. However, it is true to assert in respect of Socrates that Socrates is a two-footed man; yet when I predicated 'man' I at the same time predicated 'two-footed' since every man is two-footed. Hence it is true to say of Socrates that he is two-footed, and yet again to say that Socrates is a two-footed man; whence the predication 'Socrates is a two-footed two-footed man Socrates' becomes true. But I have just used the word 'man', and thereby yet once again named a two-footed creature, since every man is two-footed; hence Socrates is a two-footed, two-footed, two-footed man. This sort of thing, when carried on indefinitely, gives rise to an excessive waste of speech. It follows, therefore, that it cannot be taken for granted that whatsoever is additionally asserted in no matter what fashion can really be predicated conjunctively.

Amplius quoque Socrates Socrates est, et rursus homo, erit igitur Socrates Socrates homo; sed et bipes, erit igitur Socrates Socrates homo bipes; sed de Socrate verum est dicere quoniam Socrates homo bipes est, sed cum dixi 'hominem', de eo iam et 'bipedem' dixi, omnis enim homo bipes est: verum est ergo de eo dicere quoniam bipes est, sed verum erat dicere quoniam Socrates Socrates homo bipes est; vera igitur praedicatio erit, Socrates Socrates homo bipes bipes est. Sed rursus 'hominem' dixi, atque in eo aliud bipes nominavi, omnis enim homo bipes est, Socrates igitur homo bipes bipes bipes est, et hoc in infinitum protractum superflua loquacitas invenitur; non igitur fieri potest ut modis omnibus quidquid extra dicitur, id iunctum vere praedicetur: BDIG 574C–D.

These last words represent Boethius' verdict that combination of previously divided predicates cannot be assumed as a general rule, because of the regresses that may thus be set up. If this objection to the inferences is anything more than a logically irrelevant quibble arising from the stylistically unusual word-combinations, then the nature of the word-juxtapositions effected in the complex predicate inferred must represent something more than the conjunction such as the '$\cap$' characterisable thus:

(x) $[abc]: a \in b \cap c . \equiv . a \in b . a \in c$

Now Boethius describes the regresses as '*inconvenientia*' ⊖ 'improprieties', '*impossibilia*' ⊖ 'impossibilities', and adds '*et hoc in infinitum protractum superflua loquacitas invenitur*' ⊖ 'this sort of thing when carried on idefinitely gives rise to an excessive waste of speech' (*BDIG* 574B, *BDIG* 574D, *BDIG* 575D). Caietan does not speak of 'impossibilities', but says there is something 'unfitting' ('*inconveniens*') about the 'nugations' (*APH* 263). Yet both seem to agree that there is preservation of truth-value in the inferences. This is evidenced by the passage from *APH* 263 quoted above and by Boethius' '*si de eodem homine albo rursus album praedicare velis, verum est*' ⊖ 'If of the same white man you again wish to predicate "white", truth results': *BDIG* 74B–C. The point, then, is not that the inferences fail to preserve truth, but that the regresses show that the proposition containing the composite predicate is not *one* proposition.

In order to obtain the required unity Aristotle propounds the rule, discussed in detail in *n*4.72*a*, which demands that *secundum accidens* ⊖ extra-theoretical predications should be eschewed if the predicate is to have reference to *unum aliquid* ⊖ one thing. For instance, if to (x) above is added the proviso that '*b*' should be the name of an appropriate genus (cf. *n*4.2411*g*) and '*c*' that of an appropriate constituteive characteristic (cf. *n*4.22*d*) then the compound this formed, given the Aristotelian rules of definition (*n*3.800*b*) will be capable of naming *unum aliquid* ⊖ one thing in the strict sense. This, however, is only one of the several alternative provisos which would have to be added to (x) in order to cover all the cases that Aristotle appears to have in mind.

Boethius expresses the position thus:

Whatever things are asserted extra-theoretically, whether they involve two extra-theoretical features' being predicated of the same subject, or one extra-theoretical features' being	*Eorem igitur quaecumque secundum accidens dicuntur, eorem vel si duo sunt accidentia et de eodem praedicentur, vel si alterum accidens de altero accidenti dicatur, ex his non potest una fieri*

predicated of another such feature, are such as not to yield one predication, nor does the conjunction yield a [countable] unity. Thus [in the first instance] a man is white and musical, but white and musical, since they do not fall under the same theoretical structure, do not effect a single proposition. For a white is not the same thing as a musical: they are both extra-theoretical features of the same subject, without at the same time being themselves the same thing. Again [in the second instance] if we predicate *white* of the musical, i.e. an extra-theoretical feature of an extra-theoretical feature, although this may be true there is no theoretical necessity that that which is musical should be white, nor do we encounter one [countable] unity here ... Hence on the same account we must hold that *good* and *harpist* cannot constitute an identity, and that not even when they are joined together in the same object, do they make up one [countable] thing, even though each taken separately is truly predicable. Suppose, however, that somone predicates something intra-theoretically, and asserts two things separately: those things which are truly laid down intra-theoretically, although separately and in a disjoined fashion, nevertheless can comprise one proposition. For a man, being both animal and two-footed, is a two-footed animal, and from these is formed a unitary predication. This is because neither *animal* nor two-footed is extra-theoretical in relation to *man*.

praedicatio, neque erit unum si iuncta sint, ut homo et albus est, et musicus; album enim musicum, quoniam in unam formam non concurrunt, non faciunt unam propositionem. Non enim idem est album et musicum; utraque enim eidem sunt accidentia, non tamen idem sunt. Nec si album de musico praedicemus, id est accidens de accidenti, et hoc verum sit, non tamen necesse est id quod musicum est esse album, neque enim est unum aliquid ... Quodcirca eadem ratione tenetur, ut non possit idem esse citharoedus bonus, nec in unum corpus coniuncta, faciant unum aliquid, quamquam sigillatim vere praedicentur. Quod si quis aliquid substantialiter praedicet, duasque res sigillatim dicat, possunt in unam propositionem redire, quae substantialiter vere seiunctae separatimque ponuntur; homo enim, cum et animal sit et bipes, est animal bipes, et fit ex his una praedicatio. Nam neque animal secundum accidens inest homini nec bipes: BDIG 576A–B.

However, although the provision barring *secundum accidens* ⊖ extra-theoretical compoundings eliminates the regresses in cases like those covered by 3, 5, and 7, it would appear that to Aristotle's mind we are still exposed to inferences such as those based on 8a and 8b, and perhaps even to those corresponding to 4a and 4b, since he adds a further cryptic rider, a rider which brings us rather more close to Anselm's regress: *Amplius nec quaecumque sunt in alio. Quare neque album frequenter, neque homo: homo animal est vel bipes; sunt enim in homine animal et bipes* ⊖ Whatever is contained in another thing is also to be excluded. Hence we avoid the repetition of 'white', as well as the one that arises from 'man', because of the consideration that *man* is both *animal* and *two-footed*, and that hence both *animal* and *two-footed* are contained in *man*: *BDIG* 575A. The purport of this remark seems to be as follows. If one term is 'contained in' ('*inest*') another (as 'white' is contained in 'white man' and 'two-footed' in 'man') it will not be proper to repeat (in the first case) or to make explicit (in the second case) the 'contained' term, and so set up a regress. This rider is doubtless added because cases such as '*homo bipes*' ⊖ 'two-footed man' still provide potential reference to one (countable) thing (*unum aliquid*), and yet still must be expressly eliminated because of the 'implicit nugation', leading to regress, which they encapsulate. Thereby are eliminated 6c and 6d, 8a and 8b; so also, according to Aristotle, are 4a and 4b, although it is difficult to see, as the commentators admit (*APH* 269) why case 2, from which 4a and 4b spring, should be admitted in the first place, given the *unum aliquid* ⊖ one thing criterion. This point will be discussed below. Boethius' comments at this juncture as as follows:

The reason for the rider lies in the fact that whatever things are implicitly or explicitly contained in some term which contributes to the make-up of a proposition are also not to be asserted jointly. Thus 'white' is not to be predicated of a white man so that we have 'white white man' as the predication. Or again, and for the same reason, 'two-footed' should not be predicated of *man*, for although this fact is not explicit, nevertheless that which is a man is also two-footed ... Whosoever, therefore, goes on to predicate 'two-footed' of a thing having two feet, has predicated 'two-footed', so that we hence have a two-footed, two-footed man, and this in a fashion of predication which should be avoided. 'Two-footed' is contained in man, and so if you go on to predicate 'two-footed' again you are effecting a most irksome repetition.	*Addit quoque illud, quoniam nec ea iuncta recte praedicantur, quaecumque vel latenter vel in prolatione in aliquo terminorum continentur, qui in propositione positi sunt. Idcirco enim de homine albo non debet dici 'albus', ut veniat pradicatio homo albus albus, quoniam iam in 'homine albo' continetur album. Rursus de homine idcirco non debet praedicari 'bipes', quoniam licet non sit prolatum, tamen qui homo est bipes est ... Si quis ergo adhunc praedicet 'bipes' de re duos habente pedes, 'bipedem' praedicavit. Erit igitur homo bipes bipes, sed ita praedicari non debet. Continetur enim in homine bipes, ad quod si rursus 'bipes' praedices, molestissimam facies repetitionem*: *BDIG* 567C–D.

In this way, in particular, what Caietan calls the 'implicit nugations' corresponding to 6c and 6d above, are avoided (cf. *APH* 263).

Now it is just to the sort of '*molestissima repetitio*' ⊖ 'most irksome repetition' mentioned at the close of the last quoted passage that Anselm believe the Student's equation of *grammaticus* ⊖ literate with *homo sciens grammaticam* ⊖ man displaying literate commits its proponent. In 4.2413 the Tutor has obtained the Student's concession that '*homo grammaticus*' ⊖ 'literate man' is not like the kind of combination barred by Aristotle's rider which has just been discussed, e.g. it is not like '*homo animal*' ⊖ 'animal man' (*Non ... apte dicitur quia Socrates est homo animal ... Sed convenienter dicitur quia Socrates est homo grammaticus* ⊖ It is inappropriate to say that Socrates is an animal man ... but it is proper to say that Socrates is a literate man: 4.2413). In 4.2414, at present under scrutiny, the Tutor is in effect showing the Student that given the latter's definition of *grammaticus* ⊖ literate as *homo sciens grammaticam* ⊖ man displaying literacy, the locution '*homo grammaticus*' ⊖ 'literate man', which has just been passed as appropriate, becomes nugatory. Thus in the same way as the superfluous term '*bipes*' ⊖ 'two-footed' becomes repeated if the combination '*homo bipes*' ⊖ 'two-footed man' is admitted, so also the superfluous term '*homo*' ⊖ 'man' becomes repeated, if the combination '*homo grammaticus*' ⊖ 'literate man' is admitted along with the Student's definition of *grammaticus* ⊖ literate. The conclusion to be drawn is that *homo* ⊖ man should not be part of the definition of *grammaticus* ⊖ literate (cf. 4.31). And certainly it is clear that this would avoid the regress, for '*sciens grammaticam*' ⊖ '... displaying literacy', the truncated remainder of the Student's definition, if substituted for '*grammaticus*' ⊖ 'literate' in the 'apt' '*Socrates est homo grammaticus*' ⊖ 'Socrates is a literate man' yields only '*Socrates est homo sciens grammaticam*' ⊖ 'Socrates is a man displaying literacy', which is in no way, implicit or explicit, of a nugatory nature. Anselm clearly assumes, as also does Aristotle, that making explicit that which is 'contained in' a nugatory combination is a move still remaining licit even after the '*unum aliquid*' ⊖ 'one (countable) thing' restrictions have been accepted; otherwise Aristotle would not have had any need to add his rider. In any case, Anselm makes explicit the nugation by replacing *definiendum* by *definiens*, a procedure entirely at one with that of Aristotle when he exposes the fallacy of the division of '*homo mortuus*' ⊖ 'dead man' (cf. 10 above and *B* 576D–578B, *APH* 274–276).

However, although the origin and form of Anselm's regress are thus accounted for, still much remains to be clarified in Aristotle's own text. Does he allow the licitness of inferences based on 2 above? Caietan is certainly right when he settles the question affirmatively (*APH* 269), and the fact that Aristotle feels the need to check further regresses *after* the '*homo albus*' ⊖ 'white man' combination has been effected shows that at least that combination was attainable: *Amplius nec quaecumque sunt in alio; quare neque album frequenter* ⊖ Whatever is contained in another thing is also to be excluded. Hence we avoid the repetition of 'white' ...: *BDIG* 575A. What Aristotle chiefly wants to avoid, as Caietan points out (*APH* 269) are cases like '*Socrates est albus musicus*' ⊖ 'Socrates is a musical white', wherein the two predicates '*est albus*' ⊖ 'is white' and '*est musicus*' ⊖ 'is white' are united only in virtue of their accidental application to a third thing: '*albus*' ⊖ '*white*' does not "in-form" '*musicus*' ⊖ 'musical' (or *vice versa*). Whites are not a species of beings in the strict sense of 'species' (cf. *n*4.2411*h*) one, many, or all of which are sometimes or always musical. Neither is 'white' a generic word and 'musical' a constitutive characteristic (cf. *n*4.2411*g*, *n*4.22*d*):

Now the reason why *white* and *musical* do not yield a conjoined predicate is because in such conjoined predication it is necessaty that one element should be related to the other as capacity to realisation, so that therefrom a unity should be effected at least some times, such that the one may receive its name from the other ... Now *white* and *musical* taken in themselves do not form a single unambiguously countable unity, as is obvious, nor do they form a merely extra-theoretical unity. For although the two of them insofar as they are united in one subject are one in relation to that subject, nevertheless the very fact that they are united in one third subject does not mean that between them they constitute an extra-theoretical unity, and this for two reasons: first, neither is structurally related to the other (for this is demanded for an extra-theoretical unity of things among themselves, assuming that they are not connected *via* a common subject);

Causa namque quare album et musicum non inferunt coniunctam praedicationem est quia in praedicatione coniuncta oportet alteram partem alteri supponi, ut potentia actui, ad hoc ut ex eis fiat aliquando modo unum, et altera a reliqua denominetur: ... album autem et musicum secumdum se non faciunt unum per se, ut patet, neque per accidens. Licet enim ipsa ut adunatur in subiecto uno sint unum subiecto per accidens, tamen ipsamet quae adunatur in uno, tertio subiecto, non faciunt inter se unum per accidens: tum quia neutrum informat alterum (quod requiritur ad unitatem per accidens aliquorum inter se, licet non in tertio); tum quia non considerata subiecti unitate, quae est extra eorum rationem, nulla remanet inter ea unitatis causa: *APH* 269, cf. *APH* 270.

secondly, leaving out of account the unity endowed by any common subject which has nothing to do with their definitions, there remains no reason for their being so mutually related as to form a unity.

On the other hand, not only are *homo* ⊖ man and *albus* ⊖ white related as are a capacity and its realisation (as also are genus and species, according to Porphyry-Boethius) but also they are not merely combined in virtue of their informing some other third thing: '*est homo albus*' ⊖ 'is a white man' is hence a predicate which may be inferred from the correspondingly divided predicates. (On the 'third thing' see *n*4.72*a*). Here are Caietan's words:

From the fact that *man* and *white* are mutually interrelated as capacity and realisation (and hence the whiteness can affect, lend a name to, and become one with, the man insofar as any account of the latter may be given) it follows that from these divided predicates may be formed a unitary predication, so that one may assert: he is a man and is white, and is therefore a white man. Conversely it was said that from *musical* and *white* one could not infer a joint predicate because neither of these affected the other.

Ex eo enim quod homo et albus se habent sicut potentia et actum (et ita albedo informet, denominet, atque unum faciat cum homine ratione sui) sequitur quod ex divisis potest inferri coniuncta praedicatio ut dicatur: est homo et albus ergo est homo albus. Sicut per oppositum dicebatur quod ideo musicum et album non inferunt coniunctum praedicatum quia neutrum alterum informabat: APH 269.

Once '*homo albus*' ⊖ 'white man' has thus been attained, however, Aristotle's rider against the repetition of that which is 'contained in' ('*insit*') a combined term, whether that containment be explicit (as here) or implicit (e.g. '*homo animal*' ⊖ 'animal man'), comes into operation, and prevents further regress.

Other points remain to be discussed in this matter of the combination and division of predicates. How close, for instance, does Aristotle consider that combinations which fulfil his *desiderata* approximate to what we would regard as hyphenated words, or even to single words formed by composition or agglutination? Much ingenuity has been exercised on the discussion of compounds such as '*homo mortuus*' ⊖ 'dead man' (cf. 10 above). Thus Caietan says that in one way there is no mutual incompatibility here:

'Man' and 'dead' are not here incompatible, since 'man' already has its

'homo' et 'mortuus' non opponuntur, quia 'homo' transmutatus iam per

meaning changed by the disintegrative qualification implied by the word 'dead', and so does not stand for the significate required by its theory, but rather as required by the adjoined term, whereby its significate is diverted elsewhere.

determinationem corruptivam importatam in ly 'mortuus', non stat pro suo significato secundum se, sed secundum exigentiam termini additi, a quo suum significatum distractum est: APH 276.

Abelard's remarks on the matter are more suggestive. '*Homo mortuus*' ⊖ 'dead man' and '*citharoedus bonus*' ⊖ 'good harpist' are, he says, single names (*A* 116.27.29), and he mentions his mysterious *Magister* who would classify '*citharoedus bonus*' ⊖ 'good harpist' with '*respublica*' ⊖ 'commonwealth' as one of the '*cohaerentes voces*' ⊖ 'agglutinated utterances' (*A* 116.5.11). He also rightly points out that one can no more analyse the significance of '*respublica*' ⊖ 'commonwealth' into '*res*' ⊖ 'wealth' and '*publica*' ⊖ 'common' than one can analyse '*magister*' ⊖ 'master' into '*magis*' and '*ter*' (two adverbs) or '*domus*' ⊖ 'house' into '*do*' and '*mus*' (verb and noun). In fact '*res*' ⊖ 'wealth' and '*publica*' ⊖ 'common' are more like syllables, he says, than separate unitary significants ('*dictiones*'): *A* 115.16.30. Further, he appears prepared to hyphenate thus: '*homo-albus*' ⊖ 'white-man', and '*animal-rationale*' ⊖ 'rational-animal', but not in the case of the implicitly nugatory '*homo rationalis*' ⊖ 'rational man' or '*animal sensibile*' ⊖ 'sensitive animal', referring in this connection to Aristotle's remarks on '*homo animal*' ⊖ 'animal man' and '*homo bipes*' ⊖ 'two-footed man' which have been discussed above (*A* 117.10.25). Of course, one of the roots of the whole difficulty of understanding the precise sense of some of Aristotle's compoundings may arise from the great facility which exists in Greek, but tends to be more infrequent in Latin or English, for framing *sesquipedalia verba*. A similar facility is found in German, however, which is thus able to offer single-word translations for some of Aristophanes' marvellous compoundings, e.g. '*Morgendämmerungshändelmacherrechtsverdebmühwanderung*' for his 'meanly-rising-early-and-hurrying-to-the-tribunal-to-denounce-another-for-an-infraction-of-the-law-concerning-the-exportation-of-figs': *MLE* 201.

Anselm's other regresses (4.812, 4.8121) are discussed in the corresponding notes. For accounts of '*nugatio*' which date from a time slightly later than that of Anselm, see *DLM* I 205, 411–2, and II–II 174.

*n*4.2415*a*: derives its name ⊖ *denominatur*] It was explicitly stated at the opening of the dialogue (1.000) and it is repeated at the close (4.82), that the findings which result from the examples used ('literate', 'white', and so on) are to be generalised to cover the whole class of words of the same type. In the present section this policy of generalisation is being carried out in order to make manifest yet another absurd consequence which will follow from the Student's contention (4.240) which is now undergoing examination.

In the case of 'literate' that which is paronymously named is *man*, and that from which it is so named is literacy (see *n*1.000*f*).

The use of '*intelligere*' ⊖ 'to understand' at the opening of the Tutor's assertion is a reminder of the connection between '*intelligere*' ⊖ 'to understand', '*definitio*' ⊖ 'definition', and '*esse*' ⊖ 'being' (cf. 4.240 and *n*4.24120*d*).

*n*4.2415*b*: today ⊖ *hodie*] The '*id quod denominatur*' ⊖ 'that which is named paronymously' in respect of '*hodiernum*' ⊖ 'today's' is *id quod vocatur 'hodiernum'* ⊖ that which is called 'today's', and the *id a quo denominatur* ⊖ that from which it is named paronymously is *hodie* ⊖ today. Anselm's point is that '*hodiernum*' ⊖ 'today's' does not signify '*id quod denominatur*' ⊖ 'that which is named paronymously' (i.e. *id quod vocatur 'hodiernum'* ⊖ that which is called 'today's'), for should it do so it would signify something (i.e. *id quod vocatur 'hodiernum'* ⊖ that which is called 'today's') along with a time, i.e. *hodie* ⊖ today, and this sounds very much like the definition of a verb (cf. *n*4.2415*e*); but it is absurd to classify '*hodiernum*' ⊖ 'today's' as a verb, hence we must not conclude that '*hodiernus*' ⊖ 'today's' signifies both *id quod vocatur hodiernum* ⊖ that which is called 'today's' and *hodie* ⊖ today. This argument unfortunately turns on a rather contentious identification of '*consignificatio*' ⊖ 'side-import', on which see *n*4.2415*e*.

It may be noted that '*hodiernus*' ⊖ 'today's' is given as an example by Priscian when he is dealing with the similitude of certain participial functions to those of verbs, so as to show that participles are not just names:

[Participles] are prevented from being names by their taking on of various tenses in the course of their appropriate transformations, as do verbs. But should	*Prohibet ea [*sc.* participia] esse nomina temporum diverorum assumptio quae fit in propriis transfigurationibus ad similitudinem verborum. Sed si quis dicat quod nomina*

someone object that there are also to be found many names which signify time, we would reply that the difference between participles and such temporal names is as follows. Such names signify nothing apart from a time as such, and taken in itself, as in the cases of 'year', 'month', 'day', 'midday', 'today's', 'yesterday's', and this not in the course of their appropriate transformations. Participles, on the other hand, indicate some action or undergoing of an action as taking place at various times, and not a time as such, and taken in itself. Again, the same things ensue upon their case-forms as ensue from the verbs which give rise to them. Further, they possess the meanings of verbs, and are substituted for verbs. None of these features, however, is attributable to a name.

quoque multa inveniuntur tempus significantia, respondebimus, quod hoc interest inter participia et nomina temporalia, quod nomina illa nihil aliud significant nisi ipsum tempus per se, ut 'annus', 'mensis', 'dies', 'meridies', 'hodiernus', 'hesternus', 'crastinus', nec in propriis sunt transfigurationibus, participia vero actionem vel passionem aliquam in diverso fieri tempore demonstrant, non tempus ipsum per se, et quod sequuntur casus, quos ex verba, ex quibus nascuntur, et quod verborum significationes habent et quod pro verbo ponuntur, quorum nihil est suum nominis: K II 449.21–450.3.

There are resemblances, at least verbal, between this passage of Priscian's and the Tutor's doctrine, i.e. '*hodiernus*' ⊖ 'today's' is said to signify '*tempus per se*' ⊖ 'time as such' in somewhat the same way as, according to the Tutor, it signifies *per se hodie* ⊖ today as such. The '*nihil aliud significat*' ⊖ 'it signifies nothing apart from' is also redolent of Anselm's turn of expression (e.g. in 3.21, 4.4233).

*n*4.2415*c*: temporal side-import ⊖ *cum tempore*] See Donatus, *Ars Grammatica: Verbum est pars orationis cum tempore et persona sine casu aut agere aliquid aut pati aut neutrum significans* ⊖ A verb is a part of speech having a temporal import and transformations according to person, but not according to case; it signifies something either acting or being acted upon, or neither of these: *K* IV 381.15.15. Anselm's use of '*cum tempore*' ⊖ 'with a temporal side import' is designed to show that '*hodiernum*' ⊖ 'today's' becomes a verb if the Student's supposition (4.240) is generalised (cf. *n*4.2415*e*).

*n*4.2415*d*: verb ⊖ *verbum*] The name and verb (cf. *n*4.2415*c*, *n*4.2415*e*) here mentioned are the two parts of speech which according to Boethius and Priscian were the only two such parts admitted by the philosophers; this thesis was in opposition to that of the grammarians, according to whom there were many more. Both Boethius and Priscian discuss

the matter in terms of a constructional analogy. Thus Boethius says:

We must consider whether the name and the verb are the only two parts of speech, or whether there are six such parts, as the opinion of the grammarians maintains, or again whether any of these six can rightly be assimilated to the verb and noun ... The name and the verb should be held to be the only two parts of speech, and the rest not so much parts, but rather completions of speech. They are like the brakes and reins of chariots, which are not parts but act in a certain way as combining factors as it were, and as suggested above, as completions rather than parts. Thus considered conjunctions and prepositions and other things of this sort are not parts of speech, but rather have a certain connective function. That which is called a participle may be taken as a verb, since it is indicative of time. On the other hand the adverb is really a name, since its fixed meaning has not a temporal import, and the fact that it does not decline according to case is no objection to this nominal classification: being declined according to case is not a property uniquely confined to names. After all, some names are indeclinable and are called 'one-cased' by the grammarians. But all this has to do with grammar rather than with our present concern.

Utrum nomen et verbum solae partes orationis sint consideremus, an etiam aliae sex, ut grammaticorum opinio fert, an aliquae ex his in verbis et nominis iura vertantur ... Nomen et verbum duae solae partes sunt putandae, caeterae enim non partes, sed orationis supplementa sunt: ut enim quadrigarum frena vel lora non partes, sed quaedam quodammodo ligaturae sunt et, ut dictum est, supplementa non etiam partes, sic coniunctiones et praepositiones et alia huiusmodi non partes orationis sunt, sed quaedam colligamenta. Participium vero quod vocatur, verbi loco ponetur, quoniam temporis demonstrativum est. Adverbium vero nomen est, cuiusdam enim definitae significationis est sine tempore, quod si per casus non flectitur, nihil impedit. Non enim est proprium nominis flecti per casus. Sunt enim quaedam nomina quae flecti non possunt, quae a grammaticis monoptota nominantur. Sed hoc grammaticae magis quam huius considerationis est: *BC* 796C–797A; cf. *B* 766A–B.

Priscian prefers to use the analogy of a ship, rather than that of a chariot, but his words clearly belong to the same conversation:

Certain philosophers hold that the name and the verb are the only parts of speech, and that the others are merely supporting members or joints, in the same way as the parts of a ship are the planks and beams, and the remainder thereof (e.g. the caulking and nails and so on) which ensure the binding and glueing together of the parts of the ship should not be asserted to be parts. But to this thesis the objection may be raised that the wax and caulking are not made up of the same material as are the planks and beams, whereas

Quibusdam philosophis placuit nomen et verbum solas esse partes orationis, cetera vero adminicula vel iuncturas earum, quomodo navium partes sunt tabulae et trabes, cetera autem id est stuppa et clavi et similia vincula et conglutinationes partium navium, non partes navis dicuntur. Sed est obiciendum ad hoc, quod cera et stuppa non ex eadem constant materia, ex qua tabulae et trabes, coniunctiones autem et praepositiones et similia ex eadem sunt materia, ex qua et nomen et verbum constat, hoc est literis et syllabis et

conjunctions, propositions, and so on, are of the same material as that from which the name and the verb are constituted (i.e. letters and syllables, accentuations and acts of understanding). Hence even when uttered forth in isolation, they show themselves to be parts of speech. For what else is a part of speech than an utterance indicating a concept of the mind, i.e. thought? Hence we rightly say of any intelligible utterance used to signify something that it is a part of speech. If such things were not parts of speech, names could never be used in their stead, whereas the planks of a ship cannot be used instead of the wax and caulking ... And if it were said that those things which appear to act as joining between names and verbs should not be asserted to be parts of speech, then on the same grounds we should not take the sinews to be parts of the body, since they bind together members and joints; but this is wholly absurd. Hence it is much better that the name and the verb should be said to be the principal and more prominent parts, and the others their appendages.

accentibus et intellectu. Itaque etiam per se prolatae, quod partes sunt orationis, ostendunt. Quid enim est aliud pars orationis nisi vox indicans mentis conceptum, id est cogitationem? Quaecumque igitur vox literata profertur significans aliquid, iure pars orationis est dicenda. Quod si non essent partes, numquam loco earum nomina ponerentur, cum loco cerae vel stuppae in navi tabula fungi non potest ... Sed si, quia compagem videntur praestare nomini et verbo, non sunt partes orationis dicendae, ergo nec partes corporis debemus accipere nervos, quia ligant membra et articulos, quod penitus videtur absurdum. Nulto melius igitur, qui principales et egregias partes nomen dicunt et verbum alias autem his appendices: *K* II 551.18–552.14.

Priscian has other passages on this topic. Thus he mentions the *dialectici* ⊖ logicians as holding that there are two parts of speech, the Stoics as holding that there are five, and yet others as holding that there are nine, ten, or eleven: *K* II 54.5.26.

*n*4.2415*e*: temporal side-import ⊖ *consignificans tempus*] The admission that 'today's' carries with it a temporal meaning (*significat aliquid cum tempore*) or has a temporal side-import (*est vox consignificans tempus*) and is incomplex (*nec est oratio*) makes the word not a name, but a verb, and this according to the definitions both of the grammarian (cf. *n*4.2415*c*) and of the logician. In *De Interpretatione* Aristotle defines a name thus:

A name is a conventionally significant utterance without temporal import, no part of which is separately meaningful.

Nomen ... est vox significativa secundum placitum sine tempore cuius nulla pars est significativa separata: BDIL 301C.

He speaks of the verb thus:

A verb is that which has a temporal side-import, whose parts have no independent meaning.

Verbum est quod consignificat tempus, cuius pars nihil extra significat: BDIL 306B.

From these statements Boethius concludes that the special mark of a verb is its temporal *consignificatio* ⊖ side-import: *proprium autem verbi est consignificare tempus* ⊖ the special property of a verb, however, is to have a temporal side-import: *BDIL* 306C. Anselm has added the qualification of incomplexity (*nec est oratio*) as the counterpart of those sections of each of the definitions which specify the absence of that complexity which characterises an *oratio* ⊖ sentence: *Oratio est vox significativa, cuius partium aliquid significativum est separatum* ⊖ a sentence is a significant utterance whose parts are independently meaningful: *BDIL* 311D.

These definitions recur again and again in Boethius' writings, e.g. *BISC* 762D, *BISC* 765C, *BISC* 794D, *BISC* 796B, *BD* 886B–887B;

The use of both '*cum tempore*' ⊖ 'temporal' and '*consignificans tempus*' by the Tutor may be intended as a hint that his argument holds both for grammarians who follow Donatus (in whose work '*cum tempore*' ⊖ 'temporal' is used: *n*4.2415*c*) and for logicians acquainted with the expressions involving *consignificatio* ⊖ side-import which occur in Aristotle-Boethius. In this way the point remains unaffected by those differences between the logician's and the grammarian's classifications of parts of speech alluded to by Boethius and Priscian (*n*4.2415*d*). Nevertheless, Boethius himself on at least one occasion uses the '*cum tempore*' ⊖ 'temporal' form of expression in the same sentence as that in which he uses '*consignificare*' ⊖ 'to have a side-import':

The result of what has been laid down is that some significant utterances have a temporal meaning, others a non-temporal one, and the distinguishing characteristic of having a temporal meaning does not apply to the definition of a name, since verbs have a temporal side-import, whereas names do not.

Secundum positionem vocum significativarum aliae cum tempore, aliae sine tempore, et differentia quidem cum tempore nomini non coniungitur, idcirco quod verborum est consignificare tempore, nominum vero minime: BD 886D.

Aquinas, in his commentary on *De Interpretatione*, distinguishes between *significare tempus* ⊖ to signify time and *significare cum tempore* ⊖ to signify temporally (*APA* 42) and sums up his findings thus:

To have a temporal side-import is to signify something as being in the time dimension. Hence signifying time as the principal significate, as a sort of object, which can be done by names, differs from signifying temporally, which pertains not to names but to verbs.	*Consignificare tempus est significare aliquid in tempore mensuratum. Unde aliud est significare tempus principaliter, ut rem quamdam, quod potest nomini convenire, aliud autem est significare cum tempore, quod non convenit nomini, sed verbo:* *APA* 58.

This, given the distinction between *per se* ⊖ precisive and *per aliud* ⊖ oblique signification, is sufficiently close to Anselm's conclusion at 4.431 that were the oblique sense of *signification* to be understood in the definition of a name or verb, then today's would be a verb, not a name.

*n*4.2415*f*: incomplex expression ⊖ *nec est oratio*] See *n*4.2415*e* for an account of the reasons for the addition of '*nec est oratio*' ⊖ 'nor is it a complex expression' at this point.

*n*4.30*a*: literacy ⊖ *grammaticae*] The discussion adheres explicitly to the topic of *signification*, without the use of the scandalous 'is' (cf. *n*1.000*b*, 4.2341 and its notes) until 4.50, where the Student gives a further reminder of that scandal. As a result, the necessary clarification of Aristotelian usage in such matters emerges in 4.6. The central distinctions (4.23) were in fact brought forward in response to the Student's contention (4.14) that 'literate' could not signify literacy because of the evidence of *usus loquendi* ⊖ the current course of utterance (4.21). Even after those distinctions, and still on the grounds of *usus loquendi* ⊖ the current course of utterance, he maintained that *man* must be included in the meaning of 'literate' (4.240). Five arguments (4.2411–4.2415) grounded on logical requirements (as opposed to those of *usus loquendi* ⊖ the current course of utterance) have been directed against his view, with the result that literacy now appears to be the only remaining element which could be shown to be the meaning of 'literate'

*n*4.31*a*: displaying literacy ⊖ *scientem grammaticam*] Anselm's results at this point may be reproduced in detail by means of the interpretations suggested in previous notes (e.g. *n*4.2341*b*, *n*4.230*b*, *n*4.232*b*). We are now learning (4.31) that 'signifying literacy' means 'signifying having literacy' ('*sciens* (or *habens* – cf. 4.700) *grammaticam*'). But a participle such as '*sciens grammaticam*' ⊖ 'displaying literacy' is susceptible of interpretation in two manners, according to the level at which the discourse is pitched. For example in '*Omne sciens grammaticam est grammaticum*' ⊖ 'Every literacy-haver is literate' (4.2412) one would certainly have to interpret '*sciens grammaticam*' ⊖ 'literacy-haver' as 'trm$\langle\gamma\rangle$', i.e. as a nominal expression (cf. §3.11). However, in the *de re* ⊖ thing-centred correlate of statements as to the signification of 'literate' it is evident that a non-nominal argument of the higher-order '$\in$' (§3.15) is required as the interpretation of this participial form (*n*4.232*b*, cf. 4.8). This duality of interpretation can be put in various other ways. For example, definitions §3.9 and §3.11 make it plain that the following is true:

.1 $\mathbf{g} \bigcirc \mathrm{trm}\langle\gamma\rangle$

This is an identity whose arguments are names. In contrast, Anselm's statement about the *per se* signification of '*literate*' can have as its *de re* ⊖ thing-centred correlate the sentence inferentially equivalent to .1 (cf. §3.56, *n*4.232*b*) having the higher-order '$\in$' as its main functor, and open, functorial forms as the two arguments, i.e.,

.2 $\mathrm{Cl}[\![\mathbf{g}]\!] \in \mathrm{Cl}[\![\mathrm{trm}\langle\gamma\rangle]\!]$

which by the definition §3.17 could be written as

.3 $\mathrm{Cl}[\![\mathbf{g}]\!] \in \mathrm{Cl}\,\{\gamma\}$

This statement, involving parts of speech not considered by ordinary grammar, can then be seen as the counterpart of Anselm's own '*grammaticus est grammatica*' ⊖ '*literate* is literacy' (4.2341, 4.5022) which was brought forward deliberately in order to show the necessity for novel parts of speech, given the level at which the discourse of the dialogue is now supposed to be moving (cf. *n*4.2341*b*). Expression .3 also accords with the finding that from the definition of things named paronymously existential conclusions cannot automatically be drawn (3.9, 4.810). A unified conspectus of the interpretation suggested above and in the rest of this commentary is presented in *HDG* §6.3125–§6.3128; see also *HL* §3.221.

Although the '*habens grammaticam*' ⊖ 'displaying literacy' result would probably coincide with notions then commonly held about paronyms, its form, involving a participle in the way it does, makes it peculiarly susceptible in of the dual interpretation, namely nominal (cf. .1) and verb-like (cf. .2 and .3), to which Anselm quite self-consciously submits it. Priscian's statement that a participle is a kind of cross between a name and a verb is already suggestive enough (*K* II 551.4.10, cf. *HDG* 141), but Anselm's thesis that in the present context the statement '*Albus est idem quod habens albedinem*' ⊖ '*White* is the same as ... having whiteness' is not about some thing (*aliquid*) or about that which has the whiteness (*qui habet albedinem*) (4.8, 4.81) is strong confirmation of the supposition that the verb-like, predicative, possibilities of the phrase '*habens albedinem*' ⊖ 'whiteness having' are being exploited, and that the higher-order '$\in$' of .2 and .3 is therefore quite appropriate. The manner in which '*sciens grammaticam*' ⊖ '... displaying literacy' is obtained as the result of truncating '*homo sciens grammaticam*' ⊖ 'man displaying literacy' (4.30), as if to illustrate this predicative and hence open, verb-like nature, is again consonant with the interpretations now being proposed, an interpretation which moves at that predicable level of discourse appropriate when definition is being undertaken (*n*3.800*b*). Later medieval stress on the difference between *ens ut nomen* ⊖ 'being' as a name and *ens ut participium* ⊖ 'being' as a participle confirm the feasibility of this duality of interpretation (cf. *HL* §3.221).

Thus, adopting the interpretation proposed above, one can now revert to the Student's question (4.22) which inspired the distinction between *per se* ⊖ precisive signification and *appellatio* ⊖ reference, a distinction discussed in intervening notes. The position recorded in *n*4.230*b*.1 was that both the following are true:

.4 $\quad \mathrm{Cl}[\![\mathbf{g}]\!] \in \mathrm{Cl}[\![\mathbf{h} \cap \mathrm{trm}\langle \gamma \rangle]\!]$

.5 $\quad \mathrm{Cl}[\![\mathbf{h}]\!] \in \mathrm{Cl}[\![\mathbf{a} \cap \mathbf{r}]\!]$

The Student asks, in effect, why 'man' cannot be said to signify substance and quality in the same way as 'literate' was said to signify substance and quality (4.22). In the terms now available we can say that the community evinced by .4 and .5 does not extend far enough for the Student's suggestion to hold. 'Man' signifies the substantial unity made up of animality and rationality (4.231); it is in contrast not true that 'literate' signifies a substantial unity made up of *man* and literacy. This is so because, as Anselm immediately goes on to point out (4.2411), literacy is not a constitutive characteristic (*n*4.22*d*). This in turn is connected with the later assertion that 'literate' does not signify *man* and literacy *ut unum* ⊖ as a single whole (4.232). How then can the relation between *literate*, *man*, and literacy be expressed? It has already been shown just now that 'literate' cannot be said to signify *man* in the sense that *literate* is a substance part of which is *man*. We must hence say that 'literate' is merely appellative of man (4.233), and is both involved in a theory of a sort differing from that of *man* and requires defining independently of *man*. This ensures that it is not necessary to postulate a new theory with new definitions at every extension of the application by speakers and writers of the paronym 'literate': the openness of Anselm's present definition carries this into practical effect. This openness also reflects the reasonableness of asking the question as to the '*alterum aliquid*' ⊖ 'something else' question presupposed in a sentence having a paronymously-named subject (cf. *n*4.1201*a* and the whole example of the white horse at 4.41, 4.42). It reflects also the way in which substances are more susceptible of ostensive definition than are things named paronymously (*n*4.14*c*). Finally, when in 4.2411 it is denied that literacy is a constitutive characteristic (cf. *n*4.22*d*), this need not be seen as a rather obtuse insistence on the part of the Tutor that there can be only one possible type of definition, but rather as underlining the fact that paronyms cannot be defined in the same way as are substances, and this is, after all, part of what is meant by saying that 'literate' signifies (or is) a quality as opposed to a substance.

It may be noted that Anselm's verdict that 'literate' signifies man *per aliud* ⊖ obliquely and literacy *per se* ⊖ precisively has some affinity with the doctrine of Aquinas in *De Ente et Essentia* 7. Anselm's distinctions are designed to show that, as opposed to what holds in the case of *man*, 'literate' does not signify substance and quality *ut unum* ⊖ as a single whole (4.232). Aquinas likewise holds that a subject and its extra-theoretical features are not, precisively speaking, one thing: *ex accidente et subiecto non fit unum per se* ⊖ an extra-theoretical feature and its subject do not constitute an independent single whole. Corresponding to Anselm's truncated form which is at present being shown to be the

precisive signification of 'literate' we have Aquinas' teaching as to the incomplete nature of definitions of extra-theoretical features such as *literate* and *white*: *Definitionem autem habent incompletam, quia non possunt definiri nisi ponatur subiectum in eorum definitione* ⊖ They have an incomplete definition, since they cannot be defined unless some subject is presupposed in their definition. Further attention is given to these parallels in *n*4.24121*a*, *n*4.31*a*, *n*3.800*b*.

Anselm's words in the present section of text (4.31) appear to commit him to the thesis that 'signifying *sciens grammaticam* ⊖ displaying literacy' and 'signifying *grammatica* ⊖ literacy' amount to the same thing. In other words '*grammatica*' ⊖ 'literacy' is hereby shown to be the same as the '*sciens grammaticam*' ⊖ 'displaying literacy' which has emerged from the arguments of 4.24. The well-known twelfth-century grammarian Petrus Helyas, comes pretty near to accepting this same sort of equation when he takes '*facere album*' ⊖ 'white-ising' as an alternative to '*albedo*' ⊖ 'whiteness' and to signify 'form'. He, like Anselm, realises that new ways of talking are required at this level, and apologetically remarks in this connection: '*ut fingam vocabulum pro forma*' ⊖ 'if I may coin a word for the form'; *DLM* II–I 231. Such infinitives or quasi-infinitives are, like the participial form which Anselm has now produced, counterparts of the "Cl⟦ ⟧" used in .2 above.

The present association of '*sciens*' ⊖ 'knowing/displaying' and '*grammatica*' ⊖ 'literacy' occurs in Bk. III of Boethius' commentary on the *Categoriae*:

It is stressed above that such things are qualities whereby some persons are said to be 'qualified'; thus we are said to be 'literate' not because we possess knowledge in general, but because we possess literacy itself. Further, it is rightly asserted that it is our being literates which justifies our being called 'knowledgeable', rather than our being in some sense knowledgeable justifying our being called 'literates'. No one is ever called 'literate' or 'knowledgeable' because of knowledge in general; rather it is only because of some particular form of knowledge that someone is called 'literate' or 'knowledgeable'. Since it is because of these kinds of having that we

Illas esse qualitates superius confirmatum est ex quibus aliqui quales vocarentur, nos autem idcirco 'grammatici' dicimur, non quod universalem scientiam, sed quod ipsam grammaticam habeamus, et hoc vere dicitur idcirco nos dici scientes, quia grammatici sumus, potius quam idcirco grammaticos quod aliquam scientiam retinemus. Nullus enim a generali scientia grammaticus, aut sciens, nisi a singulatim scientia sciens, grammaticusque perhibitur. Igitur quoniam ex his habitudinis speciebus quales vocamur, ipsae species in qualitate numerandae sunt. Sed cum quis grammatica participat, de ea etiam genus dicitur, et secundum eam non solum ad scientiam quoque coniungitur. Dicitur enim idcirco

are called 'qualified', such kinds may be accounted qualities. But the genus is also predicated of him who possesses literacy, and hence he has a relation not only to literacy, but also to knowledge. Because of this he is said to be knowledgeable. Since he who has literacy is said to be both knowledgeable and literate, it follows that he who does not possess the particular forms of knowledge cannot be said to have a share in any knowledge at all.

sciens. Ergo quoniam habens grammaticam, et sciens, et grammaticus dicitur, non potest ulla scientia participare, qui singulas non habuerit: BC 260D–261A.

Here not only are the *habens* ⊖ having and *sciens* ⊖ knowing/displaying alternatives used by Anselm, as recorded towards the opening of this present note, to be found, but also a further means of seeing a rapprochement between Anselm and Aquinas in this matter of the definition of 'accidents'; '*sciens*' ⊖ 'knowing/displaying' occurs in Anselm's definition '*sicut genus*' ⊖ 'after the manner of a genus', as Aquinas would say (*n*3.800*b*) so that one has an imitation of the general form of substantial definitions; *tum definerentur per modum substantiarum compositarum* ⊖ then they may be defined after the fashion in which composite substances are defined; *ADEE* Ch. 7, cf. *A* 596 et seq., *APA* 85, *APH* 40.

*n*4.31*b*: literacy ⊖ *grammaticae*] The sense in which '*grammaticus*' ⊖ 'literate' can be said to signify *per se* ⊖ precisively *grammatica* ⊖ literacy has been shown: cf. the discussion in the previous note. However, the scandal of '*grammaticus est grammatica*' ⊖ '*literate* is literacy' still remains (cf. 4.5022 and *n*1.000*b*, *n*4.31*a*).

*n*4.414*a*: signifies ⊖ *significat*] The Student will give the answer to this, his own question, at 4.4241, in the light of other examples which now follow, i.e. 4.421, 4.422. He will agree that 'literate' does not signify *per se* ⊖ precisively *man*, but only *per aliud* ⊖ obliquely.

*n*4.415*a*: doesn't signify ⊖ *significativum non est*] Once again, the Student is to answer this question for himself at 4.4242. He will agree that 'literate' is appellative of man, and only signifies man *per aliud* ⊖ obliquely. His answers are, of course, framed in terms of the corresponding cases of *horse* and *white*.

*n*4.4210*a*: a white ⊖ *albus*] The various possible English translations of the Latin '*album sive albus*' in full, e.g. as 'a white object or a white person' or as 'the colour *white* or a white person', would be superfluous, and would fail to reproduce the original problem. Anselm is at odds with the implications of the gendered forms of Latin names, and is trying to escape from them in order to give his question full generality. Indeed, at 4.8, he is to expel even the Student's 'indeterminate something' (4.801) from the meaning of '*albus*' ⊖ 'white': cf. *n*4.801*c* and *HDG* §2.32. In English, in the absence of genders, this striving is unnecessary, although in some contexts the use of the adjective 'white' as in 'a white' or 'the whites' could call up men as its oblique signification. Anselm's example is a reminder of the contingency of this connection: for example it would be quite otherwise in the discourse of a man absorbed in the breeding or study of horses or ants which were either black or white.

It is amply evident from the description of the concrete speaker-hearer context which occurs here, that the deployment of 'white' in *usus loquendi* ⊖ the common course of utterance is being exemplified, as opposed to the occurrence of the same word in the course of a logical discussion. The part which the meaning determined by logicians may play in such concrete contexts will be discussed at 4.423.

*n*4.4211*a*: whiteness is usually found in such things ⊖ *in his solere esse albedinem*] This distinction between a colour and the body coloured according to the modes of signification (the colour signified *per se* ⊖ precisively and the body obliquely (*per aliud*) as the Student in effect remarks) is clearly the one which Anselm has in mind in that passage of *Epistola de Incarnatione Verbi* which is often supposed to prove him an exaggerated realist in the matter of 'universals'; *nostri temporis dialectici ... qui colorem non aliud quent intelligere quam corpus* ⊖ our contemporary logicians ... who refuse to distinguish between colour and the body coloured; *S* II 9.21.23. The same turn of expression ('*nostris temporibus dialectici*' ⊖ 'our contemporary logicians') occurs also towards the close of the present dialogue (4.83, cf. *n*4.434*a*, *n*4.811*b*). On the import of this sort of case as far as Anslem's position on the question of universals is concerned, see *HL* §3.3.

That there is no intra-theoretical connection between *colour* and *body* or *surface* is common doctrine from Aristotle onwards; the '*in*' of

Aristotle's '*quoddam album in subiecto est corpore* (*omnis enim color in corpore est*)' ⊖ 'A particular whiteness is in the body in an *in subiecto* fashion (for every colour is *in* a body)' (*BC* 169A, cf. *n*4.101*a*) and the material quoted in *n*4.2414*b* and *n*4.72*a* leave one in no doubt about this: cf. also *HL* 89.

*n*4.4211*b*: in the case of *literate* ⊖ *de grammatico*] The last sentence emphasises how, in the same way as 'literate' has been shown not to signify man *per se* ⊖ precisively (4.232) even though men happen to be the only literate beings (4.24121), so also 'white' cannot signify a body or a surface in the *per se* ⊖ precisive sense, notwithstanding the fact that whiteness occurs only in these.

The first example, involving the enclosed white horse is a response to the first of the Student's questions (4.414), i.e. we have here a case of a paronym ('white') which does not signify that which it in some sense does signify. This is because in the open, functorial, *per se* sense 'white' does not signify the horse or any other subject, and the hearer whose information is confined to that *per se* ⊖ precisive sense is unable to grasp the subject with reference to which the speaker has deployed the word 'white'. The example demonstrates how that logical, functorial, account of the precisive signification of a paronym sets up no theoretical connection with, and in principle leaves quite unrestricted, the range of objects (in the sense of 'objects' described in §4) in respect of which that paronym may happen to be deployed in ordinary speech, i.e. of which it may be appellative (4.23). It is only in the extra-theoretical, appellative, sense that 'white' may be said to signify the horse.

The suspense of the hearer in the face of the incompleteness characteristic of the precisive signification of paronyms (cf. *n*3.41*a*) is also exemplified in this example. By varying the case it is easy to bring into relief the difference between the ways in which paronyms and substance-words signify. Thus if instead of 'A white is in this building' the speaker had asserted 'A man is in this building', there would have been none of that sort of suspense in the face of incompleteness which was encountered in connection with the first of these two sentences. Questions such as 'What is the object of which the whiteness signified by "white" is the whiteness?" or 'What is it that *has* the whiteness signified by "white"?' would be perfectly apt reactions to the first sentence. In contrast, to ask

'What is the object of which the (whole) man (*totus homo*, *ut unum*: 4.23) signified by "man" is the man?' or 'What is it that *has* the manhood signified by "man"?' would, unless 'of' and 'has' were intended in senses utterly remote from those appropriate to the first two questions, be a futile move as a response to the second sentence (see *n*4.31*a*, *n*4.1201*a*).

*n*4.4231*a*: not obliquely ⊖ *non per aliud*] This is because 'horse' like 'man' is a substance name, and hence functions in the way described at 4.231.

*n*4.4232*a*: the horse is white ⊖ *equum esse album*] Compare with this the remarks of Wittgenstein about assertions such as 'I noticed he was out of humour' and 'The sky looks threatening'. Is the first about his behaviour or about his state of mind? Is the second about the present or the future? The reply to these questions is that the assertions are about both alternatives in each case, but 'not side-by-side, however, but about one *via* the other' (*W* 179).

In the present example a concrete case of the contrast between the *per se* ⊖ precisive and *per aliud* ⊖ oblique signification of 4.232 is being presented.

*n*4.4233*a*: the word ... has the same effect ⊖ *ita et nomen*] The careful phrasing of this passage leaves the reader in no doubt that the signification of words is in question (*hoc nomen* ... *haec oratio* ⊖ this name ... this complex expression), and may be compared with the similar phrasing of 4.810. Once again this signification is coupled with understanding ('*intellectum*') which is that which is constituted by signification in its *per se* ⊖ precisive sense (cf. *n*3.101*a* and the references there given). It is not until extra-linguistic features of the context (*per visum* ⊖ by means of sight) come into play that the gap-situation characteristic of the *per se* ⊖ precisive signification of paronyms (... *habens albedinem* ⊖ ... having whiteness, see *n*4.31*a*) can be remedied by the object (cf. §4) in respect of which the paronym is deployed.

Later in the dialogue we are to have a further disquisition on '*habens albedinem*' ⊖ 'having whiteness' (4.8) wherein it will be shown that this expression must not be understood as '*aliquid habens albedinem*' ⊖ 'something having whiteness/whiteness-haver'. This is also hinted at by the word '*non eius rei*' ⊖ 'not of the thing' in the present passage. In any case, Anselm's careful use of '*hoc nomen*' ⊖ 'this name' and '*haec oratio*' ⊖ 'this complex expression' displays about the only means at his disposal, until the doctrine of 4.8 has been expounded, to make clear that the sameness of *reference* of the name '*albus*' ⊖ 'white' and the phrase '*habens albedinem*' ⊖ 'having/haver of whiteness' are not in question. Every time he is talking about signification (cf. *n*4.232*b*), as his present correlated sentences in terms of '*intelligere*' ⊖ 'to understand' show (cf. *n*3.101*a*), he has also in mind the corresponding *de re* ⊖ thing-centred assertions involving the scandalous 'is' (cf. *n*1.000*b*). In the present example, were one to follow the model of '*grammaticus est grammatica*' ⊖ '*literate* is literacy' (4.2341, 4.5022) one would have '*albus est albedo*' ⊖ '*white* is whiteness' as the corresponding *de re* ⊖ thing-centred assertion. In this last assertion '*white*' and 'whiteness' are not names at all in terms of the logical grammar which thus violates *usus loquendi* ⊖ the current course of utterance (4.2341); hence the interpretation of them as arguments of the higher-order 'is' which takes functors rather than names as its arguments (§3.15). For the moment, and pending the doctrine of 4.8, he can but express his results in terms of '*intelligere*' ⊖ 'to understand', i.e. that 'white' conveys the understanding of whiteness. The contents of 4.8 and *n*4.31*a* show that '*albus est habens albedinem*' ⊖ 'white is having/haver of whiteness', which is all that is at present available on the purely *de re* ⊖ thing-centred level, nevertheless can have the same import for logical purposes as the scandalous '*albus est albedo*' ⊖ '*white* is whiteness'. Thus the possibility of interpreting '*albus est habens albedinem*' ⊖ 'white is having/haver of whiteness' in a way which does not disagree with *usus loquendi* ⊖ the current course of utterance should not lead us to lose sight of its dual intepretative possibilities.

The expression '*constituere intellectum*' ⊖ 'to establish the understanding' which occurs in the present passage is to be found at several other points in Anselm's writings. In *De Casu Diaboli* 11 '*constituo*' ⊖ 'I establish' is opposed to '*removeo*' ⊖ 'I remove' (*S* I 249.6.11) and to '*destruo*' ⊖ 'I destroy (*S* I 249.21) in the same sort of context: e.g.

For it signifies remotively while not signifying constitutively ... remotively it does not signify nothing, but something, and constitutively it does not signify something, but nothing.

Significat enim removendo, et non significat constituendo ... et destruendo non significat nihil sed aliquid, et constituendo non significat aliquid sed nihil: S I 249.19.22, cf. *HL* §6.6.

A similar opposition is expressed in the extremely interesting passage on *aliquid* ⊖ something in *SN*:

'Non-man' affects the understanding constitutively, for it brings it about that the hearer understands that *man* is not contained in the meaning of this word, but rather that it is to be removed from it.

Constituit namque intellectum 'non-homo' quia facit audientem intelligere non contineri hominem in huius vocis significatione, sed removeri: SN 43.6.8.

A more detailed discussion of the context of these uses is provided in *n*4.813*b*.

The expression '*constituere intellectum*' ⊖ 'to establish the understanding' occurs in Boethius' translation of *De Interpretatione*:

Such verbs as are used in an independent sense are names, and signify something. The speaker's understanding is established, and the hearer is satisfied.

Ipsa ... secundum se dicta verba nomina sunt, et significant aliquid. Constituit enim qui dicit intellectum, et qui audit quiescit: BDIL 309B–C, cf. *BDIG* 430C.

This same constellation of terms recurrs in Abelard's *Dialectica* (*A* 112.6.8, *A* 128.9.16, *A* 147.30, *A* 153.33–155.38). This last-mentioned reference is to an extremely interesting discussion as to what it is that is asserted by propositions. Propositions, says Abelard, are about things and not about our understanding of things:

For when we say 'A man runs', we have to do with a man and running as things, and we conjoin man and running; it is not their concepts which we conjoin. Indeed, we say nothing about concepts, but being concerned only with states of affairs, we establish them in the mind of the hearer.

Cum enim dicimus 'homo currit' de homine ac cursu rebus ipsis agimus cursumque homini coniungimus, non intellectum eorum ad invicem copulamus; nec quiquam de intellectibus dicimus, sed de rebus solis agentes eos in animo audientis constituimus: A 154.25.29.

(On the use of '*animus*' ⊖ 'mind' as opposed to '*intellectus*' ⊖ 'intellect' in this context, see *n*4.14*g* and *HL* 8).

*n*4.4234*a*: appellative of the horse ⊖ *equus appellatur*] The *linguistic* features of this, the second example (that of the white horse and the black bull) are in effect the same as those of the first (that of the enclosed white horse, 4.421). In both cases the word 'white' is deployed nominally in respect of a horse, i.e. is used appellatively of the horse. Only in the second case, however, are the features of the context of utterance sufficient to supply that oblique reference which fills the hiatus in the precisive signification conveyed by the word 'white'. In this way the interplay of

extra-linguistic context and intra-theoretical meaning, an interplay which is characteristic of paronyms, is brought into relief.

It is clearly to logicians who whish to identify *per se* ⊖ precisive signification and appellation that Anselm is referring in yet another sentence from *Epistola de Incarnatione Verbi*:

And how can he whose mind is too darkened to distinguish between his horse and its colour distinguish between one god and his many relationships?

Et cuius mens obscura est ad diiudicandum inter equum suum et colorem eius, qualiter discernet inter unum deum et plures relationes eius? S II 10.7.9, cf. *n*4.4211*a*, *n*4.811*b*, *HL* §3.32, *HAR*.

The case of the horse and its colour mentioned in this passage is of course exactly the one which is being dealt with in the present examples.

*n*4.424*a*: does not signify ⊖ *non est significativum*] The Tutor is here repeating the questions posed by the Student at 4.41.

*n*4.4242*a*: like paronyms ⊖ *similibus denominativis*] The fact that the dialogue is not a puerile quibble about a single word, but an inspection of contrasting examples for the purpose of arriving at a generalisation is made clear here as well as at 1.000 and 4.82.

John of Salisbury mentions Bernard of Chartres' fantastic comparisons which were used to illustrate the difference between '*albedo*' ⊖ 'whiteness', '*albet*' ⊖ 'whitens' and '*album*' ⊖ 'white'. They are comparisons which in no way come up to the standard of clarity exemplified in Anslem's present elucidation, yet they plainly bring into play somewhat the same set of notions:

Bernard of Chartres used to say that 'whiteness' signified an untouched virgin, and 'whitens' her entering the bedchamber or lying on the bed, while 'white' signifies her in her post-copulatory state. He said this sort of thing because the utterance of 'whiteness' signifies the quality itself – the colour which dazzles the sight – without any implication whatsoever of some subject's having a share in it. The principal meaning of 'whitens' is the same, but with the possibility of someone's sharing in it. For if one asks what this verb means in relation to a substance, the quality of whiteness will be involved in the reply, but

Aiabat Bernardus Carnotiensis quia 'albedo' significat uirginem incorruptam, 'albet' eandem introeuntem thalamum aut cubantem in thoro, 'album' vero eandem sed corruptam. Hoc quidem quoniam 'albedo' ex assertione eius simpliciter et sine omni participatione subiecti ipsam significat qualitatem, videlicet coloris speciem disgregatiuam uisus. 'Albet' autem eandum principaliter, etsi participationem persone admittat. Si enim illud excutias, quod uerbum hoc pro substantia significat, qualitas albedinis occurret, sed in accidentibus uerbi personam reperies. 'Album' vero eandem significat qualitatem,

the construction of the verb will be found to require some substance. Finally 'white' signifies the same quality, but now mixed and intermingled with a substance, and in a fashion more impure, since in respect of substance the name signifies the subject of the whiteness, whereas in relation to quality it signifies the colour of the subject having the whiteness. It seemed to him that he was supported by Aristotle and many other authorities. After all, Aristotle said that 'white' signifies only a quality. Bernard also put forward many other arguments, quarried from all quarters, in support of the thesis that things are sometimes predicated purely, sometimes obliquely; he declared in this connection that knowledge of paronymy was immensely useful. This is an opinion which has its defenders and opponents.

sed infusam commixtamque substantiae et iam quodammodo magis corruptam; siquidem nomen ipsum pro substantia subiectum albedinis, pro qualitate significat colorem albentis subiecti. Uidebatur etiam sibi tam de Aristotile quam de multorum auctoritatibus niti. Ait enim 'Album' nihil aliud significat quam qualitatem. Multa quoque proferebat undique conquisita, quibus persuadere nitebatur res interdum pure, interdum adiacenter predicari, et ad hoc denominatiuorum scientiam perutilem asserebat. Habet hec opinio sicut impugnatores, sic defensores suos: *SM* 124.21–125.14.

The 'pure' predication of the type here said to have been defended by Bernard is of the type also defended by Anselm in connection with the same type of word, i.e. the paronym. Thus Anselm's own '*grammaticus est grammatica*' ⊖ '*literate* is literacy' is in fact an exemple of such predication, as is evidenced by the forms discussed in detail by John in the next part of this passage, which is quoted in *n*4.5122*a*.

*n*4.4243*a*: oblique ⊖ *per aliud*] This extension of the distinction between *per se* ⊖ precisive signification and *per aliud* ⊖ oblique signification to verbs as well as to the names with which *De Grammatico* is concerned, is one of the prime indications of the continuity of this dialogue with the remainder of Anselm's works. Given the identity of *per se* ⊖ precisive signification with that which a word is properly (*proprie*) said to signify, and the identity of signification which is *per aliud* ⊖ oblique with that which a word cannot properly (*non proprie*) be said to signify, which is set up at 4.232 and 4.233 of the present dialogue, then the exact complementarity of a remark which occurs in Anselm's fragments on sentence-analysis becomes quite striking:

It seems to me that whenever a name or a verb is used in an improper sense, then that state of affairs in relation to which

Videtur mihi, quotiens attribuitur alicui rei aut nomen aut verbum improprie, quia illa res, cui attribuitur, est illi, de qua proprie

it is employed stands to its proper application as either a similitude, or a cause, or as an effect, or as the genus, or as the species, or as the whole, or as the part, or as the symbol, or as the thing symbolized – it should be noted that although every symbol has a likeness to the thing symbolised, the two are nevertheless not totally alike – or, as I was saying, the verb or noun improperly used signifies or is signified by, it contains or is contained by, that of which it is employed in the proper sense, or they stand to one another as the user and the thing used.

dicitur, aut similis aut causa aut effectum aut genus aut species aut totum aut pars aut idem valens aut figura aut figuratum – quamvis enim omnis figura habeat similitudinem cum re, quam figurat, tamen non omne simili est figura aut figuratum – aut, sicut incepi dicere, alio modo quam per figuram est significans illud cuius nomen aut verbum recipit, aut eius significatum, aut est in eo aut e converso illud de quo proprie dicitur, est in eo de quo improprie profertur, aut ita se habent ut qui re aliqua utitur, et res, qua utitur: SN 34.29.39.

The doctrine of *De Grammatico* is in part a particular exemplification of this lengthy and complex generalisation, whose ramifications have been examined in detail in *HL* §4, §5, §6. The *per se* ⊖ precisive and *per aliud* ⊖ oblique signification of verbs is also given detailed consideration in *SN*.

*n*4.430*a*: accidental to such utterances ⊖ *accidentalis*] This assertion that *per se* ⊖ precisive signification is essential to the word *qua* significant utterance, whereas oblique signification (for paronyms *appellatio* ⊖ reference) is merely extra-theoretical in relation to the subject-matter in question, is reiterated at 4.515 (cf. §4).

*n*4.431*a*: proper to a verb, not to a noun ⊖ *non est nominis sed verbi*] See *n*4.2415*d*, *n*4.2415*e*, and *n*4.2415*f* for the definitions now in question, and a discussion of this point. '*Vox significativa secundum platicum*' ⊖ 'An utterance conventionally meaningful' is used as the genus of name and verb in Boethius' exemplification of classification-distinctions: *BD* 886B–887C.

*n*4.501*a*: being ⊖ *esse*] The Student has reverted to the use of the logician's 'is' described in *n*1.000*b*. His expansion of this question (4.5022) turns on this 'is', and is answered by the Tutor's account of Aristotelian usage in this matter (4.603).

*n*4.5021*a*: man alone is literate ⊖ *solum hominem esse grammaticum*] This point is taken up from 4.31; cf. also 4.24121. The Student's sophism turns, at least in part, on the ambiguity of '*solus*' which is reflected by the possibility of its being translated either as 'only' or as 'alone': he takes it in the most literal sense of 'alone' throughout the passage. A distinction of the senses of '*solus*' follows at 4.51.

*n*4.5022*a*: is a quality ⊖ *qualitas*] This represents the final stage of the Student's grappling with the scandalous logical 'is' (cf. *n*1.000*b*). Whereas at 4.22 he was prepared to posit that because 'literate' signifies man and literacy, *literate* could therefore be said to *be* substance and quality (*grammaticus quia significat hominem et grammaticam dicendus est substantia et qualitas* ⊖ because it signifies man and literacy it must be said to be both substance and quality) he cannot now bring himself to make the corresponding assertion, i.e. that because 'literate' signifies literacy (4.31), *literate* is therefore a quality, namely literacy. He feels that this is not a suitable (*conveniens*) assertion to make. We are, of course, still up against the discordance with *usus loquendi* ⊖ ordinary usage envisaged at 4.2341, a discordance which will be resolved at 4.6.

The question '*Quid sit grammaticus*?' ⊖ 'What is literate?' here mentioned by the Student exemplifies one of the sorts of dialectical question mentioned by Boethius in his commentary on *De Interpretatione*. Such a question occurs, says Boethius *quando proponentes nomen, quid sit quaerimus, aut genus, aut differentiam, aut definitionem requirentes* ⊖ when we put forward the name, asking what the thing in question is; what we are then wanting is the genus, or the species, or the definition: *B* 572D. The '*quid sit?*' 'What is it?' question will be mentioned again at 4.600 and 4.610.

*n*4.511*a*: either alone or along with man ⊖ *nec sola nec cum homine*] Here the sense of '*solus*' corresponding to the English 'only' is distinguished. This sense, which Aquinas characterises as 'syncategorematic' (see *n*4.5121*a*), makes '*Solus homo est grammaticus*' into a true statement translateable as 'Only man is literate'. Anselm's technical differentiation of the meanings of '*solus*' is given in 4.5121 (see *n*4.5121*a*).

*n*4.5120*a*: no one can be literate ⊖ *nullus esse grammaticus potest*] Here the sense of '*solus*' corresponding to the English 'alone' in its fullest and most literal sense, is distinghuished. This sense, which Aquinas calls 'categorematic' (see *n*4.5121*a*) makes '*Solus homo est grammaticus*' into a false statement translateable as 'A man on his own is literate'.

*n*4.5121*a*: it's impossible for there to be a precedent ⊖ *praevius esse non potest*] In order to distinguish between the two senses of '*solus*' ⊖ 'alone' in question, the Tutor outlines sets of conditions, one of which is such that '*solus est praevius*' ⊖ 'precedes alone' holds, and one in which '*solus non est praevius*' ⊖ 'does not precede alone' holds. The first set of conditions is '*qui sequitur non est praevius nec separatim nec sic ut ex illis duobus unus fiat praevius*' ⊖ 'one who follows is not a precedent, either separately or in such a way that the two form a single precedent'. These describe a linearly-ordered couple, one of which we may call '*x*', such that *x* alone precedes (*solus est praevius*). In this way the sense of '*solus*' concerned in 4.511 is clarified. The second set of conditions, namely '*nisi sit qui sequitur, praevius esse non potest*' ⊖ 'unless there is a follower, it is impossible for there to be a precedent' ensures that *x* does not precede, and that hence *x* alone does not precede (*solus non est praevius*). The sense of '*solus*' clarified by this second set of conditions is the one rejected by the Tutor in 4.512.

Boethius had distinguished two meanings of '*solus*' thus:

'Alone' can be used in two ways. First to be unique, as when we say 'The universe is alone', i.e. there is only one. Secondly, we have the way in which we use the word to separate one thing off from another, as when someone says that a coat alone is what I have, that is, I do not also have a cloak; thus I contrast the coat with a cloak.

'Solum' autem duobus modis dicitur: semel cum aliquid unum esse dicimus, ut si dicamus 'solus est mundus' id est unus; alio vero modo cum dicimus ad quamdam ab altero divisionem, ut si quis dicat solam me habere tunicam, id est, non etiam togam, ad divisionem videlicet togae: *BC* 164C.

William of Sherwood speaks at length on sophisms turning on '*solus*' (*KSS* Ch. XI); see also *HSL* 7.36. Aquinas analyses the word as follows:

'Alone' can be taken as categorematic or as syncategorematic. A categorematic word indicates the thing signified as relating to some object without qualification, as whiteness in relation to a man when a man is said to be white. If, therefore, 'alone' were taken in this sense, it would indicate the aloneness of the thing to which it is applied. ... However, a syncategorematic word is said to be one which implies some relation of predicate

'Solus' potest accipi ut categorematica, vel syncategorematica. Dicitur enim categorematica quae absolute ponit rem significatam circa aliquod suppositum, ut albus circa hominem, cum dicitur homo albus. Si ergo sic accipitur haec dictio 'solus' ... poneret solitudinem circa terminum cui adiungeretur ... Dictio vero syncategorematica dicitur quae importat ordinem praedicati ad subiectum, sicut haec dictio 'omnis', vel 'nullus'. Et similiter

to subject, as in the cases of the words 'all' or 'no'. In this way this word 'alone' excludes all other objects from concomitant participation in the predicate. Thus when it is said that Socrates alone is writing, the sense conveyed is not that Socrates is solitary, but only that no one accompanies him in writing, even though many other things co-exist along with him.

haec dictio 'solus', quia excludit omne aliud suppositum a consortio praedicati. Sicut cum dicitur, solus Socrates scribit, non datur intelligi quod Socrates sit solitarius, sed quod nullus sit consors ei in scribendo, quamvis cum ei multis existentibus: *AST* I, q.31, art.3, c.

Finally it may be noted that *BDIG* 633–4 contains some of Boethius' theorems on things which precede and things which follow; this may have suggested Anselm's method of elucidation at this point in *De Grammatico*.

*n*4.5122*a*: Aristotle's treatise *On the Categories* ⊖ *tractatus Aristotelis De Categoriis*] The answer to the question about '*solus*' (4.5021) is completed, and now the Tutor, in response to 4.5022, changes the topic, and prepares to clarify the logician's use of 'is' (cf. *n*1.000*b*).

The Tutor's attribution of this use of 'is' (herein interpreted as the counterpart of the higher-order '$\in$') to the example of Aristotle, and the consequent dislocation of *usus loquendi* ⊖ the common course of utterance, is exactly the kind of thing against which John of Salisbury writes in Ch. 2 of Bk. III of his *Metalogicon*. John not only refers to paronyms in this connection, but also expressly combats Anselm's thesis that expressions such as '*grammaticus est grammatica*' ⊖ '*literate* is literacy' can make sense in a logical context. Only in exceptional cases does he allow locutions of this pattern to be justified. In this respect his logical acuteness scarcely rivals that of Anselm. John's attack immediately follows upon his account of Bernard of Chartres' fantasy on paronyms which has been quoted in *n*4.4242*a*. Having recorded Bernard's opinion, which Anselm certainly shares, that the study of paronyms is particularly useful in distinguishing kinds of predication, and having referred to 'pure' predication of the type of '*grammaticus est grammatica*' ⊖ '*literate* is literacy', wherein abstract is apparently predicated of concrete, John continues rather crustily:

I do not want to get at all involved in such merely verbal disputes, as I am well aware that the interpretation of an assertion should be made to depend on the reasons why it was made. And I do not

Michi pro minimo est ad nomen in talibus disputare, cum intelligentiam dictorum sumendam nouerim ex causis dicendi. Nec sic memoratam Aristotilis aliorumque auctoritates interpretandas arbitror, ut

think that the quotation from Aristotle or from other authorities should be so interpreted as to be capable of being dragged in at every verse end ... We must not, on the basis of slim excuses, distort what an author meant to say; rather, the circumstances of his utterance must be taken into account. Every assertion should not be interpreted according to a set pattern. Obviously paronyms do not convey exactly the notion of that from which they are derived, nor does the hearer's mind receive that same notion. Again, paronyms are not appellative of that from which they are derived; the two are altogether remote from eachother, and produce incompatibilities. Sometimes, however, they are mutually compatible, and the paronymous couple can then be either simultaneously predicated of the same thing or of eachother, as, for example, in the assertions 'Goodness is good', or 'Unity is one'. Normally, however, they give rise to incompatibilities; this is said to derive from their side-import rather than from their meaning. This seems likely enough; we can leave the question for the experts to settle. After all, when two things have the same meaning the incompatibility can only arise from the side-import, as when singularity is incompatible with plurality, even though the name is the same: whatever is a *man* is not *men*. Why this is so is not our business, since the logican's entire aim is to uncover the implications of words, and to attain knowledge of the true and the provable from an examination of the way in which verbal predication is carried out. This is what he is doing whenever he classifies, defines, systematises, or analyses the systematised material. Thus paronyms signify in some fashion the qualified with reference to that from which it received its qualification. The words from which they are derived signify the source of the qualification. Thus 'courage' signifies whence comes the qualification 'courageous', and 'courageous' shows how some-

trahatur istuc quicquid alicubi dictum reperitur ... Non est itaque ex leui occasione uerbi menti auctorum preiudicandum, que ex circumstantia sermonis pensanda est. Non enim omnis dictio semper eodem formatur scemate. Plane denominatiua non eundem his a quibus denominantur intellectum significant, nec in eandem rem descendit animus his auditis; nec eorundem appellatiua sunt; a se inuicem plerumque remouentur et ad ea sequitur contradictio. Interdum tamen se patienter admittunt, et de eodem simul vel de se inuicem predicantur denominatiue coniugata. Nam et bonitas bona, una unitas dicitur. Regulare tamen est ut ad ea sequatur contradictio, quod tamen ex causa consigificationis magis, quam significationis asserunt euenire. Et hoc quidem probabiliter; an satis diiudicent periti. Nam ad ea que idem significant ex causa consignificationis dumtaxat sequitur contradictio. Singularis enim numerus positus eiusdem nominis pluralem tollit, ut si quod homo est, illud homines non est. Nichil equidem refert unde proueniat, cum eo tendat dialectices tota intentio, ut sermonum uim aperiat, et ex eorum predicatione examinandi ueri et statuendi scientiam assequatur. Hoc agit, siue diuidat siue diffiniat siue colligat siue ea que fuerint collecta resoluat. Ergo denominatiua significant quodam modo qualia ex aliquibus; illa uero a quibus denominantur, notant a quibus qualia. Nam fortitudo significat ex quo quis fortis; fortis autem, qualis quis ex fortitudine; unde et fortitudinis dicitur nomen, non ut cuius, sed ut ex quo; indicat enim causam: SM 125.15–126.20.

one is qualified in relation to courage. This is why 'courage' is said to be a whence-wise name rather than an applicatory name; it shows the ground of the latter.

The extracts quoted from the same source in *n*4.2341*a* may also be consulted.

*n*4.513*a*: and so on ⊖ *et cetera*] This is a deliberately garbled version of Aristotle's statement in *Categoriae* 4:

Words considered out of relation to particular utterances signify either substance or quantity or quality or relation or place or time or position, or state or action or passion.

Eorum quidem quae secundum nullam complexionem dicuntur, singulum aut substantiam significat, aut quantitatem, aut qualitatem, aut ad aliquid, aut ubi, aut quando, aut situm, aut habere, aut facere, aut pati; B 180A.

Neither at this point, nor in the variations on this Aristotelian statement devised by the Tutor in his reply to the Student, is the list extended beyond its first two or three items, it being understood that it is familiar enough, and that its details are, in any case, not under scrutiny at this point.

The Student is deliberately ignoring the 'signifies' of the last quotation and substituting for it the logician's 'is' which is also derived from Aristotle's usage (cf. *n*1.000*b*) to present his version of the quotation: he will then combine it with a sentence turning on an 'is' derived from the consideration of *appellatio* ⊖ reference and draw a sophistical conclusion from this combination. The Tutor is to react by enlarging on the point which Boethius stresses so strongly in the preface to his commentary on the *Categoriae*, namely that the work deals with significant utterances insofar as they are significant; *Est igitur huius operis intentio de vocibus res significantibus, in eo quod significantes sunt pertractare* ⊖ It is therefore the aim of this work to deal with words which signify things insofar as those words are significative: *BC* 160A. Likewise Abelard says:

For if we survey attentively the whole of Aristotle's works, we are able to see him to be involved more with words than with things, and his words can be more liberally interpreted as having to do with utterances rather than with things; after all, his aim was to help logical study.

Si enim omnia eius opera studiose inspiciamus, magis eum in vocibus immorari quam in rebus inveniemus, liberiusque verba eius de vocibus quam de rebus exponerentur, quippe qui logicae deserviebat: A 388.11.14.

*n*4.513*b*: substance ⊖ *substantia*] Having, as remarked in *n*4.513*a*, used the logician's 'is' in his quotation of Aristotle, the Student now first therefrom infers implicitly that *homo est substantia* ⊖ *man* is substance (as contrasted with '*homo*' *significat substantiam* ⊖ 'man' signifies substance) and then makes appeal to the factual, extra-theoretical truth that only men are literate, thus yielding the present conclusion that only a substance is literate (cf. 4.510–4.5121). He will be reminded that this involves invoking a truth based on the merely accidental, extra-theoretical, oblique, coefficient of the meaning of 'literate' (4.515).

*n*4.5141*a*: of the things you mention ⊖ *horum est*] Boethius expresses himself on this point in his preface to the *Categoriae*, for instance:

He (i.e. Aristotle) reduced the limitless and boundless diversity of things within the much smaller plurality of the ten categories, so that things which, because of their limitless number, could not be the objects of knowledge, might be reduced to their ten correct headings within the fixed boundaries of knowledge.

Rerum ergo diversarum indeterminatam infinitamque multitudinem decem praedicamentorum paucissima numerositate concludit, ut ea quae infinita sub scientiam cadere non poterant, decem propriis generibus definita scientiae comprehensione claudantur: BC 161A.

*n*4.5142*a*: what things they signify ⊖ *quarum significativae sint*] Here the Tutor runs through the distinctions made at 4.23. His point is to bring *per se* ⊖ precisive signification to the fore, and to correlate its use with the logical examples (4.515) which had formerly (4.21–4.22) appeared so scandalous. The 'is' which was associated with this scandal will be confirmed as the correlate of *per se* ⊖ precisive signification (4.601, 4.602).

*n*4.5143*a*: can only signify things ⊖ *non significant nisi res*] Anselm is here probably summarising the words of Boethius:

But possibly the following question might be raised: if the discussion centres on utterances which signify things, why does he talk about things? To this the reply is that things are always correlated with their appropriate signifyings, so that whatever holds in respect of things has a correlate in the realm of the utterances used for things.

Sed forte quis dicat, si de significantibus rerum vocibus ipsa disputatio est, cur de ipsis disputat rebus? Dicendum est, quoniam res semper cum propria significatione coniunctae sunt, et quidquid in res venit, hoc quidem in rerum vocabulis invenitur: BC 162D.

At first sight Anselm's present assertion may seem to be the expression of a crude 'name-thing' theory of signification. However, it is nothing of the sort. It is made clear in 4.503 that '*grammaticus est qualitas*' ⊖ '*literate* is quality' is a *de re* ⊖ thing-centred assertion, yet it is amply clear also (cf. 4.8 and *n*1.000*b*) that the '*est*' ⊖ 'is' of such a sentence does not take names as its arguments: it hence appears to correspond to a functor such as the higher-order '∈' of Ontology (§3.15). The whole sentence now in question is an adumbration of the *de voce/de re* ⊖ word-centred/thing-centred distinction given at 4.601. From this fact the extremely wide sense of '*res*' ⊖ 'thing' may be judged: it does not always necessarily mean 'object'. As a first approximation one might define a *de re* ⊖ thing-centred assertion as one which is not merely *de voce* ⊖ word-centred. Anselm is here saying, quite rightly, that for certain *de voce* ⊖ word-centred assertions to be true (e.g. assertions about the signification of a word) certain *de re* ⊖ thing-centred assertions (including those interpretable in terms of the higher-order '∈' and which hence do not involve names at all) must also be true. '*Voces non significant nisi res*' ⊖ 'Words only signify things' hence does not mean that words only have meaning by *standing for* physical (or other) objects in the way that certain names might be taken to stand for objects. Hence on the assumption that Abelard's uses of '*significatio*' ⊖ 'meaning' (in the *per se* ⊖ precisive sense) and '*appellatio*' ⊖ 'reference' are not too remote from Anselm's, *DLM*'s suggestion that Abelard's attempt 'to free logic from ontological elements was far from successful despite the distinction he made between *significatio* and *appellatio*, since he did not pursue it consistently' becomes rather beside the point. For the grounds of this accusation are to the effect that Abelard (like Anselm) 'seems to stress the nexus of *significatio* and *res*' (*DLM* II–I 196). The manner in which the Leśniewskian approach to logic has facilitated a sympathetic elucidation of Anselm's correlation of *significatio* ⊖ meaning and *res* ⊖ things is yet another indication of the suitability of that approach as an aid in the understanding of medieval logic.

That Anselm was aware that '*res*' ⊖ 'things' need not literally mean 'object' is confirmed in the first place by his remark in *Epistola de Incarnatione Verbi* when he says; *Solemus enim dicere* '*rem*' *quidquid aliquo modo dicimus esse aliquis* ⊖ The ordinary course of utterance allows us to say that whatever is in some sense said to be something is a *thing*: *S* II 12.5.6.

It is further confirmed by his treatment of empty names (*n*4.813*b*).

John of Salisbury also has remarks on this point:

Indeed, although the things covered by affirmative and negative sentences are called 'things', and more often than not said to be true things, nevertheless they cannot be assimilated to either substances or accidents, nor can they be named either 'creator' or 'creature' ... Hence, granted that there are universals, and even that these are things, if this will satisfy the sticklers, it still does not follow from this admission that there is an increase in the number of things or a decrease in that number if it is denied that universals are to be numbered among things.	*Nam et ea que iacent sub affirmatione et negatione res dicuntur, et uera sepissime dicuntur esse, nec tamen substantiis vel accidentibus aggregantur aut nomen suscipiunt Creatoris aut creature ... Itaque detur ut sint universalia, aut etiam ut res sint, si hoc pertinacibus placet; non tamen ob hoc uerum erit rerum numerum augeri uel minui pro eo quod ista non sunt in numero rerum:* *SM* 100.26–101.7.

John's connection of '*res*' ⊖ 'thing' with affirmation and negation may stem from *BDIL* 354C. On Abelard's approach to this connection see *TA*.

*n*4.5144*a*: expressed in an incomplex fashion ⊖ *secundum nullam complexionem dicuntur*] The Oxford translation has 'expressions which are in no way composite' as the translation of the Greek text which *B* renders as '*eorum ... quae secundum nullam complexionem dicuntur*' ⊖ 'of those things which are expressed in an incomplex fashion': *BC* 180A, see also *BC* 162B, *B* 180C–181C. Boethius uses this phrase in the same way as Anselm does, i.e. to show that the *Categoriae* are concerned with significant utterances (*BC* 162B, *BC* 180–181, cf. *n*4.5144*c*).

The translation of the Latin version as 'whatever is expressed in an incomplex fashion' at least preserves some of the flavour of '*dicuntur*' ⊖ 'are asserted'. It would be totally misleading to adopt Joseph's 'terms out of construction' as a translation (*JL* 66) as this tends to carry with it the assumption that the *Categoriae* is a treatise on isolated 'terms', written expressly as a preliminary to their employment in syllogistic, an impression which *DLM* is prepared to concede as being prolonged by the earlier medieval logicians when it suggests that the contrasting 'contextual approach' was a later 'new stage of development' (*DLM* II–I 116). Now Boethius elucidates '*sine complexione*' ⊖ 'in an incomplex fashion' thus:

Those things are expressed in an incomplex fashion which are uttered forth as demanded by the incomplex sound of the name, as in the cases of 'man' and 'horse'. In contrast, those things are expressed in a complex fashion which are mingled by means of some conjunction or putting together of the features of speech.

Sine complexione enim dicuntur quaecumque secundum simplicem sonum nominis preferuntur, ut homo, equus (BC 169A*). Secundum complexionem vero quaecumque aliqua coniunctione vel accidentis copulatione miscentur:* *BC* 180C–D.

Yet the fact that concern with words '*sine complexione*' ⊖ 'in an incomplex fashion' is opposed to such words as occurring in true or false propositions does not necessarily have the consequence that those words are being treated in isolation: the whole practice of the *Categoriae* and its commentary, with the central distinction between *de subiecto* ⊖ of a subject and *in subiecto* ⊖ in a subject (*n*3.501*a*) is sufficient to show that a third alternative is in question, i.e. the theories in which the words may feature is being discussed. Thus anthropology is the theory of *man*, and the *Categoriae* shows the kind of thing that should or should not be incorporated in such a theory (cf. §4). It is to the words insofar as they are potentially enmeshed in their respective theories, as opposed to their use in concrete affirmations or denials, that the expression '*sine complexione*' ⊖ 'in an incomplex fashion' is designed to call attention. In this sense the 'contextual approach' was never totally absent. As regards the present dialogue, such an approach is prominent throughout, witness the constant allusions to the contrast between spoken ordinary usage and written logical usage (e.g. 4.210, 4.42, 4.620).

*n*4.5144*b*: 'quantity' as its appellation ⊖ *appellatur* ... *quantitas*] This is what Aristotle would have had to assert if this *Categoriae* treated of the way in which words were used in the customary course of utterance. By pointing out that Aristotle did not deal with *appellatio* ⊖ calling, Anselm is strengthening the contrast between spoken usage (*usus loquendi*) and the kind of signification which is the business of the logician (cf. 4.21, 4.2341, *n*1.000*b*).

*n*4.5144*c*: signifies a substance or a quantity ⊖ *substantiam significat aut quantitatem*] Verbally Anslem appears merely to be making the same point as that made by Boethius in the preface to his commentary on the *Categoriae*, i.e. that this latter work deals with words rather than with things:

Our claim that this work was not to deal with sorts of things, nor with things, but rather with words signifying various types of things, is borne out by Aristotle's own assertion when he says 'Those things expressed in an incomplex fashion each signify either substance or quantity'. Now were he concerned with the typology of things, he would not have said 'signify'; things do not signify, but are rather themselves signified.

Namque (ut docuimus) non de rerum generibus, neque de rebus, sed de sermonibus rerum genera significantibus in hoc opere tractatus habetur, hoc vero Aristotelis ipse declarat cum dicit 'Eorum quae secundum nullam complexionem dicuntur, singulum aut substantiam significat, aut quantitatem'. Quod si de rebus divisionem faceret, non dixisset 'significat'; res enim significatur, non ipsa significat: BC 162B.

However, Anselm's three versions of Aristotle's assertion already show that Boethius' point has now been deepened by the distinction between *significatio* (*per se*) ⊖ meaning (precisive) and *appellatio* ⊖ calling or reference (4.23), i.e. as 4.515 will shortly show, by the distinction between the intra-theoretical and extra-theoretical aspects of signification. Cf. also *BC* 180C–181C.

*n*4.515*a*: signify precisively ⊖ *per se significant*] See 4.232.

*n*4.515*b*: pertains to them essentially ⊖ *illis est substantialis*] See 4.430.

*n*4.515*c*: oblique ⊖ *per aliud*] See 4.232.

*n*4.515*d*: accidental ⊖ *accidentalis*] See 4.430.

*n*4.515*e*: signify precisively ⊖ *per se significant*] That Aristotle himself imputes *per se* ⊖ precisive signification to noun and verb in the course of their definition is an assumption resulting from logical usage (cf. the rest of the present section and 4.21–4.23) and is not given explicit statement by Aristotle. Anselm's thesis is that only by attributing the use of *per se* ⊖ precisive signification to Aristotle can one make sense not only of his definitions of noun and verb, but also of his examples. The definitions mentioned here are those reproduced and discussed in *n*4.2415*e*.

*n*4.515*f*: to show ⊖ *ad ostendendum*] The expression '*ponere aliquam vocem as ostendendum aliquid*' ⊖ 'to proffer an utterance to show something' refers to the kind of procedure exemplified by Aristotle in connection with his list of categories, as when he says:

There is substance such as, to use examples, *man* and *horse*, quantity, such as *two-feet* and *three-feet*, quality, such as *white* and *literate*.

Est autem substantia, ut figuraliter dicatur, ut homo, equus. Quantitas, ut bicubitum, tricubitum. Qualitas, ut album, grammaticum: BC 180A.

Anselm is now giving his analysis of what is involved in the proffering of examples in this Aristotelian fashion (cf. 4.211 and its use of '*ostendere*' ⊖ 'to show'). He appears to have all along presupposed that the passage just quoted authorises '*Literate* is a quality' as a logically correct assertion. This in turn involves him in having to clarify (4.6) the logician's 'is' (*n*1.000*b*) which, owing to its deviation from *usus loquendi* ⊖ the current course of utterance (4.2341) has been a stumbling block ever since the first sentence of the dialogue.

When, therefore, the expression '*ponere aliquam vocem ad ostendendum aliquid*' ⊖ 'to proffer some utterance in order to show something' is used here, the words proffered, the *voces* ⊖ utterances, are to be understood as the names of exemplifications of the various categories ('man' for substance, 'literate' for quality, and so on) and the thing shown in each case is the corresponding category. Thus '*grammaticus est qualitas*' ⊖ '*literate* is quality' is true, whence the scandal of '*grammaticus est grammatica*' ⊖ '*literate* is literacy' (4.5022) which the present phase of the dialogue is expressly designed to settle (cf. 4.5122). The statement '*grammaticus est qualitas*' ⊖ '*literate* is quality' is said to be a response to the definition-generating (and hence theory-generating) question '*quid sit*?' ⊖ 'What is it?' question, as 4.600 goes on to make clear; cf. *n*4.5022*a*.

*n*4.515*g*: and so on ⊖ *et similia*] Compare Boethius: *Sed per se qualitas, ut album neque ullius substantiam significat* ⊖ But quality taken in itself (e.g. *white*) does not signify the substance of anything: *BC* 195C. Were one to assert that *literate* is a substance (see the initial problem, 1.000) one would, in the terms adopted by Anselm, be proffering the word 'literate' to show what it signifies obliquely, namely the substance (*man*); cf. 4.232. It has now been decided that logicians deal not with oblique, but with precisive signification, so that the proffering of 'literate' to show what it signifies in a *per se* ⊖ precisive fashion, namely a quality (i.e. literacy), is the correct response. The examples here used indicate that the Student has by now absorbed the Tutor's thesis as to the parity of *white* and *literate* in their significatory functions; cf. 3.941, 4.24121.

*n*4.600*a*: what *literate* is ⊖ *quid sit grammaticus*] On this form of question see *n*4.5022*a*. The use of '*sit*' ⊖ 'is' now restores the discussion to the level of the troublesome 'is' (cf. *n*1.000*b*) of the dialogue's opening. 4.610 will claim that this 'is' can be understood in relation to either of the two ways (*de re* ⊖ thing-centred, *de voce* ⊖ word-centred) of interpreting the present question.

*n*4.600*b*: in terms of that classification ⊖ *secundum hanc divisionem*] This is, of course, a reference to the classification (cf. *n*4.2411*a*) represented by Aristotle's list of categories.

*n*4.601*a*: signifies ⊖ *significat*] The unexplained alternation between the use of the logician's scandalous 'is' (*n*1.000*b*) and the use of 'signifies' has been a feature of the dialogue up to the present point. It is **now** being made clear that this alternation was based on two inferentially equivalent ways of understanding the '*sit*' ⊖ 'is' of '*quid sit*?' ⊖ 'What is it?' (cf. *n*4.5022*a*), i.e. the *de voce* ⊖ word-centred (4.601) and the *de re* ⊖ thing-centred (4.602) ways. The same alternatives have already been envisaged in an earlier parts of the discussion: *unde intelligam te loqui, de hoc nomine, an de rebus quas significat?* ⊖ What am I to take you to be talking about: this name, or the things signified thereby? (4.1101).

*n*4.601*b*: signifies ⊖ *significare*] 'Literate' signifies literacy precisively and man obliquely (4.232). Throughout the present passage (4.6) 'signification' without any qualification must be understood in its proper, *per se* ⊖ precisive, sense.

*n*4.602*a*: word signifying quality ⊖ *vox significans qualitatem*] The 'is' of the question here mentioned (i.e. '*quid sit grammaticus?*' ⊖ 'What is *literate*?', cf. *n*4.5022*a*) may be understood as 'signifies' as here stated, i.e. in the *de voce* ⊖ thing-centred fashion. The signification in question must then be of the *per se* ⊖ precisive sort, otherwise one could equally well say that 'literate' signified substance (4.232) and this possible ambiguity is behind the remarks at 4.604. The other way of understanding the '*quid sit?*' ⊖ 'What is it?' question now follows.

*n*4.603*a*: it is a quality ⊖ *est qualitas*] This second interpretation of the 'is' involved in the '*quid sit?*' ⊖ 'What is it?' question exemplifies the use of the 'is' which violates *usus loquendi*, and which has haunted the dialogue ever since its first sentence (cf. *n*1.000*b*). This 'is', it should be noted, is still incorrigible from the point of view of *usus loquendi* ⊖ the common course of utterance, whereas the '*significare*' ⊖ 'to signify' interpretation of the '*sit*' ⊖ 'is' of '*quid sit?*' ⊖ 'What is it?' (4.602) is of course quite consonant with *usus loquendi* ⊖ the common course of utterance. Indeed '*grammaticus est qualitas*' ⊖ '*literate* is quality', the full statement of what is now being asserted, is authorised by '*grammaticus est grammatica*' ⊖ '*literate* is literacy' (cf. 4.5022) which is one of the examples of the violation of *usus loquendi* ⊖ the current course of utterance given at 4.2341.

The distinction now being made between *de re* ⊖ thing-centred assertions and *de voce* ⊖ word-centred assertions, together with the classification of '*grammaticus est qualitas*' ⊖ '*literate* is quality' and '*grammaticus est grammatica*' ⊖ '*literate* is literacy' as *de re* ⊖ thing-centred, shows how widely the word '*res*' ⊖ 'thing' is interpreted by Anselm. For while, as is evident from 4.1101, that word does not exclude concrete objects such as men, nevertheless it need not always be taken to imply literal reference to such objects. That this should be so coheres with the interpretation of the '*est*' ⊖ 'is' of the present *de re* ⊖ thing-centred assertions as the higher-order '∊' of Ontology (cf. §4 and §3.15). The arguments of such a functor are predicates, not names, although as in the present case they may be formed from names or name-like expressions. This is why a more ambiguous word such as 'circumstance' might be adopted as an alternative to 'thing' in the present context.

Confirmation that the interpretation mentioned in the last paragraph, i.e. that of the '*est*' ⊖ 'is' of the present *de re* ⊖ thing-centred assertions as the higher-order '∊', is correct is quite forcibly provided by Anselm in 4.8. It has already been clear since 4.31 that '*grammaticus est sciens grammaticam*' ⊖ '*Literate* is ... displaying literacy' could replace '*grammaticus est grammatica*' ⊖ '*Literate* is literacy' and the outward structure of the former in its Latin version gives no hint of violation of *usus loquendi* ⊖ the current course of utterance, although (as reflected in the English version suggested) the manner of its derivation, by means of a gap-creation in the Student's proposed definition, might make one suspect its arguments to be functorial in nature. And indeed, when the corresponding case of '*habens albedinem*' ⊖ 'having whiteness' is taken up in 4.8, the denial of '*aliquid*' ⊖ 'something' or '*is qui habet*' ⊖ 'that which has' as part of the meaning of '*habens albedinem*' ⊖ '... having whiteness' shows that the latter (and hence '*sciens grammaticam*' ⊖ '... displaying literacy') is certainly not being used in what might in Latin be its *prima facie* grammatical sense, i.e. as a name (cf. *n*4.31*a*, *n*4.5143*a*).

It is noteworthy that Abelard employs the *de voce/de re* ⊖ word-centred/thing-centred distinction (*DLM* II–I 205) and this in a context where paronyms are being discussed in relation to a conflict between logicians and grammarians (*DLM* II–I 203–206).

*n*4.604*a*: this particular thing ⊖ *hoc aliquid*] Compare the Migne translation of *Categoriae* 5:

It looks as though every substance signifies a this-something; this is undoubtedly true in the case of primary substances, since they signify a this-something.	*Omnis autem substantia videtur hoc aliquid significare, atque in primis quidem substantiis indubitabile et verum est, quoniam hoc aliquid significant*: *BC* 194B.

*n*4.604*b*: word signifying a substance ⊖ *vox significans substantiam*] Aristotle is here said to call names by the name of the things they signify in a *per se* ⊖ precisive fashion, and not by the names of the things of which they are appellative. The Tutor gives as an example of this usage, 'Every substance seems to signify this particular thing'. This, says the Tutor, means, 'Every word signifying substance seems to signify this particular thing'. What would count against this statement of Anselm's? Well, were Aristotle to say, 'Every quality (i.e. word signifying a quality) seems to signify this particular thing', this would be true in the sense that quality-words such as 'literate' or 'white' have substances (and hence particular things) as their *per aliud* ⊖ oblique significates: quality words do signify particular things *per aliud* ⊖ obliquely insofar as they are appellative of such things. The Tutor's immediate point is that we don't find Aristotle using true sentences such as the last one suggested, for if he did, he would be using the word 'quality' to refer to quality words insofar as they are appellative, and not insofar as they are *per se* ⊖ precisively significative. It has to be taken that the overt 'signifies' in such a context must amount to 'signifies *per se* ⊖ precisively' because of the elucidation of the special use of 'is' given in 4.514, 4.515, and 4.500–4.603, namely that special use said to be in accordance with Aristotle's *Categoriae* (cf. 4.5122 and *n*4.515*f*).

*n*4.604*c*: not appellative of them at all ⊖ *non appellativis*] A new and interesting feature is now being added to the elucidation mentioned in *n*4.604*b*, for the Tutor points out that the special use of 'is' involves the *showing* of things, rather than the *naming* of things: *sicut nominat, vel potius ostendit res… solis vocibus earum significativis et saepe non appellativis* ⊖ It is in this way that he names or rather *shows* things … by recourse to utterances which only signify them, and which frequently are not appellative of them at all. This is accompanied by a reference back (*tu paulo ante memenisti* ⊖ you reminded us just now) to cases such as '*grammaticus est qualitas*' ⊖ '*Literate* is quality' and '*albus est qualitas*' ⊖ '*White* is quality' (4.515) which are inferentially connected with '*grammaticus est grammatica*' ⊖ '*Literate* is literacy' and '*albus est albedinem*' ⊖ 'White is whiteness' (4.2341, 4.5022). This allows us to realise fully that it is in such peculiar sentences that '*res*' ⊖ 'things' are in fact *shown*, and not *named*, by the words which signify, but are not appellative of, those *res* ⊖ things (4.234). Now on the interpretation of the 'is' which occurs in these peculiar sentences suggested in §4 and defended in these notes (e.g. *n*1.000*b*) the word '*grammaticus*' ⊖ 'literate' as it occurs in those sentences is certainly not a name, since it must be taken to be an argument of the higher-order '∈', as suggested in *n*4.2341*b*.1. The use of '*ostendere*' ⊖ 'to show' in overt preference to '*nominare*' ⊖ 'to name' could well, therefore, be an index of Anselm's realisation of the nature of such sentences. The occurrence of '*ostendere*' ⊖ 'to show' also in that part of the dialogue (4.515) to which back-reference is here being made also suggests that he sees the logician's discussions as involving such *showings*, rather than *namings*.

Incidentally, the use of '*ostendere*' ⊖ 'to show' here should not lead one to suppose that Anselm's showings are what would nowadays sometimes be called 'ostensive definitions'. Where the indications of particulars are concerned, he prefers to speak in terms of '*demonstratio*' ⊖ 'pointing' and '*designatio*' ⊖ 'designation', the two of which are most significantly contrasted with '*significatio*' ⊖ 'meaning' in his *Epistola de Incarnatione Verbi*:

For when the name 'man' is uttered, only the nature common to all men is signified. However, when we say demonstratively 'this man' or 'that man', or when we use the proper noun 'Jesus', we designate a person ... Now when he is designated in this fashion, not just any man is meant, but he who was announced by the angel, is god and man, is the Son of God and of the Virgin, and whatever else is truly predicable of him insofar as he is god or man.	*Nam cum profertur 'homo' natura tantum quae communis omnibus est hominibus significatur. Cum vero demonstrative dicimus 'istum vel illum hominem', vel proprio nomine 'Iesum', personam designamus ... Nam cum ita designatur, non quilibet homo intelligitur, sed qui ab angelo annuntiatus est, qui deus et homo, filius dei et filius virginis est, et quidquid de illo aut secundum deum aut secundum hominem verum est dicere: S* II 29.4.12, cf. *n*4.14*c*.

It should be added that the one thing that the Tutor is *not* doing here is interpreting *de re* ⊖ thing-centred assertions as disguised *de voce* ⊖ word-centred assertions. He is not saying that in Aristotle's usage all assertions involving '*substantia*' ⊖ 'substance' or 'quality', and so on, and which look as though they are *de re* ⊖ thing-centred, are really *de voce* ⊖ word-centred. He is therefore not extending to 'substance' and 'quality', and so on, the treatment given by Boethius to *genus* and *species*, i.e. he is not making them into *nomina nominum* ⊖ names of names (*BC* 176D quoted in *n*4.2411*h* (ii)).

*n*4.610*a*: a quality ⊖ *qualitas*] This sentence represents the termination of the Tutor's clarification of what may be said in accordance with the usage of Aristotle's *Categoriae*. The clarification had its inception at 4.5122, in response to the Student's qualms (4.501, 4.5022) about the '*quid sit?*' ⊖ 'What is it?' question raised in respect of *grammaticus* ⊖ literate. In turn this question is directly mentioned again in the present termination. The conclusion here arrived at is that whether '*Quid sit grammaticus?*' ⊖ 'What is *literate*?' is asked *de re* ⊖ about things or *de voce* ⊖ about utterances, then the Aristotelian form of answer is simply '*Qualitas*' ⊖ 'Quality'.

The '*quare*' ⊖ 'hence' with which the present conclusion is prefaced indicates that it is connected with the previous section (4.604) wherein Aristotle's calling of words by the names of the things of which those words are significative is demonstrated. The nature of this connection, and the reasons why it permits the inference of the present final words may now be considered. How, for instance, has section 4.604 so affected the conclusion arrived at in 4.602, 4.603, that the *de re*/*de voce* ⊖ thing-centred/word-centred distinction need not now be observed when replying to the '*Quid sit grammaticus?*' ⊖ 'What is *literate*?' question in Aristotle's manner?

The answer is that Aristotle, according to 4.604, uses words such as 'substance' or 'quality' where 'word signifying (and not merely appellative of) substance' and 'word signifying quality' are strictly speaking appropriate. In other words, according to the Tutor Aristotle neglects the *de re* / *de voce* ⊖ thing-centred / word-centred distinction. Whether this neglect is supposed to be confined to cases like the one quoted by Anselm in 4.604, and in which a *de voce* ⊖ word-centred construction is clearly called for by the 'signifies' which occurs in it, is not obvious. Anselm is here drawing the conclusion that the answer 'substance' when understood as a *de voce* ⊖ word-centred reply to a '*quid sit?*' ⊖ 'What is it?' question, should mean 'word signifying (*per se* ⊖ precisively) a substance' and not 'word appellative of substance'; *this* is the important point which 4.604 allows to be inferred. Its importance lies in the facts that were this not so, were the evidence of 4.604 lacking, then '*substantia*' ⊖ 'Substance' could be a reply to '*Quid sit grammaticus?*' ⊖ 'What is *literate*?', since '*grammaticus*' ⊖ 'literate' is appellative (although not significative *per se* ⊖ precisively) of substance, as the present section goes on to remind the reader. Understood *de re* ⊖ with reference to things, however, the reply '*substantia*' ⊖ 'substance' offers no such possible ambiguity. The remarks of 4.604 are designed, therefore, to show that provided *per se* signification is adhered to, there need be no fear that a *de voce* ⊖ word-centred interpretation, where called for, of an ambiguous Aristotelian use of 'substance', 'quality', and so on, might lead to error. The '*quare*' ⊖ 'hence' which the present passage (4.610) uses as a connecting word reflects the reassurance which the previous passage (4.604) on Aristotelian usage has provided on this count.

As already remarked, one reason for going over this point at such length in the present note is to avoid the interpretation which might suggest itself, namely that for Anselm *de re* ⊖ thing-centred questions about substance, quantity and quality, and so on are really disguised *de voce* ⊖ word-centred expressions. Were this the case, then the passage on Aristotelian usage (4.604) should have come first, instead of as a corollary to a carefully worded passage (4.601–4.603) on the *de voce* / *de re* ⊖ word-centred / thing-centred distinction. In any case, Anselm in no wise states that really there are only *de voce* ⊖ word-centred questions here. His remarks in the next speech, and the whole of the discussion on *usus loquendi* ⊖ the usual course of utterance, would be rendered otiose by such a position. The sentence '*grammaticus est grammatica*' ⊖ '*Literate* is literacy' (4.2341, 4.5022) is meant to be taken seriously as a *de re* ⊖ thing-centred sentence (cf. *n*1.000*b*), and is not here, after all the distinctions which it has suscitated, being shuffled off as 'really' meaning '"*grammaticus*" *est vox significans grammaticam*' ⊖ '"Literate" is a word signifying literacy'. Finally, the assertion which Anselm makes about the parallelism between *res* ⊖ things and *significatio* ⊖ meaning goes clearly against any such assimilation: *Sed quoniam voces non significant nisi res; dicendo quid sit quod voces significant necesse fuit dicere quid sint res* ⊖ However, since words only signify things, he had, in order to indicate what it is that words signify, to indicate what those things could be (4.5143). Accordingly, 4.62 tends to confirm the attribution of *de re* ⊖ thing-centred assertions to logicians, rather than to restrict them to the use of *de voce* ⊖ word-centred statements only.

It should be clear from the foregoing notes that Anselm appears to be running in parallel, as it were, both of what *DLM* II–I 193–9 characterises as the truly logical and as the ontological elements of discussions of meaning. I see no reason to deprecate this procedure of Anselm's. Indeed, *De Grammatico* demonstrates how the distinction considered by *DLM* to be vital in separating these two aspects (*DLM* II–I 196) could be consistently maintained by Anselm, namely the distinction between signification and appellation, without at the same time eliminating consideration of *res* ⊖ things. Indeed, it is evident that for Anselm consideration of signification in its logical sense still allowed consideration of '*res*' ⊖ 'things' in the broad sense discernible by means of the sympathetic analytic tools made available by Ontology. Of course, much depends on the notions of the logical and the ontological here in question. The logical framework presupposed in the present commentary is broad and complex enough to accommodate itself to the work of Anselm and of other medievals, and does not demand the rejection as extra-logical of certain features of that work which might not be comprised within narrower notions of the logical.

*n*4.611*a*: is a substance ⊖ *est substantia*] This is because 'literate' is appellative of man (4.233).

*n*4.620*a*: insofar as they signify ⊖ *secundum quod sunt significativae*] It is understood that *per se* ⊖ precisive signification (as opposed to *per aliud* ⊖ oblique signification and *appellatio* ⊖ reference) (4.232) is here being referred to. The form of logical written sentence to which reference is here being made need *not*, as might at first sight appear to the present-day reader, be that of the type '"A" signifies B' (cf. *n*4.610*a*). For were this the type of sentence indicated here, then the scandal now in question, namely that of the violation of the current course of utterance by logicians (cf. 1.201, 4.21, 4.2341, 4.5022, *n*1.000*b*) would just not exist. True, the Tutor goes on to point out that no such scandal arises from from the grammarian's statements about the typology of parts of speech, and such statements (4.621) do indeed involve the mention, rather than the use, of words. For Anselm, however, this is a familiar enough distinction, as the following passage shows:

There are certain things which we use as their own names for signifying them, as in the case of certain utterances such as that of the letter 'a'; apart from what holds in such cases, there is no other word which appears to be so like the thing of which it is the word, or so well expresses the thing, as does that likeness which is expressed in the eye of the mind occupied in thinking of that thing.

Exceptis namque rebus illis, quibus ipsis utimur pro nominibus suis ad eandem significandas, ut sunt quaedam voces velut 'a' vocalis, exceptis inquam his nullus aliud verbum sic videtur rei simile cuius est verbum aut sic eam exprimit, quomodo illa similitudo quae in acie mentis rem ipsam cogitantis exprimitur: S I 25.17.21.

So that if Anselm wished to say that the logician's or the grammarian's practice involve the mention rather than the use of words, why did he not express himself as in the quotation just given? It seems much more probable that in the case of the grammarians shortly to be referred to, the distinction before Anselm's mind is the cognate but wider distinction between the exemplar and its exemplification, between the 'type' and the 'token'. Indeed, as John of Salisbury shows in terms most redolent of Anselm's, this distinction can usefully be invoked as an illuminating parallel in the discussion of universals:

For the soul, receiving as it were the reflected ray of its own contemplation, discovers within itself what it is that it is defining; within itself is the exemplar of what is being defined, whereas in reality are the exemplifications of that exemplar.

Anima enim, quasi reuerberata acie contemplationis sue, in seipsa reperit quod diffinit: nam et eius exemplar in ipsa est, exemplum uero in actualibus. Sicut enim cum in gramatica dicitur: Nomina que sic desinunt, femina uel neutra sunt;

This is like what occurs in the course of grammatical discussion when it is asserted that names that end in such and such a fashion are feminine or neuter; we have here laid down a sort of general account which is as it were the exemplar covering many declinable expressions; the exemplifications are shown forth in all those expressions which possess those terminations. For in the self-same fashion certain exemplars are bred within the mind, the exemplifications of which were framed by nature and perceived by the senses. ... such exemplars are the objects of thought and are, as it were, images and shadows of existents. If, however, one attempts to grasp them as existing separately apart from particular things they vanish like dreams. They are mere manifestations which are only available to the understanding.

generalis quedam prescribitur ratio, que quasi multorum declinabilium exemplar est, exempla uero in omnibus illius terminationis dictionibus manifesta sunt; sic quedam exemplaria concipiuntur in mente, quorum exempla natura formauit, et sensibus obiecit. Illa itaque exemplaria cogitabilia quidem sunt et sunt quasi phantasie et umbre existentium ... quas si quis apprehendere nititur per existentiam quam habent a singularibus separatam, uelut somnia elabuntur. Monstra enim sunt, et soli intellectui patent: *SM* 99.24–100.6.

One only has to recall the connection between *intellectus* ⊖ understanding, *significatio* ⊖ meaning and the logician's 'is', all of which demand elucidation in terms of the higher-order '∈' (cf. §3.15, *n*1.000*b*, *n*3.101*a* and references there given) to realise that the words of Anselm are converging on the same point as those of John. That '*exemplar*' is one of Anselm's interpretations of the word '*forma*' which he is to use when speaking of grammatical assertions at the end of the present sentence (cf. *n*4.620*c*) constitutes further evidence of this convergence.

Anselm's point is that when logicians are discussing words insofar as they signify ('*secundum quod sunt significativae*') they have to have recourse to sentences involving the scandalous 'is' (cf. *n*1.000*b*) which is not a part of speech encountered in the current course of utterance. In order to bring out this type-difference he will import the analogous case, the appositeness of which John of Salisbury's remarks have revealed, represented by the grammarian's 'is' (4.621). This latter, like the logician's 'is' is a functor of a semantical category diverse from the more current 'is' of ordinary speech. Although the 'is' of the logicians and the 'is' of the grammarians cannot, of course, be identified, nevertheless the latter calls to mind a familiar case of exemplarism which may be a help in coming to terms with the status of the arguments of the logician's 'is', and hence of 'universals' (cf. *n*4.811*b*).

*n*4.620*b*: given the appellative function of those words, use ⊖ *utuntur … secundum quod sunt appellativae*] The contrast between the parts of speech involved in the logician's determination of signification and those involved in *usus loquendi* ⊖ the current course of utterance, is still being maintained here. This contrast has been apparent ever since the opening of the dialogue (*n*1.000*b*) and gradually (1.201) comes to a head (4.21), being incorporated in the distinction between *per se* ⊖ precisive signification and appellation (4.23). But disquiet persists (4.5022) and is now being finally allayed by the drawing of attention to the analogous practice of grammarians (cf. *n*4.620*a*). The allusion to grammatical discourse may be of further significance in view of the opposition between the views of grammarians and logicians reflected in the dialogue's opening question, and represented by one of the Student's positions (4.21) which leads to the central distinctions (4.23; cf. *n*1.201b, *n*3.800*b*, *n*4.22*c*, *n*4.2341*a*). The '*grammatici*' ⊖ 'grammarians' of 4.21 can now scarcely be in a position to object to apparent breaches of their rules by logicians. Not only is the difference between grammarians and logicians now resolved, but given the circumstances to which allusion will next be made (4.621) the grammarian also can have no reason for accusing the logician of ungrammatical talk.

*n*4.620*c*: word considered as an exemplar ⊖ *secundum formam vocum*] An instance of Anselm's use of the word '*forma*' in *Monologion* 9, as well as the suggestions of John of Salisbury (*n*4.620*a*), supports the reading of '*forma*' in the present context as 'exemplar':

The only basis upon which someone can bring something about in a rational way involves the preexistence in the agent's mind of a sort of pattern of the thing to be done, or perhaps what could more properly be said to be a form, or likeness, or rule.

Nullo namque pacto fieri potest aliquid rationabiliter ab aliquo, nisi in facientis ratione praecedat aliquod rei faciendae quasi exemplum, sive aptius dicitur forma, vel similitudo, aut regula: S I 24.12.14.

The expression '*forma vocum*' ⊖ 'exemplary utterance' which occurs in Anselm's present text of *De Grammatico* may be an echo of Priscian's '*videntur contra vocis formam significare*' ⊖ 'they would appear to signify in a fashion at odds with the appropriate rules of speech': *K* II 376.14.15. This remark of Priscian's occurs in the discussion of examples of the sort which Anselm is next to adduce. However, Anselm is also prepared to contrast '*forma loquendi*' ⊖ 'speech-rule' with that which is actually the case ('*secundum rem*') in *De Casu Diaboli* 11:

It is in this sense that 'evil' and 'nothing' do signify something, but what is signified is not a something relative to the actuality of states of affairs, but only in relation to the rules of speech.

Hoc igitur modo 'malum' et 'nihil' significant aliquid, et quod significatur est aliquid non secundum rem, sed secundum formam loquendi: S I 251.3.4, cf. *n*4.621*c*.

This last passage is in fact dealing with a wider sort of issue, namely the whole question of grammatical as opposed to logical form, and is not confined to the topic of exemplary utterances (cf. *HL* §2.12, §6.65).

*n*4.620*d*: in relation to the constitution of things ⊖ *secundum rerum naturam*] The term '*natura rerum*' ⊖ 'the constitution of things' which figures here falls over on the side of the '*res ipsa*' ⊖ 'the thing itself' which occurs in the definition of *appellatio* ⊖ calling (4.2341) rather than on the side of the broader unqualified '*res*' ⊖ 'thing' of '*de re*' ⊖ 'thing-centred' (4.603). '*Natura rerum*' ⊖ 'the constitution of things' was in fact an expression used by grammarians in association with '*appellare*' ⊖ 'to call'. Thus in Sergius on Donatus one finds:

When our ancestors saw how things were constituted, and did not know how they should be called, they made their decisions about the names by which various things should be called. This they did so as to recall absent objects by the use of the appropriate utterances of the names, as when they said 'man', 'lion', 'bird', and so on.

Cum maiores nostri viderent rerum naturam et nescirent quem ad modum appellarent, constituerunt sibi nomina, quibus diversa appellarent, ita ut propriis nominum vocabulis absentia praestolarent, sic ut dicerent hominem, leonem, avem, et cetera: K IV 488.3.7.

Here we have not only the expressions in question ('*natura rerum*' ⊖ 'the constitution of things', '*appellare*' ⊖ 'to call') but also that association with the needs and purposes of everyday word-users which is so typical of *appellatio* ⊖ calling (cf. 4.422, 4.423) as opposed to those theoretical logical presuppositions of significant utterance which are isolated in the logician's account of *significatio* ⊖ meaning. The ancestors of which Sergius speaks were concerned with how they should call (*appellare*) the various objects, and not with abstruse theoretical matters.

Boethius, in a text certainly familiar to Anselm (Commentary on Porphyry, Bk. I) likewise uses '*rerum naturam*' ⊖ 'the constitution of things' in order to express the concrete:

Whatever the mind understands is understood in various ways: either the mind conceives that which is based on the constitution of things by means of the intellect, and delineates it for its own use by means of reason, or it depicts something substantial for itself by means of the imagination.

Omne quod intelligit animus, aut id quod est in rerum natura constitutum, intellectu concipit, et sibimet ratione describit, aut id quod non est vacua sibi imaginatione depingit: B 82B–C.

*n*4.621*a*: 'slave' neuter ⊖ *mancipium autem neutri*] This example is used by Probus, *Institutio Artium*, *K* IV 52.9.

*n*4.621*b*: neither male nor female ⊖ *nec masculum nec feminam*] Aristotle uses the grammatical counterpart of this kind of expression when recounting difficulties of the neuter 'this' in Ch. 14 of *De Sophisiticis Elenchis*:

It is because of the neuter form of 'this' that nearly all the apparent solecisms arise, as well as when the case-ending is neither masculine nor feminine, but neuter.

Sunt autem omnes pene apparentes soloecismi propter 'hoc', et quando casus neque masculinum neque femininum significat, sed neutrum: B 1023C, cf. *B* 1037B.

Priscian describes a neuter name as one which is '*nec masculinum nec femininum*' ⊖ 'neither masculine nor feminine': *K* II 141.10, *K* II 552.16.17.

*n*4.621*c*: whereas to be feared is to undergo an action ⊖ *timeri autem pati*] The '*nemo dicat*' ⊖ 'no one asserts' of this sentence is to be taken seriously. It is not just a literary alternative for 'it does not follow that' or some such phrase. We have in fact here the ultimate response to the Student's complaint (4.20) which was in effect the first strong statement of the contrast between *usus loquendi* ⊖ the common course of utterance and logical assertions (or the supposed consequences of the latter). The complaint took the form of an inference from a logical assertion (e.g. '"Literate" signifies literacy' or '*Literate* is literacy') to the possibilities ensuing for the current course of utterance ('A literate is a useful form of knowledge' should hence be sayable, for instance). The Tutor is now reminding the Student that no one is tempted to make the same kind of inference from the comparatively more familiar but nevertheless still technical assertions of grammarians.

One of the examples here used recurs in a similar connection in *De Casu Diaboli* 11:

Many things are asserted to be the case if we go by the speech-rules, but are not the case in actual fact. Thus 'to fear' is said to be active according to the rules governing speech, when according to the states of affairs here in question we are concerned rather with the passive under-going of an action.	*Multa quippe dicuntur secundum formam, quae non sunt secundum rem. Ut 'timere' secundum formam vocis dicitur activum, cum sit passivum secundum rem:* *S* I 250.21.23.

Discussion of the discrepancy between the grammatical classification of verbs and the actual meaning of verbs stretches at least from Quintilian to Wittgenstein (cf. *HL* 16). Fallacies based on diversities of word-genders are also dealt with in *DLM* I 477–481, 515–6.

In general, Anselm refers the term '*forma vocum*' ⊖ 'speech-rules' to grammarians (4.620). Priscian uses the same expression, and contrasts purely rational rules with the usage of writers:

Those things are unusual which authors are not found to use ... and such things, although they are well said according to the rules, we nevertheless refuse to say because they do not occur in the usage of authors.	*Inusitata sunt, quibus non inveniuntur usui auctores ... ea enim quamvis ratione regulae bene dicantur, quia in usus auctorum non inveniuntur, recusamus dicere:* *K* II 371.18.22.

All this seems to confirm one more that, as suggested in *n*4.620*b*, Anselm is quite consciously opposing the rational requirements of the *per se* ⊖ precisive type of signification which is the concern of the logician, to *usus loquendi* ⊖ the common course of utterance, which has been the field of the grammarian. In limiting cases, the contrast may even extend as far as the breaking of grammatical rules (cf. *n*1.000*b*).

*n*4.700*a*: signifies a substance ⊖ *significet substantiam*] Throughout this passage 'signifies' and 'is', i.e. the *de voce* ⊖ word-centred and *de re* ⊖ thing-centred forms of expression (4.601–4.603) are used together.

*n*4.700*b*: 'having' ⊖ *habere*] 'Accoutred' occurs in Aristotle's list of categories as an example of a 'having': *Habere, ut calceatus, armatum* ⊖ Having, as in *shod, accoutred*: *BC* 180a. The moderns prefer to translate 'ἔχειν' by 'state' (e.g. *JL* 49).

These questions as to variations in the categorisation of 'accoutred' and 'literate' are probably inspired by *Categoriae* 8 and 15. In the latter diverse senses of 'having' are listed. Aristotle hints that his list is scarcely exhaustive (*Sed cui consueverunt dici, pene omnes enumerati sunt*; *BC* 293B) and explicitly suggests that 'having learning' belongs to the category of 'having'. Now since literacy is a species of learning, this Aristotelian authority is the immediate ground for the Student's present suggestion that 'literate' may signify 'having literacy', and so signify 'having'; cf. *HL* 84.

*n*4.700*c*: having a quality ⊖ *habentem qualitatem*] This is a reference to 4.31, the '*sciens grammaticam*' ⊖ '... displaying literacy' of which has become '*habens grammaticam*' ⊖ '... having literacy' in 4.511. '*Habens*' ⊖ '... having' is henceforward used along with the appropriate abstract noun in the elucidation of paronyms.

*n*4.700*d*: having accoutrements ⊖ *habentem arma*] According to Peter of Spain, who takes up and discusses Aristotle's varieties of 'having', this example ('*armatus*' ⊖ 'accoutred') represents a case of 'having' in the true categorial sense:

In a third sense one is said *to have* such things as have to do with the body, such as clothes, a coat, or such as have to do with the body's limbs, such as a ring on the hand. Now *having* taken in this sense *is* one of the ten categories, and is defined thus: *having* involves closeness with respect to the body and things having to do with the body, as with accoutering and shoeing. And names are used in a similar way with respect to other things, and it is because of this closeness that one thing is said *to have* and the other *to be had*.

Tertio modo dicitur habere ea quae circa corpus sunt ut vestitum vel tunicam, aut in membris, ut in manu anulum. Et habitus isto tertio modo sumptus est unum de decem praedicamentis et definitur sic. Habitus est corporum et eorum que circa corpus sunt adiacentia ut armatio et calceatio; et similiter funguntur nomina in aliis: et secundum hanc adiacentiam haec dicuntur habere, illa haberi; HSL 3.37.

*n*4.700*e*: having learning ⊖ *habentem disciplinam*] 'Literate' may signify 'having literacy' and be categorised as a *having*, since 'having learning' is suggested by Aristotle as an example of a *having* (*dicimur enim disciplinam aliquam habere atque virtutem* ⊖ for we are said to *have* some learning or other, or some excellence: *BC* 293A) and literacy is said to be a species of knowledge (*BC* 261A, cf. *n*4.31*a* and *BC* 295C).

*n*4.710*a*: a matter of opinion ⊖ *dubitari possit*] Verbally, here is an echo of Boethius' commentary on *Categoriae* 8:

Now while it is true that one and the same thing cannot be assigned to several categories, it can however be proper to bring one and the same sort of thing under one kind in respect of one feature and under another in respect of another feature. Thus as already stated above Socrates is a substance and *being a father* a relation; although substance is not the same as a relation, there is no objection to the same Socrates being classified as a substance insofar as he is a man, and as being related insofar as he is a father. Hence there is no objection to placing any identical thing under two categories on account of diverse features.	*Nam cum sit verum unam eamdemque rem duabus diversis generibus suppositam esse non posse, illud tamen convenit secundum aliud atque aliud unam eamdemque speciem duobus generibus posse subnecti, ut in eo quod supra* [*B* 220D] *iam dictum est, cum Socrates substantia sit, pater vero ad aliquid, cumque substantia discrepet atque relatio, nihil tamen est inconveniens eumdem ipsum Socratem in eo quod homo est, substantiae supponi, in eo quod habet filium, relationi. Quocirca si secundum aliam atque aliam rem duobus generibus eadem res quaelibet diversissimis supponatur, nihil inconveniens cadit:* *BC* 261B–C; *see also BC* 220D–221A, *APA* 219, 229.

Anselm's treatment, it will be noted, is by no means a simple reproduction of the one proposed by Boethius. However, the verb '*suppono*' ⊖ 'place under' which figures in the passage cited, also occurs in Anselm's text. This latter occurrence might be taken as having some connection with the later prominent medieval doctrine of *suppositio*, especially as some of the concerns of this doctrine run parallel to those of the present dialogue (cf. *HL* §3.4, *HHS*, *HLM* III §1). Although it can be agreed that an explicit link *via* Anselm is unlikely, medieval tenacity in taking over and enlarging on the accidents of form and vocabulary of authorities may be responsible for the title of the later '*suppositio*' doctrine. After all, much of *De Grammatico* itself owes its content to just such tenacity and enlargement (cf. *DLM* II–I 180–1, 519–21).

*n*4.710*b*: brief argument ⊖ *sermocinatione*] On logic as the *ars sermocinalis* ⊖ discursive, argumentative, art, see *A* xci, note 5, *DLM* II–I 574, and the opening of the *Liber Papiensis*:

Philosophy is divided into three parts, ethics, logic, and physics. This may be expanded by saying that ethics treats of morals, logic of argument, and physics of natural objects.	*Philosophia vero in tribus partibus dividitur: ethica, loyca, et phisica. Quod sic solvitur: ethica moralis, loyca sermocinalis, phisica naturalis:* *MGH* 290 *(Leges Langobardorum).*

Since Sohm, the historian of Roman Law, assigns 1070 as the terminal date of the work just quoted, it is already plain that this type of description of logic was in circulation during Anselm's time. It is thus certainly earlier than the late twelfth or early thirteenth century suggested in *KSI* 21.

*n*4.710*c*: one word ⊖ *unam autem vocem*] A contrast appears to be drawn here between *res* ⊖ things (at the opening of the last sentence) and the present *vox* ⊖ word; this apparent contrast runs parallel to the *de voce* / *de re* ⊖ word-centred / thing-centred distinction of 4.601–4.603. The point of such a contrast, if it is in fact intended, scarcely emerges in the text which follows, unless it is that *significare ut unum* ⊖ to signify as a single whole (cf. *n*4.710*d*) and *facere unum aliquid* ⊖ to constitute one thing (cf. *n*4.72*a*) happen to represent the continuation of that contrast. If this is so, then as in the case of the *de voce* ⊖ word-centred and *de re* ⊖ thing-centred contrast, inferentially equivalent theses are in question.

*n*4.710*d*: as a single whole ⊖ *ut unum*] The locution '*significare ut unum*' ⊖ 'to signify as a single whole' has already been encountered several times in the dialogue, first of all in 4.231: *nomen hominis per se et ut unum significat ea ex quibus constat totus homo* ⊖ the name 'man' signifies *per se* and as a single whole the complete make-up of *man*. Then one sense of its opposite, i.e. *non significare ut unum* ⊖ not to signify as a single whole, occurs in 4.232: *'Grammaticus' vero non significat homen et grammaticam ut unum, sed grammaticam per se et hominen per aliud significat* ⊖ On the other hand 'literate' does not signify *man* and literacy as a single whole: in a *per se* sense it signifies only literacy, and obliquely it signifies *man*. This sense of '*non significare ut unum*' ⊖ 'not to signify as a single whole' is then expanded, in that '*grammaticus*' ⊖ 'literate' is said to be appellative of man, but strictly (*proprie*) to be significative of literacy only (4.233). However, it is in the present section (4.71, 4.72) that a second sense of '*non significare ut unum*' ⊖ 'not to signify as a single whole' is encountered, and the connection of '*significare ut unum*' ⊖ 'to signify as a single whole' and '*facere unum aliquid*' ⊖ 'to constitute one thing' made plain. This is, therefore, a more appropriate point at which to attempt to deepen the sense of 'signifying as a single whole'.

The first sense of '*non significare ut unum*' ⊖ 'not to signify as a single whole' mentioned above clearly involves the use of '*significare*' ⊖ 'to signify' in its broad sense: 'literate' does not signify *man* and literacy *ut unum* ⊖ as a single whole because it signifies man *per aliud* ⊖ obliquely and only literacy in a *per se* ⊖ precisive manner, and oblique signification in the case of names is not, strictly speaking, signification, but rather reference (*appellatio*) (4.233). In the present context (4.71) however, signification *per se* ⊖ in the precisive sense is in question, i.e. the type of signification alluded to in 4.231 (*per se et ut unum significat* ⊖ signifies *per se* and as a single whole). It now becomes evident that when 'signification' is understood in this primary and proper sense, then the mode of the signification (i.e. '*ut unum*' ⊖ 'as a single whole' of '*non ut unum*' ⊖ 'not as a single whole') turns upon whether the referent can in any way be used as a guide or pointer to the signification. Thus, in the case of both 'man' and 'white', the Tutor goes on to say, we have a complex signification: 'man' signifies substance and qualities, 'white' signifies having and whiteness. But whereas the referent of 'man' (i.e. the *res quae appellatur 'homo'* ⊖ thing that is called 'man') is *one thing* constituted of substance and quality, it is not the case that the reference of 'white' is *one thing* ('*unum aliquid*'; cf. *n*4.72*a*) constituted out of having and whiteness. The reference of 'white' is in fact the object which happens to be white: there are no objects of reference which are constituted of just having and whiteness, and as pointed out in 4.72, the list of categories contains no heading appropriate to such a compound. Only a *unum aliquid* ⊖ single whole, namely a definable, or a compound of categorially homogeneous definables, or an individual, can be an object of reference (4.72). 'Individual' and '*unum aliquid*' ⊖ 'single whole' are here taken to have recognisable pre-theoretical senses (cf. *n*4.22*d*)). Signification '*ut unum*' ⊖ 'as a single whole' is in fact the correlate of '*facere unum aliquid*' ⊖ 'to constitute one thing' (*n*4.72*a*), which in turn is closely associated with how things are for the pre-logical, pre-philosophical, pre-scientific understanding. This association is shown, in Anselm's dialogue, by his definition of reference (*appellatio*) in terms of *usus loquendi* ⊖ the current course of utterance (cf. 4.2341 and notes), and the manner in which unity of object of reference is in turn a guide to unity of signification, as expounded in the present passage.

The expression '*dicere ut unum*' ⊖ 'to assert as being a single whole' occurs together with '*unum aliquid*' ⊖ 'one thing' in *De Interpretatione* 11, cf. *n*4.72*a*, *n*4.2414*b*, *B*356–358, *B* 572–576.

*n*4.710*e*: variously categorised ⊖ *pluribus aliquando supponi*] Although the verb '*supponere*' ⊖ 'to place under' and its cognate noun '*suppositio*' ⊖ 'putting under' are to have such an interesting future history in connection with the theory of *suppositio*, they do not here appear to have acquired the places which they later occupied. Anselm's present use probably derives from that passage of Boethius which is quoted in *n*4.710*a*; cf. *HSL* tract. 6, *HLM* III §1.

*n*4.710*f*: as a single whole ⊖ *ut unum*] Cf. *n*4.710*d*.

*n*4.710*g*: which constitute ⊖ *quibus constat*] Cf. 4.230 and 4.240, and the notes appended to this latter word.

*n*4.710*h*: one thing ⊖ *unum quiddam*] Cf. *n*4.72*a* on *unum aliquid* ⊖ one thing.

*n*4.710*i*: constitued in the way I mentioned ⊖ *constans ex iis quae dixi*] The elements of the constitution to which reference is here being made are the 'substance and qualities' of the previous sentence, the relationships between which have been detailed in 4.231.

*n*4.710*j*: only the thing that has whiteness receives the appellation 'white' ⊖ *nihil appellatur albus nisi res quae habet albedinem*] The point of the present sentence as a whole will be examined in the next note (*n*4.710*k*). In the meantime it may be noted that if, in accordance with the general policy of the dialogue (1.000, 3.82) one were to generalise '*nihil appellatur albus nisi res quae habet albedinem*' ⊖ 'nothing is called "white" which does not have whiteness' then results which might at first sight appear to be at variance with what Anselm has to say in other works of his would ensue. Thus, since '*iustus*' ⊖ 'just' like '*albus*' ⊖ 'white' is paronymous, there would apparently be no objection to '*nihil appellatur iustus nisi res quae habet iustitiam*' ⊖ 'nothing is called "just" save the thing which has justice'. Yet in *Monologion* 16 one finds:

When [that supreme nature] is called 'just', it is properly to be understood as *existing justice*, and not merely as *having* justice.	*Cum [summa natura] dicitur iusta, proprie intelligitur existens iustitia, non autem habens iustitiam: S* I 30.23.24.

(For Ockham's use of this passage see *HL* §2.22). We now have a case of something (i.e. God) called 'just' and which nevertheless cannot be said to *have* justice. Therefore the '*appellatur*' ⊖ 'is called' of the present passage and the '*intelligitur*' ⊖ 'is understood' of the *Monologion* passage must be seen as differentiating factors; otherwise the exigencies of divine simplicity would cause the findings of *De Grammatico* to be insusceptible of full generalisation, since God would be an exception. There is in *Proslogion* 17 a suggestion of an alternative sense of 'having' which would also help to cover the case. God is there said to *have* mildness, but only in his own ineffable manner (*in te tuo ineffabili modo*: *S* I 113.12.13). The fact of the matter is that God could not be said to *have* his properties, since 'having' implies participation in some other thing, and it would be improper to attribute such participation to God. It was therefore necessary to say that God *is* his justice, his mildness, and so on. This is the type of problem which was dealt with at the Council of Rheims in 1148. How, for instance, are the terms '*deus*' ⊖ 'god' and '*deitas*' ⊖ 'godness' related? If the two denote two distinct objects the first of which participates in ('has') the second, then '*Deus est deitas*' ⊖ 'God is godness' does not hold, and the divine simplicity is impugned. Gilbert de la Porrée (1076–1154) denied '*Deus est deitas*' ⊖ 'God is godness' and had to be dealt with by the council. It is interesting to note that Anselm, with his doctrine in *De Grammatico* could have admitted '*Deus est deitas*' as a parallel to '*Grammaticus est grammatica*' ⊖ '*Literate* is literacy' (cf. *n*1.000*b*) on grounds quite independent of those stated in *Monologion* and *Proslogion*. Aquinas' method of maintaining divine simplicity may be seen in *AST* I q.3 art. 3.

*n*4.710*k*: having and a quality ⊖ *habere et qualitate*] The whole of the present sentence gives the reason why '*homo*' ⊖ 'man' can be said to signify '*ut unum*' ⊖ 'as a single whole' whereas '*albus*' ⊖ 'white' (and therefore paronyms in general) cannot. As a first approximation it may be said that this is because of the coincidence of the account of the signification of '*homo*' ⊖ 'man' and the account of the referent of '*homo*' ⊖ 'man' – a coincidence which not only does not obtain in the case of '*albus*' ⊖ 'white' but also should not hold in general, if a rational general account of the paronymous situation is to be provided (cf. *n*4.230*b*, *n*4.31*a*, *n*4.1201*a*). Anthropology, the theory of *man*, is a theory of objects having a unity which is not present in the case of *white* (cf. §4, *n*4.72*a*).

*n*4.711*a*: unacceptable ⊖ *inconveniens*] The unitary objecthood implied by *man* would be shattered were the supposition mentioned (i.e. *man* is both substance and quality) to be adopted, since this would amount to conveying simultaneously both completeness and incompleteness (cf. 4.231). It would also be at variance with the presuppositions outlined in §4.

*n*4.712*a*: nothing improper follows ⊖ *nihil inconveniens sequitur*] Were one to accept the thesis here rejected, i.e. that, for example, 'white' refers to whiteness and *having*, then one would have to hold that 'white' named and stood for whiteness and *having*; but it has already been rightly pointed out that 'only the thing that has whiteness receives the appellation "white"' (4.71).

*n*4.714*a*: I've already said ⊖ *supra dixi*] The refers here appears to be not so much to the Tutor's immediately preceding speech as to the main statement on 'signifying substance', i.e. 4.231, where the '*principaliter*' ⊖ 'principally' point here repeated is first made.

*n*4.714*b*: something qualified ⊖ *quale*] On '*quale*' ⊖ 'qualified' and '*qualitas*' ⊖ 'quality' Bk. III of Boethius' commentary on the *Categoriae* may be consulted:

We use the word 'quality' in only one way, but 'qualitative' is not used in one fashion. 'Qualitative' is used in respect of the quality itself and in respect of the thing which has the quality, as in the case of whiteness, which is a quality such that that which has whiteness is called 'white'. Now we not only call whiteness itself 'qualitative' (i.e. the quality properly so called) but also we say of a white object that it is qualitative and in this case we are speaking of that which participates in the quality already mentioned. It is in this way, therefore, that we call both the quality itself and the thing which

Dicimus enim 'quale' non uno modo, 'qualitatem' vero simpliciter. 'Quale' enim dicimus et ipsam qualitatem, et illam rem quae qualitate illa participat, ut albedo quidem qualitas est, qui vero participat albedinem 'albus' dicitur. Sed et albedinem ipsam communiter 'quale' dicimus, id est ipsam proprie qualitatem, et album dicimus 'quale', illud scilicet quod superius comprehensa qualitate participat. Ita ergo et ipsam qualitatem et rem quae qualitate participat 'qualia' communiter appellamus, 'qualitas' vero simpliciter dicitur: *BC* 239B.

participates in the quality by the name 'qualitative'. In contrast, 'quality' has only one sense.

It looks as though the double sense of '*quale*' ⊖ 'qualitative' mentioned in this passage is not now being presupposed by Anselm, since otherwise he would not be able, as he is at present doing, to opposed quality and '*quale*' ⊖ 'qualitative' (or 'qualified'). On this same topic cf. *BC* 248D, 257C–D, 260D, 194C, 195B.

*n*4.714*c*: dominant ⊖ *principalius*] Compare 4.231, where '*principaliter*' ⊖ 'principally' occurs with reference to the same point.

*n*4.714*d*: kind of unity ⊖ *fit unum*] See *n*4.72*a* on '*facere unum aliquid*' ⊖ 'to constitute one thing'.

*n*4.72*a*: a single whole ⊖ *unum aliquid*] The background to the expression '*facere unum aliquid*' ⊖ 'to constitute one thing' is complex and controversial. Its origin lies in Boethius' translation of chapters 5, 8, and 11 of Aristotle's *De Interpretatione*. The whole of those chapters, as well as much of the present dialogue, turns on the sense of the words '*unum aliquid*' ⊖ 'one thing'. Anselm gives his list of senses of this word later in the present section, but a full understanding of those senses must rely in the last resort on Aristotle's own sense of '*unum aliquid*' ⊖ 'one thing'.

Some preliminary remarks on this topic occur in §4, *n*4.2411*d*, *n*4.2414*b*. Full references and discussion in connection with Ch. 8 of *De Interpretatione* are provided in *HL* 54–9. The development of the same question of '*unum aliquid*' ⊖ 'one thing' in Ch. 11 of that work clearly had a great effect on *De Grammatico* as a whole, and may now be considered.

As Boethius says:

The peripatetics gave much attention to discriminating between what constitutes one proposition, and what many.

Multa peripateticis de discernendis propositionibus quae essent una, quae multae, consideratio fuit: BDIL 354C.

This constitutes his introduction to the lesser commentary on the third attempt to define propositional unity, an attempt which is complicated by the consideration of 'dialectical questions' and of the inferential force of compound terms. Throughout, the argument leans heavily on certain presuppositions as to what constitutes *unum aliquid* ⊖ one thing, with the result that it becomes more than the simple discussion of truth-functional compounds which it might at first sight appear to be. One thing, however, appears to be quite certain: it is from this Ch. 11 that Anselm has taken over what purports to be a standard drill for showing that a compound does not constitute one thing in Aristotle's sense: this drill is the method of regress which Anselm uses in 4.2414 in order to show that '*grammaticus*' ⊖ 'literate' does not have '*homo sciens grammaticam*' ⊖ 'man displaying literacy' as its meaning. The inclusion of '*homo*' ⊖ 'man' gives rise to infinite regress (4.2414) and must therefore be abandoned (4.3).

The chapter mentioned begins with the assertion that when many things are affirmed or denied of one thing, or one thing affirmed or denied of many things, then there is propositional singularity only when the many in question constitute a unity (*BDIL* 354B, *BDIG* 567D). So far, the only thing of which we are tolerably certain, thanks to Ch. 8 of *De Interpretatione*, is that compounds such as 'man-horse' do not have reference to a unity. Here in Ch. 11, however, an attempt is made to be more positive: the unity in question consists not only in unity of name. The text then continues:

Thus *man* perhaps is not only animal, but also two-footed as well as domesticated; these, however, do constitute a single thing. *White*, *man*, and *walking*, in contrast, do not constitute a unity.	*Ut homo est fortasse et animal et bipes et mansuetum, sed ex his etiam unum fit. Ex albo autem et homine et ambulare non fit unum: B*354B, *B* 567D–568A; cf. text 111, *APH* lib. II, lec. v.

The 'perhaps' ('*fortasse*') of this passage has exercised the ingenuity of all the commentators: as Caietan remarks '*obscuritate non caret*' ⊖ 'it lacks not obscurity' (*APH* 255). We expect a case of nominal unity without singularity of object, and the 'perhaps' seems to prolong this impression, but we apparently have its opposite, since 'twofooted domestic animal' is a topical definition of *man*. Boethius, following Porphyry, attaches special significance to the interposition of the conjunction '*et*' ⊖ 'and' between 'animal' and 'two-footed' as well as between 'two-footed' and 'domesticated'. It means, he says, that these names are applied on different occasions, thus giving multiplicity of object, whereas when applied together they coalesce to give unity (*BDIL* 354C–355A, *BDIG* 569C–570C). Caietan suggests a solution which, he claims, does justice to the opinions not only of Porphyry and Boethius, but also to that of Albertus Magnus (*APH* 256). However, without going into the details of this solution, we may at least agree with Caietan (*APH* 257) that the following four-fold division covers all (and perhaps more than) the cases envisaged by Aristotle, i.e. the subject or predicate or both, of an 'is'-copulated categorical proposition may be:

(i) a single name which applies to many things which do form a unity, but '*non in quantum sunt unum*' ⊖ 'not insofar as they are a unity';

(ii) the (names of) the many things which form a unity, mentioned in (i), but once again those many things are regarded as distinct (*in quantum sunt distinctae actualitates* ⊖ insofar as they are distinct realities);

(iii) a single name which applies to many things which do not form a unity;

(iv) the (names of) the many things which do not form a unity.

Of these four, (i) and (ii) refer to the Boethius-Porphyry interpretation, which need not be weighed in order to clarify the '*unum aliquid*' ⊖ 'one thing' question, while (iii) and (iv) refer to the cases which have already been discussed by Aristotle, i.e. those such as '*canis*' ⊖ 'dog' and '*tunica*' ⊖ 'garment', in Ch. 8. There it was pointed out that the case of 'dog' is a stock example of an equivocal name (it may be used in respect of the barking animal or the dog star (*APH* 260)). The 'garment' case arises, according to Aristotle, if this name used used to refer to man and to horse; under these circumstances the required singularity will be absent from an affirmation or denial having either of these names as subject-term (*B*328). The most interesting point is the assimilation (apparently) of the 'dog' and 'garment' cases to that of 'white walking man'. 'Garment' and 'dog' are alike in not having referents which constitute one thing, and now the same is being said of the compound 'white walking man': neither this compound, nor any corresponding single name, were one to be invented, signify that which constitutes a single whole.

Caietan agrees that this assimilation is taking place here:

The second case, that in which one name is applied to many things from which a unity is not constituted, is covered when he says 'from *white* and *man* and *walking*,	*Secundus autem modus, quo unum nomen impositum est pluribus ex quibus non fit unum, subiungitur cum dicit: 'Ex albo autem et homine et ambulante', etc., id est,*

etc.'; that is to say, one name's being applied to many things from which one object is not constituted can occur in a second fashion, as when 'man' 'white' and 'walking' are involved. For as there is just no way in which some single kind of thing can be constituted from these, in contrast to the constitution which *is* possible from the parts of definables, it appears obvious that if some name were to be used to refer to these things, that name would not be a name signifying a unity, as was already said of the name 'garment' applied to both man and horse.

alio modo hoc fit, quando unum nomen imponitur pluribus ex quibus non potest fieri unum, qualia sunt: 'homo', 'album', et 'ambulans'. Cum enim ex his nullo modo possit fieri aliqua una natura, sicut poterat fieri ex partibus definitivis, clare liquet quod nomen aliquid si eis imponeretur, esset nomen non unum significans, ut ... dictum fuit de hoc nomine 'tunica' imposita homini et equo: APH 256.

In a similar fashion Boethius assimilates the case of 'white', 'walking' and 'man' to that of the equivocal '*canis*':

Should anyone assert 'Socrates, the white man, is walking', then this is not one affirmation, because no species at all emerges from the combination of man, whiteness, and the act of walking. The conclusion hence is that since these many things whence one object is not constituted can no more be said to be one thing can can the barking terrestial dog, the heavenly dog, and the sea-dog, which do not constitute one thing ....

Si quis enim dicat: Socrates homo albus ambulat, non est una affirmatio, quoniam ex homine et albedine et ambulatione nulla omnino species fit. Quare conclusio est quoniam nec si de his pluribus ex quibus unum non fit, unum aliquid praedicetur, ut ex cane terreno latrabili, et coelesti et marino quoniam unum non fit ...: BDIG 570B.

Both the passages just quoted have a further common note: there is the '*ex partibus definitivis*' ⊖ 'from the parts of definables' phrase in Caietan, and the '*nulla omnino species fit*' ⊖ 'no species at all emerges' in Boethius. This is, of course, the clue to the concept of objecthood here in question: definability by means of overriding, constitutive, characteristics, as opposed to temporary, accidental, ones (cf. §4, *n*3.800*b*, *n*4.22*d*) is required, and the *definiendum* must not futilely attempt to delineate the result of a mere transformation of an identical continuant: *apud philosophos, cum fit aliquid album, non dicitur generari, sed generari secundum quid* ⊖ As far as philosophers are concerned, when something becomes white this is not a case of generation, but only of generation in a certain respect: *APH* 286. Some pretheoretical notion of object is here being distilled; thus an object having a purely notional or fanciful unity, such as that which might be possessed by the referents of 'dog' or 'garment' (in Aristotle's suppositious example) falls outside the limits of definability in this sense. All the commentators are agreed that the parts of some definition of *man* can (but need not) constitute a reference to *unum aliquid* ⊖ one thing (e.g. *BDIG* 569B, *APH* 256) and this is one of the cases cited by Anselm in his list of unities composed from multiplicities: *convenientia generis et differentiae unius vel plurius, ut corpus et homo* ⊖ the coalescence of the genus and one or more characteristics, as in the cases of *body* and *man*: 4.72.

Aristotle next points out that one form of dialectical question, namely that which asks for a 'yes' or 'no' answer to one or other of two contradictory propositions, likewise derives that unity which it should have from the unity of the subject or predicate of the contradictory pair (cf. *Topica* Bk. 8, Ch. 7, *BT* 1001B–C). In the compressed passages which follow, inferences having what could nowadays be described as the general form 'If x is a, and x is b, then x is $a * b$' (where '$*$' indicates that its terms are joined by a conjunction plus some other problematical relation) are examined with a view to typifying values of 'a' and 'b', and the relation in which they must stand, for that form to become a true thesis. For example, does the following case satisfy its requirements: if Socrates is a man and Socrates is white, then Socrates is a white man? At least thirteen such inferences are stated or implied, and these are expanded in detail in *n*4.2414*b* as they have a very close connection with the regresses which Anselm generates at the corresponding point in the dialogue. The problem itself, as Aristotle wishes to specify it, lies in the question as to what the relation between 'a' and 'b' is supposed to be, it being granted that it must be more than a mere truth-functional 'and'. This point is taken up in *n*4.2414*b*. The important fact for the present note is that '*facere unum aliquid*' ⊖ 'to constitute one thing' figures in the rule which Aristotle propounds for the validity of such conjunctive illation: those subjects and predicates, he says, which are asserted only *secundum accidens* ⊖ extra-theoretically either of some common subject or of one another, will not be *one*, and hence their combination will not satisfy the problematical form mentioned above. For example 'x is a musical white' cannot be inferred from 'x is musical' and 'x is white' since both will be extra-theoretical in respect of the x in question. Even if it is true that the white is musical, still a musical white is not one countable object, and hence an inference of the sort indicated is not admissible: the white is said to be musical only *secundum*

accidens ⊖ extra-theoretically. On this account from '*x* is good' and '*x* is a harpist' one cannot infer '*x* is a good harpist'. In contrast, from '*x* is animal' and '*x* is two-footed', one *can* infer that '*x* is a two-footed animal' since the two terms involved in the latter example are not related in a merely extra-theoretical manner:

Hence in respect of those things which are predicated or of which they are predicated, whichever of these are asserted extra-theoretically either of the same thing or one of the other, such will not constitute one thing. For example, in 'The man is white and musical' *white* and *musical* do not form an identical object, since each is extra-theoretical in respect of the other. Again, if it is true to say that the white is musical, nevertheless white and musical cannot be one thing; white and musical are extra-theoretical in respect of eachother, hence a musical white cannot be one thing. Hence also a harpist is not straightforwardly good, but *animal* and *two-footed* go together, since they are not mutually extra-theoretical.

Eorum igitur quae praedicantur et de quibus praedicantur, quaecumque secundum accidens dicuntur, vel de eodem, vel alterum de altero, haec non erunt unum; ut homo albus est et musicus, sed non est idem album et musicum; accidentia enim sunt utraque eidem. Nec si album musicum verum est dicere tamen erit album musicum unum aliquid: secundum accidens enim album musicum dicitur; quare non erit album musicum unum aliquid. Quocirca nec citharoedus bonus simpliciter; sed animal bipes; non enim sunt secundum accidens: BDIL 358B–C, *BDIG* 575A.

From this it is at least clear that only those predicates which are not asserted *secundum accidens* ⊖ extra-theoretically in respect of each-other can be combined in an illation founded on the form mentioned above; such predicates, according to Aristotle, correspond to one thing. For example, the parts of a definition formed according to Aristotelian rules (*n*3.800*b*) allow of such compounding; on the other hand 'musical white' could never constitute a definition of this sort.

Boethius has a passage which by its wording provides an implied connection between 'constituting one thing' and definition:

Hence if one says that Socrates is a musical white this cannot constitute a truly unitary proposition, for he can be other than musical and white all the time, accidents being such as to come and go. Thus if he who is musical and white is darkened by standing in the sun, he will no longer be concomitantly white and musical.

Ergo non potest hic una fieri vera propositio, ut dicatur: Socrates albus musicus est, neque enim semper musicus albus esse potest, sed hanc naturam habent accidentia, ut veniant et recedant; ergo si eius qui musicus albus est, in sole stantis autem calor fuscaverit, non erit quidem albus cum sit musicus: BDIG 575C.

In other words a *white musical* (without any other specification) is not

a countable unit. This is what lies behind the Aristotelian determination to treat as definable objects (cf. §4) only such unities as are determined by overriding, constitutive characteristics and (in the case of spatio-temporal objects) those whose coming into existence is usually recognisable as a new beginning, and not as a mere transformation of something substantial already existing (cf. *n*4.1201*a*); its perishing likewise must be more than such a transformation. The rules of definition, of which the words '*veniant et recedant*' ⊖ 'come and go' in the last passage quoted are a clear echo, demand that the constitutive characteristics employed in the definition must not, like an accident, be capable of coming and going without affecting the existence of the object; in Anselm's own words: *nec potest adesse et abesse ... praeter subiecti corruptionem* ⊖ the alternative presence and absence of which can only result in the subject's perishing: 4.2411. (See *n*4.2411*d* for an enlargement on these points).

The application of the foregoing doctrine to the part of *De Grammatico* under examination is readily apparent: Anselm has, in 4.710, contrasted the case of 'rational mortal animal' with that of '... having whiteness'. From the Aristotelian text it is clear that the first, being framed in accordance with the rules of definition (*n*3.800*b*) applies to, or delineates, a theory-worthy object (cf. §4). On the other hand '... having whiteness' does no such thing, since, as Anselm goes on to point out (4.72) it determines neither a categorially homogeneous compound nor a definable; further, 'having whiteness' does not determine even an individual object countable as a unity, such as Plato.

It is possible also, of course, to connect the texts already inspected with those works of Aristotle which were not available to Anselm, in order to glean further characterisation of the type of unity which is associated with '*facere unum aliquid*' ⊖ 'to constitute one thing'. Thus, corresponding to that part of *De Interpretatione* 11 in which the rule for the combination of predicates is laid down, one has Aristotle's remarks in *Metaphysica* Bk. Γ, 4 (1007^{a} 33–1007^{b} 17). The *De Interpretatione* text had said that not only do 'is musical' and 'is white' not combine in such a way that reference to 'one thing' is effected, but also that 'The white is musical' is a *secundum accidens* ⊖ extra-theoretical predication on account of this fact (*BDIG* 575A). Caietan further explains that this proposition is true only because of the whiteness and musicianship in a third thing – a common subject (*APH* 269). It is this point which is clarified by the *Metaphysica* text to which allusion has just been made: the white is musical, or *vice versa*, only because both are accidents of the same subject, and this is quite different, it is claimed, from the situation in cases such as 'Socrates is white'. We do not, in the latter case cast around for a third thing, a common subject of which 'Socrates' and 'white' may be predicated. Continuing this same line of thought are the many points in Aristotle's *Analytica Posteriora*, along with Aquinas' commentary, which deal with predication which is *per accidens* ⊖ extra-theoretical. As this doctrine is so often misunderstood it is most worth-while to peruse the commentary on part of this work (Bk. I, Ch. 22; 83ᵃ 1–14, *APA* 281). This commentary will be found to confirm the sense already hinted at in Caietan's already-mentioned words: '*Musicum est album*' ⊖ 'The musical is white' implied a reference to a something else ('*alterum aliquid*') such as a particular man, who happens to be musical and white. This is one reason why '*est musicus albus*' ⊖ 'is a musical white' is denied *per se* unity in *De Interpretatione*. In contrast, '*Homo est albus*' ⊖ 'The man is white' or '*Lignum est album*' ⊖ 'The log is white' imply no such reference to something else, as far as their subject-terms are concerned. All this of course ties up with the notion of substance (*n*4.1201*a*).

Again, one finds in Aquinas' commentary on *APA* yet another of the strands behind the Aristotelian definitional theory, with its overriding, constitutive, characteristics (cf. *n*4.22*d*, *n*3.800*b*) namely the stress on the way in which extra-theoretical predicates such as 'is white' (relative to e.g. *man*, as in 'This man is white') represent the outcome of a *becoming*, and hence can have no part in the definition of that which is a completely new beginning, and not the result of an accumulation of changes in a constant something else: everything which *begins to be* so-and-so, says Aquinas in the passage mentioned above, *becomes* so-and-so. If therefore it does not *become* so-and-so, it is not so-and-so unless it always was so-and-so. This last clause is the salient point: Socrates never *began to be* an animal, or rational, in the way in which he began to be musical or sunburned or literate. A person educated in the modern era, and accustomed to the dissolution of the pretheoretical world into the notional, yet practically powerful quasi-unities of the various sciences, and the linkages of these in their turn with new pictures of the biological, will feel very little sympathy with the *per se* unities, and the restrictions on definition (strictly so called) which they purport to represent. But in point of fact the opposition here is not necessarily of a head-on sort. Aquinas is, in effect, almost agnostic as regards the availability for human knowledge of definitions of such *per se* unities in nature (*APA* 43 bis, *APA* 533). The philosophical importance of pre-theoretical notions of objecthood, however, is not inconsiderable (cf. *n*4.22*d*, *n*4.2411*d*).

*n*4.72*b*: out of a multiplicity ⊖ *ex pluribus*] Compare Aquinas' corresponding statement:

'from which one thing is not effected' may be interpreted in two ways. First, it can be taken to exclude from consideration the things which may be subsumable under one universal, e.g. *man* and *horse* which come under *animal*; for this name 'animal' signifies both of these, yet not insofar as they are many and diverse from eachother, but only insofar as they join in the nature of the genus *animal*. Secondly, and more feasibly, it can be taken to exclude that which is caused to be one from many parts, whether these be notional parts (e.g. genus and characteristics, the parts of a definition) or the integral parts of some composite, as when a house is formed from stones and wood.

'ex quibus non fit unum' potest intelligi dupliciter. Uno modo ad excludendum hoc quod multa continentur sub uno universali, sicut homo et equus sub animali; hoc enim nomen 'animal' significat utrumque, non secundum quod sunt multa et differentia ad invicem, sed secundum quod uniuntur in natura generis. Alio modo et melius, ad excludendum hoc quod ex multis partibus fit unum, sive sint partes rationis, sicut genus et differentia, quae sunt partes definitionis, sive sint partes integrales alicuius compositi, sicut ex lapidibus et lignis fit domus: APH 161.

*n*4.72*c*: of a genus ⊖ *generis*] For definition and discussion see *n*4.2411*g* and the references there given.

*n*4.72*d*: characteristics ⊖ *differentiae*] For definition and discussion, see *n*4.22*d*.

*n*4.72*e*: man ⊖ *homo*] '*Corpus*' ⊖ 'body' and '*homo*' ⊖ 'man' are here given as examples of definables in the proper sense of 'definable'; cf. *n*3.800*b*.

*n*4.72*f*: Plato] Compare Anselm's words:

But when we utter the demonstrative forms 'this man' or 'that man' or when we use the proper noun 'Jesus', then we designate a person, constituted from a nature along with a collection of properties whereby *man* in general becomes individual.

Cum vero demonstrative dicimus 'istum vel illum hominem' vel proprio nomine 'Iesum' personam designamus, quae cum natura collectionem habet proprietatum, quibus homo communis fit singulus: *S* II 29.6.9, cf. *S* II 217.18.20.

Samples of Boethius' assertions on individuals are as follows:

The property of each individual is not common to many. Thus that which is proper to Socrates, such as his being bald, snub nosed, and having a tendency to be pot-bellied, and the rest of his bodily forms, along with his way of life and manner of speaking, does not fit in with any other individual.

Proprietas individuorum nulli communis est. Socrates enim proprietas, si fuit calvus, simus, propensa alvo, caeterisque corporis lineamentis, aut morum institutione, aut forma vocis, non conveniebat in alterum: *BCP* 114C.

Those things are most properly individual which are capable of being shown and indicated by the pointing finger, as in the cases of 'this stool' and 'this person approaching'.

Ea maxime sunt individua, quae sub ostensione, indicationeque digiti cadunt, ut hoc scamnum, et hic veniens: *BCP* 114A.

Boethius is prepared to use abstract nouns such as '*Platonitas*' in order to refer to the properties peculiar to one individual, in this case Plato: *Platonitas in unum convenit Platonem* ⊖ Platonicity fits only one object, namely Plato: *BDIG* 463A. He also at this point discusses the situation wherein many individuals are called by the same proper name, and in which we seem to have an alleged proper name which is really a common noun (*BDIG* 464A–B, cf. *APH* 124).

*n*4.72*g*: no unity ⊖ *non fit unum*] All these denials as to the nature of things signified by 'white' amount to the fact that *white* is not, strictly speaking and in the fullest sense, a definable (cf. *n*4.72*a*, *n*3.800*b*).

*n*4.801*a*: having whiteness ⊖ *habens albedinem*] Similarly, of course, '*grammaticus est idem quod sciens grammaticam*' ⊖ 'A literate is identical with a displayer of literacy' (4.31) or '*grammaticus est idem quod habens grammaticam*' ⊖ 'a literate is the same as a haver of literacy' (4.511, 4.700) also hold. Note the alternative *de voce* ⊖ word-centred and *de re* ⊖ thing-centred forms of expression used it the present passage (cf. 4.601–4.603).

Now that the scandal of '*grammaticus est grammatica*' ⊖ '*literate* is literacy' has been resolved (cf. *n*1.000*b*) the discussion contres round the *prima facie* non-scandalous alternatives, involving '*habens*' ⊖ 'having' (or '*sciens*' ⊖ 'knowing / displaying') which have really been available since 4.31, and which have just been mentioned. The question thus arises: why was that scandal not immediately resolved in 4.31? Why was it deliberately maintained (e.g. 4.5022) until 4.61, 4.62? The answer appears to be that in the same way as '*grammaticus est grammatica*' ⊖ '*literate* is literacy', violating *usus loquendi* ⊖ the common course of utterance as it does, and involving parts of speech pertaining to logic, was not covered by ordinary grammar, so also the '*habens*' ⊖ 'having / haver' forms now in question will be shown to involve parts of speech which need not square with the *prima facie* interpretations which might be offered by ordinary grammar (cf. *n*4.31*a*). To have settled the scandal immediately at 4.31 would have given the impression that the rift between ordinary and logical grammar was small or non-existent. Now that the main lesson has been driven home, the kindred but finer point as to the nature of the '*habens*' ⊖ 'having / haver' and similar participial forms can be made.

4.801*b*: such as a body ⊖ *velut corpus*] The connection between *colour* and *body* is not an intra-theoretical one; cf. 4.2411 and notes.

*n*4.801*c*: indeterminately some object having whiteness ⊖ *indeterminate aliquid habens albedinem*] The Student here appears to be attempting to express an approximation to the shared nominal expression 'trm $\langle\omega\rangle$' (using 'ω' for 'whiteness'). It is not a very good approximation, for while

$$[a] : a \in \mathbf{w} \,.\equiv .\, a \in \mathrm{trm}\langle\omega\rangle \qquad (\S 3.11)$$

is true, the use of '*indeterminate aliquid*' ⊖ 'indeterminately something' could make it sound as though he were trying to express something corresponding to the right-hand '*a*' as the name of a very indeterminate something, and this will not do. Whatever the interpretation one may put upon this expression, however, if one grants that 'trm$\langle\omega\rangle$' represents the sort of notion he is presenting here, then it is evident that this is a nominal argument suitable to the lower-order '$\in$', and is hence of a semantical category differing from that of arguments of the higher-order '∈', i.e. arguments which are functors, and which appear to represent better Anselm's own interpretation of '*habens albedinem*' ⊖ 'having whiteness'. 'Cl⟦trm⟨ω⟩⟧', an argument suitable for the completion of the higher-order '∈' would appear to exemplify the sense required by Anselm. (Cf. *n*4.31*a* on '*sciens grammaticam*' ⊖ '... displaying literacy'.)

The points just made would appear to be confirmed by the task undertaken in 4.81 by the Tutor. He there distinguishes between the nominal 'trm⟨ω⟩' (defined §3.11) and the functorial 'Cl⟦trm⟨ω⟩⟧' (cf. §3.11.14), or at any rate comes as near as possible to making this distinction as anyone using only natural language ever could do. The extent to which this is to Anselm's credit may be guaged from the manner in which other and more modern logicians have fumbled around the point now to be made. J. S. Mill seems to miss it altogether when he says 'there is no difference of meaning between *round* and *a round object*, it is only custom which prescribes that on any given occasion one shall be used and not the other': *MSL* I, Ch. 2, §2. Cook-Wilson comes very near to Anselm's '*albus est habens albedinem*' ⊖ 'white is having whiteness' but does not succeed in making his elucidation of an expression such as 'having whiteness' as clear as that provided by Anselm: '"Heavy" is only the adjectival form which is the word equivalent of the participial form "having heaviness". It does not, of course, mean the objective fact symbolised by the noun form "(the) having heaviness"': *WJC* 397.

A final remark as to translations from the Latin at this point in the text: it is on account of the Student's correctly motivated striving for generality that he speaks of the 'indeterminately something' mentioned above. In order to reproduce and go along with this striving it would clearly be incorrect to give a personal ('who') translation to the '*qui*' of '*qui habet albedinem*' in the present context. The grammatical accident whereby the nominative masculine form of the Latin adjective is used in discussions of its meaning clearly cannot be allowed, here or elsewhere, to obtrude in a discussion wherein one of the arguers (the Student) wants to make that adjective's reference entirely neutral and colourless (hence his '*indeterminate aliquid*' ⊖ 'indeterminately something') and wherein the other arguer wants to depict the adjective in this context as not having a referent at all (since it is a functor); cf. *HDG.* §2.32, and *n*3.6333*a*, *n*3.701*a* of the present commentary.

*n*4.8020*a*: or that which has not whiteness ⊖ *aut qui non habet*] The Tutor's reply to the present argument will consist in showing, in effect, that 'Cl⟦trm⟨ω⟩⟧' ('... *habens albedinem*' ⊖ '... having whiteness') rather than 'trm⟨ω⟩' ('*qui habet albedinem*' ⊖ 'that which has whiteness') is here in question (4.810–4.8121; cf. §3.11.14 for definitions of the interpretative forms just suggested).

*n*4.8020*b*: that which has whiteness ⊖ *qui habet albedinem*] This sentence, which could be represented as being of the form

$$[a]: a \in \mathbf{w} \,.\equiv.\, a \in \mathrm{trm}\langle\omega\rangle \qquad (\S 3.11)$$

is true, but is irrelevant to the question of the signification of 'white' in the sense in which Anselm understands 'signification' (see 4.810).

*n*4.8020*c*: must needs be something ⊖ *non nisi aliquid est*] That is to say:

$$[a]: a \in \mathbf{w} \,.\supset.\, \mathrm{ob}(a) \qquad (\S 3.3)$$

This, once again, is perfectly true, but beside the point (see 4.810).

*n*4.8021*a*: something having whiteness ⊖ *aliquid habens albedinem*] This further contention involves the confusion of two sorts of negation. This confusion is often discussed by medieval logicians. On its forerunners, successors, and on Anselm's opinion on connected topics, see *n*4.813*b*.

*n*4.810*a*: that which has ⊖ *qui habet*] In 4.8020 the Student has shown that everything white is an object (cf. *n*4.8020*c*) as well as that

$$\mathbf{w} \bigcirc \mathrm{trm}\langle\omega\rangle \qquad (\S 3.9.11)$$

is true, and these correspond respectively to the '*aliquid*' ⊖ 'something' and the '*qui habet albedinem*' ⊖ 'that which has whiteness' of the Tutor's present summary of what the Student had to say. The Tutor's point is that although the Student's statements made at 4.8020 are passably true, they are beside the point (cf. *n*4.801*a*, *n*4.31*a* on the parallel case of '*habens grammaticam*' ⊖ '... having literacy'). No further mention is made of the '*indeterminate*' ⊖ 'indeterminately' of 4.801.

*n*4.810*b*: the expression *something* or *that which has* ⊖ *hoc quod dicitur aliquid aut qui habet*] As remarked in *n*4.801*c*, the Tutor's task is now to distinguish between the nominal expression ('trm⟨ω⟩') to which the Student has been adverting, and the functorial expression ('Cl⟦trm⟨ω⟩⟧') after which the Tutor is striving. Only the Latin expression '*habens albedinem*' is at their disposal for the expression of both, at least initially, since the two protagonists agree that here is the meaning of '*albus*' ⊖ 'white'.

The discourse is now being moved in the direction of talk about the meaning of the name '*albus*' ⊖ 'white' (i.e. *de voce* ⊖ word-centred talk) instead of remaining at the *de re* ⊖ thing-centred level with which the present speech begins (cf. 4.601, 4.603). In spite of this movement, however, the words which now follow in the text make it probable, and 4.811 makes it certain, that the *de re* ⊖ thing-centred correlate of the meaning of 'white', but at the level of the higher order '∊' as opposed to at the level of the name-flanked lower-order '∊', is what Anselm is trying to express at this point.

The form of the sentence on which comment is now being made is, incidentally, apt enough to bring out the fact that the '... *habens albedinem*' ⊖ '... having whiteness' to which Anselm is attempting to draw attention is not the same part of speech as the nominal '*sciens grammaticam*' ⊖ 'displayer of literacy' ('trm⟨γ⟩') of '*omne sciens grammaticam est grammaticum*' ⊖ 'every displayer of literacy is literate' which has figured in the dialogue on a previous occasion (4.24120). Indeed, the present form may be more than merely incidental, since '*omnis qui est albus est qui habet albedinem*' ⊖ 'Every thing-which-is-white is that-which-has-whiteness' may be drawn from it, and it is exactly in this way that '*omne sciens grammaticam est grammaticum*' ⊖ 'Every displayer of literacy is literate' can be construed in order to show forth the nominal nature of its arguments. Thus it can be construed as '*omnis qui habet grammaticam est grammaticus*' ⊖ 'Every thing-which-has-literacy is literate' (cf. *n*4.801*c* on this translation). Anselm is at present saying, in effect, that sentences of this form, with their nominal arguments, are not the ones in question in the discussion which is now taking place.

*n*4.810*c*: contains ⊖ *continet*] In terms of the functors definable in

Ontology the present '*continet*' ⊖ 'contains' might be represented either as '⊂' (§3.4) or as '∈⊂⟦ ⟧' (§3.14.15). In other words the present sentence could be either

$$\mathbf{h} \subset \mathbf{a}$$

or

$$\mathrm{Cl}[\![\mathbf{h}]\!] \in \subset [\![\mathbf{a}]\!]$$

which by §3.53 are inferentially equivalent. However, the facts that no quantifiers such as 'all' occur in the text, and that definitional discussion (cf. *n*3.800*b*) is now being alluded to, suggest that the second is intended. Anselm's denial, in 4.811, that '*aliquid*' ⊖ 'something' is involved in '*habens albedinem*' ⊖ 'having / haver of whiteness' (at least insofar as the latter is an account of the meaning of 'white') strongly confirms this suggestion; this denial points to a realisation that '*habens albedinem*' ⊖ 'having / haver of whiteness') is not to be construed as a name.

*n*4.810*d*: is ⊖ *est*] If the suggestions of the preceding note are correct, then this '*est*' ⊖ 'is' is the same as that of '*grammaticus est grammatica*' ⊖ '*literate* is literacy', i.e. the higher-order '∈' (cf. *n*1.000*b*).

*n*4.810*e*: so also *white* is ⊖ *ita albus sit*] It is possible to contend that the expression '*albus est aliquid habens albedinem*' ⊖ '*white* is something having whiteness' which the Tutor is here attributing to the Student as the latter's interpretation of '*albus est idem quod habens albedinem*' ⊖ '*White* is identical with ... having whiteness' (4.801) is, given the semantical categories of the two arguments of the '*est*' ⊖ 'is', an ill-formed expression. In terms of the functors definable in Ontology it amounts to

$$\mathrm{Cl}[\![\mathrm{trm}\langle\omega\rangle]\!] \in \mathrm{trm}\langle\omega\rangle$$

or to

$$\mathrm{Cl}[\![\mathbf{w}]\!] \in \mathrm{trm}\langle\omega\rangle$$

In either case the two arguments of the '∈' are of disparate semantical category. Thus should the '∈' be taken to be of higher order (§3.15) then it should not have a nominal expression such as 'trm⟨ω⟩' (§3.11) as an argument. If, on the other hand that '∈' is of lower order, then it should not have the functor 'Cl⟦trm⟨ω⟩⟧' as its argument.

The grounds for this opinion can easily be drawn from the considerations outlined in *n*4.31*a*, but as the latter draws in part upon the assumption that the present suggestion is correct, it may be worth-while to give an independent summary of the position. Thus, when the *significatio* ⊖ meaning of '*grammaticus*' ⊖ 'literate' is being discussed, the sentence '*grammaticus est grammatica*' ⊖ '*literate* is literacy' is seriously put forward as a logical expression of the findings in that matter; but this clearly sins against *usus loquendi* ⊖ the common course of utterance (4.2341, 4.5022), i.e. involves parts of speech of which the grammar of pre-theoretical speech can give no account. However, once the disquiet aroused by such a sin has been somewhat calmed by the explanations provided at 4.5 and 4.6, the example is changed to that of '*albus*' ⊖ 'white' which is at present in question. Here, in consequence of an alternative available since 4.31, the '*albus est albedo*' ⊖ '*white* is whiteness' which follows the pattern of '*grammaticus est grammatica*' ⊖ '*literate* is literacy' is ignored and displaced by '*albus est habens albedinem*' ⊖ '*white* is ... having whiteness'. In spite of this change, however, the '*est*' ⊖ 'is' of the latter is still the same functor as the '*est*' ⊖ 'is' of '*grammaticus est grammatica*' ⊖ '*literate* is literacy', since the same question of meaning is still being discussed. This 'is' must hence be the functor represented by the higher-order '∈', which has functors and not names as its arguments. One obvious natural-language fashion in which to bring out the functorhood of the arguments of such a higher-order '∈' is to deny that they signify objects, determinate or indeterminate, i.e. to deny that they are names. This is exactly the denial which Anselm will make in the text which now follows (4.811).

Thus the Tutor will say that in the present context, i.e. in a discussion around *per se* ⊖ precisive signification, the expression '*habens albedinem*' ⊖ 'having / haver of whiteness' is not to be interpreted as '*aliquid habens albedinem*' ⊖ 'something having whiteness', thereby denying to the former the nominal side of its participial nature – a side which in other contexts would allow it to be used as a name (like the '*sciens grammaticam*' ⊖ 'displayer of literacy' of '*omne sciens grammaticam est grammaticum*' ⊖ 'every displayer of literacy is literate' (4.2412, cf. *n*4.810*b*, *n*4.31*a*)).

In the present context, therefore, '*habens albedinem*' ⊖ '... having whiteness', as an argument of the higher-order '∈', should be seen as 'Cl⟦trm⟨ω⟩⟧', and not as the name-like 'trm⟨ω⟩'. The sentence at present undergoing comment, i.e. '*albus est aliquid habens albedinem*' ⊖ '*white* is something having whiteness' is being criticised by the Tutor; the grounds of his criticism of this outwardly grammatically impeccable sentence can only lie in the inappropriateness (given the context) of the parts of speech involved, since that same sentence can perfectly well be interpreted, if one neglects that context, as

$$\mathbf{w} \bigcirc \mathrm{trm}\langle\omega\rangle$$

(cf. *n*4.8020*b*). But one has on the one hand the Tutor's denials at the opening of the present section (4.810) and in the next section (4.811) that he is concerned with '*aliquid*' ⊖ 'something' or '*qui habet*' ⊖ 'that which has' in respect of '*albus*' ⊖ 'white'. These denials yield the non-nominal functorial form 'Cl⟦trm⟨ω⟩⟧' or 'Cl⟦**w**⟧' as the first argument of '*est*' ⊖ 'is' in '*albus est aliquid habens albedinem*' ⊖ '*white* is something having whiteness'. Yet at the same time the '*aliquid*' ⊖ 'something' of '*aliquid habens albedinem*' ⊖ 'something having whiteness' in this same sentence is plainly intended to bring out the nominal form of the second argument (i.e. 'trm⟨ω⟩') of the same '*est*' ⊖ 'is'. Hence whether one interprets that '*est*' ⊖ 'is' as being of the higher or lower order, one has in either case an ill-assorted pair of arguments, yielding syntactical nonsense.

Anselm's contention that logical assertions may involve novel parts of speech (i.e. diverse from *usus loquendi* ⊖ the current course of utterance or at least not to be taken at the *prima facie* value which they would display in the current course of utterance) therefore still stands. Nevertheless, the effort involved in bringing out exactly where that novelty lies in '*albus est habens albedinem*' ⊖ '*white* is having whiteness' is much greater than that involved when the glaringly obvious novelty of '*grammaticus est grammatica*' ⊖ 'literate is literacy' is in question.

*n*4.811*a*: signifies none of these things ⊖ *nihil horum significat*] The 'necessities' here mentioned appear to be of different sorts. Since *colour* is extra-theoretical in relation to *body* (cf. 4.4211) the necessity of the first example (*omne animal necesse est coloratum* ⊖ every animal is necessarily coloured) appears to arise from universal factual truth or from associational compulsion (4.4211). On the other hand the necessity of every animal's being rational or irrational appears to be connected with the principle of the excluded middle, and is hence an exemplification of logical necessity. However, in view of the context, the general point is clear enough: the Tutor wishes to point out that he is not concerned with objects as such, or with dispositions generated by habit and custom, but with *meaning*. In our terms, only theses at the level of the higher-order '∈' (as opposed to the lower-order '∈') are relevant here. Given the connection between *significatio* ⊖ meaning and *intelligere* ⊖ to understand (cf. *n*3.101*a*), Abelard's discussion of propositional commitment (*A* 153.33–157.12) with its contrast between *res ipsae* ⊖ actual things and *intellectus* ⊖ understanding, appears to represent an analogous facet of the same topic.

*n*4.811*b*: 'white' need not signify these facts ⊖ *non tamen necesse est ut albus hoc significet*] Here is drawn a clear distinction between truths at the level of the lower-order '∈' and 'ob( )' (cf. *n*4.8020*b*, *n*4.8020*c*) and those which come within the ambit of *significatio* ⊖ meaning, and which involve the higher-order '∈', e.g. the '*albus est habens albedinem*' ⊖ '*white* is ... having whiteness' now undergoing scrutiny. The nominal arguments of the former sorts of truth do not require the amendment of the latter to '*albus est aliquid habens albedinem*' ⊖ '*white* is something having whiteness' as a consequence. True, according to *usus loquendi* ⊖ the current course of utterance, one may construe '*albus est habens albedinem*' ⊖ '[a] white [object] is [having] / a-haver-of whiteness' as '*albus est aliquid habens albedinem*' ⊖ 'a white [object] is something having whiteness', but in a discussion of *significatio* ⊖ meaning such a construction is out of place. It can be shown to be out of place in either of two ways, both of which have been considered above, i.e. it may either be irrelevant or it may be nonsense (cf. *n*4.810*e*).

Anselm's expulsion of '*aliquid*' ⊖ 'something', and hence of reference to objects, from the account of the *meaning* of '*albus*' ⊖ 'white' is entirely consonant with his distinction between appellation and signification (4.232–4.2341). Signifying is not calling, referring, or naming, and hence does not required an account of *something* named (4.234). However, this expulsion becomes immensely significant in relation to a topic only lightly touched on in the previous notes, i.e. Anselm's position in the discussion of 'universals'. It is nevertheless plain that much of the dialogue has in fact been dealing with aspects of the whole group of problems which are usually so disconcertingly lumped together under this heading.

The significance mentioned extends as far as the very example, namely '*albus*' ⊖ 'white', here being used, and the details of its discussion by the Student in 4.80. In the first place white is the colour of the horse mentioned in the example of 4.421–4.424. In the second place the Student mentions, but denies, the position that 'body' is part of the meaning of 'white' (4.4211), but later suggests the 'indeterminately something' as an explicit substitute for 'body' (4.801). This suggestion is now undergoing rejection by the Tutor. Consider now the following well-known passage from Anselm's *Epistola de Incarnatione Verbi* 1:

Those contemporary logicians of ours, heretics of logic indeed, who consider universal substances to be just the breath of an utterance, and who identify colour with the object coloured, and human wisdom with the soul, should be totally blasted out from the discussion of spiritual problems. In their minds the reason, which should be ruler and judge of all things that are within man, is so caught up in bodily imaginings that it cannot disentangle itself from them, nor is it capable of distinguishing such imaginings from those things which should simply and solely be the objects of theory. For how can he who does not yet understand how many men are specifically one *man* be capable of grasping how, in that most hidden and high nature, several persons, each of which is wholly god, can be one god? And how can he whose mind is so fogged as to be incapable of distinguishing between his horse and its colour be capable of discriminating between one god and his many relationships?

Illi utique nostri temporis dialectici, immo dialecticae haeretici, qui non nisi flatum vocis putant universales esse substantias, et qui colorem non aliud queunt quam corpus, nec sapientiam hominis aliud quam animam, prorsus a spiritualium quaestionum disputatione sunt exsufflandi. In eorum quippe animabus ratio, quae et princeps et iudex debet omnium esse quae sunt in homine, sic est in imaginationibus corporalibus obvoluta, ut ex eis se non possit evolvere, nec ab ipsis ea quae ipsa sola et pura contemplari debet, valeat discernere. Qui enim nondum intelligit quomodo plures homines in specie sint unus homo: qualiter in illa secretissima et altissima natura comprehendet quomodo plures personae, quarum singula quaeque perfectus est deus, sint unus deus? Et cuius mens obscura est ad diiudicandum inter equum suum et colorem eius: qualiter discernet inter unum deum et plures relationes eius? S II 9.21–10.9.

This passage has been quoted countless times in order to demonstrate Anselm's 'realism' in the matter of universals. Yet in fact herein recur the familiar points which have been recalled above. *De Grammatico* has shown exactly what is involved in distinguishing between a horse and its colour. The Student of the dialogue has, in fact, in 4.801, got well beyond identifying a body as its colour, so that the Tutor may carry on his campaign against the 'indeterminately something'.

Most of the other apparently new features of this passage can quite easily be accounted for in terms of the doctrine of *De Grammatico*. Thus '*universales substantias*' ⊖ 'universal substances' is surely a reference to 'secondary substances' as opposed to individuals, i.e. it need be no more 'realist' than are the arguments of the higher-order '∈' such as 'Cl⟦**h**⟧'. Again, '*quomodo plures homines in specie sint unus homo*' ⊖ 'how man men can be specifically one *man*' can be understood in the light of the following characterisation of a higher-order 'there is exactly one ...':

.1 $[\varphi]: \text{ob}\{\varphi\} . \equiv . [\exists\psi] . \varphi \in \psi$

which is analogous to §3.3. Now in contrast to what holds in the case of the lower-order '∈', one has from §3.22 and §3.56 the following thesis:

.2 $[\exists\varphi] . \varphi \in \varphi$

Thus, given the '**h**' for '*homo*' ⊖ 'man' one has as an instance drawn from .1 and .2 the thesis:

.3 ob {Cl⟦**h**⟧}

i.e. the required sense of 'There is exactly one *man*' where the 'reference' is to the species *man* or to the secondary substance *man*. This excursion into the higher-order '∈' is not at all alien to Anselm's general approach in the present dialogue, and in general there is not one statement in the passage quoted which cannot usefully be related to the doctrine of *De Grammatico*. It would be tedious to run through this coherence in detail, but when the distinction between signification and appellation is recalled and coupled with the present purging of the meaning of '*albus*' ⊖ 'white' of any element of object-hood at the level of the lower-order '∈' represented by '*aliquid*' ⊖ 'something', it is difficult to see how that text could ever be used as one of the keystones of the thesis that Anselm considered universals to be objects in a 'realist' sense.

There would thus seem to be here no reason for supposing that Anselm maintains the doctrine that universals are separate entities to be numbered as additions to the concrete individuals in the world. They may, in a sense, be '*res*' ⊖ 'things', but it is quite clear that none of them is '*aliquid*' ⊖ 'something' in a sense associable with the lower-order '∈'. The words of John of Salisbury, whom no-one would maintain to have been an exaggerated realist, might well be corollaries of Anselm's own statements at the present point in the dialogue:

Hence, granted that there are universals, or even that they are things, if this will satisfy the sticklers, it still doesn't follow from this admission that there is therefore an increase in the number of things any more than there is a decrease in that number if it is denied that universals are to be numbered among things. A thorough inspection of universals will reveal that while they are numerable, their number is nevertheless such that it cannot be added to the number of individual objects. For in the same way as corporate or other bodies and their heads cannot be totalled up together in the same numeration any more than can the heads and bodies, so also neither do universals constitute additions to individual objects, nor individual objects to universals; on the contrary, a number embraces only those things which are of the same type – things which are naturally shared out in all their variety among particular sorts of objects. There is no such thing as a universal apart from what one comes across in individual objects. Many have searched for the universal as a separate entity, but in the end they have all found themselves empty-handed. This is because the universal apart from individuals is just nothing, except perhaps in the way that truths and the other significates of word-combinations may be said to be something.

Itaque detur ut sint uniuersalia, aut etiam ut res sint, si hoc pertinacibus placet; non tamen ob hoc uerum erit rerum numerum augeri vel minui pro eo quod ista non sunt in numero rerum. Si quis autem uniuersalia seorsim recenseat, numero quidem inueniet esse subiecta, sed cui singularium numerus non aggregatur. Sicut enim collegiis aut corporibus non connumerantur capita, aut capitibus corpora, sic nec uniuersalia singularibus nec singularia numeri accessione uniuersalibus accrescunt; numerus enim dumtaxat illa complectitur que eiusdem rationis sunt et que in singulis rerum generibus natura discreuit. Nichil autem uniuersale est, nisi quod in singularibus inuenitur. Seorsum tamen a multis quesitum est, sed tamen nichil inuenerunt omnes in manibus suis; quoniam seorsum a singularibus nichil est, nisi forte qualia sunt uera aut similia complexorum significata sermonum: SM 101.4.20.

For a more detailed discussion of this question see *HL* §3, *HRE*, *HRG*.

*n*4.8120*a*: is the same as *something white* ⊖ *non est aliud quam aliquid album*] Note the continued alternation of *de voce* ⊖ word-centred and *de re* ⊖ thing-centred formulations which are embodied in the 'signifies' and 'is' which occur here (cf. 4.601–4.603).

n.4.8120*b*: and so on to infinity ⊖ *et hoc infinite*] The sources of Anselm's use of regresses have been traced in *n*4.2414*b* and *n*4.72*a*, and doubtless the same sources inspire the present exercise.

The stages of the argument may be analysed by identifying with '○' (weak identity, defined §3.9) all the occurrences of '*significat*' ⊖ 'signifies' and '*est*' ⊖ 'is' in the equation set up by the Student, i.e. one accepts what has been shown in the foregoing notes to be the level of the Student's discourse: it is at the level of nominal arguments of the lower order '$\in$' rather than at that of functorial arguments of the higher-order '$\in$'. Given the abstract noun which figures in '*aliquid habens albedinem*' ⊖ 'something having whiteness' it seems feasible to construe the latter as 'trm$\langle\omega\rangle$' (§3.11.61), whereas the non-abstract name within '*aliquid album*' ⊖ 'something white' suggests 'trm$\langle\in[\![\mathbf{w}]\!]\rangle$' (§3.11.12.60) as its counterpart. One thus has

(i) *albus significat aliquid habens albedinem* ⊖ *white* signifies something having whiteness, i.e.

$$w \bigcirc \mathrm{trm}\langle\omega\rangle$$

the latter being the *de re* ⊖ thing-centred correlate of the Latin sentence. Again, one has:

(ii) *aliquid habens albedinem non est aliud quam aliquid album* ⊖ something having whiteness is identical with something white, i.e.

$$\mathrm{trm}\langle\omega\rangle \bigcirc \mathrm{trm}\langle\in[\![\mathbf{w}]\!]\rangle$$

From these two it follows that

(iii) *albus significat aliquid album* ⊖ *white* signifies something white, i.e.

$$\mathbf{w} \bigcirc \mathrm{trm}\langle\in[\![\mathbf{w}]\!]\rangle$$

But from (iii), by using the identity therein given in order to effect continued substitutions of 'trm$\langle\in[\![\mathbf{w}]\!]\rangle$' for '**w**' one has an infinite regress; e.g. the first stage of that regress is:

(iv) $\mathbf{w} \bigcirc \mathrm{trm}\langle\in[\![\mathrm{trm}\langle\in[\![\mathbf{w}]\!]\rangle]\!]\rangle$

and this can plainly be continued to infinity.

Thus interpreted, the argument that a regress is generated under such circumstances is hence perfectly sound. However, does the possibility of such a regress prove that the Student's supposition is to be rejected? The adoption of the Tutor's alternative (in its natural language) would avoid the regress, since given only '*albus est habens albedinem*' ⊖ '*White* is ... having whiteness', where is no obvious way of getting an occurrence of '*albus*' ⊖ 'white' as a proper part of the second argument of the '*est*' ⊖ 'is' of this sentence, and so no way of performing the substitutions necessary for a regress. Similarly, if that alternative were rendered at the level of language required by the Tutor, i.e. were '*albus est habens albedinem*' ⊖ '*white* is ... having whiteness' to be interpreted as:

(v) $\mathrm{Cl}[\![\mathbf{w}]\!] \in \mathrm{Cl}[\![\mathrm{trm}\langle\omega\rangle]\!]$ (§3.11.14.15)

then while the counterparts of (ii) and (iii) above would again be derivable in the artificial language, thus:

(vi) $\mathrm{Cl}[\![\mathrm{trm}\langle\omega\rangle]\!] \in \mathrm{Cl}[\![\mathrm{trm}\langle\in[\![\mathbf{w}]\!]\rangle]\!]$
(vii) $\mathrm{Cl}[\![\mathbf{w}]\!] \in \mathrm{Cl}[\![\mathrm{trm}\langle\in[\![\mathbf{w}]\!]\rangle]\!]$

the regress could not be generated by the substitution of the first argument of the higher-order '∈' of (vii) for any proper part of the second argument which is equiform with that first argument, since there is now no such equiformity; such a substitution was, however, possible in the case of (iii).

To this extent, therefore, the intuitions of Anselm, as reflected in his refusal to allow '*habens albedinem*' ⊖ '... having whiteness' to become '*aliquid habens albedinem*' ⊖ 'something having whiteness' are remarkably confirmed. Reciprocally, these results analogous to Anselm's own, but now obtained by the use of the higher-order '∈', i.e. the functor having the semantical category attributed to his problematical '*est*' ⊖ 'is', tend to confirm that the attribution was justified. The possibility of a regress does in fact reflect the use of a functor of inappropriate semantical category (in the sense that it is not at the level of the higher-order '∈') and to that extent the rejection of the Student's equation is underpinned. However, it is not made clear in Anselm's text that this is the precise ground of the rejection. The regress is taken as a symptom of sheer defect rather than mere inappropriateness to the purpose in hand, and the exact nature of that supposed defect is left in the dark. In the artificial language, of course, the existence of some regress or other need not in itself be a symptom of any defect whatsoever. In point of fact all of the sentences (i) to (vii) are inferentially equivalent relative to the definitions available in Ontology, so that a regress could be generated from (vii) by recourse to (iii), for instance.

*n*4.8121*a*: is having ⊖ *habens est*] Here is a transformation of a predication *de secundo adiacente* ⊖ of a second component into a predication *de tertio adiacente* ⊖ of a third component. The following passage from Boethius' letter commentary on *De Interpretatione* deals with such transformations:

There are some propositions which involve predication by means of 'is'. There are others in which we cannot effect predication by means of the verb 'is', as when we assert 'A man walks' and 'A man runs'. But in point of fact it makes no difference whatsoever whether, as suggested, one says 'A man runs' and 'A man walks', or whether we effect the predication by means of 'is'; for it amounts to the same thing to assert 'A man runs' and 'A man walks' as to assert 'A man is running' and 'A man is walking'. Hence in propositions of this sort it makes no difference whether the assertion is made in terms of the verb 'is' or of some verb additional to and other than 'is'.

Sunt ... quaedam propositiones quae cum 'est' praedicantur. Aliae vero quas cum 'est' verbo praedicare non possumus, ut in eo quod dicimus 'homo ambulat', 'homo currit'. Sed in his nihil differt an ita quis dicat, ut dicitur, id est 'homo currit', et 'homo ambulat', an cum 'est' verbo eas praedicet; idem namque est dicere 'homo currit' et 'homo ambulat', tanquam si dicatur 'homo currens est', 'homo ambulans est'. Quocirca nihil differt in huiusmodi propositionibus utrum cum 'est' verbo, an praeter 'est' adiuncto verbi actu proponatur: *BDIL* 348D; cf. *KSS* 91–2 and *n*3.431*a*.

On the assumption (cf. *n*4.8120*b*) that the equations with which we are now concerned involve functors having names as arguments (as opposed to those having verbs as arguments) the first sentence of the present speech is the counterpart of

(i) $\mathbf{w} \bigcirc \mathrm{trm}\langle \omega \rangle$ (§3.9.11)

It would, of course, be more natural to translate the present '*est habens*' as 'is a haver', rather than as 'is having'. However, since the previously used '*habens albedinem*', translated as 'having whiteness' in order to show its non-nominal status, is to be invoked (cf. *n*4.8121*c*), consistency in the English version requires the maintenance of this participial form here.

*n*4.8121*b*: that which is having whiteness ⊖ *qui albedinem habens est*] The equivalence of '*habet*' ⊖ 'has' and '*habens est*' ⊖ 'is having' now yields the '*albedinem habens*' of the present speech, so leading to the next equation.

*n*4.8121*c*: this phrase is equisignificant with *white* ⊖ *non aliud significat haec oratio quam album*] This is a reference back to the equivalence which opened the discussion (4.801). On the assumption that the equations remain at the level of the noun-flanked '○' (§3.9), no logical change from the situation delineated in (i) of *n*4.8121*a* has really taken place. Of course, given the Tutor's exclusion of '*aliquid*' ⊖ 'something' from '... *habens albedinem*' ⊖ '... having whiteness', the present assertion, with its '*significat*' ⊖ 'signifies' ought to have the following *de re* ⊖ thing-centred correlate:

(i) $\mathrm{Cl}[\![\mathbf{w}]\!] \in \mathrm{Cl}[\![\mathrm{trm}\langle\omega\rangle]\!]$ (§3.11.14.15)

For the regress to arise, however, the level of language cannot be assumed to have changed in this way.

*n*4.8121*d*: that which is white ⊖ *qui albus est*] By means of the backhanded procedure described in *n*4.8121*c*, the Tutor has now obtained:

(i) $\mathbf{w} \bigcirc \mathrm{trm}\langle \in [\![\mathbf{w}]\!]\rangle$

From this, and (i) of *n*4.8121*a*, the same regress as that initiated in (iv) of *n*4.8120*b* is generated. The remarks made in the last-mentioned note on such a regress also apply here.

*n*4.8121*e*: and so on to infinity ⊖ *et sic in infinitum*] Thus ends the argument against the thesis defended by the Student in 4.802, i.e. that '*albus est habens albedinem*' ⊖ '*White* is ... having whiteness' is to be interpreted as '*album est aliquid habens albedinem*' ⊖ '*white* is something having whiteness'. The refutation has involved two stages: first the Student's interpretation is said to represent a truth, but one which is irrelevant to the discussion of signification (4.810, 4.8121). (Alternatively, it could be interpreted as logical nonsense, as indicated in *n*4.810*e*). Secondly, the two regresses (4.8120, 4.8121) are shown to result from the Student's supposition. Although the regresses obtain their results by what is probably a mixture of acute intuition and luck (cf. *n*4.8120*b*), they exemplify the presupposition that the logician's language used in connection with questions of signification should be perfect in the sense that such regresses ought not to occur.

A remarkable parallel to the present argument, using the same example and obtaining the same result, is found in the late twelfth-century *Summa Sophisticorum Elenchorum*. There it is pointed out that if *white* is taken to be identical with *white thing*, or if the word 'white' is explained by the words 'white thing', then in both cases we get a regress. The conclusion is that 'having whiteness' is the proper definitional equivalent of 'white': *DLM* I 412.

*n*4.8121*f*: repetition of *something, something* ⊖ *saepe sit aliquid aliquid*] This is a reference to the result of the first (4.8120) of the present pair of regresses.

*n*4.813*a*: when it is asserted ⊖ *si quis autem dicit*] The Student's second argument in favour of '*albus est aliquid habens albedinem*' ⊖ '*white* is something having whiteness' is now to be resolved.

*n*4.813*b*: not-something ⊖ *non aliquid*] The equation of 'nothing' ('*nihil*') with 'non-something' ('*non aliquid*') which occurs here is also to be found in *Monologion* 19 (*S* I 34.23) and *De Casu Diaboli* 11 (*S* I 249.6.7), and is a common medieval equation; cf. *HLM* III §4. It is an equation which might appear to raise quite crucial issues for someone who, like Anselm, is prepared to hold that *voces non significant nisi res* ⊖ utterances only signify things (4.5143), were it not for the fact that the present phase of the dialogue is already confirming that these '*res*' ⊖ 'things' need not be *aliquid* ⊖ something. However, for some of his predecessors the doctrine that seems to be implied by the principle quoted, certainly carried difficulty with it. Thus a simple combination of that principle with the equation of '*nihil*' ⊖ 'nothing' and '*non-aliquid*' ⊖ 'not-something' would seem to make '*nihil*' ⊖ 'nothing' into a non-significant utterance. This is because on one interpretation of '*res*' ⊖ 'thing', if '*nihil*' ⊖ 'nothing' is the same as '*non-aliquid*' ⊖ 'not-something', then '*nihil*' ⊖ 'nothing' cannot be said to signify any *res* ⊖ things: how then can '*nihil*' ⊖ 'nothing' be said to signify anything at all?

A name is an utterance. But some utterances are significant, others signify nothing. A name, however, signifies that of which it is the name.	*Nomen est ... vox. Sed vocum aliae sunt quae significant, aliae quae nihil significant. Nomen autem significat id cuius nomen est: BDIL* 301C.
If some utterance designates nothing, then it is not a name, for if it is the name of no thing, it certainly cannot be said to be a name.	*Si vox aliqua nihil designat, nullus nomen est; quae si nullius nomen est, nec nomen quidem esse dicitur: BDIG* 408D.

It is in such terms that Boethius, commenting on *De Interpretatione*, conveys the doctrine that utterances (and in particular names) cannot be significant unless they signify something. Thus, whether '*scindapsus*' is a name or not depends on whether it is a sign for something (*BDIL* 303C–D, cf. *BDIG* 423B). The discussion of signification in such terms, coupled with the classification of '*nihil*' ⊖ 'nothing' as a noun, can easily lead to the paradoxical conclusion that it is not a significant utterance.

In St. Augustine's *De Magistro* II, 3, the doctrine that words are signs, and that signs *are* signs only because they signify something, is shown to be apparently falsified by the case of '*nihil*' ⊖ 'nothing':

Augustine: We agree that words are signs?	*Constat ergo inter nos verba signa esse.*
Adeodatus: We do.	*Constat.*
Aug.: But how so? Can a sign be a sign if it does not signify something?	*Quid? Signum, nisi aliquid significet, potest esse signum?*
Ad.: It cannot ... But what does 'nothing' signify apart from that which is not?	*Non potest ... 'Nihil' – quid aliud significat, nisi id quod non est?*
Aug.: Perhaps what you say is true, but I'm prevented from agreeing with you because of what you admitted above, namely that a sign is only a sign if it signifies something; now that which does not exist cannot in any sense be something. Hence the second word in the line we are considering is not a sign, since it does not signify anything, and so we falsely concluded that all words are signs, or that all signs signify something.	*Verum fortasse dicis: sed revocat me ab assentiendo quod superius concessisti, non esse signum nisi aliquid significat: quod autem non est nullo modo esse aliquid potest. Quare secundum verbum in hoc versu non est signum, quia non significat aliquid: et falsa inter nos constitit, quod omnia verba signa sint, aut omne signum aliquid significet: PL* 32, 1196.

Fredegisus of Tours, about 800 A.D., in his *Epistola de nihilo et tenebris* (*PL* 105, 751 et seq., part reproduced in *S* I 249 *n*) produces what could well stand as the classical statement of one of the extreme positions to which considerations of this sort can lead, namely that nothing is something, since 'nothing' being significant, must signify something (cf. *HL* §6.62).

It is in *De Casu Diaboli* 10, 11, and 12 that Anselm shows his familiarity with the type of argument described. Having identified evil ('*malum*') and nothing ('*nihil*') in Ch. 9, he broaches the question of the signification of these names in Ch. 10: the utterance 'evil' is certainly a significant one, and hence signifies. But it can only signify something. How then can evil be nothing if its name signifies something? (*S* I 247.19.21). The next chapter transfers the discussion to the topic of 'nothing', since if the case of this name can be settled, clearly the same solution will be applicable to 'evil' (*S* I 248.9.12). The Student of that dialogue sketches the difficulties. If '*nihil*. ⊖ 'nothing' does not signify something, then it is no name; but it is a name, so how can it signify nothing and at the same time signify something (*S* I 248.15.30)?

The essence of the Tutor's resolution of their difficulty lies in denying that '*nihil*' ⊖ 'nothing' is a name, insofar as its significative functions are concerned. Thus, given that '*nihil*' ⊖ 'nothing' can be equated with '*non-aliquid*' ⊖ 'not-something' (*S* I 249.6.7, and cf. 4.813) this infinite name (cf. *n*4.813*c*) like '*non-homo*' ⊖ 'non-man', has a two-fold significative function, remotive and constitutive, neither of which is naming. Remotively (*removendo*) '*nihil*' ⊖ 'nothing' effects the complete removal from its import of every object which is something: constitutively (*constituendo*) therefore, the meaning which it establishes is 'no thing at all' or 'no thing that is something' (*S* I 249.6.17; compare '"*non-aliquid*" *vox nullam rem aut quod sit aliquid significat*' ⊖ 'The utterance "non-something" signifies no thing nor anything that is something' (*S* I 249.17, cf. *S* I 249.9, 250.3) with Peter of Spain's '"*Nihil*" *enim significat idem quod* "*nulla res*"' ⊖ '"Nothing" signifies the same as does "no thing"' (*HSL* 12.28)). In the first (remotive) case, '*nihil*' ⊖ 'nothing' signifies something; in the second it signifies nothing:

For these various reasons, the utterance 'non-something' in a certain fashion signifies *thing* and *something*. For it signifies them remotively while not signifying them constitutively. This is why the name 'nothing' which eliminates all that is something has a twofold significative function; remotively it does not signify nothing, but something, and constitutively it does not signify something, but nothing.

Haec vox 'non-aliquid' his diversis rationibus aliquatenus significat rem et aliquid, et nullatenus significat rem et aliquid. Significat enim removendo, et non significat constituendo. Hac ratione 'nihil' nomen, quod perimit omne quod est aliquid: et destruendo non significat nihil sed aliquid, et constituendo non significat aliquid sed nihil: *S* I 249.18.22.

The term '*constituere*' ⊖ 'to establish' (along with '*intellectus*' ⊖ 'understanding') which occurs here, and has important historical and theoretical associations, figures also in *De Grammatico* (cf. 4.4233 and notes).

After the equation of '*nihil*' ⊖ 'nothing' and '*non-aliquid*' ⊖ 'non-something' in *Monologion* 19, the fact that '*nihil*' ⊖ 'nothing' thus analysed, may incorporate the negation of a sentence is made clear in the following way. It is pointed out that in order to be true, the sentence '*Nihil me docuit volare*' ⊖ 'Nothing taught me to fly' must be understood as '*Non me docuit aliquid volare*' ⊖ 'It's not that something taught me to fly' (*S* I 34.22.24; cf. *HL* §6.66, *HLM* 86).

However, for someone who, like the Student of *De Casu Diaboli*, wishes to maintain that since '*nihil*' ⊖ 'nothing' is a name, it must have a nominal function, the account outlined will not do. In a passage which is redolent of the Student's position in *De Grammatico* it is argued that the name '*nihil*' ⊖ 'nothing' is said to be a name because it names something, because something is called by that name, yet the constitutive signification suggested provides no such reference:

That something which is in this (constitutive) way signified by this name is not named 'nothing' ... I therefore ask what it is that this name stands for ... It is the name of that the signifying of which causes it to be counted among names, and which is called 'nothing'.

Illud aliquid quod isto modo hoc nomine significatur non nominatur 'nihil' ... Illud igitur quaero quid pro quo hoc nomen ponitur ... Eius quippe nomen est pro cuius significatione inter nomina computatur, et illud vocatur 'nihil': *S* I 250.5.12.

That there is here somewhat the same confusion between meaning and reference which has been countered by *De Grammatico* (4.232–4.2341) becomes even more clear when the companion-problem of '*malum*' ⊖ 'evil' is summarised. An account of what it signifies and of what it *names* is demanded by the Student, the assumption behind the demand evidently being that these two are to be identified:

... how something can be identical with nothing. I make the same queries regarding the name 'evil': what does it signify, and what is it that is named 'evil'?

... quomodo idem sit aliquid et nihil. Illud idem quaero de nomine mali, et de eo quod significat, et quod 'malum' nominatur: *S* I 250.13.16.

The Tutor of *De Casu Diaboli* responds by invoking a distinction similar to that made in *De Grammatico* (4.62), namely that between an utterance considered as a paradigm or exemplar by the grammar of ordinary speech (*secundum formam vocum*, 4.620, *secundum forman vocis*, *S* I 250.22) and the utterance considered in relation to states of affairs as they actually are (*secundum rerum naturam*, 4.620; *secundum rem*, *S* I 250.2.3). He accompanies this distinction by an example common to both texts ('*timere*' ⊖ 'to fear' is active *secundum formam vocis* ⊖ according to the appropriate exemplary rule, but is passive *secundum rem* ⊖ in relation to states of affairs (4.621, *S* I 250.22.23)). Thus, he continues, the use of a word such as 'blindness'' follows the same pattern as the use of 'sight', i.e. it is employed in the same way as a word referring to something positive, whereas in fact the absence of something is in question:

Blindness is said to be *something* if we go by the form of speech employed, when from the point of view of how things are it is not something.

Caecitas dicitur aliquid secundum formam loquendi, cum non sit aliquid secundum rem: *S* I 250.23.24.

In other words, the rules observed in ordinary speaking are in very many cases no guide as to whether reference is actually being made to any existing thing:

Many other things are likewise said to be *something* (if we go by the form of the utterance) whereas they are not something; we just use speech in their respect in the same way as we do in respect of existing things.

Multa quoque alia similiter dicuntur aliquid secundum formam loquendi, quae non sunt aliquid, quoniam sic loquimur de illis sicut de rebus existentibus: *S* I 251.2.

A like reasoning can be extended to the cases of '*nihil*' ⊖ 'nothing' and '*malum*' ⊖ 'evil'. The form of speech which is exemplified in sentences in which they occur can be outwardly identical with that found in sentences making some positive reference. On this account one can only say that in the case of the two words mentioned a quasi-reference is effected:

Evil therefore is indeed nothing, and nothing is not something, even though they are in a certain fashion something on account of our speaking of them as though they were something, as when we say 'He is doing nothing' and 'He is doing evil', or 'What he is doing is nothing' and 'What he is doing is evil' in the same way as we say 'He is doing something' and 'He is doing good', or 'What he is doing is something' and 'What he is doing is good'.

Malum igitur vere est nihil, et nihil non est aliquid: et tamen quodam modo sunt aliquid, quia sic loquamur de his quasi sint aliquid, cum dicimus: nihil vel malum fecit, aut: nihil vel malum est quod fecit: sicut dicimus: aliquid vel bonum fecit, aut: aliquid vel bonum est quod fecit: *S* I 251.8.12.

Such quasi-references are also mentioned when four uses of '*aliquid*' ⊖ 'something' are being distinguished in *SN* (cf. *HL* §6.653).

Like Anselm, Aquinas traces the supposition that '*malum*' ⊖ 'evil' refers to some thing to the identity of the forms of true propositions in which such privation-word occur with the form in which words having a positive reference occur, and uses the same example ('blindness') in order to illustrate his point: *AST* I q.48 art. 2, ad 2.

In *HL* §6.6 (cf. *HNA*) the material described above is further examined and its relation to Anselm's general logical theories is exposed. The way in which later medieval treatment of negation rectified some of Anselm's deficiencies is outlined in *HLM* III §4. Other aspects of the significance of words such as '*res*' ⊖ 'thing' and '*aliquid*' ⊖ 'something' according to Anslem may be seen in the notes on 4.5143 and 4.811.

It may be added that any impression created by the foregoing remarks that Anselm's theory of evil lies in the simple equation of *malum* ⊖ evil and *nihil* ⊖ nothing would be quite mistaken. In addition to the *malum* ⊖ evil which is the absence of some good where that good ought to be (*absentia boni ubi debet aut expedit esse bonum: S* I 251.6.7) he also introduces the notion of *malum incommodum* ⊖ deterimental evil, which is sometimes really some thing (*S* I 274.8.24). *De Conceptu Virginali et de Originali Peccato* 5, 6, *De Concordia* Q 1, ch. 7, also deal with the question of evil. On *per nihil* ⊖ through nothing and *ex nihilo* ⊖ from nothing, see *Monologion* 6. The *facere ex nihilo* ⊖ making out of nothing which is involved in the doctrine of creation is treated in *Monologion* 6, and may be compared with *AST* I q. 45, art. 1 and 2.

*n*4.813*c*: infinite name ⊖ *infinitum nomen*] The notion of 'infinite name' is covered in Boethius' lesser commentary on Aristotle's *De Interpretatione* 3 in the following terms:

Every name signifies one definite thing: for example, when we utter 'man' we don't signify just any substance, but the rational mortal one. The same goes for all other names. Hence he who utters 'non-man' certainly removes *man*. He does not, however, define exactly what he intends to show by this meaningful utterance; a non-man may be a horse, a dog, a stone, and so on for all the things

Omne enim nomen unam rem significat definitam, ut cum dicimus 'homo', substantiam significat nec quamlibet, sed rationalem atque mortalem. Eodem modo et caetera nomina. Qui vero dicit 'non-homo', hominem quidem tollit. Quid autem illa significatione velit ostendere, non definit; potest enim quod homo non est, et equus esse, et canis, et lapis, et caetera quaecumque homo non fuerint. Quare

that are not man. Hence, since by the use of the negative prefix he removes that which can be signified in a definite way, he does not definitely say what he is committed to signifying, and any hearer merely understands a multiple infinity. This is called, he [i.e. Aristotle] says, an infinite name. This is because in saying 'non-man' the latter signifies as many things as are diverse in their definitions from that of *man*.

quoniam id quod definite significare potest, aufert in eo negativa particula, quid vero significare debeat, definite non dicit, sed multa atque infinita unusquisque auditor intelligit. Dicatur, inquit, nomen infinitum. Hoc enim quod dicimus 'non-homo', tam multa significat quam multa sunt quae a definitione hominis disiunguntur: *BDIL* 304D.

In the major commentary on the same work (*BDIG* 424D et seq.) as well as in *De Syllogismo Categorico* (*B* 795D), *Introductio ad Syllogismos Categoricos* (*B* 764D) and *Liber de Divisione* (*B* 882A–B), infinite names are also defined or discussed. There occur in addition lengthy disquisitions on inferences involving such names in both lesser and major commentaries on *De Interpretatione* (*BDIL* 342–354, *BDIG* 520–567). Aquinas' commentary (*APH* 48) deals with the same section of Aristotle's text. Cf. also *HSL* 1.04, *A* 127.8–129.5. All these make it amply clear that the theory that 'The Negative is in every case the class of the elements which are excluded from a well-defined class, but which are, every one of them, positive' (*HMN* 140) which claims to be 'a definite solution to the problem of the Negative which has haunted philosophers from Parmenides to Hegel and Mallik' (ibid.) is scarcely novel.

HLM III §4 may be consulted for general remarks on this kind of topic.

*n*4.813*d*: what has been laid down previously ⊖ *iis quae dicta sunt*] The disjunction which is here approved, i.e. '*significat aliquid habens* [*albedinem*] *aut non significat* [*aliquid habens albedinem*]' ⊖ 'It signifies something having [whiteness] or it's not that it signifies [something having whiteness]' is true in respect of '*albus*' ⊖ 'white' because in fact the first alternative is true, although not in the strict sense of 'signifies' (cf. 4.811).

Thus is rebutted the argument of 4.8021, which relies for its force on a supposed exemplification of the 'Principle of the Excluded Middle', i.e. '[p]. $p \vee {\sim} p$'. It was assumed that '*albus aut aliquid significat habens albedinem aut nihil*' ⊖ '*White* either signifies something having whiteness or nothing' is such an exemplification, and from this it is concluded that since *nothing* cannot have whiteness, 'white' must signify *something* having whiteness. The refutation takes the form of a showing that this assumption does not in fact represent the disjunction of a proposition and its negation (as should be the case if it is to exemplify the Principle of the Excluded Middle), and hence is neither exhaustive of the situation (*non est integra*) nor true (*nec vera*). The reason given for this failure is that since '*nihil*' ⊖ 'nothing' means '*non-aliquid*' ⊖ 'non-something' (cf. *n*4.813*b*) an infinite name (cf. *n*4.813*c*) is being used as one member of the disjunction, with the result that the 'non' which is prefixed to that name is confused with the 'non' which should negate one of the propositional alternants. In other words, Anselm is rightly distinguishing between the nominal negation defined at §3.21 above, and propositional negation. The former forms names from names, the latter forms propositions from propositions: they are therefore plainly not the same part of speech.

De Interpretatione and its commentaries treat of this distinction in detail, the chief texts in Boethius being *BDIL* 342–354 and *BDIG* 520–567. It is also summarised elsewhere, notably *BDIL* 363–4, *BDIG* 447B, *BDIG* 580B–D, and *BDIG* 590B–591C. In the present instance a term within the predicate is negated instead of the whole proposition, i.e. '*significat non aliquid*' ⊖ 'It signifies non-something' is taken to be the negation of '*significat aliquid*' ⊖ 'it signifies something', whereas it should be '*non significat aliquid*' ⊖ 'It's not that it signifies something'. The Tutor's remarks are a reminder of Boethius' doctrine that '*est iustus homo*' ⊖ 'he is a just man' and '*est non iustus homo*' ⊖ 'he is an unjust man' are both affirmative forms, the latter having an infinite name (*non iustus* ⊖ unjust) as part of its predicate. The true negation of '*est iustus homo*' ⊖ 'he is a just man', however, is '*non est iustus homo*' ⊖ 'it's not that he is a just man' (*BDIL* 344–348, esp. 345B, 346B; cf. *APH* 217). The transformations described by Boethius (*BDIL* 348C–349A) and noted in *n*4.8121*a*, are of course presupposed in the case of 'signifies' and other unitary verbs, in order that the distinction between the two cases (the propositional and nominal negation) can be universally extended.

The example of the blind man which occurs in the text illuminates the point at which the negation impinges when it is misplaced in a disjunction of the type described. The Student's mistake is the same as that which lies in interpreting 'The blind man either sees something or nothing' as 'The blind man either sees something or sees non-something', which leaves the blind man seeing in the cases of both alternatives. What are really required are one alternative in which it is said that he sees and one in which it is said that it is not the case that he sees, as in 'The blind man either sees something or does not see something'.

A confusion similar to that of the Student's has to be repaired by an *ad hoc* distinction in *RI* ch. XVI under the guise of the 'primary and secondary occurrences of descriptions in propositions' (*RI* 179). Again, the same chapter of *RI* contains forms of words having exactly the same form as those of the Student's (4.8021) which is now undergoing criticism, e.g. 'the description "x" describes something or describes nothing' (*RI* 170). This springs from the author's use of 'Ψx' as the formal analysis of a propositional form where such an analysis is really inadequate. Lacking the '$\in$' forms of Ontology to show forth the inner structure of 'Ψ', he has, for instance, to parse 'x is not a unicorn' as 'not-Ψx'; the former is at least susceptible of being read so as to involve the negation of the second argument of 'is' (i.e. as being of the form '$x \in \neg(b)$') so that the existence of x is required for its truth, whereas the 'not-Ψx' conveys rather '$\sim(x \in b)$', which can hold either because x does not exist or because, although x exists, it is something other than b. This confusion stems ultimately from the restricted quantification used by Russell and others (cf. §3.21, *LLE*, *HLM* 73–4). A list of medieval appreciations of this point is given in *n*4.813*c*.

*n*4.82*a*: it signifies them equally ⊖ *pariter utrumque significat*] The occasion of the present phase of the discussion has been the Student's request (4.72) for details of the doctrine laid down in 4.714, which doctrine the Student is now reiterating.

*n*4.82*b*: expressed in an incomplex fashion ⊖ *sine complexione dicuntur*] See *n*4.5144*a* for the sources of this expression.

*n*4.82*c*: does not form a single whole ⊖ *non fit unum*] See *n*4.72*a* on the meaning of '*facere unum aliquid*' ⊖ 'to constitute one thing'.

*n*4.83*a*: logicians ⊖ *dialectici*] Who are the contemporary logicians to whom Anselm is here referring? In a section of his *Dialectica* which deals with the same problem of signification as that treated by Anselm in *De Grammatico* (*A* 112–4) Abelard mentions a '*magister V*' as holding what is, in effect, the Student's position as opposed to that of a certain Garmundus whose thesis approximates to that of the Tutor, as far as one can judge (*A* 112.24.28). In the introduction to his edition of the *Dialectica* De Rijk disagrees with Cousin, in that he interprets '*magister V*' to mean '*magister Ulgerius*' and not '*magister Willelmus Campellensis*' (*A* xx). This new interpretation opens the way to tracing a line of succession which stretches back into the lifetime of Anselm (1033–1109) for it is known that in 1096 Master Marbod, of the school of the cathedral chapter of St. Maurice in Angers, was succeeded by one Geoffrey Babio, whose sucessor in 1107 was the '*magister Ulgerius*' now in question (*A* xx). On the other hand Garmundus succeeded Odo of Tournai in 1101 (*A* xxi) and although William of Champeaux may not be the '*magister V*' of the *Dialectica* he was certainly Abelard's master (*A* xxi). The *dialectici* ⊖ logicians to whom Anselm refers may therefore lie at least in any of the three lines of descent suggested by the presence of a discussion in Abelard's *Dialectica* similar to that in *De Grammatico*.

The discussion of the theme of *De Grammatico* is in fact prolonged throughout the Middle Ages and beyond, although sometimes in differing terms. For an example of such parallel cases, see the Ockham-Burleigh version of the debate, as described in *HL* §3.4.

*n*4.83*b*: stubbornly hanging on to them ⊖ *ea pertinaciter teneas*] There is a notable lack of urgency evinced here, a lack which contrasts strongly with the passionate words of *Epistola de Incarnatione Verbi* quoted in *n*4.811*b*.

*n*4.83*c*: establish different ones ⊖ *diversa valuerit astruere*] Here occurs the same opposition of '*astruere*' ⊖ 'to establish' and '*destruere*' ⊖ 'to weaken' as that of 1.21, the possible origin of which is discussed in *n*1.21*d*.

*n*4.83*d*: exercise in discussion ⊖ *exercitationem disputandi*] Compare the remarks concerning *De Grammatico* which occur in the preface to Anselm's *De Veritate*:

At various time I composed three treatises pertaining to the study of Holy Writ; they resembled eachother to the extent that	*Tres tractatus pertinentes ad studium sacrae scriptura quondam feci diversis temporibus, consimiles in hoc quia facti*

they had a question and answer structure, with the questioner denoted by the name 'Student' and the person questioned by the name 'Tutor'. I also produced a fourth treatise, similar in structure, and not altogether useless, in my opinion, for beginners in logic. Its *incipit* is *'De grammatico'*. However, as this latter deals with subject matter diverse from that of the three former, I do not want it to be counted along with them.

sunt per interrogationem et responsionem, et persona interrogantia nomine notatur 'discipuli', respondentis vero nomine 'magistri,. Quartum enim quem simili modo edidi, non inutilem ut puto introducendis ad dialecticam, cuius initium est 'De grammatico': quoniam ad diversum ab his tribus studium pertinet, istis nolo conumerare: *S* I 173.2.8.

The separating out of *De Grammatico* from the other dialogues is effected not because of its triviality, but because it pertains to a study other than that of Holy Writ. Such a separation by no means involves a lack of continuity in logical doctrine and its application. As has been shown in *HL* the doctrine continues to be applied in most of Anselm's works. The extension of the doctrine of *De Grammatico* to *all* significant utterances which takes place at 4.430 is in fact a symptom of this continuity.

INDEX

Apart from the works of Aristotle, only the titles of writings not mentioned in the bibliography (pp. 3–6) are included in this index.

SYNTHESE HISTORICAL LIBRARY

Texts and Studies
in the History of Logic and Philosophy

Editors:

1. M. T. Beonio-Brocchieri Fumagalli, *The Logic of Abelard.* Translated from the Italian. 1969, IX + 101 pp.
2. Gottfried Wilhelm Leibnitz, *Philosophical Papers and Letters.* A selection translated and edited, with an introduction, by Leroy E. Loemker. 1969, XII + 736 pp.
3. Ernst Mally, *Logische Schriften*, ed. by Karl Wolf and Paul Weingartner. 1971, X + 340 pp.
4. Lewis White Beck (ed.), *Proceedings of the Third International Kant Congress.* 1972, XI + 718 pp.
5. Bernard Bolzano, *Theory of Science*, ed. by Jan Berg. 1973, XV + 398 pp.
6. J. M. E. Moravcsik (ed.), *Patterns in Plato's Thought. Papers arising out of the 1971 West Coast Greek Philosophy Conference*. 1973, VIII + 212 pp.
7. Nabil Shehaby, *The Propositional Logic of Avicenna: A Translation from al-Shifā': al-Qiyās*, with Introduction, Commentary and Glossary. 1973, XIII + 296 pp.
8. Desmond Paul Henry, *Commentary on De Grammatico: The Historical-Logical Dimensions of a Dialogue of St. Anselm's.* 1974, IX + 345 pp.
9. John Corcoran, *Ancient Logic and Its Modern Interpretations.* 1974, X + 208 pp.

SYNTHESE LIBRARY

Monographs on Epistemology, Logic, Methodology,
Philosophy of Science, Sociology of Science and of Knowledge, and on the
Mathematical Methods of Social and Behavioral Sciences

1. J. M. BOCHEŃSKI, *A Precis of Mathematical Logic*. 1959, X + 100 pp.
2. P. L. GUIRAUD, *Problèmes et méthodes de la statistique linguistique*. 1960, VI + 146 pp.
3. HANS FREUDENTHAL (ed.), *The Concept and the Role of the Model in Mathematics and Natural and Social Sciences. Proceedings of a Colloquium held at Utrecht, The Netherlands, January 1960*. 1961, VI + 194 pp.
4. EVERT W. BETH, *Formal Methods. An Introduction to Symbolic Logic and the Study of Effective Operations in Arithmetic and Logic*. 1962, XIV + 170 pp.
5. B. H. KAZEMIER and D. VUYSJE (eds.), *Logic and Language. Studies dedicated to Professor Rudolf Carnap on the Occasion of his Seventieth Birthday*. 1962, VI + 256 pp.
6. MARX W. WARTOFSKY (ed.), *Proceedings of the Boston Colloquium for the Philosophy of Science, 1961–1962*, Boston Studies in the Philosophy of Science (ed. by Robert S. Cohen and Marx W. Wartofsky), Volume I. 1963, VIII + 212 pp.
7. A. A. ZINOV'EV, *Philosophical Problems of Many-Valued Logic*. 1963, XIV + 155 pp.
8. GEORGES GURVITCH, *The Spectrum of Social Time*. 1964, XXVI + 152 pp.
9. PAUL LORENZEN, *Formal Logic*. 1965, VIII + 123 pp.
10. ROBERT S. COHEN and MARX W. WARTOFSKY (eds.), *In Honor of Philipp Frank*, Boston Studies in the Philosophy of Science (ed. by Robert S. Cohen and Marx W. Wartofsky), Volume II. 1965, XXXIV + 475 pp.
11. EVERT W. BETH, *Mathematical Thought. An Introduction to the Philosophy of Mathematics*. 1965, XII + 208 pp.
12. EVERT W. BETH and JEAN PIAGET, *Mathematical Epistemology and Psychology*. 1966, XXII + 326 pp.
13. GUIDO KÜNG, *Ontology and the Logistic Analysis of Language. An Enquiry into the Contemporary Views on Universals*. 1967, XI + 210 pp.
14. ROBERT S. COHEN and MARX W. WARTOFSKY (eds.), *Proceedings of the Boston Colloquium for the Philosophy of Science 1964–1966, in Memory of Norwood Russell Hanson*, Boston Studies in the Philosophy of Science (ed. by Robert S. Cohen and Marx W. Wartofsky), Volume III. 1967, XLIX + 489 pp.
15. C. D. BROAD, *Induction, Probability, and Causation. Selected Papers*. 1968, XI + 296 pp.

16. GÜNTHER PATZIG, *Aristotle's Theory of the Syllogism. A Logical-Philosophical Study of Book A of the Prior Analytics*. 1968, XVII + 215 pp.
17. NICHOLAS RESCHER, *Topics in Philosophical Logic*. 1968, XIV + 347 pp.
18. ROBERT S. COHEN and MARX W. WARTOFSKY (eds.), *Proceedings of the Boston Colloquium for the Philosophy of Science 1966–1968*, Boston Studies in the Philosophy of Science (ed. by Robert S. Cohen and Marx W. Wartofsky), Volume IV. 1969, VIII + 537 pp.
19. ROBERT S. COHEN and MARX W. WARTOFSKY (eds.), *Proceedings of the Boston Colloquium for the Philosophy of Science 1966–1968*, Boston Studies in the Philosophy of Science (ed. by Robert S. Cohen and Marx W. Wartofsky), Volume V. 1969, VIII + 482 pp.
20. J. W. DAVIS, D. J. HOCKNEY, and W. K. WILSON (eds.), *Philosophical Logic*. 1969, VIII + 277 pp.
21. D. DAVIDSON and J. HINTIKKA (eds.), *Words and Objections: Essays on the Work of W. V. Quine*. 1969, VIII + 366 pp.
22. PATRICK SUPPES, *Studies in the Methodology and Foundations of Science. Selected Papers from 1911 to 1969*. 1969, XII + 473 pp.
23. JAAKKO HINTIKKA, *Models for Modalities. Selected Essays*. 1969, IX + 220 pp.
24. NICHOLAS RESCHER *et al.* (eds.). *Essay in Honor of Carl G. Hempel. A Tribute on the Occasion of his Sixty-Fifth Birthday*. 1969, VII + 272 pp.
25. P. V. TAVANEC (ed.), *Problems of the Logic of Scientific Knowledge*. 1969, XII + 429 pp.
26. MARSHALL SWAIN (ed.), *Induction, Acceptance, and Rational Belief*. 1970, VII + 232 pp.
27. ROBERT S. COHEN and RAYMOND J. SEEGER (eds.), *Ernst Mach; Physicist and Philosopher*, Boston Studies in the Philosophy of Science (ed. by Robert S. Cohen and Marx W. Wartofsky), Volume VI. 1970, VIII + 295 pp.
28. JAAKKO HINTIKKA and PATRICK SUPPES, *Information and Inference*. 1970, X + 336 pp.
29. KAREL LAMBERT, *Philosophical Problems in Logic. Some Recent Developments*. 1970, VII + 176 pp.
30. ROLF A. EBERLE, *Nominalistic Systems*. 1970, IX + 217 pp.
31. PAUL WEINGARTNER and GERHARD ZECHA (eds.), *Induction, Physics, and Ethics, Proceedings and Discussions of the 1968 Salzburg Colloquium in the Philosophy of Science*. 1970, X + 382 pp.
32. EVERT W. BETH, *Aspects of Modern Logic*. 1970, XI + 176 pp.
33. RISTO HILPINEN (ed.), *Deontic Logic: Introductory and Systematic Readings*. 1971, VII + 182 pp.
34. JEAN-LOUIS KRIVINE, *Introduction to Axiomatic Set Theory*. 1971, VII + 98 pp.
35. JOSEPH D. SNEED, *The Logical Structure of Mathematical Physics*. 1971, XV + 311 pp.
36. CARL R. KORDIG, *The Justification of Scientific Change*. 1971, XIV + 119 pp.
37. MILIČ ČAPEK, *Bergson and Modern Physics*, Boston Studies in the Philosophy of Science (ed. by Robert S. Cohen and Marx W. Wartofsky), Volume VII. 1971, XV + 414 pp.
38. NORWOOD RUSSELL HANSON, *What I do not Believe, and other Essays*, ed. by Stephen Toulmin and Harry Woolf. 1971, XII + 390 pp.
39. ROGER C. BUCK and ROBERT S. COHEN (eds.), *PSA 1970. In Memory of Rudolf Carnap*, Boston Studies in the Philosophy of Science (ed. by Robert S. Cohen and

Marx W. Wartofsky), Volume VIII. 1971, LXVI + 615 pp. Also available as a paperback.

40. Donald Davidson and Gilbert Harman (eds.), *Semantics of Natural Language*. 1972, X + 769 pp. Also available as a paperback.
41. Yehosua Bar-Hillel (ed.), *Pragmatics of Natural Languages*. 1971, VII + 231 pp.
42. Sören Stenlund, *Combinators, λ-Terms and Proof Theory*. 1972, 184 pp.
43. Martin Strauss, *Modern Physics and Its Philosophy. Selected Papers in the Logic, History, and Philosophy of Science*. 1972, X + 297 pp.
44. Mario Bunge, *Method, Model and Matter*. 1973, VII + 196 pp.
45. Mario Bunge, *Philosophy of Physics*. 1973, IX + 248 pp.
46. A. A. Zinov'ev, *Foundations of the Logical Theory of Scientific Knowledge* (*Complex Logic*), Boston Studies in the Philosophy of Science (ed. by Robert S. Cohen and Marx W. Wartofsky), Volume IX. Revised and enlarged English edition with an appendix, by G. A. Smirnov, E. A. Sidorenka, A. M. Fedina, and L. A. Bobrova. 1973, XXII + 301 pp. Also available as a paperback.
47. Ladislav Tondl, *Scientific Procedures*, Boston Studies in the Philosophy of Science (ed. by Robert S. Cohen and Marx W. Wartofsky), Volume X. 1973, XII + 268 pp. Also available as a paperback.
48. Norwood Russell Hanson, *Constellations and Conjectures*, ed. by Willard C. Humphreys, Jr. 1973, X + 282 pp.
49. K. J. J. Hintikka, J. M. E. Moravcsik, and P. Suppes (eds.), *Approaches to Natural Language. Proceedings of the 1970 Stanford Workshop on Grammar and Semantics*. 1973, VIII + 526 pp. Also available as a paperback.
50. Mario Bunge (ed.), *Exact Philosophy – Problems, Tools, and Goals*. 1973, X + 214 pp.
51. Radu J. Bogdan and Ilkka Niiniluoto (eds.), *Logic, Language, and Probability*. A selection of papers contributed to Sections IV, VI, and XI of the Fourth International Congress for Logic, Methodology, and Philosophy of Science, Bucharest, September 1971. 1973, X + 323 pp.
52. Glenn Pearce and Patrick Maynard (eds.), *Conceptual Change*. 1973, XII + 282 pp.
53. Ilkka Niiniluoto and Raimo Tuomela, *Theoretical Concepts and Hypothetico-Inductive Inference*. 1973, VII + 264 pp.
54. Roland Fraïssé, *Course of Mathematical Logic* – Volume I: *Relation and Logical Formula*. 1973, XVI + 186 pp. Also available as a paperback.
55. Adolf Grünbaum, *Philosophical Problems of Space and Time*. Second, enlarged edition, Boston Studies in the Philosophy of Science (ed. by Robert S. Cohen and Marx W. Wartofsky), Volume XII. 1973, XXIII + 884 pp. Also available as a paperback.
56. Patrick Suppes (ed.), *Space, Time, and Geometry*. 1973, XI + 424 pp.
57. Hans Kelsen, *Essays in Legal and Moral Philosophy*, selected and introduced by Ota Weinberger. 1973, XXVIII + 300 pp.
59. Robert S. Cohen and Marx W. Wartofsky (eds.), *Logical and Epistemological Studies in Contemporary Physics*, Boston Studies in the Philosophy of Science (ed. by Robert S. Cohen and Marx W. Wartofsky), Volume XIII. 1973, VIII + 462 pp. Also available as a paperback.

In Preparation

58. Robert S. Cohen and R. J. Seeger (eds.), *Philosophical Foundations of the*

Sciences, Boston Studies in the Philosophy of Science (ed. by Robert S. Cohen and Marx W. Wartofsky), Volume XI.

60. Robert S. Cohen and Marx W. Wartofsky (eds.), *Methodological and Historical Essays in the Natural and Social Sciences. Proceedings of the Boston Colloquium for the Philosophy of Science, 1969–1972*, Boston Studies in the Philosophy of Science (ed. by Robert S. Cohen and Marx W. Wartofsky), Volume XIV.
61. Robert S. Cohen and Marx W. Wartofsky (eds.), *Scientific, Historical, and Political Essays in Honor of Dirk J. Struik*, Boston Studies in the Philosophy of Science (ed. by Robert S. Cohen and Marx W. Wartofsky), Volume XV.
62. Kazimierz Ajdukiewicz, *Pragmatic Logic*, transl. from the Polish by Olgierd Wojtasiewicz.
63. Sören Stenlund (ed.), *Logical Theory and Semantic Analysis. Essays Dedicated to Stig Kanger on his Fiftieth Birthday.*

Henry, Desmond Paul

Commentary on De Grammatico

HELL ON LAND
DISASTER AT SEA

The Story of Merrill's Marauders and the Sinking of the Rhona

By Fred E. Randle
with the collaboration of
William W. Hughes

TURNER PUBLISHING COMPANY
Paducah, Kentucky

Turner Publishing Company
Publishers of America's History
412 Broadway
P.O. Box 3101
Paducah, KY 42002-3101
(270) 443-0121

Turner Publishing Company Staff
Editor: Randy Baumgardner
Graphic Design: Tyranny J. Bean

Library of Congress
Control No: 2001098726
ISBN: 1-56311-776-2

Table Of Contents

Foreword

Fred E. Randle survived some of the most perilous and punishing combat action of World War II. Concomitantly, he frequently was at the right place at the right time to witness some of military history's most absorbing events.

He saw the virtual beginning of the Space Age when history's first successful guided missile sunk the HMT Rohna, a British transport carrying more than 2,000 American veterans, some 1,047 of whom died in the waters of the Mediterranean Sea. It was the worst at-sea disaster ever to claim American military victims, the battleship Arizona losing only a few more men while moored in a state of peacetime inertia at Pearl Harbor. Randle was a few hundred feet away on the top deck of the Rohna's sister ship, the Karoa, when a German HS 293 air-to-surface missile struck the Rohna amidships. The incident, long cloaked in secrecy by the American and British governments, occurred several months before the Nazis' first VI and V2 buzz bombs hit London and the Belgian city of Antwerp after it was recaptured by the Allies and became one of their principal supply bases.

But that was only the start of Randle's exceptional wartime experience. His Mediterranean convoy of 12 ships was loaded with at least 30,000 American soldiers en route to the China-Burma-India Theater of Operations in the Great War. Upon arrival there, Randle was assigned to the 5307th Composite Unit (Provisional), later to be known as Merrill's Marauders, surely one of the most heroic infantry regiments in the history of American arms.

Randle and the other men in that regiment had to march some 800 miles over what Winston Churchill described as the world's most forbidding terrain, fighting at least 26 separate engagements against the Japanese along the way. Theirs is the story of warriors who were told by the American high command in Washington (with the concurrent knowledge of Churchill and Franklin D. Roosevelt) that they should expect at least 85 per cent casualties in their unit - a forecast that proved to be dismally accurate. Of an original force of some 3,000 soldiers, less than 300 were still on their feet when the regiment finally captured the strategic Myitkyina airstrip in North Burma, a compacted gravel runway near a village of a few hundred people, yet one which subsequently became the busiest airbase in the entire Allied war effort.

But even the sacrifices in the Marauders' long march and the capture of the airstrip were not enough. A number of those who were wounded or disabled by jungle diseases were flown to a hospital several hundred miles away, only to be forced out of their beds to assist in the capture of the village of Myitkyina itself. This became necessary when the Japanese units in the town had been strongly reinforced as the result of a costly blunder by one of America's most noted generals in the war, Joseph W. (Vinegar Joe) Stilwell. Historians are awakening to the fact that Stilwell, while justifiably heralded for his determination in the war effort, was nevertheless to be more condemned than praised for some of his most important strategic decisions, not to mention his insensitive and, at times, heartless treatment of the men in his command. The story told by Randle in this book is a devastating affirmation of this revisionist history.

Despite its many fascinating aspects, the conflict in Southeast Asia is a relatively 'forgotten war.' Ask most people to name the areas officially designated as major Theaters of Operation in World War II and they will identify only two: The European and Pacific Theaters. Similarly, they will identify only two Supreme Commanders, Dwight D. Eisenhower and Douglas MacArthur. Yet the C-B-I not only was officially designated as a third theater, but also had its own Supreme Commander who was British in his nationality, namely that colorful figure with the arresting name of Lord Louis Mountbatten.

In fact, Mountbatten was given the impressive designation as Supreme Commander of the Southeast Asia Command, which included not only the American forces in the CBI Theater, but also control of a large number of troops from the United Kingdom, Australia, Canada, India, Africa and China, the last named being a country whose control was most important to the Allies in both the Pacific and Asian regions.

Mountbatten was accurately described by his principal biographer (Philip Ziegler) as being "glamorous and almost indecently handsome." He was that and much more. He not only conducted his military command responsibilities quite competently, he later earned a batch of kudos as the Viceroy of India who almost single-handedly brought about that nation's independence, despite the fact that it was accompanied by a violent Hindu-Moslem partition that haunts the subcontinent to this day. Finally, Mountbatten received a good deal of credit for the strengthening of the British navy, both before and after the war. It is therefore quite ironic that most Americans today can identify Mountbatten only as the great uncle of Britain's Prince Charles who adored him more than any other male figure in the prince's life. Charles, in fact, was so devastated by Mountbatten's assassination by Irish terrorists that the prince's friends say it was a long time before he recovered emotionally from that tragedy in his personal life.

But Mountbatten was only one of the most impressive members in the cast of characters involved in the Southeast Asia Command of World War II. He was a man whose leadership impacted heavily on Merrill's Marauders as a group and on Randle as a commendable member of that outfit. Indeed, it would be hard to find in world history a specific place and time which held the attention or featured the activity of so many imposing leaders, all of them constantly interacting with one another and with the challenging situations facing them.

It starts with Roosevelt and Churchill.

Those two giants in the story of World War II held one of their famed conferences at Quebec in August of 1942 at which they discussed their problems with China's Generalissimo Chiang Kai-Shek and his stormy relationship with General Stilwell. But much of the meeting also was taken up with the problem of how to open the Burma Road in order to augment air transport in the movement of supplies into China, an endeavor which was essential to keep China in the war against its Japanese invaders.

Enter at this point the colorful, mysterious, and altogether fascinating personage of Brigadier General Orde C. Wingate, the originator of "long range penetration" groups. His brigade of "Chindits" proved to be the forerunner of such units as the Office of Strategic Services (O.S.S.), an American intelligence and fighting team which also operated behind the Japanese lines in Burma and which, in turn, was the predecessor of today's Central Intelligence Agency (CIA). The Marauders themselves adopted some of Wingate's tactics, as did the Green Berets who operated so dramatically behind enemy lines in the Vietnam War.

Wingate was such an eccentric character that he once appeared naked in a pep talk to some of his troops. When Great Britain was helping Ethiopia in its war against Italian invaders he lit fires under obstinate camels to make them move forward in the Ethiopian desert.

Later, he suffered such deep bouts of depression that he tried to commit suicide. But, his reputation as a strategist and tactician was so impressive that the British army not only kept him on its roster, but also gave him a tough responsibility in World War II. After he regained his mental balance, the British high command sent him to India to help Stilwell in his plans to recapture northern Burma from the Japanese.

After his arrival, Wingate took a force of about 3,000 British and Gurkha soldiers on a 200-mile foray into western Burma. His mission was never clear and the only accomplishments by his so-called "Chindits" were the blowing of a few bridges and cutting the road to Myitkyina, not anything more than an American O.S.S. detachment had accomplished earlier with a few Yanks and a handful of friendly Kachin tribesmen.

But Churchill was impressed because Wingate was one of only two British generals in Asia who had shown any desire to take the offensive against the Japs, the other being General William J. Slim whose British and Indian troops eventually defeated a large Japanese army in the south of Burma. Consequently, Churchill decided to invite Wingate to the Quebec conference along with Mountbatten. Others in attendance were American Air Corps General Hap Arnold and a number of lesser military figures. All of them were stunned when Wingate made an extremely forceful and charismatic appearance, which Arnold later described in these words: "You took one look at that face, the face of an Indian chieftain, topping a uniform still smelling of jungle and sweat and war, and you thought: 'Hell, this man is serious.' And when he began to talk you found out just how serious!"

Needless to say, FDR also was impressed, and he and Churchill decided that Wingate's Chindit force ought to be augmented by some American soldiers who would strike deep into north Burma to capture Myitkyina and its strategic airstrip. And it was in that way that the formation of the regiment later to be known as Merrill's Marauders was conceived and put into action.

As it turned out, Wingate did not get to control the regiment. Stilwell later insisted that an American regiment ought to be under American command, and he thus persuaded Chief of Staff George C. Marshall to spirit the Marauders away from Wingate but, not without Wingate's anticipated negative reaction. He told one of Stilwell's staff members that Vinegar Joe "can take his Americans and stick them up his ass."

Some weeks later, however, Wingate proved he was a team player when he took his Chindits deep into Burma to help the Marauders and lost his life in the effort. Before he died in a tragic plane crash he accomplished a feat unparalleled in military history. He loaded hundreds of men and mules onto gliders and landed them far behind Japanese lines to again cut strategic railroads and destroy a number of enemy installations.

Two other charismatic figures in the CBI Theater were aviators who conducted their work in the grand style. One of them was General Claire Chennault, originally the founder of the famous prewar Flying Tigers and later named the commanding general of the Fourteenth Air Force. His military exploits were commendable but his strategic judgments left much to be desired.

The other famous aviator was none other than Colonel Phillip Cochran, the fearless flyer who helped Wingate in his second mission by providing the planes and pilots to pull Wingate's gliders. Cochran was also the dashing American pilot who was dramatized as "Flip" Corkin in the famous Milton Caniff comic strip "Terry and the Pirates."

Among still other important personages were the political leaders of India and China, Mohandas K. Gandhi and Chiang Kai-Shek. Gandhi, of course, is regarded by many savants as one of the most admirable social and political figures in the history of the world, and deservedly so. However, he was a controversial figure to the western world during the war and allied officers and soldiers in the CBI Theater did not hold him in high regard. He had even been an Adolph Hitler admirer prior to the war, although he later changed his views toward the Nazi tyrant. More importantly, his massive demonstrations in his passive resistance to the British Raj, as meritorious as they no doubt were, could not be tolerated during the war. This was at a time when Indian soldiers were being drafted into the Allied forces to hold back the Japanese invaders of Southeast Asia, the Japs at one point crossing the Burma border into India and capturing several towns in the Imphal area. Consequently, in view of Gandhi's pacifist views and his disruptive activities, the British decided his initiatives were too great a distraction to the war effort, and decided to keep him in prison until the war ended. This decision was not compatible with Western ideals of political and social justice, but it may have been necessary in view of the war's already formidable complications.

Chiang Kai-Shek was a different cup of Asian tea. Despite the glaring deficiencies in General Stilwell's character and diplomatic skills, he did not deserve the inimical actions taken against him by Chiang and his powerful wife, known to the world as "Madam Chiang." Nor was Stilwell alone in being forced to deal with Chiang's constant insistence that the war in Burma take second place to his defense against the Japanese who had already occupied eastern China. FDR and Churchill joined Stilwell in trying to keep Chiang on track with respect to the Allied plan to take Burma as a necessary step in giving Chiang the assistance he needed, assistance which first required a land route for men and supplies into western China.

Nevertheless, Stilwell, who spoke the Chinese language fluently, finally persuaded Chiang to give him two Chinese divisions in the drive to sweep Japanese forces out of northern Burma. While he hated Chiang, Stilwell held a high regard for the potential of properly trained Chinese troops in combat situations, an assessment which later was to be confirmed in some but not all of the Chinese activity in Burma.

But Stilwell also had his failings, and they were numerous and severe. Randle covers these deficiencies in detail as he traces the general's supervision of the military endeavors of Merrill's Marauders.

In any event, the strategy confirmed at the Quebec conference was as follows:

The Southeast Asia Command was established with the understanding that the British, with the help of their Indian divisions, would move into southwest Burma and then push on east to free the country's principal cities of Mandalay and Rangoon.

Meanwhile, Stilwell and his Americans would continue their building of the Ledo Road to connect with the famed old Burma Road in east-central Burma. Concomitantly, since the road construction already was making progress in India's Assam Province, Merrill's Marauders, with the help of Chinese soldiers, would proceed down the completed part of the road which, by the time the Marauders started their march, had reached a point near Taipah Ga in the Patkai Mountains between Assam and Burma.

From that point on, the road builders would have to follow the advance of the Marauders, rather than the other way around.

All told, this meant that the Marauders, already having traversed more than two hundred miles, would then have to march another 600 miles over narrow and rough trails, through jungles and across mountains in order to achieve the objective of capturing Myitkyina which had been kept secret by Stilwell.

Meanwhile, the American air corps was to embark on the greatest airlift in history, flying many thousands of tons of supplies and weapons to Chiang Kai-Shek's western China headquarters and distribution center at Kunming. This "over-the-hump" activity across the Himalayans, the world's highest and most treacherous mountains for flying operations, subsequently became world famous, and justifiably so. The C-47 Dakotas or "Goony Birds" proved to be such great aircraft in that endeavor that they eventually were converted into the famous DC-3s, the planes which raised post-war American commercial aviation to a new level of service. Similarly, the completion of the 500 miles of the Ledo Road was certainly the greatest military construction project in the history of mankind.

In the face of all the background material presented above, it should be said that the book you are about to read is not concerned as much with great leaders and grand strategies as it is with the experiences and viewpoints of an individual soldier who fought and suffered for the causes of democracy in the Burma war. Too often the soldier himself and his contributions to victory are forgotten in the hyperbolic praises heaped upon generals and political leaders by many historians. This is not the case with this narrative, and consequently, its interest is greatly enhanced for the reader who wants to know what war really is like.

Fred E. Randle will tell you exactly what it is like and you will never forget it.

WILLIAM W. HUGHES

Prelude To War

I thought it was strange when Jude never brayed.

He surely wasn't like any mule I had worked with back in Missouri where I was born. But he was big and strong and not as stubborn as I knew Missouri mules to be.

Then I found out why Jude was so amiable. He had been through a United States army basic training course at Fort Bliss, Texas for jungle duty against the Japanese. That meant that his voice box had to be surgically removed to be sure he made no sound as we embarked on our long and arduous trek in north-east India and northwest Burma. Which made a lot of sense in the Burma jungle where, as I was soon to learn, we could stumble upon some of our enemies around any of the numerous curves in trails which snaked through dense forests and thick under-brush.

That training course did some other fine things for Jude. He became obedient and, despite the exceptionally heavy load he had to carry, usually followed docilely along when I tugged him forward. He also was trained not to buck or even shudder when he heard gunfire, no matter how close. I'll talk more about Jude later, and how I was able to survive, even if he wasn't, during our exceptionally dangerous mission against our Japa-nese foes. First a word about how I found myself in a predica-ment which, in retrospect, I could have and perhaps should have avoided.

It all began when I became a volunteer in a gamble so fool-ish that it made a drunken Las Vegas high roller look like a paragon of profundity.

My buddy, Seymour Schoenfeld, and I were suffering in the 110 degree heat in the so-called Tent City near Calcutta, India, where a large contingent of newly-arrived American sol-